INCREASING
READING
EFFICIENCY

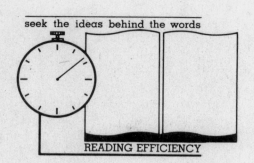

seek the ideas behind the words

READING EFFICIENCY

INCREASING READING EFFICIENCY

Fifth Edition

Lyle L. Miller

Professor Guidance and Counselor Education
Director Uniwyo Reading Research Center
University of Wyoming

Holt, Rinehart and Winston
New York   Chicago   San Francisco   Philadelphia
Montreal   Toronto   London   Sydney
Tokyo   Mexico City   Rio de Janeiro   Madrid

Library of Congress Cataloging in Publication Data

Miller, Lyle L.
  Increasing reading efficiency.

  Bibliography: p. 27
  1. Developmental reading. I. Title.
LB1050.53.M54 1984   428.4'3   82-25523

ISBN 0-03-062049-X

CBS COLLEGE PUBLISHING
Holt, Rinehart and Winston
The Dryden Press
Saunders College Publishing

Preface

Economics and efficiency

Current concerns about economic factors in our society raise serious questions about the focus of responsibility for unemployment, inflation, recession, interest rates, deficit spending, and balanced budgets. In a rapidly changing society long-range planning sometimes seems almost unrealistic. But in many cases, current problems have their roots in the lack of adequate planning, and in the subsequent waste of personal and natural resources. The obvious need for conservation and effective use of time, talent, and resources has been a continuing challenge to society for many years.

Early in my life, I became concerned about one very important resource that simply could not be recycled or reclaimed—our time! Personal experience with the sudden death of a very close boyhood friend reinforced the concern about the irrevocable passage of time and the undetermined supply of time available to any one of us.

These concerns led me to the preparation of an entry in the National IBM Essay Contest on the topic "The Value of Time in Education." Some of the ideas expressed therein must have been challenging and innovative because the essay won the state award. The profound effect was that the research on this essay started me on an extensive search for more effective ways to use time wisely, and for ways to get more done in less time. For me, the concept of *efficiency* had been born. This concept was to grow rapidly and to influence much of my personal and professional behavior in the years that followed. But the emphasis on the *quality* of work always took priority over any emphasis on speed alone.

Many years later, when a small group of students approached me and asked me to help them learn to read faster, I certainly did not anticipate the very interesting and challenging project I was undertaking. Little did I dream then that most of my professional reading and research time for many years would be devoted to the challenge of helping people to read more effectively.

Certainly I never thought of myself as a reading expert! If anything, I was very skeptical about "speed reading" programs. I was concerned with effective study skills in my capacity as a study skills instructor; and, as a counselor, I had a deep concern for helping young people define and resolve their problems. These two perspectives stimulated my interest in speed reading as a possible solution for some students' problems. Could speed be developed with no loss in comprehension or quality of achievement? Could a student become a fast reader and be a *good* student at the same time?

Resources and research

I soon found that there were few, if any, experts, and only very limited resource materials for programs in developmental reading beyond the sixth grade level. Today there is significantly more material, but still a shortage of individuals who claim to be experts in this field. So much of the reading process goes on in the eye and the brain that no one can really observe or study the real reading process to learn answers about it. All one can actually do is to observe behavior and record data in such a way that, bit by bit, one adds to knowledge and contributes to the improvement of methods and materials for developmental reading programs.

I never expect to become an *expert* on reading, but I certainly have learned a great deal about the process and I do know considerably more than I would have thought possible thirty years ago. More than anything else, I have been impressed greatly by the observed behavior of young people who have discovered new and challenging potentials for learning through their personal experience in a reading efficiency laboratory.

Needs and purposes

In an age of automation, space laboratories, and video games, we may take for granted some of our basic concepts of communication. The instantaneous transfer of ideas through radio, television, outer space satellites, and modern, constantly-improving long distance telephone services has literally brought the world into our daily lives. Today we depend more and more on looking and listening to keep us informed. In the midst of all of these modern developments, however, we find evidence of the increasing circulation of magazines, the continuous publication of new books, expanding library facilities, and an ever-increasing volume of printed material being circulated through the mail. In our high-speed world of computer technology and satellite transmission of electronic signals, we still find that *reading* is our most fundamental tool for effective interpersonal communication.

With our rapidly expanding accumulation of human knowledge, reading ability has become one of the most important factors for success in many fields today. This is true for the modern scientist analyzing the work of others through their research papers, for the business executive reading current market reports and correspondence, for busy doctors and lawyers reviewing recent developments in their professional journals, and for homemakers seeking relaxation and relief from their daily problems by reading current magazines. Reading is especially important for conscientious students who are trying to grasp an understanding of the many new concepts in their specialized curricula. None of these could achieve success without reading. More important, however, is the fact that all of them need to read *quickly and efficiently*.

Colleges are aware of the reading problems of young adults and are attempting to deal with these problems. Remedial reading programs, designed for the student with specific reading difficulties, have been available in colleges for many years. Study skills programs, including developmental reading units, have expanded rapidly in the last few decades. Many of these focus on the needs and problems of "average" or "good" readers who wish to reduce the amount of their time spent in studying. More recently, greater attention has been given to the potential value of reading efficiency programs for these "able" students.

Few readers have been able to avoid the pressures of the faster pace of living and *learning*, and the urgent need to read more effectively. Efficient reading habits are of value to any reader, and many college reading centers have engaged in extensive research on this problem. The first edition of *Increasing Reading Efficiency* (29)[1] was the product of such research in the Study Skills Center and the Reading Research Center at the University of Wyoming. Extensive use of this workbook in many other colleges and in adult reading programs since then has confirmed the value of this approach to developmental reading.

Experimental work in many universities and high schools has shown that few students are reading at speeds that even begin to approach their real reading capabilities. Although some universities and colleges still stress remedial reading, many instructors in study skills programs have come to the conclusion that this emphasis may be misleading. It may discourage students from participating in reading efficiency programs because they feel that their reading habits are "normal." Experience has shown, however, that reading efficiency programs can help any person who has a sincere desire for self-improvement. Therefore this manual has been developed primarily as a series of basic drills for supervised group activities. The individuals who need specific remedial help can usually secure this assistance in addition to the group work. Those who are interested primarily in improving their reading efficiency may devote extra time in practice on longer reading exercises such as those provided in *Maintaining Reading Efficiency* (30).

[1] All reference numbers refer to the numbered selected references on p. 27.

Letters from many teachers and students who have used *Increasing Reading Efficiency* in many parts of the United States and abroad have convinced me that this pattern of reading exercises has been of real practical value to thousands of high school and college students and adults. Its success led to the development of a companion volume called *Developing Reading Efficiency* (28), which has the same basic pattern of organization but is focused on the reading needs of middle school students, and of *Personalizing Reading Efficiency* (32) for the upper high school years. Later a manual for teachers was developed and published, *Teaching Efficient Reading Skills* (34). These publications are now distributed by Burgess Publishing Company, Minneapolis, Minnesota 55435. A supplemental workbook of longer exercises, *Maintaining Reading Efficiency* (30), a series of *Reading Efficiency Tests* for pretesting and post-testing, a *Reading Efficiency Tape*, and various other materials for study skills programs are produced and distributed by Developmental Reading Distributors, P.O. Box 1451, Cape Coral, Florida 33910 (813) 549-6562.

In producing this revision of *Increasing Reading Efficiency*, I have been careful to preserve the basic format and exercise sequence which have been so well-received. The major changes in this revision include the restandardization of some materials and the replacement of about 40 percent of the exercises in Series V, VI, VII, and VIII in order to update these materials and to provide a better reading balance. With these changes, this fifth edition of *Increasing Reading Efficiency* should continue to facilitate the development of efficient reading skills for many more students for many more years to come.

Use of the workbook

Although this workbook often may be used for self-improvement practice in individual cases, it was designed primarily for use with small groups of readers, where competition within the group may serve as a psychological motivation for increased proficiency in the drill exercises. With a planned supervision that stresses both self-improvement and competition with other readers, most individuals in the group will be pleasantly surprised by the improvement they can make in a series of reading classes. It is not unusual for many students in a group to double or triple their reading efficiency if they make a sincere effort to achieve such a goal.

Sources of inspiration and support

In developing this manual, I am indebted to many sources for ideas and inspiration. In these reading workbooks I have attempted to incorporate some of the best of the ideas on *developmental reading* and *effective study*. First of all, my interest in the field of higher level study skills and in the potential for improvement by college students was stimulated by my work at Ohio State University with Dr. Francis P. Robinson (47).

Many authors contributed to my understanding of the reading process. I was most impressed by the basic concepts and basic reading drill sequences developed by Stroud and Ammons (52). The criticisms of hundreds of students in study skills classes and in the Reading Efficiency Laboratory, and stimulating discussions with many graduate students throughout the years have contributed extensively to the depth of my understanding about reading and to the expansion and polishing of these basic concepts.

The inspiration of Oscar Causey and his work with a series of National Reading Conferences at Fort Worth, Texas (10) throughout the late 1950s was of tremendous significance. Many questions about the reading process were explored in the research efforts of a number of graduate students at the University of Wyoming throughout the years, as they selected some aspect of reading as a focus for their graduate study. These included Jeanne Taylor, James Gordon Shaw, Kristen Solberg, Robert Jones, Dudley Sykes, Paul Koziey, Martin Faber, Ed Johnson, Tom Marshall, Russell Washburn, and many others.

Many authors and publishers have been extremely generous in granting permission to use their materials and to revise these materials slightly when necessary to develop them into standard reading exercises. Those whose materials appear in this final revision have been acknowledged by the credit lines in the articles, but many others have been just as gracious in granting permission to use their material in developing the wide range of potential reading exercises from which the final sets were selected. Many of their exercises have been used extensively in the study skills classes at the University of Wyoming.

The necessity for standard lengths of articles and balance of reading difficulty determined the final choice of exercises included in this book; but without the support and encouragement of *all* of the authors and editors who granted permission for the utilization of their materials in this standardized way, these reading efficiency workbooks could never have been developed.

Evaluation and modification

Many suggestions and evaluative comments have been provided by teachers who have used these books in their reading efficiency classes throughout the country. These comments and suggestions have been very helpful in the evaluation and consecutive revisions of the whole series of Reading Efficiency books. Special thanks should go to the following group of reviewers who served as a panel to review the fourth edition of *Increasing Reading Efficiency* in detail, and to make constructive suggestions for improvements to be made in this revision: Mrs. Lorell C. Guydon, John Jay College of Criminal Justice, New York City; Dr. Charles Clark, Western Illinois University, Macomb, Illinois; Dr. Girly Cousert, Oakland City College, Oakland City, Indiana; Ms. Joyce Evans, North Carolina Central University, Durham, North Carolina; Mrs. Nancy Fillion, University of Wyoming, Laramie, Wyoming; Dr. Pauline Griskey, University of Wisconsin, Milwaukee, Wisconsin; Dr. Jeanne Anne Hull, Western State College, Gunnison, Colorado; Mrs. Garlene Lee, Ogallala, Nebraska; Ms. Judy Richardson, Virginia Commonwealth University, Richmond, Virginia; and Dr. Victoria Hunter Sanders, University of the Pacific, Stockton, California.

Special recognition should be given to the staff members of the UniWyo Reading Research Center for all of their contributions in developing the new materials for this revision and for their dedication to detail in the final organization. Especially deserving of credit for this revision are Karen Arata, Mary Ellen Latham, Jennifer Lundy, Donna Martinez, Carrie Robison, Jo Rodriguez, and Stephanie Tate.

Above all, I am most appreciative of the support and inspiration of my two children, Tom and Patty, who participated in some of my early experimental reading groups and who discussed student reactions extensively with me. Deepest appreciation goes to my wife, Grace M. Miller, who has been a continuing partner in the long-term development of the entire series of Reading Efficiency publications. Without her patient understanding, loyal support, encouragement, and hours of diligent labor on the basic materials and the final manuscript, I would never have been able to persevere through this series of revisions.

Lyle L. Miller

Laramie, Wyoming
September 1983

Contents

INCREASING
READING
EFFICIENCY

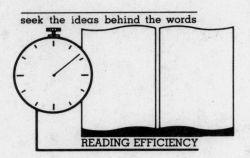

TO THE TEACHER

Survival

With the publication of this its fifth edition, *Increasing Reading Efficiency* will now have been recognized for almost thirty years in the academic marketplace. During this period, it has had a profound impact on the lives and reading habits of many thousands of individuals. By increasing their reading efficiency, they have been able to live much fuller lives and to engage in many more activities than would have been possible otherwise. Many of them have found a great deal more pleasure in reading and have come to recognize reading as one of the important keys to success in their lives. The strongest supporters of the continued use of this book are the individuals who have had a positive personal experience in the way that it can improve their individual perception and retention of verbal symbols.

In that period of time, *Increasing Reading Efficiency* has been used by several hundred teachers in public schools, colleges, and adult education programs. Many of these teachers have written back to the author to share student reactions and to make suggestions for improvement. With the benefit of those suggestions, each revision has reflected some improvements over the earlier editions.

Although it was originally designed as a workbook for use primarily with study skills groups at a college level, it has proved to be practical at many other levels and in many other types of group and individual situations. It has been a useful tool for many teachers with differing perspectives and with different purposes and patterns of use.

For those who have been behaviorally oriented, it has provided a carefully structured sequence of drill materials designed to bring about specific modifications of basic reading behavior. Such changes can be functionally defined and carefully measured to reflect the individual's attainment of his or her goals and expectations.

For those more interested in the affective aspects of learning, the materials have provided a basis for bringing about attitudinal change concerning reading, study skills, and personal responsibility. Many teachers have commented on the value of the suggestions and the application of reading skills to practical needs. Changes in self-concept often seem to be significant outcomes of the development of flexibility in reading skills. Flexible reading habits lead to broader interests and make it more possible for students to become more deeply involved in activities that they really enjoy. For many students the real "pay-off" from improved reading efficiency is the free time achieved for such activities.

The practical uses of this book seem to range from its use as *the* basic workbook in some groups or classes on reading improvement to simple use by an individual student. In the first case, it seems to serve as the basic instrument for specific behavioral change in reading habits in a sixteen- to twenty-hour structured program of carefully planned and supervised reading experiences. On the other end of the scale is its use by an individual student who purchases a single copy at the bookstore for his own program of self-structured self-improvement. Between these two extremes are many other variations of functional use in the classroom or reading resource center.

Within a wide range of experimentation and critical examination, the earlier editions of *Increasing Reading Efficiency* seem to have proved the continuing value of this material sufficiently to justify further refinement and revision in this fifth edition.

Demands for reading efficiency

The constantly increasing explosion of knowledge and the resultant publication of increasing numbers of challenging and stimulating books and periodical articles have made good reading a key to a wide range of vicarious experiences. The success of so many highly advertised commercial reading programs seems to be ample evidence that many people want to read better and faster. It has been a concern of this author for many years that public schools and colleges have not been more responsive to these needs. Surely, our schools could offer all of the best characteristics of most of the commercial reading programs at a fraction of their cost.

A focal point of attention for this author for the past thirty-three years has been the development of appropriate instructional materials for developmental reading programs with the hope that these materials might at least provide a sound basis for personal development of reading skills in a variety of settings.

A family of reading efficiency books

The popularity of *Increasing Reading Efficiency* (29),[1] first published by Holt, Rinehart and Winston in 1956 and now in its fifth edition, has demonstrated the value of such materials for college students and adults. The demand from many teachers for another workbook standardized at a less difficult level led to

[1] All reference numbers refer to the numbered selected references on p. 27.

the development of a parallel workbook, *Developing Reading Efficiency* (28), which was published by Burgess Publishing Company. This book has been very effective for younger students, primarily in grades seven through ten.

A third workbook, *Personalizing Reading Efficiency* (32), has been published by Burgess Publishing Company since 1976. With structure comparable to the other two books, this one is designed specifically for the upper high school years. It is a condensed version, with only half as many exercises as the other two and planned specifically for classroom use without the exercises for suggested outside practice.

A fourth workbook called *Maintaining Reading Efficiency* (30) was designed to provide practice in the application of flexible reading skills over longer periods of time. This book and other tests, pacing tapes, and related study skills materials are available from Developmental Reading Distributors, P.O. Box 1451, Cape Coral, Florida 33910, (813) 549-6562.

Resources for teachers

One reaction of teachers using the earlier editions of *Increasing Reading Efficiency* was that materials for teachers should be included *in the workbook itself,* rather than in a separate teacher's manual. They also suggested that the teacher's section should be expanded to cover several basic points of concern to the teacher. In response to those suggestions, this brief section for teachers has been developed, and sets of answer keys, arranged on perforated pages for easy removal, have been included at the back of the workbook.

Teachers who desire more specific suggestions on methods and materials for teaching developmental reading are encouraged to study the more comprehensive manual for teachers, *Teaching Efficient Reading Skills* (34), published by Burgess Publishing Company, Minneapolis, Minnesota.

Purpose of the workbook

Increasing Reading Efficiency originally was designed to promote the mutual development of reading speed and reading comprehension through carefully controlled group activity. Although the author since has received abundant evidence of effective and highly gratifying use of the workbook by individuals and in individualized settings in reading clinics, he still emphasizes that the materials were intended primarily for use in groups, where competition with oneself and with others in the group tends to provide parallel patterns for psychological motivation. The author is firmly convinced that this dual competitive pattern, supported by a teacher who can provide a system of both group and individual

motivation, provides a stimulus more appropriate than any specific pattern of mechanical or machine-oriented motivation.

With the primary goal of increasing rate along with a maintenance or improvement of comprehension skill, other aspects such as vocabulary improvement and critical reading skills are of secondary importance in the overall structure of the book. With full recognition of the basic importance of higher-level study skills, analytical reading, critical reading, and vocabulary development, one must recognize that any attempt to expand this book to include comprehensive coverage of all of these points would result in an extremely bulky and expensive volume and would represent a sacrifice of some currently established and meaningful sequences of exercises. Teachers seeking these other types of emphasis are encouraged to consider other appropriate materials on the market.

In summary then, this material was designed primarily for use in groups under supervision of an able teacher who can motivate people to reach beyond their current grasp. It was designed also for use with young adults and mature individuals who have mastered the basic development of language skills. Teachers of younger or less mature groups are urged to consider the use of *Developing Reading Efficiency* (30). Consideration might also be given to the shorter collection of materials at a slightly lower interest and vocabulary level. This collection is available from Burgess Publishing Company under the title *Personalizing Reading Efficiency* (32).

The concept of reading efficiency

Although both rate of reading and comprehension are recognized as important aspects of reading ability, neither one is stressed in itself. Instead, this author places the stress on a combination of the two factors that he calls *reading efficiency.* This measures what might be called a "rate of understanding." Reading efficiency is computed by multiplying the rate (in words per minute) by the comprehension score (percentage of correct answers on tested material). This yields a "words per minute" figure that serves as a measure of the amount of material understood during a minute of time. Although one recognizes that ideas cannot be measured accurately in "words per minute," this stress on efficiency does seem to overcome some of the students' concerns over comprehension loss in the early stages of reading improvement.

Early experimentation in the University of Wyoming Study Skills Center revealed that students seemed to attain lower comprehension scores for a period of time immediately after having successfully increased their reading rate. Consequently, much thought has been given to the provision of training exercises designed to bring about increases in *both* rate and comprehension. After years of observation and comparison, however, research seems to show that most students can make very substantial increases in reading rate with no significant loss in scores on comprehension.

During the years in which *Increasing Reading Efficiency* has been used in the Study Skills Center, group evaluations have revealed an increase in both rate and comprehension on comparable standardized tests administered at the beginning and end of the ten-week training period. *Maintaining Reading Efficiency Tests* (31) is published by Developmental Reading Distributors, Cape Coral, Florida 33910. With five different forms, these tests can be used effectively for such pre- and post-comparisons. Also available from this source is the *Reading Efficiency Tape,* which can be used for individual pacing, or can be used with the group to free the teacher for more careful observation of individual behavior during reading activities. Simultaneous improvement of rate and comprehension results from such a careful integration of speed-reading skills and higher-level study skills.

This can be accomplished best by introducing students to techniques of self-recitation, reading for ideas, and recognition of textbook clues. The materials in this workbook are organized in such a way that the effectiveness of this approach is easy to illustrate to the students.

Do not expect these characteristics

No one book on developmental reading can be all things to all people. Therefore, one should consider some of the things that this book is *not*.

It is not a ''speed-reading'' workbook. The author believes that teachers should deal cautiously with the idea of ''speed'' in reading. The gullible public often is given the idea that all reading difficulties are essentially problems of ''speed.'' The multitude of commercial programs and specialized materials for the improvement of rate suggests that rapid improvement in reading rate alone will produce miracles. This may be a misinterpretation of potentially serious problems. A slow reading rate very easily may indicate other reading difficulties such as weaknesses in basic word recognition, interpretation skills, study skills, or even more serious physiological problems. It may be simply a problem of personal attitude toward schools and education. The author already has indicated his concern for a balanced approach and for supervision by a teacher who is observant of, and sensitive to, symptoms of other problems.

It is not a remedial workbook. The materials are designed for older adolescents and adults who already have mastered basic language skills. Many other good materials are available on the market that emphasize the basic language skills and remedial techniques.

It is not primarily a vocabulary builder. Vocabulary training needs to be an essential supplementary activity. Exercises in this book allow for the basic identification of some potential vocabulary problems, but practice on vocabulary improvement is a matter of individual emphasis. The author would recommend a supplemental practice book such as *Basic Vocabulary Skills* by Davis (13) or *Developing Vocabulary Skills* by Joffe (19).

It is not a book for reading improvement through concentrated applied practice. This book involves much basic drill material. For those who prefer direct practice in reading content-oriented materials, the author would recommend either *Maintaining Reading Efficiency* (30) or *Efficient Study Skills* (35).

Basic concepts of reading

One of the confusing points to students and teachers alike is the absence of a universal definition of the term *reading*. Consequently, many people are writing and talking about *reading* and not meaning the same thing. Let us first explore the much-quoted statement that no one can possibly read at a rate of more than 800 words per minute. This statement seems to be based on the following steps of logic:

1. Readers identify and recognize visual material only during eye pauses or fixations.
2. Research indicates that the average adult reader can recognize clearly only 1.1 words during such a fixation and that the most able readers seldom recognize over 2.7 words per fixation or stop.
3. Efficient readers require at least a one-fifth second duration to recognize any symbols during any fixation or stop.
4. Efficient readers, therefore, cannot hope to make more than five stops per second.
5. Therefore, it can be mathematically calculated that the very efficient reader who can see 2.7 words per fixation and who makes five stops per second will be able to read only 810 words per minute ($2.7 \times 5 \times 60$).

Thus the 800 words per minute maximum is established—based on a concept of *deliberate reading,* which is defined as the act in which the reader *contacts all of the words visually and strives for complete comprehension.* Of course, this does not discount the fact that people can ''skim'' or ''scan'' at much more rapid rates, but to the ''purist'' these activities are *not* reading. For those with more practical interests, however, questions exist about all but the first step in the logic outlined above.

Considering the many demands for varied types of reading in modern society, however, one can see why most teachers and students find acceptance of such an extreme definition impractical. But no other definition has been accepted universally. Therefore, each author should feel an obligation to make clear his own concepts of the term. As used in this book, *reading* means *that process of communication of ideas from one individual to another through the medium of writing or printing.* More concisely, the purpose of reading is seen as *seeking the ideas behind the words.*

Within this definition, skimming and scanning can be viewed as effective types of the total reading program, and the concept of reading rates beyond 800 words per minute is much more understandable and acceptable.

Basic points of reference

Any development of materials is dependent upon concepts developed for other purposes. Materials in this book are dependent for meaning upon two basic concepts in addition to that of "reading efficiency" as previously described.

The basic vocabulary around which reading exercises in Series I, II, and III are built is the *Teacher's Word Book of 30,000 Words* (55) developed by E. L. Thorndike in 1944. Considering the publication date, one can see that many words of recent vintage are not included. The scope of these exercises is somewhat limited, therefore, by the basic word list. The author is unaware, however, of any comparable current word list composed by an authority of similar reputation.

The measurement of reading difficulty in all exercises in Series V through VII has been done with the careful use of the Flesch formula (14). Although limited to only two basic factors, sentence length and syllable count per hundred words, this has been viewed for many years as the most efficient measure of reading difficulty for adult materials. Although it has been criticized widely by teachers of English, no one seems to have come forth with any comparable formula that seems any better for the same purpose. So, with due recognition to its obvious limitations, this author has continued to use it in all of his *Reading Efficiency* publications as the best available instrument for establishing a standard basis for comparison of the relative difficulty of materials used in reading exercises.

Development of the reading exercises

Of basic importance to the exercises in this manual is a provision for increasing eye span and for establishing rhythmic eye movements. Also basic is an emphasis on increasing the mental perception rate of understanding what is read and thus reducing the eye fixation time. In addition, the difficulty of the exercises has been standardized sufficiently to allow for comparisons within and between Series in sequences of gradually increasing difficulty.

Standardization of the materials

One of the major difficulties a few years ago in evaluating the results of a training program in developmental reading was the lack of standardized materials. The materials used in this book are now standardized as much as possible in order to make exercises comparable.

In Series I and II, answer frequency per column has been standardized, so that in each exercise the right answer will occur five times in each column.

In Series I and II, all key words occur in Thorndike's list of 10,000 most frequently used words (54), and all words in the answer columns occur in Thorndike's list of 30,000 most frequently used words (55). Therefore, these exercises may serve also as vocabulary drills for high school or college students.

In the phrase and sentence meaning drills, the key words have been checked against the same word list. These exercises have been arranged in an order of gradually increasing length and difficulty.

The paragraph reading material in Series V, VI, and VII has all been reduced to standardized lengths so that rates may be obtained easily from tables. This material has been rated by the Flesch formula (14) and has been arranged in order of increasing difficulty—from fifth grade through the upper college level, with most of the material falling in the range of the upper high school years.

Arrangement of materials

Although these materials are arranged by groups in the sequence believed to be most advantageous, the groups are designed for some overlapping in class practice. For example, practice on "word meaning" exercises should be started when the class is only about 30 percent through the "word recognition" section. This overlapping in the four basic groups of exercises provides better continuity. The "idea reading," "exploratory reading," and "study reading" drills should be started at least by the second or third period of training and should be used regularly thereafter.

If time is limited, the odd-numbered exercises may be used for individual practice and the even-numbered ones for group work. If time permits, however, all the exercises may be used for group practice.

The purpose and method of procedure for each set of exercises is given immediately preceding that set of exercises. These include "Suggestions" for students to think about. Students should be urged to read these before they start the Series, and then to go back and review the suggestions again after having done one or two exercises in the Series.

Progress Charts are provided on pages 297–305 for maintaining daily records of reading progress for the period of training. Keeping this daily progress chart is an important aspect of self-motivation. Suggestions for effective use of these Progress Charts are presented in Section V for the reader. Teachers should clarify the use of these Progress Charts very early in the program and should check frequently to see if students understand and use these to set goals for self-improvement.

Types of exercises

The first exercises are designed primarily as speed exercises. In Series I, the major emphasis should be on the establishment of rhythmic eye movements and increased eye span. In Series II, understanding is emphasized, and most readers will slow down. Each error indicates a possible misunderstanding of three words that may become reading blocks. The key word obviously may be a problem as well as the one marked in error. But the correct answer that was overlooked also might be a clue to a vocabulary problem. Hence students should be encouraged to develop vocabulary lists and to study words missed to increase vocabulary.

Series III continues this stress on understanding but deals with groups of words and emphasizes the increasing eye span and the perception of ideas rather than words. In this sequence, stress is put on gradual increase of eye span in both a horizontal and a vertical direction.

Series IV concentrates on rapid scanning for basic ideas in a sentence.

Series V provides practice in high-speed reading for basic ideas. The tests on these materials consist of two questions relating only to basic thoughts or ideas in the material. Here both rapid reading and correct understanding are important. The questions are of the same type for each exercise. Questions are designed to pick up recurrent thoughts, basic themes, or overall purpose in the article. The primary purpose of this series, however, is to emphasize the development of high-speed reading with minimal emphasis on comprehension.

Series VI places stress on more accurate reading for short periods of time. Here again, the tests follow similar patterns for each exercise; but, in this case, they require more attention to detailed ideas and facts presented in the material.

Series VII demonstrates an application of the Self Recitation technique and helps students develop a better understanding of that process. It emphasizes the importance of *thinking* as they read. These units are matched with those in Series VI for readability, length, and types of questions asked, but here the reader is required to stop, think, and respond to questions at intervals throughout the exercise.

Series VIII provides some initial practice in critical thinking and is designed to help develop an inquiring and critical mind. A series of short excerpts from undisclosed sources is presented with basic questions for consideration on each. Keys reveal the sources and purposes of each selection.

Sequence of exercises

This book can be used for reading improvement in many types of training groups. In general, the writer recommends a ten-week training period to provide time for additional practice and application. A five-week training period has been demonstrated to be less satisfactory but still productive. Periods shorter than five weeks may have limited carry-over value.

As an illustration of a procedure for the overlapping of exercises—for college students or adults—one might consider the sequence used in many of the extension classes at the University of Wyoming. The pattern shown on page 333 is that used in a class that meets once weekly for one-and-a-half to two-hour sessions.

During the last half of the course, workbook practice should be supplemented by longer reading exercises from current materials or from standardized ten-minute reading exercises. The supplementary workbook *Maintaining Reading Efficiency* (30) provides a collection of standardized reading exercises appropriate for this purpose. *Efficient Study Skills* (35) provides a series of standardized reading exercises in which the content is related to the building of more effective study skills.

Motivation

Experience has shown that giving the exercises in overlapping sequence usually proves stimulating to the students. Precise timing and pacing are essential to help readers achieve maximum progress in reading efficiency. All exercises should be monitored by a stop watch or a standard pacing tape, and the time of completion, in seconds, should be given out to each student as soon as he finishes an exercise. Pacing will provide motivation if time intervals are called out regularly on a five-second or ten-second basis. The Reading Efficiency Tape mentioned earlier provides a standard pattern of pacing at five-second intervals for a ten-minute period with instruction for effective use. Many teachers find these tapes helpful for general classroom use with a reading class or for check out to individuals who want to practice under some pressure outside the class.

The instructor must be available constantly to provide encouragement and motivation, not only to the group as a whole, but to individual students as well. In addition to using pacing techniques as mentioned before, one should suggest goals. For example, in Series I, one can suggest that most students should be able to finish in 30 seconds or less. In Series V, the instructor can suggest that all students should strive to complete these exercises in 60 seconds or less. Accuracy in setting realistic goals in different exercises depends upon the developmental pattern of any particular group as well as the teacher's experience with the materials. Students always should be urged to improve their own scores. Encouraging competition with other specific members of the group also is quite effective in many cases, especially in study skills classes designed for athletes or for highly motivated able students.

Watching the fastest readers and calling finish times a few seconds before they are through helps to keep them working at a maximum. Calling out time intervals a few times after the slowest readers have finished may help them to avoid feeling that the whole class was waiting for them. If one or two slow readers hold up the whole class to the point that others are getting restless, however, something may need to be done to help both the individuals and the class. Rather than keep the whole group waiting, individual assignments can be made for slow readers. For example, one might ask them privately to complete only half an exercise. Extremely slow readers who retard the whole group should be removed from the group if possible and given individual help.

Emphasis should be placed on keeping individual progress graphs up-to-date and encouraging students to compare results of the trends in the various Series of exercises and to make frequent comparisons to their pretest scores. During the period between exercises, staff members should move around the classroom and provide individual comment and encouragement.

If reading machines are available, a short class demonstration with two or three class members may be an effective way of demonstrating to some skeptical individuals what their potential for eye movement really is. Thus, they may be stimulated to increase their self-motivation.

Scoring of questions

Series I is self-scoring because identical words were to be selected. Keys for scoring all of the other exercises are located on pages 317 to 332. In the completion exercises, individual teachers should use their own judgment in accepting "equivalent terms" for full or half credit.

These perforated key pages may be left in the book for self-scoring or may be removed by the teacher to discourage advance study of the answers. These keys are grouped according to odd and even numbers since some teachers like to make one set available for student use and to keep the other set secure for standardized testing in class.

Variations in use

Many teachers have reported a wide range of application of *Increasing Reading Efficiency* and *Developing Reading Efficiency* in their classes. The two books are developed in exactly the same form and pattern but at different levels of difficulty. Several teachers have reported the use of both books in the same classroom to meet the needs of a range of readers but with an efficiency of teacher time and supervision.

Innovative experimentation with different combinations or different sequences of exercises may produce more positive results for some teachers. The author is always interested in hearing from teachers who have developed new and interesting ways to use these materials.

TO THE READER

Can you spare the time?

Do you have the time to do what you want to, or are you running a little behind schedule? Have you missed any deadlines lately? Do you sometimes get desperate and wonder if you can keep up the pace in this fast-moving world?

Can you survive?

Every day thousands of students are facing the decision to drop out of school before graduating. On the college scene, only four out of every ten students who start ever attain their academic goals. In the daily routine, thousands of individuals lose their jobs because they cannot do all that their employers 100 expect. Often the problem is one of verbal communication. Frustration and failure lead many people into depression that may result in hospitalization or even suicide. How are you keeping up with all the conflicting expectations of family, friends, teachers, supervisors, employers, and community responsibilities?

Life in an exploding society

Survival is complicated by the rapid change that you encounter all around you. No previous generation faced the problems that confront you today. *The population explosion* has created many problems of competition for jobs, high unemployment, and increasing demands for flexibility in placement. *The knowledge explosion* overwhelms 200 many by the mere quantitative aspects. The world body of knowledge now doubles every six or seven years. Each year over 1,000 books per day are published. *The technology explosion* has plunged our world into a super industrial revolution. Over 90 percent of *all* scientific inventions have been developed within the last twenty years, most of them since you were born! Within your lifetime there has been more technological progress than the world has seen in 50,000 years. Culture changes faster than individuals can adjust. Many fall by the wayside. How good are *your* survival skills?

Could you use a time-stretcher? 300

Does the end of the day catch you with unfinished tasks regretfully laid aside? Do you sometimes need just a little more time to get things done? Would you really like to "stretch" your days? Do you really have time for reading newspapers, magazines and other recreational materials you'd like to? Like many others you may find that at least one third of your time is required for reading of some kind. At the same time, you probably recognize that your reading habits are not adequate to meet these demands, and

400 you may become depressed when you cannot keep the pace and complete the amount of reading you feel that you should.

No one has developed a "time-stretcher" to lengthen your days for you, but for years many educators have studied the problem of slow reading habits. Research since World War II, however, has led to many improvements in techniques and has encouraged new approaches to achieving greater reading efficiency. Reading centers today are using many techniques and group exercise materials that represent great advances over those used twenty years ago.

Developmental reading services are now available to many high school and college students and adults. Many participants in these classes have made 500 astonishing improvements in reading skills without any serious loss in comprehension. Thus one is able to do, in five hours, the reading that once took ten hours. Many individuals have increased their reading efficiency much more than this. Saving these five hours for other activities may give you the "time-stretcher" for which you may have wished.

One reading authority once computed that the saving in time required to do all the reading in the nation, computed at only 50 cents per hour, would be more than five billion dollars if every American 600 over fifteen years of age were given reading training for at least a month (8).[1] Many industrial concerns have recognized this potential saving of manpower and have subsidized reading programs for their employees with very gratifying results. Many students have found free time for greater enjoyment of their school activities by registering for classes in reading efficiency. What benefits could you obtain if you were to double your reading efficiency? Would that help you to survive?

Are you ready to be exposed to a program to increase your reading speed? Some individuals who have become faster readers have not necessarily 700 become better readers. If you have difficulty understanding what you read now, you will not be helped by learning to misunderstand faster. If you have a very inadequate vocabulary, you will not be helped to learn to skip any faster through unknown or vaguely defined words. In either case, you have the challenge of developing some basic skills and knowledge before you really can benefit from a reading efficiency program. But first, let us explore a few attitudes you may have about reading.

---

[1] All reference numbers refer to the numbered selected references on p. 27, with the second number, if any, identifying the page number.

Exploding some myths

Before going further in your exploration of the reading process, you should consider some of the myths that students often use to rationalize their failure to improve their reading skills: $\overset{800}{\leftarrow}$

1. *No one can really read over 800 words per minute.* They can quote many authorities, especially those who have been critical of some of the commercial reading programs in recent decades. This statement is based on an analysis of typical eye movement patterns and typical eye fixations. If one accepts a definition of reading that involves an *actual eye contact with every word* in the material, then this limitation of 800 words is a fairly accurate statement. Most people $\overset{900}{\leftarrow}$ use the term *reading* in a much broader sense, however. Reading is a communication skill used to *communicate ideas by means of the written or printed message.* In this sense, the upper limits of speed in communication have not been identified.

2. *Skimming and scanning are bad habits that I should avoid.* Again this is based on a misinterpretation of the critics of speed reading. Within the broader concept of reading, these skills are very valuable and essential aspects of efficient reading and effective study.

3. *My comprehension will drop if I read fast or skim.* $\overset{1000}{\leftarrow}$ There is no foundation in research to support this. Raygor and Schick (46) made the following comment after an extensive review of research: "It is relatively easy for most people to make very significant increases in the rate at which they read without any loss in reading comprehension."

4. *Machines are necessary to improve my speed.* This idea is perpetuated by salesmen for some media companies, but again Raygor and Schick (46) report: ". . . experimental studies have shown no difference between the various methods and, in fact, have shown no advantage for any of the devices over the use of the book." $\overset{1100}{\leftarrow}$

5. *My eyes won't let me read fast.* With the exception of a very few persons with severe physiological handicaps, research has shown that most people have the potential in the brain and the eyes to function at much higher levels of reading than they have ever tried.

6. *It is wrong to skip passages in reading.* This is an old-fashioned idea still perpetuated by some teachers and guaranteed to make reading a deadly dull experience. All modern concepts of reading and study skills stress the importance of being selective and using judgment in deciding what to $\overset{1200}{\leftarrow}$ read and the extent of detail needed.

7. *I must read every word to get meaning.* Many words are necessary to sentence structure or to an author's style, but are not essential in the $\overset{1700}{\rightarrow}$ communication of basic ideas. Good readers learn to seek out those words that convey meaning and give minimal attention to many supporting words.

Set your own goals

You should realize, however, that your ability to increase your speed and comprehension significantly depends upon many variables—intelligence, physiological and psychological traits, general background of knowledge, motivation, previous reading $\overset{1300}{\rightarrow}$ experience, diligence in doing recommended practice, and general attitude toward reading and toward the reading group with which you work. No one can predict how much you will improve from the pretest to the posttest. People love to quote "averages" or outstanding achievements that seem dramatic, but there always are individuals all along the scale. Only you can determine your own achievement!

You must recognize also that there is no one speed of reading that you attain and maintain. There are many speeds that must vary with the nature of the reading activity and with your own familiarity $\overset{1400}{\rightarrow}$ with the materials. You should have a purpose in mind as you read. This purpose should help you understand more and remember better. The purpose is a determining factor in *how* you read. You may have many good and logical reasons for reading, but, at any one time, you should know *why* you are reading *that* particular material in *that* particular way.

Different people cannot and should not read at the same rate. You establish your own unique patterns of reading. You probably will be able to achieve a significant improvement by using these materials, but it takes a lot of self-discipline, hard $\overset{1500}{\rightarrow}$ work, and often monotonous practice to replace old reading habits with new, more effective ones.

When you finish this work, you should be able to identify substantial personal growth. Whatever your measured rate at that time, you should have achieved the flexibility of at least *four* rates. Your slower rate will be the one to use when you have to pay close attention to detail for later retention. You can have another (about twice that fast) when you read for relaxation.

When you skim for new ideas, you can go about four times as fast as your slower rate; and when you $\overset{1600}{\rightarrow}$ scan to locate specific material for specific purposes, your rate may be much higher.

Much more could be said about the reading process before you start your program, but perhaps a few suggestions and ideas thrown in along the way will be more helpful. At least some students who used this material before thought so! On the introductory pages for each new series of exercises, you will find "suggestion" sections. May I suggest that you read these again *after* you have done the first few exercises. In that way we can "keep in touch" as $\overset{1700}{\rightarrow}$ you read your way through this workbook.

I

How Do We Read?

Good reading is a key to new information and ideas. It opens the door to many opportunities to enrich your life. Your reading skills are essential aspects of self-preservation in a dynamic society. You probably place great importance on becoming a successful reader.

But what are the characteristics of successful readers? You might say that they are the ones who keep up with their fair share of the millions of words of printed material that is created in the world each day. This means that they are able to keep up with all of their personal and professional correspondence and to keep informed on significant developments 100 in their society from skimming newspapers and news magazines. They must find the time to deal with their daily mail and to keep up on developments in their business or professional field through many specialized professional publications. For a balanced life, they also find time for reading for pleasure in areas of their own personal interests.

For most students, success in reading those materials essential to all of their academic course work is merely a preparation for the challenge of the deluge of reading materials they will face when they leave the academic field and go out into the world of work. 200

Even if your plans do not include intense specialization for a professional field of work, you will still find that successful reading is an essential for coping with many daily problems in the modern world. Operating instructions for cars, boats, machines, appliances, and household equipment are a challenge to everyone. Unless you can read application forms, insurance policies, sales contracts, and employee memos effectively, you may miss many of the opportunities for personal improvement and protection open to you. You also may find yourself vulnerable to many unscrupulous salesmen or promoters. You have a real stake in your 300 long-term effectiveness as a successful reader. You may find it very helpful to give some thought to how you became the kind of reader you now are, and to how you can move toward a higher level of success in your own reading.

Good reading involves not one skill, but many. Although some individuals can increase their rate of reading without specific training, few can improve—without such help—their comprehension, analytical skill, judgment, skimming and scanning skills, and the technique of adjusting their habits of reading to their purpose and the nature of the material. These 400 skills require thorough understanding of the reading process and practice in a carefully planned program.

The first fact that must be recognized is that your present reading habits are the result of your early experiences in learning to read and your continuing experiences in reading over a period of years. These habits, practiced for many years, are hard to break. You may encounter many feelings of insecurity while you are in the process of substituting new habits for old. Therefore, you should give some attention to how you may have developed some of 500 your present reading habits.

Development of reading habits

Many articles in popular periodicals have criticized public schools and current methods of teaching reading. You should be cautious in placing the blame for your habits on the schools you attended, however, and should consider several other factors that have affected your own particular reading habits. Consider the following factors and see which of them may have had an effect on your habits of reading:

1. Reading is not demonstrable as are speaking, walking, or problem solving. It is impossible to *show* someone how you *read*. It involves recognition of many symbols that have no meaning 600 in themselves and that must be combined in innumerable combinations in order to convey meaning to others. The visible eye movements and fixations are only a small part of the total reading process involving a continuous invisible mental process.

2. The irregular supply of well-qualified developmental reading teachers in the last few decades has resulted in the assignment to reading classes of many teachers who possessed only limited interest, desire, or skill in the teaching of reading. Such teachers may have overlooked individual needs and problems in reading development. Unintentionally, they may have reinforced some negative self-concepts and 700 created negative attitudes toward reading. Such teachers may have stressed reading every word, oral reading, vocalizing, and enunciating every syllable. Overemphasis on such factors may make some students feel guilty about any attempts to develop efficient silent reading skills. Under these circumstances, many young people continue to pass through our school systems

without developing a sound pattern of basic reading skills.

3. Schools have been developing better methods of teaching. The children in elementary schools today are getting better basic training in reading than their parents in the past. Many teachers now have greater understanding of the factors of reading and of the learning problems of the ←800 1200→ individual student. In all periods, however, some schools have developed programs that are more effective than those in other schools.

4. We have come through a period of conflicting philosophy about the basic approach to reading. Some teachers insisted that the ''phonics'' approach of sounding out syllables was the best method. Others were completely dedicated to the "sight reading" approach of recognizing words as units of meaning and developing a vocabulary by visual association. As a result, we had a great variation between different schools and even between teachers in the same school, with a resulting confusion on the part ←900 1300→ of the students. Fortunately, today most of our elementary teachers are recognizing that both "sight reading" and "phonics" have a place in developing reading skills. Unfortunately, they still are not in complete agreement on the best combination or sequence of application of these two ideas.

5. Our population has become increasingly mobile, and, as a consequence, many children do not follow the planned sequence of courses in a single school, but attend many schools during their elementary years. Thus they may miss a basic part of their reading instruction because it has not yet been reached in one school, but ←1000 has already been covered in another school to which they transfer.

6. Overcrowded schools, in many instances, contributed to poor reading because the problems of the individual student were overlooked and the teaching was directed toward the assumed average of the class. Better schools attempt to discover individual problems in reading through testing programs and observation, and try to provide special attention for slow readers by means of remedial reading classes.

7. Specific instruction in reading has placed emphasis on oral reading, and limited attention has been given to helping the student discover various techniques to be used in silent reading. ←1100 Consequently, some people have carried oral reading habits into silent reading practice.

8. Instruction in reading skills often is terminated after the fourth or fifth grade. It was assumed by both teachers and parents that, having mastered the basic skills of reading, the student 1600→

could make the adaptations of those skills to the different reading needs he would face later. Unfortunately, many individuals made few adaptations, and many adults today try to read adult-level materials, using reading skills appropriate for a fifth-grade level of reading.

9. Many students who feel that they are poor readers really are expressing an attitude rather than a limitation in skill. At some time, they may have had a very frustrating experience in a reading program, and they may still continue to carry bad feelings about reading that make them feel inadequate in facing current reading problems.

10. Many adolescents and adults avoid activities involving reading because they are self-conscious about some reading problems. As a consequence, lack of practice has made their existing habits even more ineffective.

The process of reading

A second important fact to recognize is that we do not read while our eyes are moving. Just as the motion picture is made up of many still pictures flashed before us rapidly, so our reading is a series of visual impressions carried to our brain in a rapid sequence. We stop for each glance and then move on for another glance at another word or phrase. Reading rate, then, is a combination of the amount we see at each glance, the length of time we hesitate for each eye fixation, and the speed with which the eye can move and focus on another unit of material.

The first of these factors is referred to as *eye* 1400→ *span*—the quantity of reading material one can see at one glance. For some people this may be a single word; for others, one complete phrase; and for others, still larger units of thought. For the very rapid reader, this may be several lines or a paragraph.

The second factor is closely related to the thinking process. It is referred to as a *rate of perception*. How long does it take to register the impression of what you see and to transmit it to your brain, and how long does it take the brain to 1500→ interpret what was seen? Unless one has had an injury resulting in damage to brain tissue, he probably is capable of a great deal of acceleration in this thinking process.

The third factor of rate is that of eye movement in shifting from one point of focus to another. This is primarily a physical factor requiring the acceleration of rhythmic habits of eye movement.

The average individual is not aware of his complex pattern of reading habits and, therefore, makes little effort to coordinate the factors affecting his reading efficiency. Recognition of various types of reading and adjustment of reading habits to the 1600→ type and purpose of specific reading assignments are essential. Most individuals have developed a rather limited range of reading efficiency, however, and therefore have little leeway in adjusting to different types.

One of the greatest contributions of a reading program is that of increasing the ceiling on reading speed. As one increases this upper limit of reading speed, of course, he also increases his range of reading efficiency and develops greater flexibility in his reading habits. By focusing attention on reading habits and placing an individual in a position where he is stimulated to operate at his maximum, teachers find that most persons are capable of reading at least 1700 twice as fast as they had been doing. Thus the normal adult who may be reading at a rate of about 250 words per minute actually may be capable of reading 500 words per minute or more if properly stimulated. With practice and concentrated personal effort, this individual may learn to read at 750 to 900 words per minute. Many individuals have made even greater improvements; reading class records reflect many persons who have read 2,000 or 3,000 words per minute. Some reading centers have reported individuals who have achieved rates as high as 50,000 1800 words per minute on certain types of material. The potential maximum reading speed of any individual is unknown. The possibilities for any normal adult seem to be limited only by his own interest and his determination to improve. Only *you* can determine just how fast you can read, but you can be assured that you should be able at least to double or triple your present reading rate and perhaps to achieve much more than that.

How do we read faster?

Slow readers may possess any one or a combination of poor reading habits. Most of these habits 1900 can be changed by recognizing the factors involved in the habit. Glance over the list of poor reading habits below and see which ones may apply to you; then consider what you might do to change these habits.

Vocalizing. Sounding out each word as if you were reading aloud slows you down to a snail's pace. This may be only a mental pronunciation process, but frequently it is accompanied by the moving of the lips as you read. If you do this, try placing your finger tightly on your lips as you read until you have broken the habit of lip movement. Once the lip 2000 action is broken, you will find it easier to push yourself to faster rates where mental vocalization decreases considerably.

Word-by-word reading. Looking at one word at a time to be sure you understand it may obscure the overall meaning of the sentence or paragraph. Remember the old adage about the man who could not see the forest because of the trees. To break

yourself of this habit, try reading for ideas instead of words. Try to grasp whole phrases in a glance and sense their meaning.

Word blocking. Stopping to worry about an 2100 unfamiliar word breaks the rhythm of your reading and makes you lose the trend of thought or miss some of the main ideas. If you do this often, you probably have a poor vocabulary and need to work intensively on building up a greater understanding of commonly used words. In many instances, you can find the meaning of a certain word in the context, however, if you will just keep reading with an emphasis on ideas instead of words. Later on, after you have finished reading, you can go back and check the dictionary for some of the words that 2200 troubled you. After looking them up, think about their meaning and try to use them several times in conversation or writing that same day. This will fix the meaning in your mind. But do not let new words upset you and make you feel self-conscious. Most people encounter new words in their reading and take them in stride, identifying their meaning from other words or phrases with which they are associated.

Number attraction. Some readers come to a complete stop every time they reach a number. They seem to want to study it carefully as if it were 2300 a completely different concept of communication. Unless you are studying thoroughly for detailed content, dates, and quantitative ideas, you should try to generalize the numerical idea into verbal symbols such as "many" or "few," "long ago," "recently," "next year," or similar clues that will help in getting general ideas from the material.

Word analysis. Stopping to analyze a strange word as to its origin, structure, prefixes, and suffixes may be a sound vocabulary building exercise, but it 2400 destroys the trend of thought in reading and may lead to many false impressions, as meanings of many words vary with the context in which they are used. We must look for the larger ideas. *Seek the ideas behind the words.*

Monotonous plodding. Keeping the same pace of reading in all materials, from light fiction to heavy study, is tiresome. You need flexibility in reading habits. Let yourself go on some reading materials and do not worry about comprehension. You are missing much of the enjoyment of recreational reading by applying to it the same type of reading used for study. Learn to adjust your rate to the type of material and the purpose for reading it. Good readers 2500 may read at a very slow rate if they want detailed understanding, but read at a rate of several thousand words per minute on fiction, light correspondence, and other materials they are reading for main ideas or for recreation.

Finger following. Following a line of print with a finger or with a guide of some kind always slows down the reading process because fingers can not move as fast as eyes. To break this habit, keep both hands in your lap if reading at a desk, or hold the book in both hands. Rely solely on your eyes to follow the printed page.

Head swinging. Moving the head from side 2600 to side as one reads is much more laborious than moving the eyes. In addition to slowing down reading, this increased muscular activity will hasten fatigue. If you have this habit, try holding your head firmly in place with your hands and force your eyes to do the moving until the habit is broken.

Clue blindness. Like the driver who is too busy watching the road to see the signposts that direct him to his destination, many readers become too involved in word reading to notice such things as headings, subtitles, styles of type, listings, illustrations, introductions, and summaries. These 2700 all are important clues put in by the author to help you understand his concept of what is important. Try looking through some materials, reading only the headings and the ideas set off by a different style of type or by listings, and see how much you can really get from these clues alone. Use the introductory paragraphs and lead sentences as clues to organization and the summary statement as a review of material read. Try to develop the ability to glance over some material and get an understanding of the author's style and the types of signposts he 2800 has erected for you.

Backtracking. Going back to reread words or phrases is an indication that you doubt your own ability to pick out the important material. It slows you down a great deal because you are constantly thinking back instead of looking ahead to spot new ideas. Consequently, you miss ideas until you have gone past them, and then you have to go back to pick them up. The more you backtrack, the more necessary backtracking becomes to you. Try to concentrate on reading everything *only once.* You will be surprised to find that you get an overall 2900 understanding of it without the mental underlining.

Rereading. Closely associated with backtracking is the habit of going back to read the whole assignment over again to be sure you understand it. Studies have shown that rereading is a fairly ineffective method of reviewing immediately after study (39). If you concentrate on doing a good job of reading in the first place, a few minutes of thinking about what you have read will be far more valuable than rereading. Try laying the reading material aside after you have finished it and thinking over what you have read. This not only will develop a better 3000 understanding of the material, but also will serve as an aid to remembering it later.

Daydreaming. Allowing your attention to wander to other things while you read leaves you with the feeling of having covered pages but having no knowledge of what you have read. To overcome this, you must develop the ability to concentrate on one thing at a time. This matter of concentration is complex and will be discussed in detail in Sections III and IV.

Programs for improvement

Unless a person has a serious physical or mental handicap, none of the habits mentioned above 3100 is serious. All can be overcome with concentrated practice. Thousands of people have overcome them and established flexible reading habits that enable them to read several times more efficiently than they did before. Some individuals find that bifocal glasses limit their reading speed. Usually, this problem can be overcome by changing to reading glasses.

Colleges and businesses have come to realize the benefits that can be obtained by providing a training situation in which individuals can be motivated to achieve such changes of reading habits. Such reading programs try to force the individual to 3200 read faster by applying pressure of various kinds.

Some training centers rely heavily upon me-chanical devices such as the reading films, tachistoscopic devices, flash cards, reading-rate controllers, and reading accelerators of various types. Some use these devices for group work; others provide them for individual practice. The reading center in your vicinity may have one or more of these types of training devices with which you can practice if you are interested in them.

Other centers rely largely upon group drill methods and the psychological pressure of competition within the group as a motivating device. In such situations, the instructor usually will use 3300 pacing techniques and a great deal of urging to get students to read faster.

Regardless of the program, much of the prog-ress depends upon the motivation of the individual. Unless you really want to improve your reading and are willing to try out new ideas in an attempt to break old habits, you will gain but little from the experience. If you really want to improve and will try new approaches to reading, the possibilities seem unlimited for your improvement in reading rate.

How do we understand more of what we read?

All of the techniques discussed above are 3400 designed primarily to increase rate of reading, but reading is a complex process, of which the rate is only one factor. In this workbook, emphasis is placed upon *reading efficiency,* which is a combination of factors. In order to understand this term, we should first define clearly what is meant in this book by certain other terms, such as rate and comprehension.

Rate of reading is a numerical expression of the amount of material covered in a unit of time. It is expressed in words per minute. Thus a normal adult reading rate of 250 means that a normal adult should be able to cover 250 words of the material he is 3500⇆ reading each minute.

Just covering words or pages would mean little if you did not grasp some meaning from what you read. Comprehension, therefore, is an essential factor 4000→ in good reading. Let us stress, however, that perfect comprehension is not the ideal of good reading, for perfect comprehension would be almost synonymous with memorization of the material, and this is seldom essential. The degree of understanding is measured more commonly in terms of the understanding of the main ideas and basic facts expressed in the reading. In some reading, it is more important to get a fairly 3600⇆ thorough knowledge of these facts than in others. Therefore, comprehension also should be flexible and should be adjusted to the type of material read and the purpose of reading. One hundred percent comprehension is seldom needed unless one is memorizing material. For most reading, a 60 to 80 percent comprehension is adequate. For light recreational reading, detailed comprehension is even less important. In studying, you should be concerned with more detailed comprehension, but should not depend on reading alone. Here you need to use a balanced study approach that will make use of other techniques of understanding and remembering material. 3700⇆ These are discussed in some detail in Section IV.

One of the most important factors in improving comprehension is that of having a purpose for reading. This purpose must be personalized to be effective. Mere reading of material because an instructor assigns it is not sufficient. You, personally, must see some reason for reading the material and must be looking for something in the material read. There are several ways of developing this personal interest.

First of all, you should *think* before starting to read. Think about the subject matter covered in the material. What do you already know about it? What 3800⇆ would you like to know about it? What do you know about the person who wrote the article? Is the author an authority? Is he or she well-known for personal prejudice on this subject? Will the presentation be biased? Can you depend on statements being accurate and complete, or is the author likely to try to persuade you in certain ways by presenting only partial facts or distorting views of the problem? These are just some of the questions which you should ask yourself before starting to read, but thinking about them will help to establish a good 3900⇆ mental attitude toward reading the article with interest and concentration.

After having spent a few seconds in thinking before starting to read, glance over the article quickly to look for clues. The headings and boldface print will tell you the direction that the article will take in presenting the ideas. This helps prepare you to recognize important points as they are presented.

A third point in helping improve concentration and retention of material is to concentrate on small units, one at a time. Intense concentration on the portion between two headings with a slight pause to rest your eyes and think about the material before going on to the next section will provide relaxation as well as help to organize your thinking.

Take a few seconds after each unit, and a longer time at the end of the reading period, to think over what you have read and to fix a mental impression. This will help you to retain that impression for a longer period of time. In short, an alternation of reading and thinking provides a greater comprehension of what is read.

In order to measure comprehension, you must 4100→ be tested in some way to see how much you remember of what was read. Comprehension usually is expressed numerically as a percentage score. *The comprehension score is the percent of questions answered correctly in a test on the material read.* A good reader should be able to score at least 60 to 80 percent on such a test, depending on the number of questions asked and the amount of detail involved in the questions.

What is reading efficiency?

Many students, in trying to increase their reading rate, become disturbed when their comprehension drops. Others trying hard to improve 4200→ comprehension slow down in an attempt to get better understanding. Many reading teachers have found that the faster readers often secure better comprehension scores than the slower readers. Similarly, they find that, at the end of a reading training program, students often read at several times their original rate with comprehension as great as or greater than they did before starting training. Although most of them go through a period of decreased comprehension while they are working hard on increasing rate, they find that, as they become adjusted to reading at a faster rate, they are able to build up their comprehension again.

4300→ Neither rate nor comprehension really gives us the complete picture of reading skills. Reading at a rapid rate is of little value if you understand very little of what you have read. On the other hand, reading with a high degree of comprehension is of little value if you never have time to read all the material you are expected to cover. The most important factor is *neither* the speed at which you read *nor* the amount you can remember of what you read, but a combination of these: *the amount you can read and remember* per unit of time. In an attempt ←4400 to express this factor and place an emphasis on the importance of this combination of skills, we use the term *reading efficiency* to represent the amount of material comprehended per minute of reading time. Efficiency is computed by taking the product of the *rate* of reading (expressed in words per minute) and the *comprehension* score (expressed as the percent of correct answers on a test over the material). *Efficiency*, then, is a numerical expression of rate of effective reading represented in words per minute. Let us compare the following sequence of scores to see how this works.

	1st test	2d test	3d test	4th test
Rate	150	200	400	600
Comprehension	80	70	60	70
Efficiency	120	140	240	420

←4500 ←4900

If this individual were to consider only the decreasing comprehension scores during practice, he might become discouraged and stop pushing his rate improvement. By stressing the efficiency score instead of rate or comprehension, he gets a better picture of his real progress, however; and although his final comprehension score is still below his initial one, his efficiency score gives a better picture of the amount of material he can grasp in a unit of study time. This individual probably would find that he was ←4600 accomplishing at least three times as much work in his periods of reading as was possible before, and the slight difference in comprehension could be offset by other techniques of remembering.

Throughout this book, stress will be placed upon the efficiency scores on reading exercises because efficiency seems the best expression of the effectiveness of reading habits.

Conditions for improvement

In this chapter you have been urged to explore some new possibilities for reading improvement, recognizing some of the bad habits that may slow you down, some of the factors that influence these reading habits, and some of the terms used to describe the ←4700 results of reading habits. We have presented the idea that anyone is capable of improving his reading efficiency unless prevented from doing so by physical or mental handicaps. The question remains: How can *you* improve your reading efficiency? Three conditions are needed to make satisfactory progress in the improvement of reading efficiency.

First of all, you must be convinced that you want to become a better reader. You must be willing to put in several hours of hard and sometimes monotonous work in reading practice. You must be 4800→ willing to face the problems of being compared with others, of competing with others, and of working under pressure that may be irritating. You must be willing to cast aside established habits in order to try new ones. You need to be convinced that the time to be saved in the future, when more satisfactory reading habits have been established, is worth the sacrifice of several hours of your time now. If you can see the long-range value and are willing to work, your possibilities of improvement are practically unlimited.

Second, you will need to work with appropriate materials from which comparisons can be made to determine improvement. Unless the exercises you use are of comparable difficulty, misunderstanding and discouragement may follow. Unless all sets of questions are made in comparable forms, your scores in comprehension may vary because of the difficulty of the test rather than your degree of understanding. There will be a better chance of progress if you work from a workbook that has been standardized and that has comparable tests. The materials used in this workbook represent the results of many years of experimentation and revision in order to develop the best possible sequences of exercises. Note that all 5000→ exercises are marked with a readability score. These scores are determined by the application of the Flesch formula (14) to the material. Exercises are arranged in a gradually ascending order of difficulty so that, as you learn to read faster, you also learn to read material of a little greater difficulty.

Finally, you must feel a sense of progress and satisfaction. Using your scores from one exercise to set goals for the next one will help sustain your motivation. You must compare results of today with those of yesterday and then set higher goals for 5100→ tomorrow. The reading progress charts in this book help you to do that. They are organized in such a way that you can compare results on any particular exercise with others in that series, or with different types of exercises. Keeping your reading graphs up-to-date will help you to get an overall view of progress in increasing your reading efficiency. The extent of your growth in effective reading skills will depend upon your desire, your attitude, and your concentration.

A combination of motivation, concentration, and comprehension should lead you to a deeper level of understanding and to more effective retention of 5200→ the materials you read.

II

Kinds of Reading

Recognize types of reading

If you want to evaluate your success as an effective reader, you might look at your ability to adjust your reading to the different types of materials and to your different purposes in reading. The greater the range of reading efficiency you have, the greater possibilities you have to judge what types of reading skills are most appropriate for what materials. Limited space in this workbook prevents the presentation of detailed analysis of the various types of reading and their application. However, a brief consideration of some of the major types of reading may help you to understand your present reading 100 habits and your reactions to some of the work you will do in this book.

Purpose for reading

Some authors see only two major classifications for your purpose for reading. Either you are reading for ideas or reading for facts. Either of these purposes has specific implications for you. These may be reviewed in considerable detail in two pairs of books: *Reading for Ideas* (40) and *Reading for Facts* (39) by Pauk and Wilson, or *Reading for the Main Idea* (44) and *Reading for Significant Facts* (45) by Alton Raygor.

In addition to these major classifications, one 200 might add the purpose of "light" reading for entertainment and that of "heavy" reading for aesthetic appreciation of style, content, or philosophy. This type of reading involves a combination of intense concentration and uninterrupted contemplation that is not readily measured in terms of rate or comprehension.

Regardless of your basic purpose in reading, you constantly should use reading as a channel to improve vocabulary. Some good resources to help you improve your process of vocabulary development are *Basic Vocabulary Skills* by Davis (12), *Developing Vocabulary Skills* by Joffe (19), and *The Teacher's Word Book of 30,000 Words* by 300 Thorndike (55).

Skimming and scanning

These two terms are used interchangeably by many writers. They are denounced as inappropriate labels for reading by many critics of speed reading. Some writers refer to these activities as "semi-reading" skills. Many writers in the developmental reading field do recognize them as types of reading that have very significant meaning in the total reading process. They feel that these types are essential to

the total development of flexible and efficient reading skills.

Both techniques involve reading by the "signposts"—the clues set up by the author. By using 400 these you can learn to skip materials that are not of immediate interest to you and to locate more quickly those that you really wish to read in detail. Most textbooks are organized to make intelligent skimming possible. All devices such as chapter titles, sectional headings, **boldface** or *italicized* type, and underlining are clues to help you with this technique. Take time to think before you start to read, and get a good idea of just what you are looking for. Then clues can save a great deal of reading time by leading you 500 right to the sections in which you are interested. This allows you to skip over the rest.

In recent years, some writers have attempted to establish a difference between the two terms. There is no general agreement on this distinction, however. Emphasis on scanning as a search for main ideas and on skimming as a search for specific facts or details is presented by both Norman (38) and Pickett (42). They are presented in exactly the opposite pattern by Adams (1), Maxwell (26) (27), and Thomas and Robinson (53). This latter position seems to be more widely accepted, however. It will be used in 600 this publication. *Skimming* is that technique of rapid reading designed to identify the major ideas and relationships discussed in an article. *Scanning* is that technique used to locate and utilize specific facts or ideas related to a predetermined goal. Both skills require preplanning and intense concentration to be effective.

Skimming is the basic first step in the well-known SQ4R method of study discussed in Section IV. Skimming also can be very effective as a preliminary step to reading something more thoroughly. It gives an overview of what you can expect in the material.

Scanning is an essential aspect of any search for 700 specific information. Use it in sources such as telephone books, encyclopedias, dictionaries, or general reference sources. It also is an essential aspect of the self-recitation study technique, which emphasizes reading to seek answers to predicted questions.

Idea reading

Idea reading extends use of skimming techniques beyond the heading into the content paragraphs. It involves more comprehensive coverage of total word content, but in a highly selective fashion. It is most essential in many types of business and professional reading as well as in much incidental and recreational reading. The basic meaning of many published articles could be condensed into several simple statements.

This reading for the main ideas is a technique 800 of rapid reading in which the eyes move rapidly. They catch large phrases at each glance and register with the brain only the most significant words or ideas in those phrases. Successful idea reading is perhaps one of the most difficult types of reading to master. It is also one of the most efficient. One can develop extremely rapid rates of reading with it. It means being familiar with the makeup of the English language as a means of communication. Rapid recognition of key sentences, illustrative words and phrases, and the skeletal structure of the sentence is 900 essential to discovering the basic meaning. Idea reading means making quick decisions as to the relative importance of different sentences and paragraphs as you read. It means quick recognition of the author's clues and rapid association with ideas you already understand that relate to this material.

Exploratory reading

Exploratory reading, or general content reading, involves more detail than the two types mentioned before. This type of approach is appropriate for longer articles in magazines, for descriptive literature, and for light fiction. It may be used for similar reading in which you wish to pick up a better 1000 understanding of some new ideas. You should use this technique on many outside references in which you wish to find background material, but in which you will not be tested for detail. Emphasis here should be placed on recognizing and understanding main ideas more thoroughly. You should relate them to other ideas in the article or to previous knowledge of the subject.

Study reading

Study reading is a type in which you must get a maximum understanding of the main ideas and their relationships. This is the type you must apply to your textbooks. You may apply it to contracts, legal papers, technical manuals, instructions, and other similar materials. Here you frequently deal with materials that you must read and understand 1100 *now* and also remember for future use.

Clues are important. A preliminary scanning may be quite helpful. The actual reading process, however, needs to be an alternating activity between reading for ideas and thinking about those ideas. The actual reading process itself may be quite rapid, but greater skill must be developed in thinking and organizing the ideas for long-term retention. Many different study skills must be used to supplement the reading process. These are discussed in more detail in Section IV.

Critical reading

Another type of reading that must sometimes 1200 be applied wisely is that of critical reading. You may find a certain article that tends to stir you to action. You may feel you should write to your congressman or rush downtown to buy some new and indispensable household appliance. Then you should stop and consider what you have read more carefully. Many periodical articles, books, and advertising materials are loaded with carefully worded propaganda devices. These are designed to sway your opinion or to sell you on some particular idea or product. Be careful that a rapid reading of the main ideas does not lead to false conclusions.

To apply techniques of critical reading, you 1300 should go back and consider carefully what you know about the source of the reading material. What are the possible biases or ulterior motives that its publisher or author may have? You also should consider what you know about the author's background experience and potential knowledge of the subject. You should watch the reading material for inconsistent logic or false analogies. Particularly important is an awareness of emotionally loaded words that appeal to basic emotions. With experience, you soon can learn to spot some of these types of appeals through quick scanning for the clues the author 1400 provides. Then you can beware of these techniques before beginning to read. In any reading, you should frequently ask yourself: "What is the author trying to make me believe and why?"

Analytical reading

Certain sections of study materials require a much more thorough type of reading than those mentioned before. Mathematical theorems and problems, scientific formulas and certain definitive statements of key ideas require careful attention to each word and to its relative importance. You must approach such reading with a questioning mind, seeking complete clarification. You can learn to recognize such passages and to slow your reading 1500 pace to deal with such sections more adequately.

Identify and adjust

By learning to recognize different types of reading and to judge what types of reading skills to apply to them, you may become more effective in your overall use of reading time. Streamline your reading activities to meet the needs of the time and the material to be read. Such judgment can be developed only from practice. This workbook will provide an opportunity to practice several types of reading, but you must apply the principles of efficient reading to the materials that you read every day if 1600 you hope to maintain really efficient reading habits.

III

Is Reading Enough?

Reading is what *you* make it. You can make your reading hard work, or you can make it an exciting adventure. It can be drudgery or relaxation. From the previous chapters you should have developed a better understanding of *how* you read, and *why* you read that way. You understand *how* you can control further development in your reading skills to make them more effective for you. Your eyes and your brain have the potential to make reading skills work in any way you desire.

Only you can determine the ultimate effectiveness of your reading skills. But a word of caution is 100 perhaps appropriate.

Overdependency on reading

No one would question that reading is essential to personal development. Too many persons jump to the conclusion, however, that reading is the *only* respectable approach to learning. They tend to depend *entirely* on reading for gaining new ideas and for understanding them. They frequently consider audiovisual devices as mere recreational gadgets of momentary interest but of little lasting value. Such persons may completely ignore the possibilities of note making from speeches, conferences, seminars, and telephone conversations as an effective technique. They often consider note making in conjunction with reading as too much extra work.   200

Extreme dependency on reading may make you fearful of any techniques that might lower your reading comprehension even temporarily. This fear is the basis of much hesitancy in learning.

You may be afraid that if you develop faster rates of reading, you will lose some comprehension accuracy. Research shows that this is not a matter for concern (38). Most people are able to make very significant increases in their reading rates without any significant loss in comprehension. Many fast readers maintain comprehension levels much higher than the average for their age or grade.

But reading still has its limitations in compari- 300 son with some other means of communicating ideas. For most people, reading is one of the slower techniques of picking up ideas. A picture sometimes can convey as much information in one glance as several pages of descriptive literature could do. The oral statement often can be made to convey much more meaning than the same statement in print. The speaker can do this through the changes of tone or inflection and the verbal stress on certain words.

Identification with the author

One way to get more understanding from the 400 printed page is to seek a better understanding of authors as unique individuals. Find out more about who they are and what they have done. Use the title page or introductory comments to try to get a feel for their attitudes and enthusiasms. Try to visualize these authors as persons like yourself. They want to express themselves clearly to you, but they need your help to do it effectively. As you read, try to identify their attitudes, interests, and biases. Watch for their use of tone and inference. Study how they use words and figurative language to individualize 500 their presentations. Seek evidence of their use of critical judgment. Watch for evidence of their distinction between fact, fiction, and personal opinion. Seek help if you need assistance in developing these skills of personal identification with the author. You can find many detailed suggestions in *Developing Reading Versatility* by Adams (1) or in *Reading for Ideas* by Pauk and Wilson (40).

Some supplements to reading

One reason some people feel so self-conscious about their reading may be that they are too dependent upon it. They may fail to associate it adequately with other means of communication. 600 Think about some of the techniques that can be used to enrich its meaning.

Listening involves skills often overlooked and ignored. A speaker uses many "signposts" just as the writer does. He or she uses introductions and summaries during which you should be thinking. Relate what you hear to what you already understand. Changes of tone, pitch, and rate of speaking are used to emphasize certain points. Speakers use lead statements as headings to new topics. They frequently list or itemize points they think are important. The listener who is alert to these clues can learn a great deal during these concentrated periods of listening.

Thinking is the conscious process by which you try to control some of the activities of your brain. Thinking seems to be a very rapid, continuous process that may or may not be in tune with your reading or listening activities. Because thinking seems 700 to go on at a speed so much greater than reading or listening, you must make a special effort to achieve some congruence in these activities.

Perhaps your thinking process can be focused on three phases of learning activity. First is the recognition of facts that are significant to you for some reason. Second is the fusing of your understanding of the purpose, function, and specific relationships of these facts with your existing knowledge. Third is the classification and filing away in the brain for future application and use.

Learning may be enhanced by a three-stage classification system. First, you identify the general topic of the author. What or who is he or she writing ⤺ 800 about? Next, what special area within that topic is the focus of this unit of reading? Finally, what attitudes is the author expressing about this special area of this topic? Such an approach may help you in seeing relationships and achieving long-term retention of significant information.

Note making is a very important technique for the busy student. By relying on brief notes, you can relieve the stress of detailed mental comprehension of many minute facts of temporary importance. Brief, well-organized notes taken on important reading assignments provide an excellent basis for review at ⤺ 900 a later time. An important aspect of good notes, however, is that they are *made* in the writer's own words rather than *taken* as a few random excerpts from the speaker's terminology (6).

Self-recitation of important points helps to keep them in mind. This process of predicting questions to which answers must be found requires occasional pauses to think over what is being read. The questions posed serve as a goal for reading. The pauses for thinking provide brief relaxation for the eyes.

Frequent review of important materials is an invaluable aid in remembering and will make later ⤺ 1000 rereading unnecessary. Well-organized notes are a much more effective basis for review than reliance on rereading or on skimming again the material originally read on the subject.

Improving comprehension

In the previous chapter, reference was made to several techniques that might be used to improve comprehension. These are all supplementary techniques not actually a part of the reading process itself but closely related to it. At this time, let us consider more carefully the actual steps involved in these activities.

Orienting oneself to the reading assignment

Most efficient individuals operate on some sort of schedule. They plan a certain time of day for ⤺ 1100 reading. By having regular times for certain types of reading work, they get into habits of thinking about these things at regular periods. This helps to establish a "mood" for reading. This can be intensified by

taking a few minutes to survey the reading to be done, to arrange it according to importance, and to anticipate the questions that must be answered in the reading.

Getting the overall view

In the consideration of any particular item of reading, rapid skimming of pages looking for key ideas will set up general idea goals to be attained. This will make the task more meaningful.

Reading to find answers to questions

In the preview of the material, you will recognize several main topics. As you approach each topic, try to pose questions for yourself to give you a purpose for reading. You will find that looking for 1200 → answers does much to focus your interest more sharply. This helps you attain faster rates of reading.

Visualizing and making associations

As you pause, at intervals, try to form a mental picture of the things about which you have been reading. Relate the ideas to something you already know and understand. Establishing associations with known facts will provide a more thorough understanding

Making notes from materials read

If you are reading to organize material for a speech or a report or if you want some deails for later use, take some notes *in your own words* during 1300 → your pauses. Brief notes with personalized expression help you to organize verbal concepts more clearly. These notes should have more lasting meaning for you. If you have difficulty concentrating on important material, making notes forces you to think about it.

Reviewing

Use some time *regularly* to think over materials read during the previous few days and to pull together the important ideas from various sources. This is an invaluable supplement to the reading process. Ideas picked up from very rapid reading can be fixed more firmly in your mind for later use.

In summary

These techniques will serve to strengthen your 1400 → comprehension of what you read. They will make it easier for you to relax. They will allow you to read at a maximum rate without fear of losing comprehension. The time you save in rapid reading should provide an opportunity to use some of these techniques so important to remembering ideas and their 1450 → relationships.

IV

A Program for Effective Study

The ideas in the previous sections are basic to any sound program of study. You need to develop sound habits of study if you hope to live a balanced life and to survive in the competitive academic world today. You must provide time for both academic requirements and social opportunities. Many colleges are attempting to help students establish such habits by the provision of classes in "Study Skill Techniques." Such courses recognize reading as one aspect of study, but also point out that efficient reading *alone* is not enough to meet the competition of college classes today.   100 ←

Let us look at some of the factors that are important in study. We might consider them by asking five questions about effective study:
What? Who? Where? When? How?

What is effective study?

Many students, even some of those who receive good grades regularly, spend a' great deal more time in study than is necessary. These students have developed study techniques that are laborious and time-consuming. Other students spend many hours in study, but seem to get little out of the time spent. They frequently complain about difficulties in certain courses, and the only remedy they can think of is to spend more time on that subject. In both cases 200 ← the students probably are ignoring some basic principles about fatigue and span of interest. Instead of spending *more time* in study, they need to make *better use of the time* they do spend. You need to get the most possible good out of each hour spent on a course. This is what is meant by *effective study.* If you have effective study habits, you will spend *less* time on the same material and will understand it better than one who has not learned effective methods.

Whose responsibility?

In high school, parents and teachers usually try 300 ← to encourage study habits by providing certain times and places for study, and by trying to reduce possible interruptions. As you grow older, however, you find yourself more "on your own." Especially at college you will find that no one seems to exert much effort to *make* you study. By now you are supposed to be mature enough to realize that study is essential to success in school. One very important aspect of maturity is the personal assumption of responsibility

for control of your time. Achieving freedom from control by others implies developing greater self-control and exercising self-discipline. Therefore, it 400 → is your responsibility to see that you provide adequate time for study. Other school activities will place many demands on you, and you will find it easy to devote to them time that should be given to study.

Some students realize too late that they have been neglecting their studies and try desperately to cram all their study and review into the last few days before examinations. When they fail the exams, they frequently rationalize and blame the instructor, their roommates, or someone else for their inability to keep up with the requirements of the course. With 500 → the keen competition present in college, poor study habits can undermine the entire enjoyment of a college program. An early recognition of this could save much unhappiness.

If you wish to improve your academic record, you must assume the responsibility *yourself* for keeping up-to-date in all your school work. The sooner you accept this responsibility seriously, the more likely you are to succeed in your school program. Specific suggestions to help you establish better study habits are given on the following pages.

Where to study?

Some students are able to study almost anywhere. While walking or resting, they may be 600 → mentally organizing ideas. Many students, however, do not have this ability to concentrate in the midst of other activity. Even when seated at a study desk, you may find other ideas creeping into your mind to keep you from thinking about the school work waiting to be done. You may find it helpful to consider some of the factors that *you can* control to make that study desk a more effective place to work.

Auditory distractions usually can be controlled by selecting as quiet a place as possible. You can reduce, to some extent, distraction from outside 700 → noises. This may mean working out arrangements for study hours with your roommate and making an agreement not to have guests in the room during certain hours. If you find yourself unable to eliminate these distractions in your own room, then consider the scheduling of study hours in the library, where the atmosphere is kept as quiet as possible. Another possibility is the use of a vacant classroom for those free periods between classes.

Some students find that a radio or stereo set playing continuous music and set at a minimal volume creates a sound barrier sufficient to block out the variety of outside distracting noises. By careful selection of the station or of recordings, you can establish a stable sound background to which you can adjust and thus be protected from the uncontrolled sounds of your environment. In doing this, however, you need to keep your volume low enough to avoid creating sound distractions for others who work near you.

Visual distractions frequently are present without being recognized. The picture of a friend on your desk may take you off on a chain of pleasant memories every time you glance at it; the souvenir ash tray you picked up on your vacation trip last summer may recall many pleasant experiences; the colorful new sport jacket you wore to the last ball game may revive the excitement and competition you enjoyed then; the letter you got from home yesterday may start you worrying about the situation at home; the advertising on the desk blotter may stir thoughts of the good times you could have if you only followed the suggestions printed there. The curling smoke from the cigarette in your ash tray may attract your attention and lead your thoughts astray. These and many other items frequently found on study desks may lead you to many minutes of daydreaming during the hours when you *think* you have been studying.

One of the first essentials in improving the place of study is to clear the desk of as many of these diverting influences as you can. If possible, the study desk should be cleared of everything except the textbook you are studying at the moment and the necessary papers and pencils for taking notes.

Next, consider what disturbing items lie in your range of vision as you sit at your desk. Consider carefully any objects that lie in the area of distraction. To do this, check the *angle of distraction* from your study desk. Any object falling within a 60-degree angle on either side of the forward view from your desk is likely to interfere with your concentration. Mirrors are especially disturbing as they expand the area of distraction to include a reflected area as well as the actual one. How many things in your room fall within this range? What do they make you think about? To improve your concentration you would be wise to move your desk so that the space included in this area of distraction is at a minimum and so that most of the wall surfaces included are blank. Ideally, then, a study desk should be placed in a corner, and the wall above it should be kept clear of distracting influences.

Lighting is also an important factor in concentration. Eye strain and general fatigue are the logical results of poor lighting. Do not depend on a single overhead light. You need a good desk lamp that will provide indirect lighting in your working area. Desk lamps that cause a glare on the books and papers should be avoided. In addition to a good study lamp on the desk, some other light in the room is needed to prevent sharp contrasts between a brightly lighted desk and a dark room. Extreme contrasts make the eyes tire more rapidly. A combination of a good, indirect desk lamp and an overhead light is considered ideal for effective study conditions.

Ventilation and temperature are important, too. There should be some provision for fresh air without a draft. If you cannot work with a window open, make a point of airing out the study room once a day. A warm room develops drowsiness and makes studying difficult. Usually, you can study best in a room that is slightly cooler than the normal living room temperature.

Avoid physical relaxation when trying to study. If you pick the easy chair or the bed as a place to study, do not expect to be able to concentrate very long. By relaxing physically, you invite mental relaxation as well. A good straight chair at a study desk is the ideal location for effective study.

Having one place for study *and study only* is important. If you study at the same place that you play games, do your nails, write your letters, or plan dance programs, you will find it more difficult to get to work. If, however, you use one desk exclusively for studying, you will find it natural to start concentrating when you sit there.

You can control the environment in which you try to study. Do not blame others for distractions. Take time to check out your study area, and do some reorganization to make it an atmosphere more conducive to effective study.

When to study?

Your school program is one of your most important obligations and requires more time than you are likely to give to it without careful planning. The best protection against late assignments and the necessity for "cramming" is to budget your time as you go along and to plan a proper balance between work, study, and recreational activities. One of the best ways to do this is to use a *Time Budget Sheet*. A sample *Time Budget Sheet* is shown on pages 23 and 24. Copies of these usually can be obtained through your school bookstore. The success of such a time budget will depend on how carefully you plan it and use it. Several points should be considered. The suggestions on the back of the *Time Budget Sheet* are worthy of careful consideration. Read them thoughtfully; think about their meaning to you. Discuss them with your advisor or with a counselor if you need help in applying them to your own planning.

How to study?

Probably no two students study in exactly the same way. You have learned certain techniques that seem easiest for you. If these techniques bring you understanding of the materials with a minimum expenditure of time, then you are probably satisfied with these study habits. If, however, you feel that you are not getting the desired results or that your methods are too time-consuming, then you should consider a change. If your present study habits are leading only to poor grades and discouragement, they should be discarded and replaced by a new set that may lead to more effective use of your time.

Many students fail to make effective use of new techniques of study because they are unwilling to give up the old techniques, even though these older ones have not produced the desired results. Often it is necessary to *unlearn* poor work habits before you can establish good ones. If you wish to develop a greater efficiency in your study, you must be willing to release some old habits in favor of some new ones.

Space in this book does not allow a detailed discussion of all techniques of study. You will find many good references on study skills in your library or your bookstore. For detailed suggestions on note making, you may read *Learning More by Effective Study* by Charles and Dorothy Bird (6). For specific suggestions on classroom and examination skills, you will find *Effective Study* by F. P. Robinson (47) very helpful. For detailed information on the preparation of reports and term papers, you can find assistance in *The Research Paper* by Hook and Gaver (18). *Tips to Improve Personal Study Skills*, prepared by the New York State Personnel and Guidance Association (37), is a concise pamphlet—an excellent reference to keep in your notebook. Other references with detailed suggestions to improve study habits are *A Time to Learn* by Bandt, Meara, and Schmidt (4), *Study Skills* by Carmen and Adams (9), and others (2), (7), (13), (21), (22), (35), (48), (56).

Three "S. R." techniques

Three major techniques presented by Francis P. Robinson in his book *Effective Study* (47) have proved to be so helpful to many college students that they merit a presentation here. These techniques provide an excellent means of establishing important ideas in one's mind and retaining them. These may be identified as the three "S.R." techniques because these letters can be used as common memory clues. All three require a high level of personal self-discipline and planning. Only you can make them work for you. In brief, these techniques may be applied as follows:

A. **Self-Recitation.** Ask questions of yourself as you study and as you review. Be alert at all times

to the questions suggested about major ideas, and try to read for answers to them. In reviewing, ask yourself questions, and see if you can answer them; then check your answers against your notes. In studying for exams, try to predict the questions that the instructor may ask, and be prepared for these questions in the examination.

B. **Spaced Review.** Review briefly immediately after study; then review again within a week. Each week, schedule review periods where you can review all the material presented thus far in the course. These brief weekly reviews will reduce the necessity for any last-minute cramming before examinations.

C. **The SQ3R Method.** Originated by Robinson (47), this method frequently has been called the SQ4R Method for purposes of clarification. The following explanation of the six steps of this method has been presented by Miller and Seeman (36).

The SQ4R method of study

1. **Survey.** Glance over the headings in the chapter to see the few big points that will be developed. This survey should take only a few seconds and will show the several core ideas around which the discussion will be developed. This preview will prepare you for more effective study of the details in the following steps.

2. **Question.** Turn the first heading into a question. This should arouse your curiosity and thus aid comprehension. It will help to bring to mind information that you already know. In this way, your understanding of that section will be increased. The question will make the important points stand out.

3. **Read.** Read to answer the question. Make this an active search for the answer. You will find that your eyes tend to move more rapidly over the material, slighting the unimportant or explanatory details while noting the important points.

4. **Recite.** Try to recite the answer to your question without looking at the book. Use your own words, and think of an example. If you can do this, you know what is in the book; if you cannot, glance over the section again. If you jot down "cue" phrases in outline form as you do this, you will have an excellent basis for later review and study.

5. **Repeat.** Repeat steps 2, 3, and 4 on each succeeding section. Turn the next heading into a question, read to answer that question, and recite the answer by jotting down "cue" phrases in an outline. Read in this way until the lesson is completed.

6. **Review.** Look back over your notes to get a bird's-eye view of the points and their relationships.

Check your memory as to the content by reciting on the major subpoints under each heading. This checking of your memory can be done by covering up the notes and trying to recall the main points, then exposing each major point and trying to recall the subpoints listed under it. Save these notes for later use in *Spaced Review* activity.

SQ4R applied to problem solving

A modification of the SQ4R Method to apply to mathematical-type reading that involves problem solving might be summarized as follows:

1. **Survey.** Look over the problems to see what types of logic they require and what basic formulas will 2700 be used. Try to make associations with practical situations in which similar problems might be encountered.
2. **Question.** Looking at the first problem, think through it to be sure you understand what is the unknown factor which you are to find and what are the known facts with which you can work.
3. **Solve.** Work through the problem to find the unknown factor.
4. **Check.** Substitute the answer you have found for the unknown in the original statement and see if it makes sense. Check through the basic formula to see if it balances with this value. 2800
5. **Repeat.** Apply steps 2, 3, and 4 to each successive problem in the assignment.
6. **Review.** Check over the whole assignment again to be sure you have completed all the assigned work and that your answers were reasonable. Be 3100 sure you understand the purpose of such exercises, and try to think of practical applications of principles involved in the problems.

Concentrate on end results

The application of these three "S.R." techniques will free you from much of the tension associated with trying to get thorough comprehension from the reading alone. Frequently, students depend 2900 on one reading of the material to grasp its entire content. The methods outlined above decrease the stress on detailed comprehension in initial reading. They provide other study techniques—skimming, questioning, reciting, and reviewing—to develop the understanding of material. This frees you to read as rapidly as possible with a major emphasis on *seeking the ideas behind the words*.

Improving comprehension requires a constant awareness of your own goals and a sensitivity to the ideas and organization of the author.

As you develop this technique of rapid reading, you usually will find that comprehension will improve 3000 also. But more important than either is the efficiency of reading—that is, the amount you understand per unit of study time. By increasing the efficiency of the initial reading, you can find time for the other techniques, which will help build a more permanent comprehension of the whole body of material. More than that, a combination of efficient reading with effective study techniques should enable you to get more studying done in less time. So you should have more time to spend on other things you want to do. This is your ultimate reward for exercising self-control of your own study habits and environment.

TIME BUDGET SHEET

COLLEGE FORM

Name

(Study the suggestions on the back before making out budget)

Prepared by
Lyle L. Miller
UNIVERSITY OF WYOMING

S R STUDY PROGRAM — Self-Recitation / Spaced Review / SQ4R Method

SELF-RECITATION

	MON	TUES	WED	THUR	FRI	SAT	SUN	TOTAL
12-2								
2-4								
4-6								
6-7								
7-8								
8-9								
9-10								
10-11								
11-12								
12-1								
1-2								
2-3								
3-4								
4-5								
5-6								
6-7								
7-8								
8-9								
9-10								
10-12								
CLASS								
STUDY								
TOTAL								

S P A C E D   R E V I E W

These three evening plans interchangeable

SURVEY   QUESTION   READ   RECITE   REPEAT: QRR   REVIEW

Original Copyright: 1955 by Lyle L. Miller; Revised Edition Copyright: 1969

SOME HINTS ON PLANNING A BETTER TIME SCHEDULE

Lyle L. Miller

Professor of Guidance and Counselor Education, University of Wyoming

The effectiveness of your time schedule will depend on the care with which **you** plan it. Careful consideration of these points will help you to make a schedule which **you** can control and which will **work for you.**

1. **Plan a schedule of balanced activities.** College life has many aspects which are very important to success. Some have fixed time requirements and some are flexible. Some of the most common which you must consider are:

   FIXED: eating   organizations   classes   church   work
   FLEXIBLE: sleeping   personal affairs   recreation   relaxation   study

2. **Plan enough time in studying to do justice to each subject.** Most college classes are planned to require about three hours work per week per credit in the course. By multiplying your credit load by three you can get a good idea of the time you should provide for studying. Of course, if you are a slow reader, or have other study deficiencies, you may need to plan more time in order to meet the competition of college classes.

3. **Study at a regular time and in a regular place.** Establishing habits of study is extremely important. Knowing what you are going to study, and when, saves a lot of time in making decisions and retracing your steps to get necessary materials, etc. Avoid generalizations in your schedule such as "STUDY." Commit yourself more definitely to "STUDY HISTORY" or "STUDY CHEMISTRY" at certain regular hours.

4. **Study as soon after your lecture class as possible.** One hour spent soon after class will do as much good in developing an understanding of materials as several hours a few days later. Review lecture notes while they are still fresh in your mind. Start assignments while your memory of the assignment is still accurate.

5. **Utilize odd hours during the day for studying.** The scattered one-hour or two-hour free periods between classes are easily wasted. Planning and establishing habits of using them for studying for the class just finished will result in free time for recreation or activities at other times in the week.

6. **Limit your blocks of study time to no more than 2 hours on any one course at one time.** After 1½ to 2 hours of study you begin to tire rapidly and your ability to concentrate decreases rapidly. Taking a break and then switching to studying some other course will provide the change necessary to keep up your efficiency.

7. **Trade time—don't steal it.** When unexpected events arise that take up time you had planned to study, decide immediately where you can find the time to make up the study missed and adjust your schedule for that week. Note the three weekend evenings. Most students can afford no more than two of them for recreation, but may wish to use different evenings on different weeks. This "trading agreement" provides for committing one night to study, but rotating it as recreational possibilities vary.

8. **Provide for spaced review.** A regular weekly period when you will review the work in each of your courses will help to keep you up to date. This review should be cumulative, covering briefly all the work done thus far in the quarter. Such reviews will reduce the need for "cramming" later.

9. **Practice self-recitation as a device for increasing memory.** Organize your notes in a question and answer form and think in terms of questions and answers about the main ideas of the material as you review weekly. When preparing for exams, try to predict the questions the instructor may ask.

10. **Keep carefully organized notes on both lectures and assignments.** Good notes are one of the best bases for review. Watch for key ideas in lectures and try to express them in your own words in your notes. Watch for headings and bold face type in your reading to give you clues of main ideas for your notes. Take down careful notes as to exactly what assignments are made and when they are due.

11. **Always try to improve your study efficiency.** The SQ4R method of study is a very sound approach to improving comprehension. Details on this method can be found in the library in Chapter IV of "Increasing Reading Efficiency," published by Holt, Rinehart, and Winston, New York City 10017 or in Chapter IV of "Developing Reading Efficiency," published by Burgess Publishing Co., Minneapolis, Minnesota 55415.

Publisher:

DEVELOPMENTAL READING DISTRIBUTORS

1944 Sheridan Ave.
Laramie, Wyoming
82070

Using This Workbook

The exercises in this workbook have been grouped according to types, each of which plays a distinct part in the development of more efficient reading habits.

On the page preceding each series of exercises, you will find instructions and illustrations of the type of work to be done in that series and further suggestions about the purpose and use of that material.

Series I
Word recognition exercises

Word recognition exercises are designed to accelerate rate and to establish some rhythmic patterns of eye movement. As you proceed through these exercises, you will find yourself dealing with longer words. Here you will have an opportunity to break ←100 the habit of syllabication and to learn to pick up longer words at a single glance.

Series II
Word meaning exercises

Word meaning exercises, involve you in thinking processes as you are expected to identify synonyms at a rapid pace. The arrangement is the same as before, except that you now must think about word meanings. In addition to eye span and rhythmic eye movements, the factor of rate of perception has been added. Because all of the words used in these exercises have been taken from Thorndike's list (54) of the 30,000 most frequently used words in ←200 our vocabulary, these exercises also serve to point up potential weaknesses in your vocabulary list, which may need study. Any words missed here should be placed on a vocabulary list and studied carefully so that they will not remain as stumbling blocks to your reading.

Series III
Phrase meaning exercises

The third series introduces phrases and is designed primarily to increase eye span. At the same time, you continue to practice on rhythmic eye movements and perception of meaning under time pressure. These are exercises in which you should begin to sense an improvement in rate of ←300

reading as you learn to pick up several words at one glance. These exercises begin with short phrases and gradually build up in length until the last few exercises are composed of phrases of several words.

Series IV
Sentence meaning exercises

The fourth series consists of exercises in recognition of sentence meaning. Here increased eye span is further stressed, and, in addition, you are expected to recognize the key words that provide meaning for a sentence. This is basic training for the idea-type of reading, in which you strip the sentences of their 400→ verbal padding to pick up the basic ideas. This series provides basic training in quick recognition of key ideas, which is essential to developing your skills in skimming for new ideas or scanning to pick up specific content.

Series V
Idea reading exercises

Series V is made up of short articles from which you are to pick up the main ideas or basic themes as quickly as possible. On these you should apply your techniques of *idea reading* to attain maximum rates with only a general comprehension of the more basic ideas being presented. Primary 500→ emphasis in this series is on the extension of your upper limits in reading rate.

Series VI
Exploratory reading exercises

The sixth series is composed of readings of longer length and greater complexity. They provide practice in *exploratory reading*. In these exercises you develop skill in reading at a fairly rapid rate, while concentrating for greater detail in terms of general content and ideas, rather than specific facts.

Series VII
Study reading exercises

Here you must stop and *think* to answer some questions at intervals in your reading. The basic purpose is to demonstrate how rapidly material can be covered even when you take time for thinking and 600→ answering questions. Although not an exact duplication of the *study* reading, in which you develop idea outlines, these exercises will provide an objective comparison of this type of reading. You can build skills in reading shorter units more intensively and in interrupting your reading with short periods of thinking and note making. These exercises provide opportunities for application of alternating patterns of studying: think . . . read . . . think . . . write . . . think . . . read. . . think . . . write . . . and so forth.

Series VIII
Critical thinking exercises

Here you must think critically about all of the materials presented to you. Exercises are identified only by a number, and you have to try to detect the $\overset{700}{\leftarrow}$ purpose and intent, author bias or propaganda, and attempt at emotional appeal. Emphasis here is not on rate, but on the quality of your thinking skill in dealing with unidentified material.

Computing scores and recording progress

On each exercise throughout the book, you are to record time, rate, comprehension, and efficiency. Tables are provided for looking up your reading rates. Each exercise refers you to the table for rates for that exercise.

Keys for scoring exercises are located in the back of the workbook. After computing the comprehension and efficiency scores, you should compare these with scores on other exercises to $\overset{800}{\leftarrow}$ determine your progress.

Progress Charts are provided starting on page 297 to record your scores on each reading exercise. Keeping these charts up-to-date will help motivate you to seek continued improvement.

If you record your current score and connect it with a line to your previous score on the same Series, you will get a broken line graph which will be your Progress Chart on that Series. For maximum motivation, record both your rate and your efficiency scores. Some students prefer only to plot the efficiency scores. When both scores are plotted, however, the $\overset{900}{\leftarrow}$ variation between the lines tends to emphasize the balance maintained in the comprehension as well.

Progress Charts for Series I, II, III, and IV are set up on the same page, 297, to make comparisons easy. The normal pattern of progress in Series I and II is quite similar with the scores for Series II staying about half as high as those for Series I. In both cases the scores will vary up and down slightly as you experiment with different ways to achieve your best efficiency. The general pattern should show a slight upward pattern as you move through each Series. $\overset{1000}{\leftarrow}$

Series III scores should start off at about the same level as Series II. These should climb much more rapidly as you develop confidence in your eye span.

Series IV scores should start slightly above Series II. These should show a consistent rise throughout the Series, but probably not as sharp a rise as you find in Series III.

The Progress Charts for Series V, VI, VII and for the supplemental longer reading exercises also are set up on the same pages for comparison. These begin $\overset{1100}{\rightarrow}$ on page 299, with extensions on the following pages.

The initial scores on Series V should be much higher than on any of the other Series. Your chart should show a rapid rise throughout this series as you develop self-confidence in rapid skimming and scanning skills.

In Series VI, your scores should start off lower than in Series V and build up much more gradually. When you maintain your comprehension at 60% or above, however, you should feel safe to push yourself to higher rates on each succeeding exercise. You should observe a consistent improvement in your progress charts here.

$\overset{1200}{\rightarrow}$ Series VII emphasizes the alternation of reading, thinking, and writing, so your scores here will be much lower at the beginning of the Series. As you gain confidence, you probably will find that you can read the short sections much faster and have more time for the thinking and writing. As you do so, you may be amazed to find these scores getting more and more like those in Series VI. Some students who have mastered the SQ4R method of study have found that their scores on Series VII sometimes exceed those on comparable exercises in Series VI.

Setting personal goals

As you move through each Series, you can help $\overset{1300}{\rightarrow}$ motivate yourself by setting goals of consistent improvement. Before starting a new exercise, look back at the time on the previous one in that Series, and try to cut your time a little bit.

You probably will find that your comprehension scores remain fairly constant as you increase your rate gradually. Errors in comprehension should be used to help expand your vocabulary. You *will not* automatically increase your comprehension by slowing down. Avoid the tendency to read more slowly whenever comprehension scores drop. Instead, go back and try to understand *why* you missed the specific items.

$\overset{1400}{\rightarrow}$ Effective use of these exercises should enable you to increase your reading speed at the same time that you are increasing your vocabulary and improving your skill in concentration.

You may develop your effective reading skills further by practicing on longer reading exercises such as those in *Maintaining Reading Efficiency* (30) or $\overset{1450}{\rightarrow}$ *Efficient Study Skills* (35).

Selected References

1. Adams, W. Royce. *Developing Reading Versatility*. 2d ed. New York: Holt, Rinehart and Winston, 1977.

2. Askov, Eunice M., and Karlyn Kamm. *Study Skills in the Content Area*. Boston: Allyn and Bacon, Inc., 1982.

3. Bamman, Henry A.; Midori F. Hujama; and Delbert L. Prescott. *Free to Read*. San Francisco: Field Educational Publications, 1970.

4. Bandt, Phillip L.; Naomi M. Meara; and Lyle D. Schmidt. *A Time to Learn*. New York: Holt, Rinehart and Winston, 1974.

5. Bieda, Margaret R., and Vinola S. Woodward. *Realizing Reading Potential*. New York: Holt, Rinehart and Winston, 1971.

6. Bird, Charles, and Dorothy M. Bird. *Learning More by Effective Study*. New York: Appleton-Century-Crofts, 1945.

7. Bragstad, Bernice J., and Sharyn Stumpf. *Study Skills and Motivation*. Boston: Allyn and Bacon, Inc., 1982.

8. Brown, James I. *Efficient Reading*. Boston: D. C. Heath and Company, 1952, 1965.

9. Carman, Robert A., and W. Royce Adams. *Study Skills*. New York: John Wiley & Sons, 1972.

10. Causey, Oscar S., ed. *Exploring the Levels of College Reading Programs*. Ft. Worth, TX: Texas Christian University Press, 1956.

11. Danks, Joseph, and Kathy Pezdek. *Reading and Understanding*. Newark, DE: International Reading Association, 1980.

12. Davis, Nancy B. *Basic Vocabulary Skills*. New York: McGraw-Hill Book Company, 1969.

13. Devine, Thomas G. *Teaching Study Skills*. Rockleigh, NJ: Longwood Division, Allyn and Bacon, Inc., 1981.

14. Flesch, Rudolph. *The Art of Readable Writing*. New York: Harper & Row, Publishers, 1949.

15. Fry, Edward B. *Reading Drills for Speed and Comprehension*. Providence, RI: Jamestown Publishers, 1975.

16. Gerow, Joshua R., and R. Douglas Ling. *How to Succeed in College*. New York: Charles Scribner's Sons, 1975.

17. Hess, Karen M.; Robert E. Shager; and Lanny E. Morreau. *Developing Reading Efficiency*. New York: John Wiley & Sons, 1975.

18. Hook, Lucyle, and Mary Virginia Gaver. *The Research Paper*. 4th ed. Englewood Cliffs, NJ: Prentice-Hall, 1969.

19. Joffe, Irwin L. *Developing Vocabulary Skills*. Belmont, CA: Wadsworth Publishing Company, 1971.

20. Joffe, Irwin L. *Finding Main Ideas*. Belmont, CA: Wadsworth Publishing Company, 1970.

21. Langan, John, and Judith Nadell. *Doing Well in College*. New York: McGraw-Hill Book Company, 1980.

22. Lenier, Minnette, and Janet Maker. *Keys to College Success*. Englewood Cliffs, NJ: Prentice-Hall, Inc., 1980.

23. Locke, Edwin A. *A Guide to Effective Study*. New York: Springer Publishing Company, 1975.

24. McNinch, George H. *Comprehension: Process and Product*. Athens, GA: The American Reading Forum. 1981.

25. Maker, Janet, and Minnette Lenier. *College Reading*. Belmont, CA: Wadsworth Publishing Company, 1982.

26. Maxwell, Martha J. *Improving Student Learning Skills*. San Francisco: Jossey-Bass Publishers, 1979.

27. Maxwell, Martha J. *Skimming and Scanning Improvement*. New York: McGraw-Hill Book Company, 1969.

28. Miller, Lyle L. *Developing Reading Efficiency.* Rev. ed. Minneapolis: Burgess Publishing Company, 1967, 1972.

29. Miller, Lyle L. *Increasing Reading Efficiency.* New York: Holt, Rinehart and Winston, 1956, 1964, 1970, 1977, 1984.

30. Miller, Lyle L. *Maintaining Reading Efficiency.* Rev. ed. Laramie, WY: Developmental Reading Distributors, 1962, 1967, 1973.

31. Miller, Lyle L. *Maintaining Reading Efficiency Tests.* Laramie, WY: Developmental Reading Distributors, 1967, 1970.

32. Miller, Lyle L. *Personalizing Reading Efficiency.* Rev. Ed. Minneapolis: Burgess Publishing Company, 1976, 1981.

33. Miller, Lyle L. "Speed Reading in the Seventies." *Educational Leadership,* Vol. 30, No. 7, 623–627.

34. Miller, Lyle L. *Teaching Efficient Reading Skills.* Minneapolis: Burgess Publishing Company, 1972. (A revision of "Accelerating Growth in Reading Efficiency.")

35. Miller, Lyle L., and Nelda Hernandez. *Efficient Study Skills.* Minneapolis: Burgess Publishing Company, 1984.

36. Miller, Lyle L., and Alice Z. Seeman. *Guidebook for Prospective Teachers.* Columbus, OH: The Ohio State University Press, 1948.

37. New York State Personnel and Guidance Association. *Tips to Improve Personal Study Skills.* Albany, NY: Delmar Publishers, 1968.

38. Norman, Maxwell H. *Successful Reading: Key to Our Dynamic Society.* 2d ed. New York: Holt, Rinehart and Winston, 1975.

39. Pauk, Walter, and Josephine Wilson. *Reading for Facts.* New York: David McKay Company, 1974.

40. Pauk, Walter, and Josephine Wilson. *Reading for Ideas.* New York: David McKay Company, 1974.

41. Phillips, Anne D., and Peter E. Sotiriou. *Steps to Reading Proficiency.* Belmont, CA: Wadsworth Publishing Company, 1982.

42. Pickett, Thomas. *Guide to Efficient Reading.* Minneapolis: Burgess Publishing Company, 1969.

43. Pugh, A. K. *Silent Reading.* London: Heinemann Educational Books, 1978.

44. Raygor, Alton L. *Reading for the Main Idea.* New York: McGraw-Hill Book Company, 1969.

45. Raygor, Alton L. *Reading for Significant Facts.* New York: McGraw-Hill Book Company, 1970.

46. Raygor, Alton L., and George B. Schick. *Reading at Efficient Rates.* New York: McGraw-Hill Book Company, 1970.

47. Robinson, Francis P. *Effective Study.* New York: Harper & Row, Publishers, 1946, 1961, 1970.

48. Spargo, Edward. *The Now Student.* Providence, RI: Jamestown Publishers, Inc., 1971.

49. Spargo, Edward. *Selections from the Black.* Providence, RI: Jamestown Publishers, 1970.

50. Spargo, Edward. *Topics for the Restless.* Providence, RI: Jamestown Publishers, 1974.

51. Strang, Edward; James A. Giroux; and Livia J. Giroux. *Voices from the Bottom.* Providence, RI: Jamestown Publishers, 1972.

52. Stroud, James B., and Robert B. Ammons. *Improving Reading Ability.* New York: Appleton-Century-Crofts, 1949; 3d ed., 1970.

53. Thomas, Ellen Lamar, and H. Alan Robinson. *Improving Reading in Every Class.* Boston: Allyn and Bacon, Inc., 1972.

54. Thorndike, Edward L. *The Teacher's Word Book.* New York: Bureau of Publications, Teacher's College, Columbia University, 1921.

55. Thorndike, Edward L., and Irving Lorge. *The Teacher's Word Book of 30,000 Words.* New York: Bureau of Publications, Teacher's College, Columbia University, 1944.

56. Walter, Tim, and Al Siebert. *Student Success.* New York: Holt, Rinehart and Winston, 1981.

Word Recognition Exercises

Instructions

Series I exercises are designed to help you develop control of your habits of eye movement. The exercises are of equal difficulty, and you should be able to reduce the time necessary to complete them quite rapidly. Keep practicing on them until you are able to complete an exercise in 20 seconds or less.

In these exercises are two columns of words, one with a single word and the other with five words. The first column contains the key word. On each line this key word is repeated somewhere among the five words in the other columns. You are to locate this identical word as rapidly as possible and underline or check it. Then you proceed to the next line and so on till you have finished. As soon as you have finished, check your time with the instructor or with a watch or timing tape. Record this time,

and look up your rate in the table on page 307. (Find your time in Column I, and then look in Column II for your rate.)

Next go back, and check your work to see if you have marked any words that were not identical with the key. Count your errors, and record them at the bottom of the exercise. Compute your comprehension by multiplying the number of correct answers by four (4). Compute your reading efficiency on this exercise by multiplying the rate you secured from the table by this comprehension score. Round off the efficiency score to the nearest whole number. Record both the rate and the efficiency on the Progress Chart for Word Recognition Exercises on page 297.

These exercises begin on page 31; rate tables are on page 307; progress charts, on page 297.

Example

22.	six	six	hexagon	fix	kiss	sex
23.	oxen	often	toxin	shown	oxen	boxes
24.	rite X	kite	ritual	right	rate	rite
25.	were	ware	we're	were	wear	went

Time 32 Sec. RATE (from table on page 307): R. 281
No. Correct: 24 COMPREHENSION (4% for each correct answer): (4 × 24) C. 96
I-0 EFFICIENCY (R × C): (281 × .96) = 269.76 E. 270

Suggestions

Although the primary purpose of this type of reading exercise is to break up old habits of rigid use of eye muscles and to develop your control of more rapid rhythmic eye movements, there is also an aspect of logical reasoning and sound study skill application that you may begin to apply.

The practice of speeded recognition of exact duplicates in words tends to reduce the thinking process requirements and to allow one to concentrate on eye movements.

You might want to consider this as a game in quick recognition of symbols, however, and begin to apply some logical thinking to the activity. Man lives in a world of symbols and must learn to identify quickly a wide variety of items by size, shape, color, or location in relationship to other symbols. Thus we can "read" a highway sign by its shape long before we actually can see the words on it. We often

can tell what brand of gasoline a station sells by the shape of its signs long before we can make out the words on those signs. Symbols help us to select our food, clothing, and recreational activities. Words are only verbal symbols, and we learn to recognize and use many of them as such without question or without deep thought process.

If this were a game in which you had to find boxes of an appropriate shape to pack something in, you would apply many skills once developed to help you in early learning experiences. Size and shape would be most important to you in selection. Although you cannot read words while your eyes are moving, you can form some impressions of size and shape. If you have a particular size and shape in mind, a word will sometimes seem to stand out from a group for you. The secret is in knowing what you are looking for so you can recognize it when you find it!

Let us consider the word in the first column as a symbol that we need to pack in the right size box. If we study it carefully as to size, shape, and unique irregularities in form, then we have some idea of what we need to look for in our "box pile" in the other column. A quick scan eliminates several of our choices because they obviously are too large or too small. So we have only one or two that have possibilities and that we might look at more carefully. A quick glance is often enough to convince us that one will do or will not do, and we quickly narrow our choice to the specific one that will fit our key word exactly. When we find the box that fits it perfectly, we do not have to search further.

Even if we did not understand meaning of words, we could still play this matching game with verbal symbols. Let us consider the basic rules of the game:

1. Concentrate first on the key symbol to be matched. Form a visual image of its appearance, its size, shape, and specific characteristics. Know what you are looking for!
2. Scan the answer section quickly for possible matching materials. Sometimes the perfect match will stand out clearly and can be identified without

detailed searching. If not, the scanning at least eliminates some choices that obviously do not fit.
3. Look individually at those most likely prospects identified in the scanning. Mentally match each one to your key, and discard it quickly if it does not fit.
4. Concentrate on your key symbol and matching it. Do not take time to study in detail all of the five choices. When you have found the match for the key symbol, *stop* your search. There is no point in looking at other empty boxes when you have already selected the right one for your key symbol.

Even simple exercises like these can be more than visual activity. Routine reading process is more than eye movement and word recognition. It can be a challenge to logical thinking as well. Time spent in thinking and establishing goals can pay off in quick identification and selection from the alternatives presented. Scanning as a rapid reading technique is effective only if you *think first* and have some idea for which you are seeking. You can use these exercises to help develop your goal-setting and scanning skills.

Reading can be fun if you think ahead and plan as you read.

Exercise I-1

1. beech   beast   beach   beetle   write   beech

2. civil   meat   civilian   civil   evil   civic

3. desist   desire   desist   design   resist   'shoe

4. fabric   fabulous   fabricate   ruining   fabric   fable

5. gun   gun   foil   gum   sun   gunnery

6. supple   supply   support   supplicate   minister   supple

7. miner   concern   miner   diner   mine   mineral

8. pebble   pebble   peddle   treble   medal   flout

9. redden   fish   reddish   gladden   redden   ratify

10. shrub   grub   tangle   shrub   scrub   rub

11. talcum   vacuum   talcum   annoy   welcome   falcon

12. unveil   bewail   unwieldy   object   sail   unveil

13. begot   forgot   begone   beget   begot   friend

14. clasp   clasp   head   clap   chap   class

15. cheat   cheapen   photo   cheat   check   chess

16. deer   dear   beard   dare   ever   deer

17. hadn't   haven't   hadn't   haddock   sign   aren't

18. meed   meed   rose   need   seed   mean

19. minus   minute   plus   case   minus   minor

20. peg   leg   pug   peg   few   pig

21. refer   reference   confer   dealt   defer   refer

22. random   random   ranger   ransom   rankle   medal

23. tape   tap   tape   stun   taper   ape

24. six   six   kiss   hexagon   sexton   sex

25. we're   ware   let's   we're   were   we've

Time 31 Sec.   RATE (from table on page 307):   R. 29

No. Correct: 24   COMPREHENSION (4% for each correct answer):   C. _____

I-1   EFFICIENCY (R × C):   E. _____

Record on Progress Chart on page 297

Exercise I-2

1. adopt   adapt   adopt   arrange   clot   adoption

2. belle   bell   bowl   peal   belle   belt

3. blight   light   oblige   punch   blight   blind

4. devout   devour   vault   devout   bout   about

5. farce   face   false   race   rigid   farce

6. hammer   hamper   stammer   hammer   midst   pound

7. job   syne   job   bog   jog   sob

8. he'd   held   she's   he   he'd   would

9. per   per   par   stir   pet   pert

10. pillar   pillage   pillow   pillar   pill   coarse

11. smelt   felt   rode   smell   melt   smelt

12. thine   time   thine   forest   thing   thin

13. he'll   she   hell   held   he'll   we'll

14. bent   bent   broad   scent   regard   tent

15. closet   cabinet   closed   tabby   clothes   closet

16. mud   muddy   dumb   mud   cud   muddle

17. fatal   fatal   futile   fated   frost   total

18. hap   hop   joy   hole   haste   hap

19. jolly   jelly   jolly   holly   haste   jam

20. mitten   hidden   smite   mitten   often   more

21. pirate   pistol   piracy   pilot   pirate   rate

22. sneak   ratify   sneak   neat   snake   sneer

23. sinful   fully   almost   sinister   awful   sinful

24. teeth   beneath   teem   aback   teeth   tee

25. villa   villa   void   silly   tell   house

Time_____Sec.   **RATE (from table on page 307):**   R. _____

No. Correct:_____   **COMPREHENSION (4% for each correct answer):**   C. _____

I-2   **EFFICIENCY (R ✕ C):**   E. _____

Record on Progress Chart on page 297

Exercise I-3

1. abuse   bruise   cord   abuse   bus   about

2. betake   betake   take   better   trace   rush

3. germ   fish   stern   worm   germ   gem

4. dilute   delude   dirt   dilute   rain   dish

5. scrap   bandy   scrip   rap   scrap   scrape

6. harlot   hauteur   harlot   lot   harlequin   marry

7. jumble   mumble   gore   jungle   rumble   jumble

8. stud   stud   study   extra   stub   studio

9. attain   sustain   rock   attain   attend   attach

10. cast   caste   fast   casting   true   cast

11. cycle   bicycle   cycle   master   cymbal   cyclist

12. gilt   silt   gild   gift   gilt   silk

13. pulp   pulp   pulse   pup   pulpit   town

14. beyond   below   beyond   yonder   frost   bead

15. cog   cog   fog   cogent   many   got

16. dirt   skirt   funny   ditty   dirge   dirt

17. felon   simple   fell   long   felon   felt

18. hast   last   hast   masque   haste   aster

19. jury   hurry   junk   jury   juror   fix

20. monkey   monkey   key   money   monarchy   skunk

21. style   mess   study   stile   stylish   style

22. remove   remodel   remnant   remove   move   take

23. wager   bet   wages   wag   wager   wagon

24. ten   tend   ten   bend   fen   ace

25. volume   rescue   voluntary   voluble   luminous   volume

---

Time_____Sec.   RATE (from table on page 307):   R. _____

No. Correct:_____   COMPREHENSION (4% for each correct answer):   C. _____

I-3   EFFICIENCY (R × C):   E. _____

Record on Progress Chart on page 297

Exercise I–4

1. awe   stop   awe   aware   awake   await

2. bog   log   bogus   bog   affix   dog

3. eschew   escort   shrew   screw   topped   eschew

4. ditch   ditty   ditch   witch   mansion   itch

5. flash   moral   flak   flash   lash   flask

6. herd   curd   heard   hero   herd   bird

7. massy   massy   stock   massive   mash   master

8. sultan   pending   sulk   sulky   sultry   sultan

9. plane   true   pane   plane   lane   plain

10. babe   baboon   babble   mercy   babe   baby

11. sober   sobering   sober   bolder   cold   sob

12. etch   etch   civil   etc.   catching   catch

13. goody   good   scorch   goodly   goodman   goody

14. bonny   sonny   bondage   bonny   risk   bone

15. racer   racer   race   eraser   south   tracer

16. dizzy   discreet   forth   divulge   dizzy   fuzzy

17. fleece   maximum   fleece   flee   fleet   feet

18. sunny   summon   summary   verbal   sunken   sunny

19. lard   lard   land   lord   hard   roll

20. muster   mustard   muster   accede   must   master

21. wean   wear   bean   luxury   weak   wean

22. revery   revery   revere   message   very   review

23. solder   rescue   older   solder   soldier   sold

24. thump   thumb   under   hum   hump   thump

25. weekly   meekly   weak   week   weekly   read

Time_____Sec.

No. Correct:_____

I–4

RATE (from table on page 307):

COMPREHENSION (4% for each correct answer):

EFFICIENCY (R × C):

R. _____

C. _____

E. _____

Record on Progress Chart on page 297

Exercise I–5

1. anybody   anybody   mixing   anywhere   anyhow   nobody

2. bumble   twist   bundle   bumble   bungle   bumblebee

3. cottage   cotton   phrase   pottage   cottage   cot

4. easily   eagerly   easily   easy   surgery   ease

5. freight   yearling   freighter   eight   free   freight

6. hurtful   hurtful   saddles   healthful   hurt   hurry

7. liver   livid   livery   liver   live   candy

8. notebook   cookbook   pawning   note   notebook   noted

9. prelate   preach   prelude   township   prelate   precede

10. saber   safer   sable   sober   wing   saber

11. stag   staff   vain   stag   stage   tag

12. trespass   tress   trespass   clocking   trestle   trespasser

13. appall   appall   appeal   apparel   misery   appear

14. burner   force   burn   bureau   burner   bunker

15. couple   coupled   reserve   couplet   coupe   couple

16. eddy   edify   eddy   yank   edge   edit

17. frighten   fright   hairpin   freighter   afraid   frighten

18. iceberg   ice   iceboat   iceberg   cooking   icebox

19. lock   lock   locker   idle   loch   local

20. novice   sucker   novice   novel   novelist   novelty

21. sailboat   iceboat   macaroni   sailboat   sailor   soil

22. staple   staple   mixture   stable   table   fable

23. triumph   triumphant   triumph   mulberry   trial   triumphal

24. worry   hurry   stock   worldly   scurry   worry

25. preservation   presentation   preservative   journalistic   preservation   reservation

---

Time_____Sec.   **RATE (from table on page 307):**   **R.** _____

No. Correct:_____   **COMPREHENSION (4% for each correct answer):**   **C.** _____

I–5   **EFFICIENCY (R ✕ C):**   **E.** _____

Record on Progress Chart on page 297

Exercise I–6

1. action   faction action fact act actor

2. colt   coax volt colt cotton mother

3. discord   disclose cord discourage discord office

4. feud   turn feud feudal futile rude

5. hawthorn   hawthorn hawk hauser fording thorn

6. kettle   mettle kernel kettle ketch morning

7. mope   mop hope scope rather mope

8. repine   sent repine repose pine reprove

9. sled   led slowed lead sled moist

10. theater   theater thaw heater theatrical fooling

11. adieu   mess die adieu adjure address

12. blank   blast lower blink last blank

13. disguise   disgust nesting dish guise disguise

14. fifteen   sixteen purple fifth fifteen teens

15. heap   leap heap heart heaven chair

16. kindred   kindness slacks hindered kind kindred

17. mosquito   moss faintly mosquito quite mosque

18. picker   lost picker picnic ticker pick

19. repulse   repulse repulsive repel pulse gauntlet

20. sling   slang sing sling slink force

21. therein   therefore in fiddle therein wherein

22. wampum   wanton wander pumice course wampum

23. comforter   comforter blanket fixture comfort fort

24. philosophic   philosophy microscopic physiology philosophic earnestness

25. birthright   birthright daintiness right birthplace birthday

---

Time_____Sec.   RATE (from table on page 307):   R. _____

No. Correct:_____ COMPREHENSION (4% for each correct answer): C. _____

I–6   EFFICIENCY (R × C):   E. _____

Record on Progress Chart on page 297

Exercise I-7

1. brand   brand   ran   branch   student   brandy

2. doz.   mature   dozen   doz.   buzz   oz.

3. foolish   cool   keelson   fooling   foot   foolish

4. holder   hole   holder   letter   hold   older

5. ledge   led   ledger   perform   ledge   edge

6. necklace   necktie   neck   necklace   marauder   lace

7. polite   polite   politic   light   polish   depart

8. rite   dully   rite   right   kite   ritual

9. spade   valve   space   paid   span   spade

10. alphabet   alkali   alphabet   faintness   allegation   alpha

11. breath   breath   breather   council   beneath   breast

12. drawback   drawer   heading   back   draw   drawback

13. fore   mat   four   ore   fore   forty

14. honest   modest   hornet   honest   honey   punch

15. leisure   leisure   pairing   leisurely   composure   sure

16. Negro   shirk   Negroid   neglect   neither   Negro

17. pony   pond   pony   pooh   puny   smug

18. robe   robes   oboe   toxin   rob   robe

19. special   special   serial   perfect   facial   specify

20. tonight   tonic   versus   tonight   tone   night

21. whoever   whatever   whom   twenty   whoever   who

22. constancy   horseback   constraint   constant   constancy   fancy

23. tolerable   rabble   tolerate   tolerable   review   total

24. consecration   journalistic   consecration   consecrate   conservation   secret

25. allowable   masterful   allows   allowable   lowly   allot

---

Time_____Sec.

No. Correct:_____

I-7

RATE (from table on page 307):

COMPREHENSION (4% for each correct answer):

EFFICIENCY (R × C):

R. _____

C. _____

E. _____

Exercise I-8

1. audience   auditor   audible   quadrant   audience   audibly

2. caught   casual   caught   caucus   fish   cauldron

3. damn   damn   dame   prince   dam   damp

4. entrails   entrance   trails   entrails   jackass   entreat

5. glassful   glassful   grateful   locality   glass   glassware

6. inflict   inflame   gossip   afflict   inflict   influx

7. mare   care   mare   halter   hare   margin

8. purity   purify   jurist   pure   destroy   purity

9. subtle   suckle   subtlety   snatch   subtle   subtly

10. celery   celery   celebrity   celebrate   salary   plant

11. daring   dare   punch   darning   darling   daring

12. epitaph   epitaph   epistle   epithet   rating   epoch

13. glory   gory   lorry   glory   gloria   grate

14. initial   initiate   initial   milestone   initiative   inimical

15. marrow   fact   maroon   tomorrow   marrow   marry

16. oven   over   make   oxen   oval   oven

17. quake   quack   fuse   quake   quick   wake

18. seemly   seemingly   seemly   seer   gaunt   see

19. universe   universe   union   occupancy   unit   universal

20. warmth   warmly   warm   warn   destiny   warmth

21. sufferance   suffrage   suffice   sufficient   sufferance   contacting

22. automobile   automotive   auto   automobile   plenteous   automatic

23. ungrateful   ungainly   ungrateful   originality   ungentle   grateful

24. secondary   stand   seclude   second   primary   secondary

25. outlandish   outlaw   land   outlandish   moldboard   outlive

---

Time_____Sec.

No. Correct:_____

I–8

RATE (from table on page 307):

COMPREHENSION (4% for each correct answer):

EFFICIENCY (R X C):

R. _____

C. _____

E. _____

Record on Progress Chart on page 297

Exercise I–9

1. angry   angry   finish   anger   angel   argue

2. brownie   brow   brownie   browse   brown   courage

3. coo   cook   coax   cue   coo   rue

4. duration   durable   horseman   duration   during   curable

5. fountain   fountain   foundation   neither   fount   fountainhead

6. howl   cowl   fowl   record   jowl   howl

7. lilac   lilt   prime   like   lilac   lily

8. nobility   section   nobility   nobody   mobility   noble

9. pounce   pour   pound   sphinx   pouch   pounce

10. ruby   ruby   rubber   rubble   silk   rub

11. spouse   next   souse   spouse   spoil   spout

12. annual   courage   annul   annuity   annual   annually

13. bud   bed   bud   lion   budget   buddy

14. core   corn   cork   core   corner   each

15. dwindle   dwindle   study   dwell   wind   dwarf

16. linoleum   linseed   scorch   linnet   linden   linoleum

17. noontide   noodle   midnight   noontide   eventide   noonday

18. preacher   preacher   preamble   preaching   tombstone   reach

19. rump   such   rumple   lump   rump   rummage

20. spun   vale   spun   spurn   spur   pun

21. trash   rash   track   trash   paper   trace

22. woke   wolf   walk   kink   wake   woke

23. humankind   mankind   humankind   human   disgust   humane

24. framework   housework   stronghold   frame   framework   franchise

25. transfigure   horseradish   transfer   torment   transfix   transfigure

---

Time_____Sec.   **RATE (from table on page 307):**   R. _____

No. Correct:_____   **COMPREHENSION (4% for each correct answer):**   C. _____

I–9   **EFFICIENCY (R × C):**   E. _____

Record on Progress Chart on page 297

Exercise I-10

1. ambition   ambiguity ambition ambitious hurrying amble

2. brighten   brighten gauntlet bright bring light

3. drip   hook drift dribble drip trip

4. forgave   forgive genus forage gave forgave

5. hornet   horn hornet honest figure horse

6. level   level lever shelve levy levee

7. portal   port gouge postal portal portage

8. romp   romp rump purple roam jump

9. sphere   horrible sphere spherical sphinx here

10. tortoise tortuous torpedo tortoise famous torture

11. ample   amble sample future amplify ample

12. broaden board secure road broaden broad

13. forsook forsooth riding force forsake forsook

14. hostile   occupant hostel host hostile fierce

15. lid   fly lie lied did lid

16. nickel   nasty nickel fickle sickle nick

17. postage hostage comment postal age postage

18. rosette   rosary phrase rosette rosy rosin

19. spite   cache spit pit spite spice

20. trace   trace train track race traceable

21. windy   kindly windy window wind winch

22. drunkenness drunkenness militarism drunk drinking sunken

23. contradict contradiction letterhead contradict contractor contraction

24. nevertheless nevermore insistently nevertheless unless never

25. contemplation contemptuous temptation contemplation content hieroglyphic

---

Time_____ Sec.   **RATE (from table on page 307):**   **R.** _____

No. Correct: _____ **COMPREHENSION (4% for each correct answer):** **C.** _____

I–10   **EFFICIENCY (R X C):**   **E.** _____

Record on Progress Chart on page 297

Exercise I–11

1. aisle   air   ailment   first   isle   aisle

2. bosom   handsome   ran   boss   bosom   some

3. domestic   enthusiastic   rolling   dome   domestic   mystic

4. flop   flop   lop   flow   float   ruler

5. hillock   capsize   hilltop   bullock   hill   hillock

6. lava   lavatory   lava   have   lave   mason

7. nameless   nameless   namesake   blameless   name   decorous

8. plow   plod   slow   plow   plot   too

9. riches   muse   ditches   rickety   riches   rice

10. somewhat   eighteen   what   some   somewhere   somewhat

11. timber   timber   eager   limber   time   climber

12. alert   ale   alert   avert   ascent   mercy

13. bouquet   shortly   bouquet   boast   croquet   book

14. dost   pretty   does   dost   lost   dust

15. fluid   fluid   flush   lurid   remain   fluent

16. lea   leaf   lea   leeward   smug   leave

17. nativity   horse   activity   nativity   native   naive

18. sorry   sorrow   sorry   morrow   sore   today

19. tip   in   lip   tip   top   tipple

20. whenever   topple   whichever   whatever   whenever   ever

21. righteous   headache   rightful   rightly   cautious   righteous

22. pneumonia   pneumonia   moustache   ammonia   pneumatic   monetary

23. historian   historical   custodian   history   glycerin   historian

24. congenial   congressional   regional   gentile   congenial   feudalism

25. confession   confusion   tricking   confession   confess   confessed

---

Time_____Sec.   **RATE (from table on page 307):**   R. _____

No. Correct:_____   **COMPREHENSION (4% for each correct answer):**   C. _____

I–11   **EFFICIENCY (R × C):**   E. _____

Record on Progress Chart on page 297

Exercise I–12

1. button   button   buttress   suit   buttons   butter

2. cowslip   bulls   coward   slip   cowboy   cowslip

3. fruitful   fruitless   looking   frugal   fruitful   fretful

4. illegal   ill   lawful   illicit   illegal   illness

5. loom   school   loom   loon   loan   look

6. oaken   oaken   type   oxen   oak   oakum

7. prick   prickly   medal   price   pick   prick

8. sample   noose   trample   sample   simple   ample

9. stave   starve   staves   staff   stave   perch

10. truant   truck   truant   ring   truculent   truce

11. arbor   scare   labor   arbor   ardor   arbiter

12. calamity   calcareous   calcite   disastrous   calculus   calamity

13. crash   crash   rash   crass   crater   smash

14. eldest   roost   elderly   oldest   eldest   elder

15. lovable   feasible   force   lovable   lovely   legible

16. obscure   cattle   cur   obscene   obscurity   obscure

17. printer   stark   prince   pint   printer   princely

18. sandy   sandal   sandy   sundry   task   sand

19. stem   stem   stern   stench   stencil   corset

20. tube   tubular   ebb   tube   tuck   tub

21. writhe   mate   whether   wither   with   writhe

22. immediate   immediate   occupancy   mediator   intermediate   immediately

23. fundamental   function   fundamental   prescription   mental   functional

24. efficient   posterior   efficient   proficient   efficacy   effigy

25. appreciation   apprentice   painstaking   appreciation   depreciation   appreciate

---

Time_____Sec.   RATE (from table on page 307):   R. _____

No. Correct:_____   COMPREHENSION (4% for each correct answer):   C. _____

I–12   EFFICIENCY (R × C):   E. _____

Record on Progress Chart on page 297

Exercise I-13

1. bawl   tour   bowl   bale   bald   bawl

2. chord   chord   foot   chore   choice   choral

3. denounce   announce   denounce   dense   punctual   denote

4. exploit   explicit   expect   sparse   exploit   exotic

5. groove   groove   groom   grove   root   salad

6. irrigate   irradiate   irritate   tragic   irrigate   obligate

7. mid   mild   vile   middle   mix   mid

8. pastry   paste   pastry   pantry   pastel   cord

9. shingle   shining   shingle   treaty   single   shingles

10. swim   taxi   swam   whim   swim   twin

11. variable   variable   varied   variance   variegated   messing

12. beaten   sweater   deaden   beater   mice   beaten

13. churl   church   more   churl   curdle   curl

14. deposit   despot   deposit   depot   withdraw   depose

15. extent   tent   extensive   intent   extent   opposite

16. itch   itch   rip   ache   scratch   etch

17. mild   supper   mold   mild   milk   mill

18. pattern   lantern   patty   patter   cushion   pattern

19. shorn   fork   short   shorn   shown   shun

20. vein   vain   vein   feign   veined   prose

21. wig   met   wag   wig   fig   fib

22. syndicate   syndicate   ringing   synthetic   symbol   mental

23. recognition   reception   reclamation   reckless   recognition   sanguinary

24. guarantee   warranty   guaranty   guardian   vicinity   guarantee

25. recapture   salutation   capture   recapture   recapitulate   rapture

---

Time_____Sec.   **RATE (from table on page 307):**   R. _____

No. Correct:_____   **COMPREHENSION (4% for each correct answer):**   C. _____

I-13   **EFFICIENCY (R × C):**   E. _____

Record on Progress Chart on page 297

Exercise I-14

1. camera   cameo   camera   trust   camel   cam

2. creed   creed   creek   cried   creep   erase

3. elm   ton   elk   alms   emblem   elm

4. gad   gadfly   horse   gad   gadget   fad

5. lukewarm   lucrative   lukewarm   luckily   warm   vacancy

6. o'clock   since   ocean   occult   ooze   o'clock

7. product   product   vulgar   produce   prodigy   productive

8. satyr   satin   satisfy   satyr   satire   imply

9. stir   handle   stirrup   skin   stir   stare

10. turnip   turnpike   skip   turn   urn   turnip

11. arrogant   missing   arrogant   ignorant   arrow   arrogance

12. canned   canner   yacht   canned   cannon   canopy

13. criminal   crime   crimp   trucking   criminal   crimson

14. embody   embody   embellish   embattle   head   body

15. gallows   allows   gallows   gallon   gallop   truism

16. official   officiate   vicinity   officious   official   office

17. savory   serve   savor   crouch   savory   save

18. stork   full   stork   stark   store   tore

19. twill   aspic   twice   rill   twirl   twill

20. yoke   bore   yolk   yoke   woke   yogi

21. progressive   progressive   academical   program   aggressive   progress

22. luxuriant   screwing   luxury   sumptuous   luxurious   luxuriant

23. impossible   impose   finishing   impossible   improbable   probable

24. imperative   imperturbable   sticking   impertinent   imperative   imperfect

25. aristocratic   aristocratic   aristocracy   studiously   aristocrat   arithmetic

---

Time_____Sec.   **RATE (from table on page 307):**   R. _____

No. Correct:_____   **COMPREHENSION (4% for each correct answer):**   C. _____

I–14   **EFFICIENCY (R × C):**   E. _____

Record on Progress Chart on page 297

Exercise I-15

1. bargain   bargain   sacking   margin   barge   bargainer

2. chest   quest   cheat   chest   chaste   slot

3. defy   deify   defied   deny   mild   defy

4. execute   executive   execute   occupant   excite   example

5. gravy   gravy   grow   gravity   grave   gravel

6. mention   mental   mansion   attention   mention   element

7. parch   parch   bib   porch   pouch   arch

8. ratify   rational   ratify   rectify   cart   railing

9. usurp   usher   bear   usury   usurp   us

10. bashful   bath   bashful   recount   baseball   basal

11. chill   chide   still   hill   magnify   chill

12. deliver   livery   signora   deliver   delirium   delay

13. mess   mull   table   mass   mess   message

14. readily   readiness   reading   salute   readily   ready

15. sheen   afraid   teen   shine   sheep   sheen

16. sweeper   sweeping   swim   sweeper   sweetly   treatise

17. vagabond   vagabond   thence   vagary   vagrant   vague

18. whilst   white   whittle   victim   whilst   while

19. intricate   phosphorus   intrigue   intricate   intrinsic   intimate

20. shapeless   shameless   happiness   quadrant   shiftless   shapeless

21. suspicious   roughness   suspension   suspicious   susceptible   suspicion

22. exhortation   exhortation   exhort   stronghold   exhilaration   exhibition

23. greenwood   tomahawk   greenback   greenhouse   reduced   greenwood

24. investment   inversion   investment   invention   invitation   vaccination

25. partaker   partition   partaker   particular   yearling   parted

---

Time_____Sec.   **RATE (from table on page 307):**   R. _____

No. Correct:_____   **COMPREHENSION (4% for each correct answer):**   C. _____

I–15   **EFFICIENCY (R × C):**   E. _____

Record on Progress Chart on page 297

Exercise I–16

1. ashore   fruit   shore   ashen   aside   ashore

2. caper   capes   near   caper   capital   caprice

3. crucify   crucify   crucible   cruise   dabble   crucifix

4. employ   employer   employ   capable   empower   employee

5. gas   gorge   gash   gasoline   gas   gasp

6. madman   madly   madness   dorsal   madame   madman

7. omen   omission   men   amen   omen   exit

8. scarlet   scarlet   scar   scarcity   scarcely   purple

9. ugly   win   fly   urge   glee   ugly

10. assent   assent   ascent   consent   assert   accede

11. carcass   dirge   canvass   confess   carcass   canvas

12. cube   cub   cubic   high   cube   tube

13. gem   germ   gem   gee   gin   force

14. string   strung   sting   coarse   string   ring

15. virtual   vital   virtual   eraser   virtuous   virulent

16. unceasing   uncertain   mechanize   increasing   cease   unceasing

17. property   frivolity   property   proper   prophet   propaganda

18. incense   incentive   incendiary   incense   license   courage

19. scientific   scientist   scientific   filler   science   terrific

20. magnify   sturdy   magnitude   magnificent   magnetic   magnify

21. encounter   encounter   encumber   counter   encourage   skirmish

22. prosperity   prospective   largeness   prosperity   prosperous   property

23. operation   operation   operator   observation   operate   inducement

24. incurable   curable   incumber   incurable   touring   incursion

25. strawberry   straw   blueberry   strawberry   raspberry   headstrong

---

Time_____Sec.

No. Correct:_____

I–16

RATE (from table on page 307):

COMPREHENSION (4% for each correct answer):

EFFICIENCY (R × C):

R. _____

C. _____

E. _____

Record on Progress Chart on page 297

Exercise I–17

1. affront   affair   carding   affront   affect   front

2. certify   certify   risking   certain   certified   certificate

3. daybreak   daylight   daytime   schedule   break   daybreak

4. godlike   godlike   phrase   golden   godly   manlike

5. inquiry   inquisitor   inquiry   inquest   wailing   query

6. overseer   oversee   overseer   critic   over   overseas

7. quicken   question   battery   quickly   quick   quicken

8. reunion   review   fixing   reunite   union   reunion

9. deathbed   dearth   death   decadence   deathbed   deathless

10. mattock   haddock   mattress   buttocks   merry   mattock

11. conclude   include   conclusion   conclave   conclude   yearling

12. heroism   erosion   zealot   heroism   heroine   hero

13. playground   barometer   playing   playhouse   ground   playground

14. aggravate   aggravating   aggravate   wanderer   aggregate   grave

15. thriftless   thriftless   footlights   shiftless   thrift   thrive

16. murderous   vacantly   murky   murder   murderous   hideous

17. lamentation   legislation   lamenting   lamentation   undeveloped   lame

18. comprehend   comprehensive   tabernacle   hen   comprehend   compromise

19. unspeakable   doubtfully   unstable   speak   unspoiled   unspeakable

20. sepulcher   spectacle   sepulcher   entering   spectator   sepulchral

21. oxen   oxen   often   toxin   sown   box

22. inspector   instance   spectator   touring   inspector   inspire

23. chandelier   chant   chanticleer   chandelier   courtesy   chevalier

24. unpleasant   unpack   unpleasant   pleasant   unpaid   columnist

25. sensation   sensation   sensitive   sensual   busybody   compensation

---

Time_____Sec.   **RATE (from table on page 307):**   R. _____

No. Correct:_____   **COMPREHENSION (4% for each correct answer):**   C. _____

I–17   **EFFICIENCY (R X C):**   E. _____

Record on Progress Chart on page 297

Exercise I–18

1. carrion   carried   carrier   carriage   carrion   switch

2. engrave   engrave   engross   engraving   ruling   engage

3. coachman   mansion   coat   scarlet   coachman   man

4. orchard   orchard   orchestra   orchid   ordeal   pencil

5. prudent   prune   student   prudence   telephone   prudent

6. feature   creature   feature   feat   federal   academic

7. moisture   moist   mixture   moisture   peculiar   hoist

8. undergo   underground   false   underwent   undergo   undergone

9. sixpence   twopence   roofing   sixpence   sixteen   sextette

10. enormous   enough   enormity   immense   courage   enormous

11. tenement   tendency   sentiment   rudiment   tenement   extreme

12. manifest   manifold   manifesto   recorder   manipulate   manifest

13. scullion   stallion   scullion   meaning   scull   scuffle

14. perverse   perverse   perhaps   verse   pervert   rolling

15. skirmish   shrimp   skirt   rescue   skirmish   mission

16. accordingly   accordingly   cablegram   across   cross   accord

17. remainder   remain   remainder   extreme   rejoinder   schooling

18. perseverance   perseverance   pursue   persevere   ransoming   backwoods

19. undoubted   doubted   undo   undesirable   undoubted   prescribe

20. originate   oriental   crowning   origin   original   originate

21. inevitable   inequality   pensively   inevitable   ineffable   inexcusable

22. malicious   impromptu   malice   malicious   delicious   malignity

23. indignation   indignant   indignation   snatching   indigestion   indigenous

24. curiosity   currency   curio   pensively   curiously   curiosity

25. astronomy   astronomical   astronomy   astrology   noontide   astray

---

Time_____Sec.

No. Correct:_____

I–18

RATE (from table on page 307):

COMPREHENSION (4% for each correct answer):

EFFICIENCY (R × C):

R. _____

C. _____

E. _____

Record on Progress Chart on page 297

Exercise I–19

1. abandon   band   abuse   abandon   bandanna   backward

2. disperse   dispersion   disperse   dispel   identify   purse

3. mission   missive   permission   passion   sylvan   mission

4. silvery   silver   slavery   silvery   silvered   saunter

5. taxicab   cab   taxicab   toxin   ability   tropical

6. bluebell   blue   resting   bell   bluebell   blueberry

7. firmness   firmness   firm   first   foolishness   pacifism

8. laborer   excuse   laboratory   bore   laborer   labor

9. dictate   direct   detect   estate   roseate   dictate

10. perfume   perfume   refuse   perhaps   fuming   perfect

11. rejoice   quaint   rejoice   voice   join   revolve

12. thorough   finish   thought   thorough   though   borough

13. abominable   tabernacle   abandoned   abominable   fundamental   practically

14. adversity   adversity   adverse   folding   advisable   verse

15. financial   jealously   final   financial   facial   finance

16. watermelon   salutation   melon   waterfall   watermelon   water

17. responsible   responsive   quadrangle   response   sponsor   responsible

18. dissolution   soluble   dissuade   dissertation   occupancy   dissolution

19. compensate   comparison   compensate   compensation   necessary   pension

20. regardless   retard   regardless   homeless   relative   joyousness

21. resistance   resist   machination   resolute   assistance   resistance

22. mountaineer   maintain   kindergarten   mountain   mountaineer   mount

23. knighthood   knighthood   largeness   night   neighborhood   knight

24. clergyman   clergyman   candlelight   salesman   minister   accountant

25. commonwealth   common   commotion   hallucination   commonwealth   wealth

---

Time_____Sec.   **RATE (from table on page 307):**   R. _____

No. Correct:_____   **COMPREHENSION (4% for each correct answer):**   C. _____

I–19   **EFFICIENCY (R × C):**   E. _____

Record on Progress Chart on page 297

Exercise I–20

1. balance — balance   charge   balcony   balanced   lance

2. charity — chariot   cherish   charge   drift   charity

3. decisive — decision   decisive   exclude   declension   derisive

4. gradual — radiate   graduate   grad   invest   gradual

5. meantime — heading   meander   meanwhile   meantime   text

6. painter — painful   painter   headache   pointer   painted

7. raiment — railway   soldier   raiment   regiment   rainbow

8. janitor — janitor   jangle   jungle   sloppy   banister

9. verdict — convict   vindicative   predict   verdict   allow

10. bandage — occupant   band   bandanna   bandy   bandage

11. faithful — faithful   fitful   faithless   convince   fateful

12. insurance — insurance   insular   dressing   insure   insult

13. grandpa — grandma   grandpa   python   grandfather   father

14. servitude — service   servitude   servile   serve   vomiting

15. pancake — panacea   sturdy   pan   pancreas   pancake

16. uppermost — upper   insistence   uppermost   upraise   underneath

17. surgeon — surgery   surge   highland   surly   surgeon

18. witchcraft — witchery   feudalism   handicraft   witchcraft   craft

19. sideboard — sideways   headboard   sideboard   eighteen   boardwalk

20. vexation — sensation   vexation   fixation   vegetation   syllable

21. interchange — interchange   recharge   intercept   exchange   hydrophobia

22. destroyer — battleship   distraught   destine   destroyer   destroy

23. jeopardy — perfidy   jeopardize   leopard   jeopardy   schedule

24. examine — exaggerate   lobbying   examine   exasperate   example

25. everybody — everyone   frivolity   everybody   evermore   anybody

---

Time_____Sec.   RATE (from table on page 307):   R. _____

No. Correct:_____   COMPREHENSION (4% for each correct answer):   C. _____

I–20   EFFICIENCY (R × C):   E. _____

Record on Progress Chart on page 297

SERIES II

Word Meaning Exercises

Instructions

In these Series II exercises, the emphasis shifts to a rapid recognition of *meaning*. Here each key word is followed by five others, one of which means almost the same as the key word. This exercise is the first to give you practice in reading for meaning. Here you want to scan as rapidly as you can, looking for similar meanings.

The directions are the same as for the preceding exercise. Look at the key word in each line, and then find the one in the answers that has most nearly the same meaning. Underline or check that answer, and go on to each succeeding line as rapidly as possible. When you have finished, ask for your time, and look up your rate in the table on page 307. Use the keys on pages 317 and 325 to check your errors. Odd numbered exercise keys are on page 317, and even numbered exercise keys are on page 325. Find your number of errors and compute your comprehension by multiplying the number of correct answers by four (4). Compute your efficiency to the nearest whole number, and record scores on the Progress Charts for Series II on page 297.

Remember that your scores probably will be much lower than they were on Series I. Thinking about meaning requires much more time than simple recognition. In comparing scores on your Progress Charts, recognize that most readers' efficiency scores for Series II are only about half as high as they were for Series I. But with practice you should be able to reduce your time on these exercises as you move through the Series.

Because all of these words have been taken from the 30,000 most frequently used words, you can use these exercises also to help develop your vocabulary skills. List on the vocabulary lists at the back of the book all key words you missed, all correct answers you did not underline, and all words underlined in error. Look up the meaning of these words, try to develop an understanding of them, and then practice using these newly discovered words in a variety of ways, in both reading and speaking, until you develop confidence in them as part of your own vocabulary.

These exercises begin on page 53; rate tables are on page 307; keys are on pages 317 and 325; Progress Charts are on page 297; vocabulary lists begin on page 293.

Example

22.	prefer		refer	preface	confer	peace	<u>choose</u>
23.	dent	X	spent	bend	dens	<u>split</u>	dines
24.	night	X	might	dark	nigh	<u>blight</u>	evil
25.	film		<u>haze</u>	craze	limb	kiln	finest

Time 63 Sec.
No. Correct: 23
(Key on page 317)

RATE (from table on page 307):
COMPREHENSION (4% for each correct answer) (4 × 23)
EFFICIENCY (R × C): (143 × .92) = 131.56

R. 143
C. <u>92</u>
E. <u>132</u>

II–0   Words to add to vocabulary list to help improve your vocabulary.

dent	night
split	dark
bend	blight

Suggestions

These exercises are much like the ones in the first series, but the same game does not apply because you have to know the *meaning* of the symbols in greater detail. Now you must recognize that symbols have various meanings and that your skill in playing the game depends on previous experience and knowledge.

Thinking about what you are doing is essential to success in these exercises, but to improve reading skills you must learn to think fast and effectively.

Many students waste time by doing unnecessary thinking that has no direct bearing on the rules of the game. Some dash off mentally in search of an answer without knowing what they are really looking for. Some become disturbed over the meaning of six words when the instructions stress the importance of only *one* key word.

Again the logical thing to do is to concentrate on the *key* word before beginning the search for synonyms. Just studying its physical characteristics of size and shape is not appropriate this time though. You must add another dimension of meaning *to you*.

If the key word has no meaning to you, there is no need to go on to the answer columns. You have found a word that you need to add to your vocabulary; and until you do, it has no value to you as a symbol or a tool. If the key word has no meaning to you, just check it as an error to add to your vocabulary list for further study, and move on quickly to the next line.

In most cases, the key word will have some meaning for you. It may have several meanings. You have to sort out the various meanings it might have and to project in your mind these various possibilities.

Armed with several possible synonyms, you are ready to scan the answer columns. You may recognize one of these synonyms immediately and be ready to go on to the next line. If you do not see any of them at once, you may need to go back to the key and think of other possible meanings. Again you may be faced with a new meaning for this word, which you will need to add to your vocabulary.

There is little reason for you to take each of the five choices in the answer column and think about each one intensively, however. You may not need to read some of these choices at all if you are able to identify quickly and confidently the match for the key word. If you know what you are looking for and then find it, you can stop and go on to the next line.

Do not be afraid of making errors. They are a natural part of the learning process. But each error can be a means of improving your understanding of the language and your reading skill. Look upon errors as a means of pinpointing ideas that need further study and application in your communicative skills.

Use your errors in this series as steps to learning. *Think* about the key words that bothered you, that you guessed at, and that you missed! All of these words in these exercises are common words in your native vocabulary. If you do not understand them, they may become barriers that may inhibit your effective communication skills.

This book is not intended as a workbook in vocabulary building, but there are many such publications available. Ask your teacher or your librarian to suggest good materials for vocabulary development. An analysis of errors made in these exercises might help to identify the kind of vocabulary help that you need most. Your directions suggest that for each word missed, you should add three words to your vocabulary list for effective study.

If you really want to improve your vocabulary, however, do not stop with just putting them on a list! Think about each one. Try to decide why you missed it. Review your earlier experiences with the word. Do you have any feelings about it? Have you avoided or resisted it for some reason? Do you really want to add it to your vocabulary?

Your vocabulary list can be a real help in specific vocabulary expansion, but it will require time and effort on your part to accomplish this. There are no magic tricks for sound vocabulary development, but these words probably will come up again in some unexpected time and place, and you will feel more secure and comfortable if you recognize them.

Use your dictionary as a first step. Most of these words are in a standard college dictionary. If you do not have a copy of your own, you should get one, and you should use it regularly. If a word is not in your desk dictionary, go to the library and seek it out in the larger dictionary there.

Once you find it, look at all the possible meanings presented. You will probably find that your experience has exposed you to only a limited aspect of the total use of the word. Write down several of the synonyms of the word. Take notes on the basic definition and derivation of the word, and then consider the various extensions or modifications of the term.

Thinking about words is not enough. You need to use them in speech and writing to make them functional. Try using your newly found vocabulary in various ways.

Some people like to use library "cue cards" to help develop fluency with new words. Setting up the word on one side of a card and the definitions and synonyms on the back of the card provides a good practice card that can be carried in your pocket and used frequently until the word has become firmly set in your vocabulary.

Constructive thinking and planned vocabulary development can make reading more interesting and meaningful. Logical thinking on these exercises can help you set up goals in reading and become more selective in your skimming and scanning activities.

Developing skills in rapid recognition of similar ideas or recognition of new concepts will do much to help you become a more efficient reader and will save you many hours of time that you may now be spending on unnecessary reading.

Exercise II-1

1. brow   sow   forehead   now   bow   scow

2. bully   fully   pulley   gully   tulip   tease

3. cot   bed   rot   tot   bought   aught

4. ease   tranquillity   knees   difficulty   squeeze   sleep

5. freeze   lizard   job   ice   care   ire

6. noise   choice   mount   notice   source   sound

7. lively   lovely   brisk   liver   blithely   vile

8. notch   crotch   foam   gulch   dent   dotage

9. noble   head   bobble   fine   foal   hobo

10. rag   tatter   fag   tag   gag   bag

11. staff   raft   stick   laugh   quaff   show

12. trend   send   bend   tend   drench   direction

13. worn   born   sworn   mourn   tired   foreign

14. woeful   armful   mournful   artful   baleful   manful

15. dad   bad   cad   father   fad   gad

16. dart   dish   dash   disc   disk   cart

17. errand   trip   head   ferret   wand   tang

18. goal   foal   sole   soul   score   role

19. inn   fin   gin   hotel   skin   hinge

20. meal   feel   peal   peel   powder   seal

21. pagan   sage   fagot   patron   hag   heathen

22. raft   craft   draft   graft   abundance   aft

23. scant   rant   pant   rare   faint   banter

24. catch   match   adapt   crack   cattle   trap

25. tyrant   pirate   hydra   scour   dictator   dysentery

Time___ Sec.   **RATE (from table on page 307):**   R. _____

No. Correct:_____   **COMPREHENSION (4% for each correct answer):**   C. _____
(key on page 317)

II–1   **EFFICIENCY (R × C):**   E. _____

Record on Progress Chart on page 297

Exercise II–2

1. bed   fed   red   head   cot   bred

2. civil   devil   shrivel   swivel   level   polite

3. arise   mount   size   maize   nice   barge

4. fable   falsehood   table   stable   staple   gable

5. gum   bum   resin   sum   dumb   hum

6. jam   dam   damn   lamb   predicament   ham

7. mind   find   rind   memory   hind   bind

8. camel   dromedary   cancel   sample   trample   dame

9. weigh   weird   well   measure   sleigh   mellow

10. shroud   conceal   loud   crowd   bowed   proud

11. taint   contaminate   faint   quaint   saint   paint

12. verdant   aunt   veranda   pant   green   shank

13. amateur   sure   pure   cure   dabbler   lure

14. bribe   tribe   scribe   price   five   live

15. cone   phone   lone   roan   bone   shell

16. dogma   hog   bog   cog   doctrine   foggy

17. flit   hit   dart   kit   slit   bit

18. lucky   duchy   touchy   much   fudge   fortunate

19. lease   please   grease   contract   tease   peace

20. neat   heat   tidy   peat   beat   seat

21. pace   taste   gait   case   haste   chase

22. reside   beside   aside   decide   tide   dwell

23. slap   cap   map   slop   straight   pat

24. occur   fur   befall   sir   stir   burden

25. wallet   pallet   mallet   pocketbook   palate   palette

Time_____Sec.   **RATE (from table on page 307):**   R. _____

No. Correct:_____   **COMPREHENSION (4% for each correct answer):**   C. _____
(key on page 325)

II–2   **EFFICIENCY (R × C):**   E. _____

Record on Progress Chart on page 297

Exercise II–3

1. airy   light   dairy   diary   fairy   lira

2. back   lack   support   tack   sack   sac

3. stink   blink   smell   think   wink   summer

4. dome   cupola   come   foam   home   comb

5. turkey   turnkey   murky   slack   fowl   furl

6. yield   furnish   wield   sealed   reeled   field

7. laurel   honor   quarrel   sorrel   moral   haul

8. naked   sake   slaked   bare   baked   caked

9. plow   allow   plot   cut   how   slow

10. rich   pitch   wealthy   ditch   bit   wick

11. sack   back   ravage   lack   hack   rack

12. tilt   slope   lilt   silt   kilt   gilt

13. wait   fate   date   rate   stay   saith

14. abase   erase   degrade   taste   case   dash

15. beckon   reckon   second   hexagon   seclude   signal

16. defer   confer   refer   postpone   affair   peevish

17. eager   beaver   meager   lever   agent   avid

18. fury   flurry   jury   brewery   aura   anger

19. pen   few   threw   hew   cage   cession

20. mad   bad   bade   crazy   fad   cad

21. olden   golden   stolen   den   ancient   alter

22. prone   phone   drone   gnome   liable   lone

23. rub   dub   tub   scour   tug   sub

24. paste   waste   waist   taste   dastardly   dough

25. trance   dance   enhance   glance   branch   daze

Time_____Sec.

No. Correct:_____
(key on page 317)

II–3

RATE (from table on page 307):   R. _____

COMPREHENSION (4% for each correct answer):   C. _____

EFFICIENCY (R × C):   E. _____

Record on Progress Chart on page 297

Exercise II-4

1. glance   lance   manse   glimpse   dance   enhance

2. quack   lack   rack   charlatan   back   cub

3. colony   call   loan   loon   sol   settlement

4. stairs   start   tear   fares   steps   stress

5. fetter   hamper   letter   debtor   hew   better

6. yell   yes   cry   bell   knock   yellow

7. keen   seen   sharp   bean   dean   lean

8. mop   pop   sop   cop   pout   flop

9. turban   hat   turbine   suburban   fat   ban

10. rack   backward   tack   jack   afflict   repeat

11. slayer   thrill   player   clay   killer   kitty

12. thaw   melt   haw   jaw   law   maw

13. wage   salary   adage   beige   cage   sage

14. amity   calamity   aim   absurdity   friendship   family

15. baby   fade   child   bake   lady   dabble

16. brief   grief   belief   sheaf   fief   short

17. dump   jump   drop   bump   chunk   dumb

18. fought   sought   aught   struggled   fault   ought

19. drill   fill   grill   bill   pill   practice

20. lit   ignited   fit   bit   kit   itch

21. horn   born   corn   mourn   morn   cornucopia

22. prefer   close   preamble   creditor   confer   choose

23. retort   resort   deport   answer   fort   aerial

24. spent   rent   exhausted   bent   cant   dent

25. tight   light   fight   taut   sight   night

Time_____Sec.   **RATE (from table on page 307):**   R. _____

No. Correct:_____   **COMPREHENSION (4% for each correct answer):**   C. _____
(key on page 325)

II–4   **EFFICIENCY (R × C):**   E. _____

Record on Progress Chart on page 297

Exercise II–5

1. torrid   parched   horrid   florid   morbid   porridge

2. bad   wad   tadpole   had   gad   inferior

3. cowl   hoof   hook   hood   hoop   howl

4. wind   mind   bind   kind   twist   tinder

5. frugal   nominal   struggle   stubble   economical   frustrate

6. ignore   floor   door   overlook   roar   ogle

7. avert   assert   pervert   convert   prevent   habit

8. nymph   goddess   lymph   symphony   limp   gym

9. prey   pray   victim   fray   day   voyage

10. salve   save   have   soothe   halve   delve

11. carol   barrel   song   oral   laurel   sorrel

12. taint   faint   feint   blemish   rant   bailiff

13. writer   fighter   scribe   girder   lighter   stab

14. bat   rat   mat   fat   sat   stick

15. char   mar   far   car   scorch   share

16. endure   cure   bear   sure   pure   benumb

17. gain   gabardine   gander   gauge   get   gentlefolk

18. gown   frown   down   dress   abound   round

19. map   nap   chart   lap   cap   gap

20. menace   dentist   finesse   apprentice   tenacious   threat

21. parade   pageant   tirade   scourge   braid   chard

22. rash   headlong   rare   flash   crash   hash

23. scour   power   dower   tower   courage   clean

24. strut   nut   glut   stray   brutal   brace

25. undefiled   pure   mild   wild   tile   pun

Time_____Sec.

No. Correct:_____
(key on page 317)

II–5

RATE (from table on page 307):

COMPREHENSION (4% for each correct answer):

EFFICIENCY (R × C):

R. _____

C. _____

E. _____

Record on Progress Chart on page 297

Exercise II–6

1. baker   cook   shaper   shaker   rook   took

2. abode   mode   rode   node   pod   house

3. salmon   fish   lemon   salad   balsam   fallow

4. trough   rough   gutter   sought   soft   golf

5. flare   dare   care   bare   blare   blaze

6. herb   grass   barb   bard   bird   garb

7. grade   fade   raid   cage   level   staid

8. insult   affront   cult   result   stint   basal

9. plait   plate   late   rate   place   braid

10. meant   rent   intended   sent   dead   fed

11. sob   weep   rob   mob   rod   bob

12. thrifty   rift   cliff   whiff   shriek   saving

13. weed   seed   ready   really   plant   udder

14. appeal   seal   prayer   real   apple   peel

15. bust   rust   chest   must   cuss   dust

16. cove   rove   dove   hove   inlet   ion

17. edit   reveal   eddy   merit   rain   revise

18. frown   down   scowl   town   sound   sown

19. affirm   blurt   worm   assert   squirm   skirt

20. luck   due   duck   duct   chance   cluck

21. occidental   accidental   rental   western   wobble   sleep

22. proceed   procure   recess   advance   desist   arrow

23. role   roll   dole   foal   part   pole

24. shell   help   swell   cover   bell   relish

25. torn   thorn   worn   ripped   born   rope

Time____Sec.

No. Correct:____
(key on page 325)

II–6

RATE (from table on page 307):

COMPREHENSION (4% for each correct answer):

EFFICIENCY (R × C):

R. _____

C. _____

E. _____

Record on Progress Chart on page 297

Exercise II-7

1. bauble   bubble   stubble   trouble   gobble   trifle

2. blur   whir   stir   our   obscure   endure

3. denote   remote   rote   vote   quote   mark

4. haven   port   raven   leaven   sort   sport

5. groom   manservant   room   broom   croon   doom

6. knelt   felt   belt   cent   centaur   bent

7. mice   rodents   rice   lice   trice   ice

8. motor   mortar   tartar   carter   snow   dynamo

9. recall   stall   remember   fall   ball   gall

10. shin   bin   fin   gin   leg   grin

11. sworn   vowed   worn   horn   corn   born

12. vapor   taper   mist   caper   maker   favor

13. allay   alley   alloy   ally   relieve   lay

14. boyish   fish   dish   coy   youthful   toy

15. comply   yield   die   dye   fry   cry

16. dance   ants   ball   danger   dandy   anger

17. flank   rank   rancor   thigh   hank   thank

18. habit   bit   rabbit   costume   fit   hit

19. regal   legal   lately   beagle   stately   fate

20. mystic   ritual   mist   stick   physic   enigmatic

21. plod   clog   clod   drudge   pod   fog

22. repentance   pence   penitence   pants   stance   lance

23. sinner   system   sister   criminal   dinner   hysterics

24. temptation   location   generation   seduction   inspiration   nation

25. volcano   canoe   eruption   volt   cameo   canto

Time_____Sec.   **RATE (from table on page 307):**   R. _____

No. Correct:_____   **COMPREHENSION (4% for each correct answer):**   C. _____
(key on page 317)

II-7   **EFFICIENCY (R × C):**   E. _____

Record on Progress Chart on page 297

Exercise II–8

1. shrill   keel   keep   still   frill   keen

2. clergy   energy   clerk   allegory   clear   ministers

3. devour   eat   devout   devote   devoid   sour

4. vacant   dummy   cant   empty   rant   pant

5. ham   pork   cam   dam   jam   lamb

6. jingle   tingle   jangle   simple   jungle   single

7. misplace   space   lace   lose   race   trace

8. pepsin   resin   lessen   medicine   lesson   tension

9. regarding   retarding   guarding   lauding   harboring   concerning

10. silverware   fair   fare   sliver   bare   cutlery

11. taxation   ration   relation   levy   sensation   station

12. vile   disgusting   file   tile   pile   guile

13. ammonia   pneumonia   phone   bony   bone   gas

14. broom   loom   brush   doom   boom   tomb

15. conquer   her   stir   vanquish   whir   burr

16. dove   love   pigeon   done   rove   move

17. folder   moulder   holder   solder   bolder   boulder

18. hock   dock   lock   rock   pawn   sock

19. lesser   smaller   dresser   fester   tester   jester

20. net   bet   met   yet   trap   new

21. port   sort   harbor   sport   wart   snort

22. rage   sage   fury   page   cage   beige

23. sly   furtive   cry   high   rye   try

24. thicken   thicket   sicken   chicken   coagulate   lichen

25. waste   taste   washer   waist   squander   haste

Time_____Sec.

No. Correct:_____
(key on page 325)

II–8

RATE (from table on page 307):

COMPREHENSION (4% for each correct answer):

EFFICIENCY (R × C):

R. _____

C. _____

E. _____

Record on Progress Chart on page 297

Exercise II-9

1. alligator   agitator   fascinate   crocodile   mediator   cliff

2. brand   stigma   sand   grand   hand   land

3. consecrate   devote   secret   freight   locate   donate

4. wage   stage   wager   salary   dot   aged

5. fondness   soundness   largess   affection   afoot   jolt

6. hoist   foil   ghost   moist   lift   loiter

7. lecture   picture   fracture   conjecture   discourse   decry

8. necessity   perplexity   need   city   complexity   nationality

9. policy   police   rule   docility   folly   mollify

10. risk   danger   frisk   brisk   wrist   disk

11. spacious   vast   gracious   specimen   narcissus   vacillate

12. token   broken   spoken   army   sojourn   sign

13. buzz   fist   his   jazz   hum   hive

14. assume   room   pretend   doom   broom   psyche

15. statute   statue   flute   random   law   stature

16. crook   brook   book   shook   look   hook

17. emit   permit   remit   submit   venal   voice

18. garnish   varnish   vanish   adorn   vanquish   aroma

19. ability   adversity   legality   power   illiterate   pillory

20. make   male   form   drake   slake   fake

21. oral   sorrel   floral   moral   morale   verbal

22. prow   sow   now   how   row   bow

23. rural   pastoral   fuel   full   gruel   purchase

24. squirrel   quarrel   chipmunk   whirl   furl   square

25. tremble   thimble   assemble   shake   bungle   semblance

---

Time_____Sec.   **RATE (from table on page 307):**   R. _____

No. Correct:_____   **COMPREHENSION (4% for each correct answer):**   C. _____
(key on page 317)

II–9   **EFFICIENCY (R ⨯ C):**   E. _____

Record on Progress Chart on page 297

Exercise II–10

1. ashamed   claimed   humiliated   named   tamed   rash

2. cape   shape   headland   grape   tape   hap

3. crow   row   stow   boast   bow   dough

4. empire   spire   inquire   dominion   bier   dire

5. refute   deny   refund   lute   rest   male

6. incapable   traceable   escapade   enable   enchant   incompetent

7. madden   sadden   dampen   gladden   each   enrage

8. stubborn   stung   inflexible   subsequent   escape   ice

9. property   proper   density   prosperity   possessions   prophetic

10. scarf   muffler   scoff   slough   harp   maze

11. straw   draw   thaw   paw   stalks   ball

12. udder   rudder   shudder   utter   buddy   bag

13. zoological   tropical   biological   topic   surgical   book

14. behold   fold   gold   see   sold   bold

15. chisel   sizzle   cheat   drizzle   gizzard   look

16. deity   lemon   preen   divinity   screen   problem

17. expedite   hasten   extradition   condition   tradition   hexagon

18. grocer   dealer   poacher   roach   brooch   loafer

19. idea   for   flee   concept   sea   cease

20. mince   since   quince   rinse   hash   hind

21. peal   resound   deal   feel   fealty   real

22. recovery   delivery   covertly   mockery   recalcitrant   restoration

23. semblance   blanch   dance   arrogance   form   female

24. suitor   neuter   looter   cuter   wooer   wry

25. unnecessary   commissary   crazy   student   ugh   useless

---

Time_____Sec.

No. Correct:_____
(key on page 325)

II–10

RATE (from table on page 307):

COMPREHENSION (4% for each correct answer):

EFFICIENCY (R ✕ C):

R. _____

C. _____

E. _____

Record on Progress Chart on page 297

Exercise II–11

1. audible   beard   trouble   word   stirrup   heard

2. cattle   tatter   fetter   tattle   bovine   wine

3. dame   woman   wane   same   fame   luminary

4. fashion   style   file   fasten   false   snub

5. glare   flare   gaze   graze   raze   raise

6. inflammation   fervor   information   cleaver   fever   flyer

7. marble   marvel   warble   limestone   tomb   larceny

8. outing   boating   doubting   flouting   excursion   eunuch

9. purify   clear   purchase   hear   testify   rectify

10. seclude   prelude   conclude   isolate   date   fate

11. subterranean   suburb   years   hidden   bidden   terrace

12. ungracious   dude   rude   lavish   hood   food

13. acorn   nut   ache   adorn   hut   torn

14. bin   came   sin   win   box   name

15. clearness   friendliness   closeness   cleverness   limpidness   lesson

16. develop   envelop   mature   gallop   manure   lope

17. famish   furnish   furnace   carve   family   starve

18. halloo   shout   bald   look   small   too

19. jug   tug   rug   pitcher   slug   richer

20. modify   solidify   grange   change   defy   deify

21. perpetuate   perpetrate   endure   penetrate   sure   awake

22. relic   frolic   soon   clip   croon   ruin

23. sham   slam   room   tan   doom   pretense

24. suspect   respect   distrust   must   rust   trust

25. useful   awful   baleful   capsule   doubtful   helpful

Time_____Sec.   RATE (from table on page 307):   R. _____

No. Correct:_____   COMPREHENSION (4% for each correct answer):   C. _____
(key on page 317)

II–11   EFFICIENCY (R ✕ C):   E. _____

Record on Progress Chart on page 297

Exercise II–12

1. abash   sash   flash   crash   ado   embarrass

2. certificate   testimony   alimony   antimony   delicate   triple

3. dawn   faun   fawn   sand   morn   lawn

4. eruption   corruption   temptation   outbreak   snake   rake

5. gall   fall   stall   cemetery   prosperity   temerity

6. inquire   require   ask   task   fire   fin

7. massive   lassie   flighty   tryout   dread   weighty

8. overseas   oversee   mourn   torn   foreign   tree

9. quest   adventure   best   west   test   wrest

10. senior   elder   junior   juniper   fell   enigma

11. sulphur   suffer   element   cement   sultry   couple

12. pity   flighty   conversation   conversion   compassion   city

13. admit   admire   deceive   receive   calendar   purple

14. bled   fed   lead   read   injured   extinguish

15. club   rub   stud   staff   raft   dub

16. dig   rig   fig   delve   shelve   big

17. fawn   yawn   cringe   spawn   singe   ridge

18. hardware   tools   swear   fool   tear   rare

19. kennel   fennel   stutter   mutter   house   flannel

20. moonbeam   seam   ray   day   deem   say

21. phase   aspic   raze   aspect   beige   craze

22. supervisor   sector   reflector   nectar   factor   director

23. shown   threw   through   mew   guest   manifested

24. swollen   pollen   expanded   expend   boll   strand

25. vanquish   conquer   varnish   swish   vanish   query

Time_____Sec.

No. Correct:_____
(key on page 325)

II–12

RATE (from table on page 307):

COMPREHENSION (4% for each correct answer):

EFFICIENCY (R ✕ C):

R. _____

C. _____

E. _____

Record on Progress Chart on page 297

Exercise II-13

1. barefoot   bear   shoeless   root   shoot   care

2. calculate   regulate   coagulate   rate   estimate   nominate

3. defraud   laud   hod   paw   caw   cheat

4. excuse   refuse   refuge   condone   amuse   news

5. gravity   laxity   morality   seriousness   anxiety   casualty

6. intoxicated   liberated   sated   concentrated   waited   drunk

7. mental   rental   dental   gentle   intellectual   lent

8. parcel   marcel   bundle   cell   par   trundle

9. rate   date   hate   gate   estimate   fate

10. sage   wage   rage   age   beige   wise

11. suspicion   uncertainty   position   transition   condition   resolution

12. usher   rush   user   she   escort   bush

13. ahead   dead   front   red   said   bed

14. boost   roost   boot   lift   coot   door

15. commit   comment   entrust   comma   comet   come

16. disobey   refuse   hay   hey   bay   say

17. film   haze   craze   helm   limb   kiln

18. heavily   heave   vile   heat   dully   villa

19. lame   dame   infirm   blame   came   fame

20. municipal   principal   munificent   city   cipher   cider

21. plaintive   plainness   captive   plane   deceptive   melancholy

22. relish   lucky   dish   taste   fish   rely

23. silken   soft   welcome   sill   ken   bill

24. tassel   tuft   rascal   vessel   pass   castle

25. vigor   victor   snicker   liquor   stricter   strength

Time_____Sec.   **RATE (from table on page 307):**   R. _____

No. Correct:_____   **COMPREHENSION (4% for each correct answer):**   C. _____
(key on page 317)

II–13   **EFFICIENCY (R × C):**   E. _____

Record on Progress Chart on page 297

Exercise II–14

1. abundant   bun   plentiful   abuse   abusive   dance

2. bet   met   beta   stake   belt   get

3. coach   coachman   teach   broach   roach   loath

4. diligent   industrious   dilute   dilate   dilemma   lie

5. feather   father   farther   gather   weather   plume

6. hark   harp   listen   ark   dark   bark

7. juicy   interest   loosely   ruthless   succulent   ruefully

8. moisten   mosaic   wet   moss   choice   ten

9. persecutor   persevere   perspective   tormentor   persist   person

10. rely   depend   deny   lye   relax   relay

11. situation   site   sit   abbreviation   caption   carnation

12. tenderness   tend   actress   compassion   alertness   aloofness

13. vacillate   late   vacancy   ventilate   violate   oscillate

14. alter   altar   alto   change   halter   falter

15. bride   bridge   ride   pride   wife   side

16. consul   official   consult   council   counsel   con

17. dresser   presser   bureau   dress   lesser   jester

18. foresee   anticipate   fore   see   forearm   forest

19. hopeless   hop   hostess   bottomless   useless   boundless

20. likely   lively   literally   like   lightly   probable

21. nag   fag   bag   keg   torment   gag

22. pouch   couch   pout   pour   bag   vouch

23. resign   design   sign   resin   repine   quit

24. soak   sock   joke   broke   oak   drench

25. threw   drew   flue   flung   shrew   brew

Exercise II–15

1. ado   flew   grew   sad   fuss   adore

2. bloom   strew   flower   stew   few   flew

3. commonplace   comma   comment   truism   tomato   place

4. dispense   distribute   expanse   expense   tribute   defense

5. financial   romance   pinafore   pecuniary   dance   monkey

6. heavy   levee   weighty   levy   weave   bevy

7. watch   leap   over   observe   patch   wall

8. mound   hill   round   sound   around   hound

9. pillage   oil   pill   village   sill   spoil

10. resist   oppose   desist   sister   fist   pose

11. smear   pulley   fear   beer   rear   sully

12. tacit   silent   facet   tact   tack   sac

13. waterfall   cascade   water   cater   fall   waterfowl

14. anoint   appoint   annoy   ran   rub   sleep

15. bulb   tub   bulk   bull   flower   tuber

16. corrupt   interrupt   truck   rupture   vicious   connect

17. earnest   furnace   ear   serious   sardine   nest

18. freedom   dome   free   kingdom   liberty   leeward

19. hurl   curl   throw   swirl   twirl   turkey

20. lone   bone   solitary   stone   son   condone

21. nursery   servant   every   purse   incubator   ivory

22. pretext   prefix   apology   text   prepaid   pretense

23. rib   bib   crib   fib   tiara   bone

24. sovereign   souvenir   ruler   rein   rain   dominant

25. tact   fact   back   diplomacy   rapt   lack

Time_____Sec.   **RATE (from table on page 307):**   **R.** _____

No. Correct:_____   **COMPREHENSION (4% for each correct answer):**   **C.** _____
(key on page 317)

II–15   **EFFICIENCY (R × C):**   **E.** _____

Record on Progress Chart on page 297

Exercise II-16

1. astray   bay   bayou   day   wrong   wasteful

2. carrier   bearer   terrier   ferry   lexicon   barrier

3. cure   lure   heal   pure   sure   hurdle

4. engineer   guide   sheer   fear   rear   gnaw

5. cloth   there   close   back   crepe   century

6. indignant   filament   angry   pant   rant   andirons

7. malice   spite   talon   louse   shallow   callous

8. orbit   ascribe   fit   hit   path   prayer

9. prudence   prune   wisdom   fence   ascent   wrung

10. safe   secure   waft   missive   saber   salutary

11. stuck   adhered   luck   truck   rude   attune

12. underfoot   undertook   route   below   root   boar

13. absurd   work   foolish   heard   lurid   fabricate

14. beset   debt   let   kept   perplex   session

15. circumference   conference   inference   tense   piratical   perimeter

16. describe   date   rate   fate   relate   rescue

17. earn   burn   ear   learn   garnet   get

18. gulf   rough   chasm   golf   charm   fluff

19. jade   fire   raid   jewel   fade   tadpole

20. mishap   nap   tap   mist   aisle   accident

21. pent   spend   rent   confined   sent   cent

22. refusal   trial   file   denial   filial   defunct

23. server   soothe   lever   weaver   howsoever   tray

24. wise   shrew   show   shrewd   shrank   shred

25. untouched   unhappy   untie   flush   couch   unaffected

Time_____Sec.

No. Correct:_____
(key on page 325)

II-16

RATE (from table on page 307):

COMPREHENSION (4% for each correct answer):

EFFICIENCY (R × C):

R. _____

C. _____

E. _____

Record on Progress Chart on page 297

Exercise II–17

1. affright   terrify   alight   align   alike   taffeta

2. charitable   mesa   variable   benevolent   cant   rant

3. decision   revision   temptation   terror   incision   conclusion

4. evermore   forever   swore   tore   sever   boar

5. lamentable   tableau   table   mournful   men   mama

6. murderer   killer   mud   shudder   death   sturdy

7. retreat   react   readjust   recede   reappear   defeat

8. painful   hurtful   armful   baleful   careful   deceitful

9. railway   rail   railroad   railing   doorway   highway

10. servile   revile   subservient   defile   violent   revelry

11. supplant   haunt   case   race   replace   daunt

12. unusual   hair   fair   rare   snare   air

13. ignorant   ignore   finger   illiterate   rant   significant

14. chopper   hopper   cutter   robber   stopper   copper

15. college   colleague   ledge   league   university   varsity

16. disciple   tipple   ripple   molar   scholar   cider

17. fertile   specific   pacific   tile   ferment   prolific

18. explanation   excavation   relation   donation   sense   constitution

19. irresistible   irresponsible   digest   combustible   powerful   iridescent

20. pastoral   moral   sorrel   floral   choral   rural

21. district   restrict   construct   stricken   disc   region

22. lattice   trellis   lettuce   radish   cabbage   latter

23. believe   deceive   trust   receive   conceive   relieve

24. taffeta   sordid   fete   staff   fact   fabric

25. faraway   sway   distant   stay   tray   quay

Time_____Sec.

No. Correct:_____
(key on page 317)

II–17

RATE (from table on page 307):

COMPREHENSION (4% for each correct answer):

EFFICIENCY (R × C):

R. _____

C. _____

E. _____

Record on Progress Chart on page 297

Exercise II–18

1. ambiguous   antipathy   hurt   obscure   pinch   omelet

2. convene   concave   conceal   assemble   concede   sonorous

3. contemplate   con   consider   conclusive   plate   contempt

4. housework   household   homemaking   horse   homelike   homemade

5. forfeiture   fortune   forefather   feather   penalty   pore

6. nostril   nosegay   trill   fill   nose   trail

7. lettuce   vegetable   terrace   fruit   certify   date

8. neutrality   frugality   lake   rocky   immunity   grey

9. bearable   quarterly   notable   relax   tolerable   tortoise

10. romantic   gigantic   fanciful   frantic   you   save

11. somebody   somber   someday   pomegranate   person   dome

12. respect   depreciate   help   reciprocate   epoch   esteem

13. efficiency   competency   leniency   regent   frog   cedar

14. lookout   flout   watch   doubt   mount   woodland

15. statute   statue   stature   law   match   latch

16. cupboard   closet   headboard   cupola   rubber   clad

17. deceive   receive   beguile   perceive   rod   because

18. eventual   evenly   effectual   fact   fennel   final

19. indictment   foment   indicate   statement   torment   sincerity

20. instructor   factor   adapt   teacher   toy   rector

21. outcast   outbreak   mast   last   duteous   degraded

22. purchaser   pursuer   purser   chase   burden   buyer

23. compound   unite   ponder   pound   around   competition

24. stately   grand   lately   greatly   slightly   quietly

25. disturbance   turbid   turbine   cistern   ran   confusion

---

Time_____ Sec.

No. Correct:_____
(key on page 325)

II–18

RATE (from table on page 307):

COMPREHENSION (4% for each correct answer):

EFFICIENCY (R × C):

R. _____

C. _____

E. _____

Record on Progress Chart on page 297

70

Exercise II–19

1. angrily   inwardly   silly   indignantly   candidly   fully

2. anxious   noxious   concerned   gracious   rapacious   canyon

3. convince   quince   convert   fence   rinse   onward

4. durable   curate   insure   lasting   fable   lurch

5. hurricane   bean   flurry   cyclone   sour   curriculum

6. however   yet   bower   sour   never   youthful

7. likewise   also   bait   dike   size   bill

8. prejudice   reproduce   bias   fudge   juice   breezy

9. poultry   chickens   sully   paltry   motley   courtly

10. rubbish   publish   pugilist   litter   furious   lubber

11. spotless   seedless   senseless   shameless   stainless   shapeless

12. transfer   convey   defer   confer   refer   gopher

13. banquet   feast   croquet   shut   quit   fang

14. backbone   tone   telephone   phone   sack   spine

15. cataract   contract   waterfall   catarrh   fact   watch

16. ceremonial   testimonial   crane   money   formal   ferment

17. ensnare   ensue   ensure   pare   trap   tart

18. abandon   band   ranch   renounce   don   bank

19. infernal   thermal   hellish   internal   vernal   hermit

20. masonry   fashion   ration   occasion   sash   stonework

21. overlook   book   cook   rover   disregard   dove

22. birthplace   birth   earth   place   dearth   origin

23. satiate   retaliate   prelate   nominate   gather   satisfy

24. discontinue   disc   disk   con   stop   sister

25. philosophical   philanthropy   rhapsody   abdominal   beneficial   rational

---

Time_____Sec.

No. Correct:_____
(key on page 317)

II–19

RATE (from table on page 307):

COMPREHENSION (4% for each correct answer):

EFFICIENCY (R × C):

R. _____

C. _____

E. _____

Record on Progress Chart on page 297

Exercise II–20

1. desirous   rouse   covetous   liars   cypress   iris

2. peasant   rustic   pheasant   resent   sent   scant

3. credulous   duly   louse   credit   greed   naive

4. redbreast   quest   west   wrest   robin   best

5. gabardine   grenadier   sardine   cloth   grandee   cabin

6. impenetrable   abominable   bachelor   inscrutable   baronial   imaginable

7. highness   elevation   fineness   lightness   sickness   weakness

8. thankful   healthful   grateful   uneventful   vengeful   wakeful

9. produce   process   reduce   conduit   manufacture   modulus

10. satisfy   multiply   petrify   deny   gratify   gather

11. confess   dress   fuss   acknowledge   rest   anywhere

12. floor   mooring   base   booing   doing   cornice

13. highway   day   high   say   road   bay

14. calamity   disaster   salad   credulity   forcibly   formality

15. chemistry   chemise   history   science   dentistry   shelves

16. creator   theater   crater   meditate   producer   preacher

17. exchange   range   flange   trade   derange   text

18. gratitude   thankfulness   servitude   multitude   food   trash

19. interview   consultation   made   one   twinkle   toes

20. impartial   imperial   marshal   martial   farthing   fair

21. sportsman   worst   hunter   abortive   dart   horse

22. rebuild   skilled   filled   trilled   meat   mend

23. sadness   gladness   confess   redress   daddy   depression

24. subsist   resist   exist   consist   desist   eulogy

25. everywhere   mountainous   tree   fuss   obey   omnipresent

---

Time_____Sec.

No. Correct:_____
(key on page 325)

II–20

RATE (from table on page 307):

COMPREHENSION (4% for each correct answer):

EFFICIENCY (R × C):

R. _____

C. _____

E. _____

Record on Progress Chart on page 297

SERIES III

Phrase Meaning Exercises

Instructions

In these Series III exercises, the emphasis on meaning is extended from words to phrases. They also should help to increase your eye span as you are to try to grasp the meaning of each phrase at a single glance. Do not read them word for word; treat each group of words as a unit of meaning. Each of the phrases is set off by spaces to allow for concentration on group meaning with a single eye fixation.

Look at the key phrase, and think about its meaning. Concentrate on the ideas you associate with this phrase. Then glance at the phrases that follow until you find one that means approximately the same as the key phrase. Try to shift rhythmically from each phrase to the next until you find the right one.

Mark this correct answer by underlining or checking it, and go on to the next line. As soon as you have finished the last line, check your time and look up your rate in the table on page 309. Use the keys on page 318 or page 326 to check your errors. Compute comprehension and efficiency scores as indicated in the scoring directions, and record your rate and efficiency on the Progress Chart on page 297.

Here again the key words in a phrase are a measure of your vocabulary. Take the key words from any phrases you miss, and list them in your vocabulary list for further study.

These exercises begin on page 75: rate tables are on page 309; progress charts are on page 297. Keys are on pages 318 and 326.

Example

17. unite in a body	join in a group of the present day	a lag from	tend to avoid the reason why
18. state of silence		basic to all for other forms	does not mean	any other kind absence of sound
19. being sincere	may be both have claim to it	honesty of mind	the fault of learns most from
20. roughly sketched X		a correlate of not completed	no small part	some part of some are operated

Time 70 Sec.	RATE (from table on page 309):	R. 257
No. Correct: 19	COMPREHENSION (5% for each correct answer): (5 × 19)	C. 95
(key on page 318)		
III–0	EFFICIENCY (R × C): (257 × .95) = 244.15	E. 244

Suggestions

These exercises should provide you with the greatest challenge and the greatest satisfaction of any of those you have done thus far. Here the game of reading becomes more complex. Rate of eye movement, increased eye span, and mental processing of verbal symbols become interinvolved; and you should begin to see your first real indication of *seeking the ideas behind the words*.

Here you should try to free yourself from the compulsion of word-by-word reading and to see that many words are more meaningful in groups than they are alone. You need to focus on the *phrase* as the unit of meaning and to learn to recognize such blocks of words as meaningful units in your vocabulary. As you learn to think in phrases you should find it much easier to increase your eye span at the same time.

The first phrase is still the key unit to think about and to be sure you understand. From it you must organize your ideas and goals so that you know what you are looking for as you move to the answer block of phrases.

One of the major features of this series is the emphasis on increasing your eye span. From beginning to end, the phrases become progressively longer. If you can increase your eye span enough to continue to read all phrases in a single eye fixation, you should achieve real carry-over value to other reading activities.

Several changes in structure have been set up in this series to encourage you to develop some flexibility in your eye movement pattern. The phrases in the answer column are now set in two lines so that you have to change your patterns. Odd and even number lines are staggered in positions so that you can move quickly from one item to the next with a minimum of confusion. Choices are set up with some a single line entry and some a combination of two choices in a paired vertical position. This provides for personal experimentation in various applications of eye span and eye movement. Some readers find it easier to skim the three phrases on the first line and then return for a sweep of the two on the second line. Others find they can identify the two in the vertical pair at one glance and then move across to the single central phrase and then to the final vertical pair. Experiment with different ways to locate the best response and find which patterns seem to work best for you. This should help develop your skills for skimming and scanning.

You may find that when one phrase is located immediately below another, you can scan them both in one glance, thus increasing your vertical eye span as well as your horizontal eye span.

About midway through this Series the emphasis on vertical eye movement is extended by arranging the materials in a column fashion so that your eye movement is from top to bottom as you seek the correct match for the key phrase. This structure is designed to begin practice in reading the shorter column structure used in most newspapers and periodicals. Exercises 10 and 11 are transition exercises with fairly short phrases set up in a close vertical structure. Then exercises 12 to 20 are arranged in a similar vertical fashion but with wider vertical spacing and with increasingly longer phrases to challenge you to increase your eye span.

In the latter part of this Series, where phrases are arranged in vertical order, the ideas are more important than the specific words; and you should practice vertical movement of your eyes, focusing on the center of the line and trying to expand your eye span enough to get meaning from the whole line at one glance. Such skills are very helpful in newspaper and news magazine reading for new ideas and current information.

Practice with the vertically organized materials shifts your emphasis on key materials from the first to the top position; and you can see how headlines, headings, and lead questions are designed to help focus your thinking on theme ideas in preparation for the materials that follow.

Vertical skimming and scanning techniques become more important as you consider this type of reading. Some individuals begin to develop a vertical eye span that enables them to perceive and transmit to the brain larger units of verbal symbols.

This series of exercises offers you the opportunity to experiment with a variety of adjustments in your eye span and eye movement. Feel free to try out various ways of looking at these exercises to find ways that are easiest and most effective for you. Study your records on the Progress Charts and see how well you do on various ways of reading. Try to develop skill in those patterns that seem most effective in improving your efficiency scores. You may be surprised to find that your brain is much more efficient than you thought in being able to handle larger blocks of verbal symbols.

This series of exercises should also provide a real challenge to your reading and thinking skills. Here you should begin to see the first real evidence of significant increase in rate of reading, but at the same time you should begin to appreciate the depth of meaning behind various word combinations. Quick thinking and sensitivity to a breadth of meaning variations become essential aspects of good reading skills.

Taking time to think about key ideas and to anticipate possible answers will make your reading much more interesting and should enable you to get a great deal more done in less time than before.

This process is very significant in improving study habits and is a key to the success of the "self-recitation" approach to initial study and review.

Exercise III–1

1. diamond ring — in these days — an average — a precious stone
   short period — is obvious

2. spoken word — to say something — will provide — be used to
   against him — full extent

3. a passageway — little less than — practical way — to all
   an opening for — perhaps this

4. share equally — that reason — divide evenly — almost here
   with those men — have their

5. very joyous — is taken — never again — other hand
   quite happy — may compensate for

6. in the middle — judgment of — such as — about medium
   as assumed by — plan to go

7. a mature person — one fully grown — is merely — benefit all
   away from — to wait long

8. an outrage — another day — plan to go — so you can
   does not require — a violent wrong

9. to precede — college life — to go ahead of — affect all
   to believe — not in here

10. human speech — make adjustment — may record — too loud
    articulate sound — not yet heard

11. to inspect — same always — likely to — view critically
    it is also — tend to do

12. a scamp — a rascal — fine person — looks ahead
    can be expected to — always able to

13. not very full — to ignore — of the group — have said
    decline to state — rather meager

14. to droop over — may sound — to lean down — are near here
    near the top — to be seen by

15. to play — which occur often — are used by — these words
    rates low — to amuse

16. large plant — so that he — might be — a big tree
    green grass — under no conditions

17. nose of a man — for smelling — such terms as — can define as
    you can make — does not imply

18. a meek person — along with her — wanted to go — has some kind
    may be ahead — has mild temper

19. church song — to be given — morning hymn — one can go
    many more that — not wish to

20. act of hunting — free time — never will go — to enjoy life
    lead to — a search for game

Time _____ Sec. RATE (from table on page 309): R. _____

No. Correct:_____ COMPREHENSION (5% for each correct answer): C. _____
(key on page 318)

III–1 EFFICIENCY (R × C): E. _____

Record on Progress Chart on page 297

Exercise III-2

1. to remember   set it up   to enjoy life   to recognize again
    might lead again   can be

2. pure gold   is equal to   worth more   living alone
    has shown to be   precious metal

3. bright luster   can read by   great care of   to play as
    a high polish   it may happen

4. drain off   to empty out   be considered   perhaps others do
    in this sense   what is this

5. an opinion   the use of   a belief held   state support of
    because of   good life

6. a short novel   to advance   of the new   prose fiction
    to put into   need for more

7. rather narrow   the result of   more than ever   other means than this
    of little breadth   too active

8. a member of   in time of   to expend   the story of
    in every way   to belong to

9. without limits   infinite in size   his limited views   new order of
    most of us   subject to

10. act as host   best way   entertains another   for that
    his school   let that do

11. the ground   surface of earth   can be seen   the four levels
    all above   blue sky

12. to jab   about half of   to poke something   on each day
    to increase some   method of

13. given freedom   to obtain all   as with   made independent of
    as with him   be sure to

14. end hostilities   we profess   it appears   he said
    to make peace   their names

15. omit something   present time   until later   is made
    public life   leave it out

16. a noble person   possessing dignity   the work of   was able to
    was urgently   his own

17. large monster   way of   an enormous animal   its cause
    the facts   was absent

18. hold court   last year   come down from   administer justice
    be said   make wise

19. be inaccurate   should be   it also   lack of
    not correct   without loss of

20. hopeful person   he argued   the needs of   stand upon
    to guide   one who expects

Time____ Sec.   **RATE (from table on page 309):**   **R.** _____

No. Correct:_____   **COMPREHENSION (5% for each correct answer):**   **C.** _____
(key on page 326)

III–2   **EFFICIENCY (R × C):**   **E.** _____

Record on Progress Chart on page 297

Exercise III–3

1. sign of force   physical vigor   to say so   for those
   he grows up   afraid of war

2. looks flat   can develop   even surface   very rarely
   their jobs stop   no one could

3. sign of famine   in the period   fine school   scarcity of food
   they are   near to home

4. showing spite   was reached   low point of   could be
   exhibiting envy   in an age

5. always near   high rent   the future   has also been
   rural area   close at all times

6. to expose   to reveal openly   to describe as   leave alone
   along the way   return to

7. is desperate   not knowing   in great need   look for work
   buying in   showing off

8. of good humor   design for   can often be   a cheerful person
   at work   take more

9. in reality   true to life   may assume   in each class
   method of work   of this type

10. a shy fellow   on the surface   a new home   to build
    in conflict   a modest person

11. without delay   to forget   after these   other times
    less than his   with promptness

12. act of haste   we learn   the sense   quickness of action
    be a factor in   four days

13. will float   miles away   the point   higher rates
    a real income   lighter than water

14. marked faulty   no ambition   cited as   has become great
    made imperfectly   the rest

15. to be exposed   open to view   due to this   arise from
    to increase   for the aged

16. ruling over   for reasons   act of dominating   coming of age
    can afford now   upper limit

17. being partial   the ideal of   in which   show preference
    more alike   as defined by

18. as a result of   in the future   to report   believe in
    too soon after   brought about by

19. to startle   as a sign   for many days   to do with
    to frighten suddenly   to search for

20. to acquit   to assemble   to set free   certain cue
    likely to   one part of it

Time_____Sec.   **RATE (from table on page 309):**   **R.** _____

No. Correct:_____   **COMPREHENSION (5% for each correct answer):**   **C.** _____
(key on page 318)

III–3   **EFFICIENCY (R X C):**   **E.** _____

Record on Progress Chart on page 297

Exercise III-4

1. proper place   be sold at   because of   correct position
   one year   an election day

2. tame horse   gentle animal   to do better   this age group
   in a box   a few years

3. a gentle slope   useful to   a sort of   a hot day
   a gradual decline   instead of him

4. to grow small   to control   diminish in size   they give
   led by you   no one can

5. ample food   began in   few if any   a long look
   to do good   abundant harvest

6. to be confused   child's life   to consider   be flustered
   is well to   must not be

7. standing erect   upright position   to walk to   over the top
   first period   has called

8. very durable   they are   the source   a large part
   to be stable   for peace only

9. being drowsy   as well as   rather sleepy   part of this
   term used   said that

10. to be desolate   first day   his life is   sort of damp
    to revert   ruinous condition

11. be delinquent   in spite of   which are   neglect of duty
    strong arm methods   goes on

12. to groan   expressive of pain   a form of   pay for all
    the desire for   any later

13. a fixed limit   the center of   may lead   for less
    are some more   marked boundary

14. cease to exist   two weeks   to annihilate   to a degree
    so often   the behavior pattern

15. present time   number of   at one place   more usual
    this very instant   this is not

16. trudge about   our purpose   by himself   ramble along
    as a whole   is easier to

17. chief concern   most valuable part   to assert   in some
    new plan of action   are able

18. without grace   under the   to serve fish   made upon
    being clumsy   value to us

19. to break down   to secrete   to collapse   most basic part
    on the stage   is obvious

20. make difficult   as fast as   who can be   the content of
    calls for   to complicate

Time_____Sec.   **RATE (from table on page 309):**   R. _____

No. Correct:_____   **COMPREHENSION (5% for each correct answer):**   C. _____
(key on page 326)

III–4   **EFFICIENCY (R × C):**   E. _____

Record on Progress Chart on page 297

Exercise III–5

1. prompts an action
 go beyond it more to be done some incentive
 in some form   possible to define

2. a forward step
  brought to light seldom mention the rank order
  will be found here   to move ahead

3. on being decisive
 pride and joy in some cases from the rest
 man of decision   give us the word

4. a careless mistake
  not using care when he comes to leave home
  number of men   of this group

5. a catastrophe
 can set up a sudden calamity to represent all
 a passing phase   all afraid to

6. unable to recall
  to indicate the cause of act of forgetting
  it is possible to   of modern life

7. beginning point
 real danger here go to college among this group
 a little older   the threshold

8. of no value
  of all sorts will have less to earn part
  completely worthless   may be presented

9. to understand
 gain full meaning to be desired an expert in
 in social events   for that reason

10. no fixed value
  which relates to no set price they can help
  have been listening   be alert to

11. great enjoyment
 show satisfaction to think so the time being
 to talk about him   to come down

12. to verify the act
  comes to mind confirm the deed of this nature
  an end result   well known

13. to alternate
 we talk about tentative period to take turns
 perhaps in a sense   complex part of

14. rather peculiar
  taken for granted too high upon the basis
  on the party line   something odd

15. most likely
 when they agree at the end of lags far behind
 in all probability   become more fixed

16. making attack
  on the offensive provide for for some reason
  also appear to be   final answer

17. drive with force
 on this point make a thrust less selective
 a better risk   by such action

18. little importance
  in this process often possible a trivial matter
  study made by him   in any aspect

19. being unlimited
 almost half of the greater part he should help
 can best be   have no boundary

20. pattern to go by
  need to know the third session back them up
  serve as a guide   did not know about

Time_____Sec. RATE (from table on page 309):   R. _____

No. Correct:_____ COMPREHENSION (5% for each correct answer): C. _____
(key on page 318)

III–5   EFFICIENCY (R × C):   E. _____

Record on Progress Chart on page 297

Exercise III-6

1. rushing for help | be taken as <br> hurrying for aid | has been paid | tends to change <br> in this area

2. almost as simple | keep in mind <br> rate as superior | nearly as easy | high level of <br> legion of others

3. more than enough | the next series <br> on the test | he may not | in their review <br> more than needed

4. in minute amount | very small quantity <br> below average | to possess manly | exist among <br> who rates low

5. either of the two | may accept this <br> fortunate enough | there are two | one or the other <br> in a study

6. a colossal mistake | as a starting point <br> a great error | in the light | later than <br> as a sort of

7. it became obvious | may be assumed <br> a state of health | plain to see | in terms of <br> a clear example

8. not concerned with | the most interested man <br> not interested in | to predict what | what things <br> the most effective

9. shameful action | scandalous conduct <br> in the session | would not accept | less accurate <br> new to them

10. on the contrary | loss to himself <br> grain of salt | more and more | just the opposite <br> try to classify

11. from the origin | as an agency <br> at the beginning | provides a chance | the influence of <br> are held to

12. a small fragment | no matter how <br> to make sure | a surviving part | an excuse for <br> to feel superior

13. being transparent | whole new area <br> to be fewer | a small number | they may turn <br> obviously clear

14. break of day | about dawn <br> by the same token | it is interesting | the power to <br> called to account

15. guilty of crime | advantage of <br> is usually bound | it may appear | he who is a criminal <br> low nor high

16. to strongly desire | can be aided <br> craving something | some new ones | may thus help <br> be more able

17. willing to serve | may be overt <br> there is trouble | offer your service | may observe <br> an effort to

18. keeping clear of | described as <br> what extent | not at exactly | just before the <br> avoiding something

19. true to history | being historical <br> do occur together | the progress of | has failed to <br> does not deny

20. of a lazy nature | who are already <br> average age of | in summing up | dislike to work <br> years earlier

---

Time_____ Sec.

No. Correct:_____
(key on page 326)

III–6

RATE (from table on page 309):

COMPREHENSION (5% for each correct answer):

EFFICIENCY (R × C):

R. _____

C. _____

E. _____

Record on Progress Chart on page 297

Exercise III–7

1. place of union — to bring out / a broad interest — a study of — a common junction / for college life

2. a parting wish — to bid farewell / he can learn — within the law — eager to protect / the advice is

3. an endless time — no matter how / on the side — may only be — give everything / eternal existence

4. to set free — for their money / to the contrary — act of liberation — has to talk / no one expects

5. being confidential — in the night / keeping a secret — little interest — without him / a message from

6. that which ceases — we are here / just as it was — would not hurt — comes to an end / in the capacity

7. display of wit — an exhibit of humor / it is difficult — to state this — in any type / aid in general

8. appropriately placed — in the office / what he knew — major cause of — this is done / in correct position

9. out of reach — not even if / the passing of — that which is beyond — the form of / is not clear

10. full of activity — there may be / being very busy — only a step — has the best / the same was true

11. hold spellbound — best interest of / point of view — all but one — to fascinate / much depends upon

12. an angry dispute — likely a quarrel / another type of — sets of forms — were not used / one item of

13. great quantity — who will fail / considerable amount — some phases of — of the function / the purpose of

14. without delay — all are omitted / the larger task — with promptness — all too many / there is much

15. general routing — to build up / regular procedure — from the office — be extended to / first of all

16. threatening aspect — the latter plan / does not require — be given first — a severe look / will secure

17. unite in a body — join in a group / of the present day — a lag from — tend to avoid / the reason why

18. state of silence — basic to all / for other forms — does not mean — any other kind / absence of sound

19. being sincere — may be both / have claim to it — honesty of mind — the fault of / learns most from

20. roughly sketched — a correlate of / not completed — no small part — some part of / some are operated

---

Time_____Sec.

No. Correct:_____
(key on page 318)

III–7

RATE (from table on page 309):

COMPREHENSION (5% for each correct answer):

EFFICIENCY (R ✕ C):

R. _____

C. _____

E. _____

Record on Progress Chart on page 297

Exercise III–8

1. promoted in rank | but hardly more | be wise to | may suggest
any given day | rising in power

2. should be granted | working hard | should be allowed | barely escaped
to describe | to leave alone

3. concerning truth | in assuming | as late as | as most likely
according to facts | is far from home

4. to do away with | to be elected | allowed to search | to dispose of
held until notice | died instantly

5. achieve the summit | to reach the peak | must fall back | able to go
to avoid going | not innate

6. produced by means of | all has been | trying to climb | always able to
it may be true | brought about by

7. ready to proceed | is confronted | prepared to go on | in this case
not the thing | tend to do

8. all by oneself | are all obvious | will refuse to | he is afraid
exclusive of others | to participate in

9. lull in activity | they may be | how to play | not very busy
to do something well | as is usual

10. act of slaying | death by violence | if he has | habit of refusing
is crucial to | who reads poorly

11. worthy of respect | what to expect | it may be | so far as
in some places | decent in character

12. without a spot | may differ from | free from reproach | high level
the most part | so much more

13. hold in position | most sinister man | not in accord | has stopped
keep from falling | annoyed to find

14. a loud clamor | may be made to | a decided drop | a great outcry
could be observed | the effect of

15. something vital | very necessary | in low esteem | the bottom of
which was done | the only solace

16. over fatigued | in the future | happens often | very fact of
not so clear | completely exhausted

17. mountain lodge | social dancing | place for vacations | counter to
the other end of | were less active

18. a prompt person | most crucial | an area in which | in our culture
one who is punctual | turn the dial

19. brave person | little relation to | be helpful | a motive for
same classroom as | one who is courageous

20. broken to bits | shattered to pieces | in all events | show as great
does not support | are found to

Time_____Sec. | **RATE (from table on page 309):** | **R. _____**

No. Correct:_____ | **COMPREHENSION (5% for each correct answer):** | **C. _____**
(key on page 326)

III–8 | **EFFICIENCY (R × C):** | **E. _____**

Record on Progress Chart on page 297

Exercise III-9

1. jumble things up — to conclude by saying / an opportunity for / pave the way to / to mix confusedly / invite your attention to

2. mark of distinction — to be outstanding / some of these issued / remains to be done / a major obstacle / need for a system

3. a time of crisis — can be relied upon / a decisive moment / awarded to each / free to choose / cost of providing information

4. an abundant supply — the lack of time / one school of thought / more than is needed / a large section / to synthesize methods

5. contrary to reason — an emergency situation / result of experience / will profit / the required ability / thought to be absurd

6. very appropriate — be allowed to participate / in order to learn / will not remain / especially suitable / in cooperation with

7. comprehensive in scope — capacity of anything / a disturbing failure / gaining more / an adequate answer / covering all phases

8. grasp the meaning of — on a large scale / to comprehend / to approve / able to speak clearly / in relation to the city

9. an acquired habit — secret sign / the greater interest / usual way of doing something / return in the fall / to organize

10. place of residence — to be washed away / to remove from sight / which seemed to him / the other / where one lives

11. lowest in a rank — a word of caution / marked by failure / held responsible / the last in the series / process of defining

12. that which confines — boundary line / to gain prestige / no right to expect / in other instances / for what he plans to do

13. indicative of grief — kinds of pressure / a sound like a moan / not too subtle / the first activity / conferred with the group

14. picture of a landscape — cannot be disrupted / deserves mention / a scenic painting / standard practice / the final word

15. a state of privacy — a joint responsibility / person being referred / a kind of service / usually small / not in public nature

16. to make a recess in — will want to know / a simple question / for his own needs / to set back / an explanation

17. living a lonely life — a solitary existence / at a casual level / a small group / a type of program / to destroy the function of

18. furnish with a subsidy — achieve the goal / provide financial aid / tend to disappear / to express oneself / a nursery school

19. neat in appearance — an appropriate suggestion / center of it / a tidy person / a separate volume / examine the situation

20. display of kindness — the rapid growth of / a sense of balance / best way out / few specific changes / an act of good will

---

Time_____Sec.

No. Correct:_____
(key on page 318)

III–9

RATE (from table on page 309):

COMPREHENSION (5% for each correct answer):

EFFICIENCY (R × C):

R. _____

C. _____

E. _____

Record on Progress Chart on page 297

Exercise III-10

1. forced to pay a fine   punishment for an offense   to be commended   level of skill
   remains to be done   the basic terms used

2. be granted admittance   avoid the difficulty   no one can doubt   an act of entering
   used for centuries   a thing observed

3. a definite difference   really consistent   sort of estimate   method of improving
   in only one situation   in complete contrast

4. act of condemning   an economic necessity   to pronounce guilty   to be stressed
   not a part of   obtaining accurate data

5. make more difficult   universally accepted   a radical change   relationship between
   to complicate matters   one point of view

6. an innocent person   free from blame   one of the essentials   to fill in a gap
   to be arranged   very accurately described

7. to hurl into space   of the plan   degree of freedom   to throw with violence
   of special importance   some previous prejudice

8. henceforth from now   the same problem   a number of ideas   with the real issue
   the valid use of   from this time forward

9. looked upon as an enemy   are less expensive   a military foe   an estimated budget
   should be made   type of floor covering

10. cease from being   the important ingredient   the rate of speed   the principal reason
   to come to an end   after much searching

11. to shape by cutting   words of wisdom   kind of a tree   the art of carving
   after much searching   taking over too much

12. a flat-bottomed boat   the immediate circle   a large river barge   to discover when
   meet the test   certain satisfactions

13. an object of dislike   beyond the bounds   to get pleasure from   be supported by
   to have an aversion to   motivated by love

14. admittance to a hearing   to be part of an audience   may be acute   contacts in business
   with wear and tear   a new example

15. belonging to antiquity   feeling of hostility   to help others   anything very old
   a staff member   time before midnight

16. gruff in appearance   a dominant factor   to stop growing   varying needs of pupils
   rough in countenance   be initiated at

17. a friendly greeting   an ancient landscape   father and son   a losing battle
   the new building   pleasant salutation

18. the angry canine   one mad dog   to go forward   misunderstood husband
   not to be seen   a disgusted feline

19. move forward in haste   at one time   to rush someplace   would be favorable
   likely to wander   superior to long periods

20. secure from danger   found to promote   to retard forgetting   forced to check
   particularly effective   to be in a safe place

Time____Sec.

No. Correct:____
(key on page 326)

III–10

RATE (from table on page 309):   R. _____

COMPREHENSION (5% for each correct answer):   C. _____

EFFICIENCY (R × C):   E. _____

Record on Progress Chart on page 297

Exercise III–11

Directions: In the following exercises, the answers appear in a vertical column beneath the key phrase. Read the key phrase, and then let your eyes drop, trying to keep them centered on the line and trying to grasp the meaning of each phrase by a single glance. Place a check mark beside the phrase most nearly the same as the key.

	KEY PHRASE READ DOWN TO FIND MATCH	7.	guilty of crime cross section of society a parallel effort of to help answer one who is a criminal a chain of events	14.	not completed in detail roughly sketched with whom we deal often accused of will readily recognize may be expressed
1.	a craving for water field of endeavor not willingly change a feeling of thirst not to be disturbed must guard against	8.	to vanish in thin air by this time born of a need too many people to be defensive against pass quickly from sight	15.	considerable strength from time to time state of being strong one of the solutions a couple of hours the human factor
2.	rather indefinite regarding the other to know something ability to exist not certain to occur resolution of conflict	9.	fitting and proper to be in right accord our greatest fault apt to respond the latter part of on the way toward	16.	only a glimpse a big boon for no particular merit source of irritation a short hurried view give every indication
3.	execute the commands discuss the alternatives a source book of dispense with it dealing with students to be obedient	10.	on his own accord might be applied to of his own free will was addressed to more obvious signs our basic insecurity	17.	that which is unique become less concerned it is essential only one of a kind jammed with affairs to appear at ease
4.	something in the future that which is to come to take the raps a sense of resentment a complex program may come from	11.	making a selection stating our strengths in a rough way choosing from several reactions of others much more to be said	18.	different from usual everything possible of the group reason why the largest amount of changed in appearance
5.	a boisterous laugh result may decrease showing hilarity excellent argument for not easy to accept have more control	12.	causing to assemble much to learn because of long life for what they are to come together as a young profession	19.	cease from motion to stand still thoughtful interest in act of coming to in one common connection we cannot assume
6.	exemption from work some simple rules from the office an acquired holiday a direct outgrowth of trustees of human values	13.	plainness in manner beneath the surface suffer a kind of most other fields from exterior behavior simplicity of style	20.	sign of gratitude for all that happens to be thankful never seem to feel a very perplexing thing the liability of

Time_____Sec.

No. Correct:_____
(key on page 318)

III–11

RATE (from table on page 309):

COMPREHENSION (5% for each correct answer):

EFFICIENCY (R × C):

R. _____

C. _____

E. _____

Record on Progress Chart on page 297

Exercise III-12

Directions: In the following exercises, the answers appear in a vertical column beneath the key phrase. Read the key phrase, and then let your eyes drop, trying to keep them centered on the line and trying to grasp the meaning of each phrase by a single glance. Place a check mark beside the phrase most nearly the same as the key.

KEY PHRASE
READ
DOWN
TO
FIND
MATCH

1. entitled to reverence
should be an aid
a key phrase
visualized form
distraction to thinking
consecrated as sacred

2. to commit treason
level of popularity
betray a trust
the same experiment
to leave school
be allowed to decide

3. a wrong statement
it should always be
in the environment
much of the work
not according to facts
content of a book

4. the lowest point
bottom of the scale
respect for
cannot be helpful
contribute to misunderstanding
given careful attention

5. an act of exercising
newly decorated
operate effectively
training for an event
not a valid one
economical manner

6. in terms of largeness
more beautiful than
form of publicity
to make contacts
very good reason
that which is immense

7. to impart knowledge
lowered into the sea
an act of teaching
simply lay limp
love the out-of-doors
did not appear

8. act of justifying
state of excitement
await the results
to get an education
prove to be right
the village school

9. set form of procedure
an orderly arrangement
in a distant city
across the fields
ask his advice
the day before

10. a division of the year
a closely knit group
corn in the fields
one of the seasons
a short period
under no obligation

11. article of furniture
a table in a room
time to study
in order to present
conscious effort to look
train of thought

12. state of being near
recreation is fun
a sense of humor
in a close-by vicinity
give the keynote address
it is apparent

13. an affirmative reply
concerning the role
to change human nature
prone to limit
structure of society
to answer yes

14. be in opposition to
to enhance the quality
to be against
groping for words
be frightened by
bit of conversation

15. a gallant person
assigned to work
during slack period
more natural light
one noble in spirit
easily identified

16. state of inattention
lack of attention
usually enough
type of position
something hard to believe
near the state line

17. the inside of anything
pleasant experience
in the home
that which is interior
a great honor
compelled to study

18. keep possession of
a brave life
born in slavery
good deal of expense
to live in a small town
retain ownership of

19. to make an offer
almost immediately
to present for acceptance
almost like a dwarf
a great name
to show skill

20. hesitant to answer
not at all pleased
soon to be at home
an immediate appeal
to pause undecidedly
type of occupation

Time_____Sec.

No. Correct:_____
(key on page 326)

III-12

RATE (from table on page 309):

COMPREHENSION (5% for each correct answer):

EFFICIENCY (R × C):

R. _____

C. _____

E. _____

Record on Progress Chart on page 297

Exercise III–13

Directions: In the following exercises, the answers appear in a vertical column beneath the key phrase. Read the key phrase, and then let your eyes drop, trying to keep them centered on the line and trying to grasp the meaning of each phrase by a single glance. Place a check mark beside the phrase most nearly the same as the key.

1. related to the newspaper

    a thirst for great fame
    a working compromise
    associated with the press
    dependence upon authority
    emphasis upon scholarship

2. the general run of things

    a withdrawal from life
    a method of study
    the force of the spoken word
    to be determined about
    usual course of events

3. quality of being sensitive

    wrote for publication
    learned men of the past
    very sensible activity
    capacity of receiving impressions
    the unlimited activity of

4. a very robust person

    a comparison of translations
    an ideal preparation for
    to be greatly praised
    to study mathematics
    one who displays strength

5. a person who is altruistic

    cultivation of the body
    the development of good citizens
    one who is not selfish
    a sense of danger
    material to be memorized

6. a state of bewilderment

    overwhelming amazement
    soon to become a famous man
    as head of the school
    during the hot summer months
    a quality of good speech

7. characterized by kindness

    a means of eloquence
    simplified method of study
    dynamic and aggressive
    cruel action
    an amiable person

8. sufficient to satisfy

    the language of instruction
    a leader in public affairs
    service to the state
    an ample amount of anything
    a model of best style

9. something which is distinct

    excellent skill in logic
    a liberal education
    to cover a large area
    one of the unstable elements
    set apart from others

10. following a given course

    acquired fame as a teacher
    adhering to a set plan
    a method of discipline
    due to organization of
    close personal relations

11. throughout the universe

    the aim of the school
    the most striking contrasts
    best for the purpose of
    all over everywhere
    a careful use of words

12. be concerned with the result

    to make a new demand
    of the many studies made
    to anticipate the outcome
    a variety of accomplishments
    along new lines

(continued on next page)

13.   increasing in difficulty

      becoming more complex
      an occasional work of charity
      to vary widely in capacity
      conditions of the time
      in their prime condition

14.   to be scattered abroad

      to discover the nature of
      the scientific method
      that which is dispersed
      rights of the individual
      in the same way as before

15.   looked upon as important

      to be equipped with pins
      thought to be significant
      on the part of others
      training in manual skills
      to delay the growth of

16.   according to the facts

      related to the truth
      to lack of facilities
      no provision is made by
      it is encouraging to note
      should be considered now

17.   an official announcement

      the administration of the plan
      authorized by proclamation
      a consensus of opinion
      a successful program
      a series of serious talks

18.   to be denied an opportunity

      the most unusual feature
      the plan in operation
      to prove very helpful
      to withhold a privilege
      out of the picture

19.   a violation of the law

      on a less extensive scale
      an act which is illegal
      social opportunity for all
      suggested by tradition
      forcing a rule upon men

20.   that which might be available

      to be potentially obtainable
      the proper thing to do
      helps to limit cost
      to fulfill their purpose
      the best chance of success

Time_____Sec.   **RATE (from table on page 309):**   **R.** _____

No. Correct:_____   **COMPREHENSION (5% for each correct answer):**   **C.** _____
(key on page 318)

III–13   **EFFICIENCY (R X C):**   **E.** _____

Record on Progress Chart on page 297

Exercise III–14

Directions: In the following exercises, the answers appear in a vertical column beneath the key phrase. Read the key phrase, and then let your eyes drop, trying to keep them centered on the line and trying to grasp the meaning of each phrase by a single glance. Place a check mark beside the phrase most nearly the same as the key.

1. at a marked disadvantage

    possessed with a severe handicap
    a tendency to evasion
    an opportunity to learn
    included in this report
    unable to attend now

2. process of becoming essential

    does not rank very high
    soon to be indispensable
    a genius for memorization
    an active force
    the better choice

3. as frequently as needed

    to think through a problem
    to gain a great deal from it
    as often as necessary
    a conflict in the soul
    to sacrifice truth

4. occurring once each year

    welcoming the newcomer
    more than this number
    not upon a class basis
    an annual event or happening
    to be isolated from fear

5. matter added to a book

    helpful in this regard
    be adopted generally
    the appendix of a book
    less important than the other
    of like-minded friends

6. to apply oneself to a task

    to engage with close attention
    to work and play together
    necessary for the future
    is being done carefully
    take the part of

7. approximate or nearly exact

    in the attainment of
    close to correctness
    the sense of belonging to
    sharing in a common cause
    on the honor system

8. to hear and then decide

    a varied social program
    the most recurrent problem
    brief word of warning
    to submit to arbitration
    the poorest showing

9. body of men armed for war

    by those who instruct
    securing more cooperation
    a military organization
    far more recent origin
    about every two years

10. that which is artless

    validity of the argument
    the average length of time
    implied or stated power
    equip the new engine
    something made without skill

11. a violent onset or attack

    to assault another person
    a qualified worker
    more suited to serve
    a different view of the matter
    open to criticism

12. act of taking for granted

    found most effective
    the acceptance of an assumption
    to use up excess energy
    advantage in keeping open
    in their own planning

(continued on next page)

13.   outrageously cruel or wicked

resentment of authority
a building program
used for special occasions
occur in another year
quality of being atrocious

14.   to attempt to do something

the central part of
a wholesome program
the equalizing of cost
to make trials or experiments
social event of the year

15.   activities at an auction

cutting down the cost
a drain on the resources
the most vexing problem
a series of
sale of goods to highest bidder

16.   having a genuine origin

to better existing conditions
that which is authentic
on a less extensive scale
voluntary pay into a fund
opportunity for all

17.   to clothe with legal power

definite limitations
a philosophy of life
in an assured manner
to establish by authority
more difficult to attain

18.   manuscript of an author

widely adopted means
may not be included in it
that written by his own hand
three times each hour
to arrange a date

19.   a desire to turn away

feeling of aversion toward something
fairly well integrated
the most powerful force
a successful plan
noted by many

20.   strong conviction of truth

an artificial separation
it is quite obvious
one can learn to swim
all learning situations
a belief of some sort

Exercise III–15

Directions: In the following exercises, the answers appear in a vertical column beneath the key phrase. Read the key phrase, and then let your eyes drop, trying to keep them centered on the line and trying to grasp the meaning of each phrase by a single glance. Place a check mark beside the phrase most nearly the same as the key.

1.   a radiant brightness

     considered to be brilliant
     in response to the question
     a change in personnel
     over a period of years
     to receive the benefits

2.   to inflict a bruise on

     a surface injury to flesh
     a little more under control
     to be derived therefrom
     the extent to which
     included in the survey

3.   to confer or bestow upon

     the value of democracy
     principles of sound health
     that which is awarded
     in the given order
     to decide a given policy

4.   not adapted to its purpose

     opposing points of view
     belief on any matter
     something awkward or unhandy
     those elected to office
     learn by living

5.   directed or turned backward

     rights of others
     in a contrary or reverse way
     social changes take place
     a mode of behavior
     must be so guided

6.   a baffling situation

     wholesome way of life
     adapted to local conditions
     a major purpose
     a perplexing and frustrating experience
     it becomes true

7.   barracks used by the army

     to select wise leaders
     the amount of power
     complete control of
     concerns itself with
     buildings for lodging soldiers

8.   a tract of barren land

     has general oversight
     under this type of
     may lack knowledge
     be present at all times
     not capable of producing vegetation

9.   combat between two persons

     a possible disadvantage
     serve to remind us
     a battle between two individuals
     important details
     eligible to vote

10.   lives by asking alms

     be reduced to a state of beggary
     in terms of its needs
     in an advisory capacity
     a well-rounded opinion
     must be decided

11.   rhythmical flow of language

     a fair representation
     rise and fall of the voice
     may safely be regarded
     a negligible role
     in the drama of life

12.   to strike or cross out

     on the highest level of thought
     cancel out the effects of
     a tenth of the total
     indicate the bases for
     the most emphasis

(continued on next page)

13.   the seat of government

a fair scholastic record
rely on personal appeal
for the best interest of
the capital city of a state
to compete for office

14.   exercising or taking care

an equal chance to
the great majority of
a position of dominance
a state of being careful
one most capable of working

15.   that which effects a result

can be considered good
by making such mistakes
will learn for the better
one can hardly say
the cause of an event

16.   a numbering of the people

certain other problems
taking a census of the population
merit specific attention
its primary purpose
to hold public office

17.   thoroughly established

in an unsatisfactory manner
with serious consequences
can solve the problem
to keep a diary about
that which is indisputable

18.   to be challenged to a duel

involved in the process
is to be arranged at once
a summons to fight
better than doing nothing
for the most part

19.   to gather into one body

suggested by the title
a valid philosophy
based on two categories
to assemble or accumulate together
may be expressed adequately

20.   a contest between rivals

to contend in rivalry
under what conditions
types of development
two principal aspects of the job
can be separated

Exercise III–16

Directions: In the following exercises, the answers appear in a vertical column beneath the key phrase. Read the key phrase, and then let your eyes drop, trying to keep them centered on the line and trying to grasp the meaning of each phrase by a single glance. Place a check mark beside the phrase most nearly the same as the key.

1. to maintain possession of

learn to cooperate
one's own behavior may be good
product of his experience
be limited to
to have and to keep

2. causing acute suffering

result in desired learnings
effort should be made
never takes place singly
that which is tormenting
purposive in nature

3. without the least delay

in any given situation
that which is done instantly
must be borne in mind
to win high marks
means to desired ends

4. an embarrassing situation

some sort of an award
the joy of participating
oriented at the time
a chance to appreciate
a confusing predicament

5. to beware of something

be on your guard
by which it may be achieved
most vital to everyone
covered by study last year
from time to time

6. that which is deducted

cuts across all activities
a search for friends
the part that is taken away
represented to all
be well aware of

7. to wander from direct course

a brief description of
the form of inquiry
to designate all functions
a degree of guidance
having gone astray

8. a main division in a book

to mold public opinion
a somewhat greater degree
to arrange into chapters
to learn by doing
keep in touch with

9. talk in an informal manner

promote greater interest
idle chat in a conversation
a result of many requests
to grant freedom
to try to stop it

10. the chief of the group

giving some trouble to
a definite tendency
to prevent for safety's sake
the leader of the organization
in a hurry to go

11. to make pure and clear

to clarify the issue or report
an intelligent outcome
a radical group
a difficult time existing
to make a necessity

12. the act of classifying

a chance to learn
spent to good advantage
the end of the year
to group or segregate in classes
not in itself harmful

(continued on next page)

13.   a device for measuring time

instrument such as a clock
made for the sake of
to be unbiased and fair
to keep before them
a period for study

14.   a systematic body of law

closely related to
the one just discussed
to find some way
the wrong attitude toward
any system of rules or principles

15.   of the farther side of

a distinct advantage
that which is beyond
in the graduate school
problems which arise daily
on various issues today

16.   land adjacent to a border

help to the committee
obviously of little value
that which lies next to
duplication of work
very easily accomplished

17.   that which is borrowed

at a later period
to receive with intention of returning
a primary advantage
chosen for their ability
only in one sense

18.   the lowest part of anything

that which is the bottom
a possible opportunity
to learn democracy
unable to practice
a higher standard of living

19.   a device used for stopping

not very probable
among the most important
in a very sincere sense
to apply a brake to
highest total number

20.   shortness of duration

to be circulated
combine to control members
characterized by brevity
change from previous form
true in many cases

Exercise III–17

Directions: In the following exercises, the answers appear in a vertical column beneath the key phrase. Read the key phrase, and then let your eyes drop, trying to keep them centered on the line and trying to grasp the meaning of each phrase by a single glance. Place a check mark beside the phrase most nearly the same as the key.

1. a king who rules over a kingdom

an act of binding up wounds
extending to a great distance
in the direction of the wind
a group of related plants
the monarch of a kingdom

2. situated below the normal level

all under one household
to suffer extreme hunger
that which is relatively low
having intimate knowledge of
may not be interfered with

3. to magnify or to exaggerate

quality of being impure
not of any one style
an act of impelling force
an addition that improves land
to enlarge either in fact or appearance

4. anything suggestive of a map

land used for crops
conducted in a false manner
a representation of the surface of the earth
to affect the conscience
printed for several issues

5. one who voluntarily suffered death

an approaching obstacle
with excellent qualities
along the sandy shore
being of a very quiet nature
a martyr for the sake of principle

6. recalling what has been learned

surrounded by fresh water
using the faculty of remembering
in some other place besides this
an act of the legal officer
precise indication of results

7. represented on a small scale

closely resembling someone
as frequently as needed
not knowing what to do now
responding to the loud noise
reproduced on a miniature level

8. a time unit of one minute

working in pleasant surroundings
the sixtieth part of an hour
commenting on the subject
tend to produce sleep quickly
allowed special privileges

9. to be considered as moderate

marked by serious crimes
a resting place at night
short pause in reading prose
which is within reasonable limits
a bell-shaped flower

10. that which instills moral lessons

a joint at this point
a system of teaching morals
open hearth of a furnace
in place of military services
pertaining to feudalism

11. to be classified as a moron

no possible hope for the future
a moderately feeble-minded person
showing a liking for all
a desire to conceal something
realizing the real danger

12. something difficult to explain

planned according to specifications
to go out and search for work
qualified for some type of work
a complex situation or mystery
at a severe disadvantage

(continued on next page)

13.   have but a little margin

    to have very narrow limits
    a method of storing up energy
    including most of the past
    forgiving that which was done
    anticipate an approaching event

14.   not engaged on either side

    acquire a sense of belongingness
    part of the life at home
    being in the same situation
    quality or state of being neutral
    involved to such an extent

15.   to name as a candidate for office

    a state of being nominated
    usually not returned too soon
    serious and of sincere purpose
    forced to leave school
    to clarify their own thinking

16.   that which is counted normal

    various phases of the project
    go toward their new job
    of some value to others
    does not deviate from the average
    development in growth

17.   an obstacle or hindrance to

    that which stands in the way
    to be of some service
    having a large vocabulary
    one of the better opportunities
    act according to arrangements

18.   a type of fashion out-of-date

    necessary for successful learning
    instead of the other
    counted as obsolete in style
    being careful in what one does
    in the light of changed plans

19.   to prove or show to be just

    an object of special devotion
    decorations for festivals
    to vindicate or justify an act
    dapper hero of a great drama
    a member of an organization

20.   a cruel exercise of authority

    under the oppression of a tyrant
    one who usually does his best
    for those who understand
    before the opening performance
    the one who is never on time

Time_____Sec.

No. Correct:_____
(key on page 318)

III–17

RATE (from table on page 309):

COMPREHENSION (5% for each correct answer):

EFFICIENCY (R ✕ C):

R. _____

C. _____

E. _____

Record on Progress Chart on page 297

Exercise III–18

Directions: In the following exercises, the answers appear in a vertical column beneath the key phrase. Read the key phrase, and then let your eyes drop, trying to keep them centered on the line and trying to grasp the meaning of each phrase by a single glance. Place a check mark beside the phrase most nearly the same as the key.

1. the act or process of explaining

   a salutation or greeting
   to combine in a group
   a network of pipes
   operated by gravity
   to make plain by means of interpretation

2. having an intimate knowledge of

   state of being unbleached
   a large citrus fruit
   a grainlike particle
   closely acquainted or familiar with
   to act or serve as a governess

3. conventional usage in dress

   for extinguishing a fire
   the gloom or melancholy
   that which is in fashion
   goal made by a drop kick
   to catch a glimpse of

4. that which is frail or flimsy

   any plant of a family
   that which is without strength or solidity
   divided into two equal parts
   often used in police work
   that which gathers

5. something that floats on water

   a kind of a watertight structure
   a tale of adventures
   the center of the earth
   an entire range or series
   a transaction involving risk

6. the terminal part of the leg

   the foot of an animal or a person
   an increase in profits
   to silence by authority
   the functions of a public office
   to hit a foul ball

7. valid or existing at all times

   a large amount of light
   to be eternal or infinite in duration
   to receive and retain
   any of the various weeds
   an opening through anything

8. the event which takes place

   to impose restraint upon
   a score made by playing
   that which happens or occurs
   the person in possession of
   the acts of one who hoards

9. one who acts as a witness

   a place of business
   a tight hold or grasp
   a narrative of events
   a person who gives evidence as to what happened
   a natural elevation of land

10. quality of being excellent

    to receive payment of
    deviating from the common rule
    in some future time or state
    to form or put into a herd
    extremely good of its kind

11. state of going beyond limits

    extent to which sound may be heard
    destitute of courage
    in a state of good health
    operated by the hand
    that which exceeds what is usual

12. suitable to the end in view

    sudden stroke of success
    to hit the right note
    a cart pushed by hand
    personal conduct motivated by expediency
    where prisoners are confined

(continued on next page)

13.   contrary to natural instincts

      state of being important
      intensity of the stimulus
      something considered as abnormal
      careful denoting the action of
      occupy the same position

14.   living in a state of disguise

      of the essence of mental concentration
      living under false pretenses
      to follow as a pattern
      quality of being immense
      not separated in time or space

15.   following in consecutive order

      sequence with no interval or break
      manage with frugality
      the flower of the plant
      pertaining to water power
      regards for the interests of others

16.   delightful in a high degree

      in the nature of an enchantment
      an uncertain state of mind
      marked by a lack of food
      turn in such a state or position
      to be held as hostage

17.   devoted to a sacred and holy cause

      found on old walls and roofs
      consecrated to a noble purpose
      become the head of a family
      passing through the earth
      the character of a person

18.   the customary thing to do

      the famous place of execution
      considered as promising too much
      a habitual course of action
      belonging to a larger order
      of some remote ancestor

19.   of the nature of an illusion

      a tank holding green liquid
      in order of arrangement
      avoid an embarrassing position
      that which has a deceptive appearance
      an exclamation of surprise

20.   near the beginning of a period

      so that all are included
      arising from bad character
      a restricted portion of space
      plants of related genera
      that which happens early

Exercise III-19

Directions: In the following exercises, the answers appear in a vertical column beneath the key phrase. Read the key phrase, and then let your eyes drop, trying to keep them centered on the line and trying to grasp the meaning of each phrase by a single glance. Place a check mark beside the phrase most nearly the same as the key.

1. the planet which we inhabit

    the earth upon which we live
    divisible by two or four
    what might not be expected
    in about the same place
    the period from sunset to darkness

2. the act or process of educating

    the melting or freezing point
    to develop and cultivate the mental processes
    triumph over a discovery
    a motor fuel
    to present on the stage

3. excessive love and thought of self

    the practice of referring overmuch to oneself
    in commendation of someone
    the science of moral duty
    a river current
    form an opinion of

4. to feel resentful toward another

    a literary composition
    to be envious of the other person
    one who writes essays
    to gain complete control
    ideally perfect or complete

5. exactly the same in measure

    a mode of behavior
    the fulfillment of the conditions
    to be equal in quantity or degree
    equivalent to a triangle
    with intent to deceive

6. belief in what is untrue

    an error in the way a person thinks
    state of being erected
    from some particular date
    an instant of time
    to complete the plan of the work

7. that which no longer exists

    due to external causes
    that which becomes extinct
    a way of winning the peace
    belongs to the newly formed group
    preceding the owner's name

8. that which is very convincing

    a case demanding action
    testing all possibilities
    to be supported by evidence based on facts
    for use as evidence
    to reveal by signs

9. to be in the nature of a formula

    a perceptible effort
    that which is exhaled
    be given off as a vapor
    to have a prescribed or set form
    to release from some liability

10. to throw into a state of alarm

    terror excited by sudden danger
    serving as a warning
    given in excess of actual loss
    a model or a pattern
    any person earning his living

11. holding all it can contain

    that which justifies a fault
    to be full or complete in quantity
    permission to practice
    an officer of the state
    extremely good of its kind

12. the act of gaining something

    a bill of exchange
    to go beyond the limits
    the accumulation or increasing of profits
    a testing of knowledge
    ascertaining the truth of

(continued on next page)

13.   motion intended to express an idea

      condition of being fit
      a sending forth
      making an excursion
      a gesture used to enforce an opinion
      suitable for the end in view

14.   the act of giving a present

      connected with an institution
      to evaporate moisture from
      sold under eminent domain
      that which is expected
      to give a gift to someone

15.   to move gently and smoothly

      a laying out of money
      a particular study or work
      to unfold the meaning of
      one who has special knowledge
      the act or action of gliding

16.   the mark set to bound a race

      that which is exported
      by means of a probe
      the goal to obtain in winning the race
      to search for a discovery
      the influences of climate

17.   in the nature of an interview

      that which exemplifies
      a common expression
      usually followed by with
      a meeting face to face with a client
      a public exhibition or show

18.   act or process of irrigating

      indicative of character
      expected to do his duty
      delusions of greatness
      beyond the established limits
      to supply water to the land by canals

19.   tract of land surrounded by water

      seized to secure payment
      to understand the void of space
      commence or enter upon
      unable to speak intelligibly
      that which is regarded as an island

20.   the first month in the year

      without a sense of fear
      the embodiment of joy
      cast light on a surface
      January, named after the Latin deity, Janus
      being in the first category

Time_____Sec.   **RATE (from table on page 309):**   **R.** _____

No. Correct:_____   **COMPREHENSION (5% for each correct answer):**   **C.** _____
(key on page 318)

III—19   **EFFICIENCY (R × C):**   **E.** _____

Record on Progress Chart on page 297

Exercise III–20

Directions: In the following exercises, the answers appear in a vertical column beneath the key phrase. Read the key phrase, and then let your eyes drop, trying to keep them centered on the line and trying to grasp the meaning of each phrase by a single glance. Place a check mark beside the phrase most nearly the same as the key.

1.   to grant or pay a pension to

an allowance to one retired from service
various points along the way
soon after the movie
seeking a helping hand
those often in distress

2.   an involved state of affairs

shortly after the rain
absorbed in international affairs
believed to be of sound mind
that which is perplexed
going inside the house

3.   related to the matter in hand

as far as that goes
pertinent to the present condition
in many ways the best
this is advisable to all
not interested in stirring up doubt

4.   capable of being molded or modeled

to return to something
concerned with the truth
formative in nature as clay or plastic
should be removed at once
in detailed reply

5.   suitable to the public in general

quality or state of being popular
a small decrease in enrollment
recent influx of workers
should not be tolerated
for an hour or more

6.   one who carries luggage for hire

many still stand in line
a lack of responsible help
wired for a public address system
at the same time each day
the duties of a porter

7.   the state of being possible

to make better personal adjustment
within the powers of performance
on the part of the college
within each building
one of long standing

8.   an act of safety taken beforehand

a feeling of security
able to make the grade
spoken of in various ways
a precaution taken in advance
who has learned to help others

9.   a question proposed for solution

the prime purpose of
in reaching this goal
a query relative to a problem to be solved
a set of new conditions
satisfied with everyone

10.   under the protection of providence

safeguarded by divine care and guidance
an overall plan
seriously looking forward to
it was evident to everyone
his greatest error

11.   to solve or discover by ingenuity

a state of being frozen
combined with another element
to puzzle out a mystery
a railroad baggage car
an inevitable conclusion

12.   a measure containing two pints

expressed in algebraic symbols
a glimpse of the future
the first in time or in place
a measure in music
a vessel holding one quart

(continued on next page)

13. to go from place to place

an inflated ball to be kicked
to ramble or wander with no set goal
support for the feet
to waste precious time
one in charge of an office

14. the purpose of a reservoir

one who loads a ship
prescribed manner of behaving
a person who seeks a fight
a place where anything is kept in store
to make a defense

15. made in the likeness of a robe

to attempt to defeat
the plot of a dramatic poem
action which is extravagant
that which is not expected
a long loose outer garment

16. a sample portion of the whole

a sudden hostile movement
the pupil of the eye
one expert in penmanship
a part presented for inspection
to form a mental image of

17. to scatter or distribute widely

the orbit of the eye
to separate in different directions
a very poor person
vessel with a narrow stern
a thing to be regretted

18. preceding in the order of time

coming first in logical order
a contest for a reward
of standard quality
to translate or paraphrase
prompt in action or thought

19. not ready or prompt in moving

wreck due to a collision
a thickly populated street
to be slow or tardy in action
water pent up behind a floodgate
part of a railroad

20. to patrol a given territory

his first voyage to Europe
should arrive any day now
please come whenever possible
he never will do that again
the guard going the rounds

Time_____Sec.　　　RATE (from table on page 309):　　　　　　　　　R. _____

No. Correct:_____　COMPREHENSION (5% for each correct answer):　　C. _____
(key on page 326)

III–20　　　　　　　EFFICIENCY (R × C):　　　　　　　　　　　　　　E. _____

Record on Progress Chart on page 297

102

SERIES IV
Sentence Meaning Exercises

Instructions

You should now be ready to combine some skills and to deal with total meaning of sentence units. The Series IV exercises are designed to develop still further your eye span and ability to recognize similar ideas quickly. This ability is of importance especially in skimming for similar ideas, or in reading to find the answer to questions. Quick recognition of basic meaning is essential to developing rapid reading through skimming and scanning techniques.

In these exercises you are given a key statement that expresses a certain idea as the basic part of that sentence. Read this statement carefully, and identify the key words that give meaning to the idea. Then think quickly and carefully about its meaning. Ten

statements follow this key statement. With each of these ten, you are to scan quickly, looking for key words and ideas. Then decide whether the basic idea is quite similar to that of the key sentence or whether it is basically different. If the idea is the same, place the letter *S* in the space after the number. If the idea is different, place the letter *D* after the number of the sentence. As soon as you have completed the last sentence, check your time, and look up your rate in the table on page 311. Then correct your answers by using the keys on pages 321 or 329, and compute comprehension and efficiency as indicated. Then record rate and efficiency on your Progress Chart.

These exercises begin on page 105; rate tables are on page 311; progress charts are on page 297. Keys are on pages 321 and 329.

Example

It is difficult for a woman to be a great mother unless her children have serious problems and need her help.

7. Unless problems occur in the family, a mother has little chance to demonstrate her true value.	7. S
8. Few women have problem children.	8. D
9. A woman may never have an opportunity to show her real greatness. X	9. D
10. It is easier for a mother to gain recognition and appreciation in times of stress.	10. S

Time 54 Sec. RATE (from table on page 311):   R. 200

No. Correct: 9 COMPREHENSION (10% for each correct answer): (10 × 9):   C. 90
(key on page 321)

IV–0 EFFICIENCY (R × C): (200 × .90) = 180.00   E. 180

Suggestions

With this series, you move to the recognition of meaning in still larger blocks. This series is designed to help you become sensitive to clues and content. Concentrate first on the key sentence. Be sure you understand and relate it to your previous knowledge and experience with this topic. Then you can begin to sort out ideas relating to it.

With the large bulk of mass mailing, extensive reading assignments, and the maze of periodical literature, you must be discriminating in what you read. There is no need to read variations of the same basic idea over and over again, unless, of course, you are doing extensive research on that topic. In that case, a good reader will be screening carefully for new ideas or different interpretations. In either case, assessing *what* you know first will speed the process of identifying new material.

Reading materials for new ideas or new perspectives can be done fairly rapidly if you already have an understanding of your own starting point. Skimming techniques can be used to help you pick up new concepts quickly and to decide which materials deserve more careful attention for more detailed information to extend your knowledge and understanding of the topic.

This series provides good practice in the basic steps of good study practice. Emphasis is on careful thought about the key ideas to be studied—relating them to your personal orientation and previous experience.

This group of exercises should provide good vocabulary experience, good experience in a variety of sentence structures, and good application of concentrative skills. Practice should incorporate into your reading rate a high degree of perception and comprehension in grasping ideas.

Application of this type of reading to research papers or general reading can produce some real time saving and some much deeper understandings. By setting up a theme idea that you want to support or to challenge, you can provide a focus and a purpose for related reading. This then enables you to do much more effective scanning and skimming to select materials appropriate for more detailed study.

Reading, in this sense, is much more than seeing words in a passing parade across a page. Reading is thinking, comparing, setting goals, questioning, and weighing the relative values of new ideas as they are found. Reading rate and efficiency in this type of reading involve much more than the traditional word-by-word measurement of progress on a printed page.

Perhaps this type of reading is best characterized by the advice:

Think first . . . then read . . . then react!

Exercise IV-1

Some statistics, startling as they may sound, are not unusual.

1. Startling statistics are not always as unusual as one might think.   1. _____

2. Unusual statistics are usually startling to the reader.   2. _____

3. Some compiled data may sound arresting and yet, in reality, be rather commonplace.   3. _____

4. Statistics are unusual to a person engaged in research.   4. _____

5. Students interested in studying many of the college subjects will find a course in statistics mandatory.   5. _____

6. The statistics that we have here may sound startling, but they are really quite usual.   6. _____

7. Unusual facts are more interesting than common ones.   7. _____

8. A table of statistics is very useful in many fields of study.   8. _____

9. Startling facts make startling statistics as a rule.   9. _____

10. Statistics are not unusual just because they attract considerable attention.   10. _____

Time _____ Sec.

No. Correct: _____
(key on page 321)

IV–1

RATE (from table on page 311):   R. _____

COMPREHENSION (10% for each correct answer):   C. _____

EFFICIENCY (R × C):   E. _____

Record on Progress Chart on page 297

Exercise IV-2

There are no special tricks for concentrating, and they are unnecessary.

1. One of the first things that a college student must learn is the knack necessary for concentrating.   1. _____

2. Concentration is an art that college students will find very necessary in their studying.   2. _____

3. Special tricks for concentrating are not especially needed.   3. _____

4. Concentration, although difficult, does not require the use of particular tricks.   4. _____

5. Necessary tricks for concentration are special ones and not easily learned.   5. _____

6. It is necessary to learn to concentrate quickly.   6. _____

7. There are tricks necessary in learning to concentrate well.   7. _____

8. There are tricks to all trades.   8. _____

9. Special tricks are not necessary in developing an ability to concentrate.   9. _____

10. Concentration is a result of a series of special studies by a student.   10. _____

Time _____ Sec.

No. Correct: _____
(key on page 329)

IV–2

RATE (from table on page 311):   R. _____

COMPREHENSION (10% for each correct answer):   C. _____

EFFICIENCY (R × C):   E. _____

Record on Progress Chart on page 297

Exercise IV-3

Spaced reviewing develops better understanding of material.

1. Spaced reviewing is another name for rote reviewing.   1. _____

2. The best way to understand a lesson is to read it and reread it frequently.   2. _____

3. Review is necessary in order to pass the course.   3. _____

4. Reviewing once each week or at regulars intervals is a good way to improve one's comprehension of a subject.   4. _____

5. Reviewing at intervals brings about better understanding.   5. _____

6. Teachers use rote learning as a principal method to help students understand material. 6. _____

7. Better understanding is developed by frequent reviewing at regular intervals.   7. _____

8. The time of the reviewing of material is an important factor.   8. _____

9. To better understand material, one should read it carefully at least twice.   9. _____

10. Better understanding is a goal of all good teachers.   10. _____

Time_____Sec.   RATE (from table on page 311):   R. _____

No. Correct:_____   COMPREHENSION (10% for each correct answer):   C. _____
(key on page 321)

IV-3   EFFICIENCY (R × C):   E. _____

Record on Progress Chart on page 297

Exercise IV-4

Power equipment is not essential to productive activity on a farm.

1. Modern farming methods require mechanization on the farm.   1. _____

2. A farm may be able to produce quite well without power machines.   2. _____

3. Productive activity on farms can be accomplished without the use of tractors or similar equipment.   3. _____

4. Power equipment is not essential for production on a farm.   4. _____

5. Horses were once used for farming purposes, but since the widespread use of electricity they have become obsolete.   5. _____

6. Marginal farms are those that have no power equipment.   6. _____

7. Some farms may become productive without the use of power equipment.   7. _____

8. Most farms in the United States are not really self-sustaining.   8. _____

9. The high cost of modern farming machinery has kept many farmers from developing their farms into productive units.   9. _____

10. Good lighting is not necessary on a farm.   10. _____

Time_____Sec.   RATE (from table on page 311):   R. _____

No. Correct:_____   COMPREHENSION (10% for each correct answer):   C. _____
(key on page 329)

IV-4   EFFICIENCY (R × C):   E. _____

Record on Progress Chart on page 297

Exercise IV–5

Geographical factors have something to do with the mode of living.

1. The way we live depends on where we live.   1. _____

2. There is no connection between geography and living habits.   2. _____

3. Man's living is modified by physiographic influences.   3. _____

4. The geography of a country will tell a great deal about the people residing in that country.   4. _____

5. Climatic influences are quite apparent in weather maps.   5. _____

6. Geographical environment may affect society indirectly by changing the human physique.   6. _____

7. Geographical environment is one of the factors in determining one's standard of living.   7. _____

8. Religious faith is a result of geographical location.   8. _____

9. Human behavior varies according to the weather.   9. _____

10. The cultural developments that affect one's way of living are often determined by the
    topographical conditions in any given locality.   10. _____

Time_____Sec.   RATE (from table on page 311):   R. _____

No. Correct:_____   COMPREHENSION (10% for each correct answer):   C. _____
(key on page 321)

IV–5   EFFICIENCY (R × C):   E. _____

Record on Progress Chart on page 297

Exercise IV–6

Contrary to popular opinion, forgetting is not simply a weathering away of once known impressions.

1. Forgetting is a loss of memory.   1. _____

2. Many people seem to have the mistaken idea that forgetting is merely a gradual loss of
   impressions once held.   2. _____

3. The process of remembering is complicated.   3. _____

4. Forgetting is not as simple a process as many people think.   4. _____

5. Popular opinion is often the incorrect opinion.   5. _____

6. Psychology is a subject in which one studies many things.   6. _____

7. Impressions which are gained during life make up what we call memory.   7. _____

8. Popular opinion on a subject shapes our opinions on that same subject.   8. _____

9. Impressions of a thing are the same as opinions about that same thing.   9. _____

10. Forgetting consists of more than just losing impressions once held.   10. _____

Time_____Sec.   RATE (from table on page 311):   R. _____

No. Correct:_____   COMPREHENSION (10% for each correct answer):   C. _____
(key on page 329)

IV–6   EFFICIENCY (R × C):   E. _____

Record on Progress Chart on page 297

Exercise IV-7

The process of change is one in which the invention comes before we anticipate its social effects.

1. The social effects of the inventions that occur are relatively unimportant.   1. _____

2. Instead of creating stability, inventions force us to unanticipated adjustments to the effects they create in our society.   2. _____

3. Technological developments always precede the social process of adjustment which they cause.   3. _____

4. A moratorium should be declared on invention and scientific discovery until the social institutions of man catch up.   .4. _____

5. The inventions already in existence have exerted little influence on our social order.   5. _____

6. We seldom know what social effect will take place due to an invention.   6. _____

7. Before this process of change can be controlled, it must first be anticipated.   7. _____

8. Social effects are generally not only not anticipated; they are not recognized.   8. _____

9. The problem of the control of social change resolves itself largely into the problem of the control of the effects of the environment.   9. _____

10. Inventions come before the social effects which they inevitably cause.   10. _____

Time_____Sec.

No. Correct:_____
(key on page 321)

IV-7

RATE (from table on page 311):   R. _____

COMPREHENSION (10% for each correct answer):   C. _____

EFFICIENCY (R × C):   E. _____

Record on Progress Chart on page 297

Exercise IV-8

Biological man is fortunately very adaptable, more so than most other animals.

1. Man is capable of making physiological adjustments to environment more readily than most animals.   1. _____

2. Biological man's adaptability is not infinite.   2. _____

3. Famine is one of the adjustments that man finds very difficult to meet.   3. _____

4. For thousands of years man was adjusted to an environment which called for muscular activity in the open air.   4. _____

5. Cities are a radically different type of environment from the country.   5. _____

6. Few animals could become adjusted to a variety of living conditions as easily as man.   6. _____

7. Adjustment between man and his culture always will exist as a very serious problem.   7. _____

8. Laborers are able to become better adjusted to factory machines than animals such as the saber-tooth tiger were able to adjust to changing conditions.   8. _____

9. Down through the ages it has been seen that the human animal is the most adaptable of the animal kingdom.   9. _____

10. It is fortunate that all animals have learned to adapt themselves quickly.   10. _____

Time_____Sec.

No. Correct:_____
(key on page 329)

IV-8

RATE (from table on page 311):   R. _____

COMPREHENSION (10% for each correct answer):   C. _____

EFFICIENCY (R × C):   E. _____

Record on Progress Chart on page 297

Exercise IV-9

Man's inherited nature changes exceedingly slowly via the germ plasm, whereas culture changes more rapidly.

1. Heredity plays a big part in shaping our nature, but environment plays an equally important part.   1. _____

2. Our culture changes radically and rapidly, whereas the genes mutate slowly in individual reproduction.   2. _____

3. Innate personal changes do not come about rapidly, whereas cultural changes may take very little time.   3. _____

4. Social and cultural changes come about more quickly than do changes in human beings.   4. _____

5. We find that man's nature is inherited from both parents and is modified by his culture.   5. _____

6. Man is a creature of habit and, therefore, affects society's actions.   6. _____

7. Studies show that man can change his inherited personality but very little solely by his own efforts.   7. _____

8. A cause of social disorganization is the lack of adaptation of man's inherited nature to the environment of group and culture.   8. _____

9. The changes in man's nature are difficult to understand.   9. _____

10. Changes via the germ plasm are difficult to understand and explain.   10. _____

Time_____Sec.	RATE (from table on page 311):	R. _____
No. Correct:_____ (key on page 321)	COMPREHENSION (10% for each correct answer):	C. _____
IV-9	EFFICIENCY (R × C):	E. _____

Record on Progress Chart on page 297

Exercise IV-10

Careful selection in the breeding of dairy stock will pay dividends in increased milk production.

1. The mating of good bulls and good cows will result in more milk from their offspring.   1. _____

2. Farmers should be more careful in selecting their dairy breeding stock if they wish higher milk records.   2. _____

3. It is necessary to have good dairy livestock for breeding if one expects a good milk production record.   3. _____

4. Dairy farmers find it financially advantageous to invest in high quality stock for breeding purposes.   4. _____

5. Increased milk production is the aim of every dairy owner.   5. _____

6. Adequate food is required for all breeds of dairy stock.   6. _____

7. Certain types of cattle are better for dairy stock than other breeds.   7. _____

8. Breeding of dairy stock must be done carefully to increase milk production.   8. _____

9. It is no wonder that many farmers have low milk production from their dairy stock because the quality is so poor.   9. _____

10. Careful selection in breeding of all livestock will pay dividends in increased production.   10. _____

Time_____Sec.	RATE (from table on page 311):	R. _____
No. Correct:_____ (key on page 329)	COMPREHENSION (10% for each correct answer):	C. _____
IV-10	EFFICIENCY (R × C):	E. _____

Record on Progress Chart on page 297

Exercise IV-11

Although imbeciles learn to talk, there is great lack of ideas among them.

1. Imbeciles can be taught to talk, but we find that they have relatively few ideas.　　1. _____

2. All that a true imbecile can learn to do is to talk and not to think.　　2. _____

3. Although talking, imbeciles have few ideas.　　3. _____

4. Most people think that because imbeciles learn to talk, it is a sign that they can have a great many ideas.　　4. _____

5. Ideas are relatively foreign to imbeciles, but speech is not.　　5. _____

6. The study of imbeciles is to be found in abnormal psychology.　　6. _____

7. Although imbeciles learn to talk, there is great variety of ideas among them.　　7. _____

8. It is little use to teach imbeciles to talk because after they learn the language, they find it difficult to express ideas.　　8. _____

9. The lack of ideas is one mark of an imbecile although he may have a working knowledge of the language.　　9. _____

10. Imbeciles may learn to use the language, but find few ideas to express.　　10. _____

Time_____ Sec.　　RATE (from table on page 311):　　R. _____

No. Correct:_____
(key on page 321)　　COMPREHENSION (10% for each correct answer):　　C. _____

IV–11　　EFFICIENCY (R × C):　　E. _____

Record on Progress Chart on page 297

Exercise IV-12

The blueprints for the new schoolhouse are deficient in that they fail to provide for adequate fire protection.

1. The new school building is a firetrap.　　1. _____

2. Blueprints for buildings are difficult to read without training.　　2. _____

3. In making the school plans, provision of minimum safety facilities to be used in case of fire apparently was overlooked.　　3. _____

4. Adequate fire protection has not been provided for in the plans for the new school.　　4. _____

5. The architect did not provide adequate fire safety plans for the schoolhouse.　　5. _____

6. The blueprints for the new schoolhouse are inadequate in at least one aspect.　　6. _____

7. In general, good blueprints for buildings provide adequate fire protection for all occupants.　　7. _____

8. The blueprints as drawn by the architect for the new school building are not adequate in that they fail to provide for protection from fire in some cases.　　8. _____

9. The city law states that all schools must be fireproof and entirely safe.　　9. _____

10. Adequate fire protection for the blueprints of the new schoolhouse has been neglected.　　10. _____

Time_____ Sec.　　RATE (from table on page 311):　　R. _____

No. Correct:_____
(key on page 329)　　COMPREHENSION (10% for each correct answer):　　C. _____

IV–12　　EFFICIENCY (R × C):　　E. _____

Record on Progress Chart on page 297

Exercise IV–13

The assets of the business have increased threefold within the last decade.

1. Business has been unusually good in the last three years.   1. _____

2. By studying records of the business we find that its assets have grown three times greater in the last ten years.   2. _____

3. Successful businesses must have assets greater than their liabilities.   3. _____

4. In a boom, business does well whereas in a depression, business does poorly.   4. _____

5. Increases in assets over a span of years are indications that the business is prospering.   5. _____

6. During the last decade the business has increased its assets 300 per cent.   6. _____

7. The increase in the assets of a business is a good indication of how well the business is doing.   7. _____

8. Careful records must be kept for a business so that the owner can tell how much his assets have increased.   8. _____

9. A threefold increase of assets of the business is shown in the last ten years.   9. _____

10. The balance sheet for the business shows that the assets have tripled within ten years.   10. _____

Time_____Sec.   RATE (from table on page 311):   R. _____

No. Correct:_____   COMPREHENSION (10% for each correct answer):   C. _____
(key on page 321)

IV–13   EFFICIENCY (R × C):   E. _____

Record on Progress Chart on page 297

Exercise IV–14

Horseback riding is beneficial to the physique in general, but may have detrimental effects on the leg bones.

1. When we ride horseback, the horse buffets the rider violently.   1. _____

2. A number of horses make up a herd.   2. _____

3. Horseback riding is good for one in spite of the fact that one's legs may be adversely affected.   3. _____

4. We receive some benefits from horseback riding, but may become bowlegged.   4. _____

5. Riding horseback is healthful exercise, but has a tendency to cause curvature of the legs.   5. _____

6. Dancing requires a certain amount of work plus natural talent in timing and balance.   6. _____

7. Horseback riding is good exercise, but it may develop undesirable changes in the lower appendages.   7. _____

8. "A donkey can walk between his legs without its ears being touched" is frequently said of the people who ride horseback a great deal.   8. _____

9. When one approaches the horse, the rider is expecting to indulge in an enjoyable exercise.   9. _____

10. Riding generally is unhealthy from the standpoint of general physical condition.   10. _____

Time_____Sec.   RATE (from table on page 311):   R. _____

No. Correct:_____   COMPREHENSION (10% for each correct answer):   C. _____
(key on page 329)

IV–14   EFFICIENCY (R × C):   E. _____

Record on Progress Chart on page 297

Exercise IV-15

History has shown that it is difficult for a president to be a great man unless some crisis occurs in his administration.

1. Presidents usually do not secure lasting prominence unless there has been a serious crisis during their administrations.   1. ____
2. Social and economic control is generally exercised by or through the president in time of crisis.   2. ____
3. The history of many a country shows a period of particularly great prestige which is usually associated with the administration of an outstanding president.   3. ____
4. We tend to overestimate the originality, initiative, and even the ability of the president in times of stress.   4. ____
5. Presidents of the United States have often taken credit for prosperity when it was due to favorable rainfall or to the discovery of gold mines.   5. ____
6. It is natural that presidents are blamed for business depressions which they play little part in making.   6. ____
7. Unless a crisis occurs during his administration, a president seems to have little chance of becoming famous.   7. ____
8. The difficulty of becoming president prevents many great men from securing the office.   8. ____
9. A man may become president who is not destined for greatness during his term.   9. ____
10. It is easier for the man in office to be a great president in time of crisis.   10. ____

Time____Sec.

No. Correct:____
(key on page 321)

IV–15

RATE (from table on page 311):   R. _____

COMPREHENSION (10% for each correct answer):   C. _____

EFFICIENCY (R × C):   E. _____

Record on Progress Chart on page 297

Exercise IV-16

It has been pointed out that it is sometimes necessary to adjust yourself to those who fail to adjust to you.

1. People often find it necessary to make adjustments in their lives in order to satisfy other peoples' idiosyncrasies.   1. ____
2. It is sometimes necessary to force all others to adjust to one's desires for certain periods of time.   2. ____
3. We have learned in various life situations that sometimes we must follow other people's ways since they can't seem to follow our ways.   3. ____
4. International tension could be lowered if each nation could learn to adjust itself to other nations.   4. ____
5. Adjustment is a constant problem to the spider monkey.   5. ____
6. Imitation is one way of adjusting one's life to that of others with whom one wishes to live happily.   6. ____
7. Other people in order to get along well with a certain individual may have to learn to adjust to him.   7. ____
8. It has been pointed out that there are always two sides to every problem which must be considered.   8. ____
9. Instead of going our own way when someone does not agree with us, it may be necessary to learn to make adjustments to his wishes.   9. ____
10. It has been pointed out that people like to have their own way.   10. ____

Time____Sec.

No. Correct:____
(key on page 329)

IV–16

RATE (from table on page 311):   R. _____

COMPREHENSION (10% for each correct answer):   C. _____

EFFICIENCY (R × C):   E. _____

Record on Progress Chart on page 297

Exercise IV-17

Surveying the site for the new highway was very difficult because of the rugged terrain.

1. The presence of surface irregularities made mapping out the new highway very difficult.   1. _____
2. Surveying for the new highway took almost three months due to the moisture in the soil.   2. _____
3. George Washington when a young man went on a surveying party for the site of the new Cumberland Road over difficult and rugged terrain.   3. _____
4. The new highway would have been relocated to go through a certain section of the country if the terrain had been smoother.   4. _____
5. Many severe eroded gulleys and prominent outcroppings of rock provided extreme obstacles in the preliminary work on the new highway.   5. _____
6. The final location of the new highway is always of vital interest to the people through whose land it might go.   6. _____
7. The rugged terrain made difficulties in surveying the site for the new highway.   7. _____
8. Engineers had great difficulty in surveying the land for the new highway because of the very rugged terrain over which they worked.   8. _____
9. Surveying is not a difficult thing to do if the land is smooth and the landowners are cooperative.   9. _____
10. Broken and irregular topography caused the engineers a great deal of trouble in surveying for the new highway.   10. _____

Time_____Sec.	RATE (from table on page 311):	R. _____
No. Correct:_____ (key on page 321)	COMPREHENSION (10% for each correct answer):	C. _____
IV–17	EFFICIENCY (R × C):	E. _____

Record on Progress Chart on page 297

Exercise IV-18

The home economics courses taught in our high schools can be of great use to the boys and girls who take them.

1. Boys and girls who take courses in home economics probably will find them useful.   1. _____
2. The home economics courses taught in high schools are too impractical to be of real use.   2. _____
3. The boys and girls who take home economics in high school learn many things that will be of value to them.   3. _____
4. The equipment found in the high school for the home economics course is so different from what the students have at home that they gain no real value from using it.   4. _____
5. One of the most difficult courses offered in high school is economics.   5. _____
6. Since most girls marry, home economics should be taken by them.   6. _____
7. Students in high school will find that home economics can be a very useful subject.   7. _____
8. Throughout the years of high school life the students should take those subjects which will be of the most use to them after they graduate. 8. _____
9. The boys and girls will find that the things they learn in home economics can aid them greatly.   9. _____
10. Home economics as taught in present day schools is of little practical value to boys.   10. _____

Time_____Sec.	RATE (from table on page 311):	R. _____
No. Correct:_____ (key on page 329)	COMPREHENSION (10% for each correct answer):	C. _____
IV–18	EFFICIENCY (R × C):	E. _____

Record on Progress Chart on page 297

Exercise IV–19

One of the student's problems is recognizing what should be known and then fixing it in memory so that it will be there when wanted.

1. One student problem is knowing what facts are important and then being able to remember them.   1. _____
2. The success of an individual depends on how well he adjusts to the new school environment.   2. _____
3. Rote learning is highly desirable for students so that they may have the facts needed always in mind.   3. _____
4. Learning the important things is a problem and remembering them in order to use them is a part of that problem.   4. _____
5. A good way to study is to read the lesson at least twice, and then listen closely to the instructor in class.   5. _____
6. Recognizing key ideas and establishing systems for retaining them are two important problems in learning how to study.   6. _____
7. Many students find that one difficulty in studying is their inability to recognize what is important and to apply effective techniques for remembering ideas.   7. _____
8. Students find that it is important to analyze the salient facts and keep them in mind for later use.   8. _____
9. Universities are good places to learn what is important.   9. _____
10. The solving of problems is the best way to learn important facts.   10. _____

Time_____Sec.   RATE (from table on page 311):   R. _____

No. Correct:_____   COMPREHENSION (10% for each correct answer):   C. _____
(key on page 321)

IV–19   EFFICIENCY (R × C):   E. _____

Record on Progress Chart on page 297

Exercise IV–20

To look upon the faces of high school seniors, one would never guess that at least one out of twenty eventually will be found in a hospital for the insane.

1. The chances of a child being placed in a mental hospital sometime during his life are about 1 in 20.   1. _____
2. Insanity is just another form of illness, no more reprehensible than physical disease.   2. _____
3. High school students are very inclined to become mentally ill.   3. _____
4. Sentiment seems to prevail that insanity is increasing in our society.   4. _____
5. Every individual who shares group life with others develops a personality.   5. _____
6. By looking at the faces of the high school seniors one can tell that at least one belongs in a hospital.   6. _____
7. Hospital space should be enlarged to meet the heavy demands now being made on it.   7. _____
8. The tragic fact that five out of a hundred of the high school seniors will eventually find their way to a mental hospital is hard to realize.   8. _____
9. The high school seniors should face the fact that of their group half of them will become mentally ill.   9. _____
10. One can't tell by looking at high school seniors that a certain ratio of them will enter a hospital for the mentally disturbed.   10. _____

Time_____Sec.   RATE (from table on page 311):   R. _____

No. Correct:_____   COMPREHENSION (10% for each correct answer):   C. _____
(key on page 329)

IV–20   EFFICIENCY (R × C):   E. _____

Record on Progress Chart on page 297

114

SERIES V
Idea Reading Exercises

Instructions

Series V should help you to develop the upper potential of your reading rate.

These exercises are designed to help you to read for ideas in short selections of material. These articles are all standardized at 900 words in length and should be read as rapidly as possible—preferably in one minute or less. In reading, you should try to grasp the main ideas, the recurrent theme, and the purpose for which the author seems to have written the article. Remember that headings frequently provide clues to this.

At the beginning of each article you will find the length of the article and the readability scores as computed by the Flesch Formula (14). The higher this score is, the easier the material is to read. General levels of readability are as follows:

READABILITY SCORE	GRADE LEVEL OF READING DIFFICULTY
0-30	College Graduates
30-40	College Juniors and Seniors
40-50	College Freshmen and Sophomores
50-60	High School Students
60-70	Junior High Students

Exercises are arranged so that each successive exercise will be a little more difficult than the one preceding it. Therefore, you will be striving to increase both your reading speed and your reading level. Spaced at intervals down the center of the page are numbers indicating the number of words read to that point. If the instructor calls time intervals, you can glance quickly at these numbers and note your approximate speed.

Read each article as rapidly as possible, and check your time when you have finished. This time will be given in seconds, and you then can find your rate of reading by using the table on page 313, which will give you your *rate of reading in words per minute.*

Then answer the two questions that deal with the main ideas of the article. You should have no difficulty in answering these correctly. On the true-false (T–F) questions, circle either the "T" or the "F" to indicate your understanding of the accuracy of the statement. In the multiple-choice (MC) questions, select the answer that seems most appropriate to you, and then place a check on the line before that answer. If you answer both of the questions correctly according to the key, your comprehension will be 100 percent, and your *efficiency* score will be the same as your rate. Missing one question cuts your efficiency to one half of your rate; so you should concentrate on the main ideas as you read.

When you have computed your efficiency, turn to page 299, and record this score on your Progress Chart. If you have missed a question, you should record both rate and efficiency to show both scores for comparison. Keys are on pages 321 and 329.

Suggestions

This series provides experience in the type of high-speed reading or skimming that is most frequently used in our daily lives when we want a preliminary processing of masses of reading material for later use or immediate disposal. Personal mail, business correspondence, professional journals, news magazines, and other current newspapers or news digests can be processed in this fashion.

The general purpose of this series is to help you get a quick identification of general content, general ideas, and author viewpoints and to use this quick review as a basis for your own selective judgment as to subsequent use of the materials. Often reading for further detail is unnecessary and it may be a waste of time.

Effective use of idea reading involves use of headings and context clues in searching out key ideas. Posing questions from titles or headings helps you to set personal goals for reading.

Thinking first about the topic and what you already know about it will provide a mental setting in which you can best evaluate the general content that follows.

In this workbook, this series is provided as an opportunity for you to free yourself from the compulsion for detailed comprehension. Comprehension scores are relatively unimportant here, and you should not be disturbed if you occasionally miss both questions. You should push yourself to improve reading rate as much as possible in this series. Try to eliminate all backtracking. Experiment with new and expanded ideas of eye span. Consider the bad habits discussed in "How Do We Read?" on page 9, and concentrate on trying to overcome such habits as you practice on these exercises.

Let yourself go! See how fast you can breeze through these exercises without any concern for retaining content for any future use. You may be pleasantly surprised at how much you do remember even then. In the process, you may discover some flexibility of eye movement and eye span that you had not recognized or used before.

Exercise V-1

Curse of the Pharaohs
by DONNA MARTINEZ

(Reprinted from an original article of the Uniwyo Reading Research Center
by permission of the director.)

—————————— WAIT FOR SIGNAL TO BEGIN READING ——————————

The curse on Carnarvon

The sun outside beat down heavily on the sand and the rugged stone sides of the ancient pyramid. Inside it was dry and stuffy. Every move of the crew working deep in the interior seemed to stir up more clouds of arid dust.

For three months Lord Carnarvon and his crew had been working through underground passages and anterooms of the tomb of King Tutankhamen. Each night the tunnels mysteriously seemed to fill with hoards of bats which had to be cleared out each morning before the work could be started. Impatient to locate the main chamber of the tomb, they had 100 cursed the bats and the time they lost each day in clearing them out.

But on this particular day, February 17, 1923, the excitement was extremely high. Lord Carnarvon was sure that the new entrance they had discovered that morning was different from any other. As they worked through it and on into a larger chamber, he knew that, at last, they had reached the king's tomb. After years of eager anticipation, he finally had found one of the great prizes for which the Egyptologists had been searching for years.

But even as Lord Carnarvon flashed his feeble 200 light around the walls of this newly discovered chamber, he began to feel uneasy and found breathing more difficult. He decided to close up the room for the day and climb back to daylight.

The pain continued, however, and soon he was suffering acutely from breathlessness, headache, lassitude and swelling around some of his glands. He decided to return to Cairo to the Continental Hotel, where he had rooms. He did not respond to any medical aid, however, and soon developed a serious case of bilateral pneumonia. A few weeks later, on April 6, he died. All the natives who had 300 been on his work crew were sure that he was a victim of the ancient "Curse of the Pharaohs."

The conditions of his death certainly suggested the supernatural. According to some reports, all of the lights in the Continental Hotel blacked out completely at the moment of his death, then came back on momentarily, only to go out abruptly shortly thereafter.

Although no medical cause of the illness that led to his death ever was established, some journalists conjectured that he must have been bitten by a mosquito that caused blood poisoning which in turn 400 weakened him too much to fight off the pneumonia. But the local residents remembered the centuries-old legend of the "Curse of the Pharaohs."

Mace and Benedite follow

In the succeeding months, Arthur Mace, assistant director of the New York Department of Egyptian Antiquities, came to Egypt and visited the Tomb of Tutankhamen. Shortly thereafter he died very suddenly of unexplained causes. George Benedite, an Egyptologist from the staff of the Louvre in Paris also visited the famous tomb. He, too, died mysteriously soon after that visit. These deaths reinforced the superstition and led many others to 500 believe that there was some substance to the mystical "Curse of the Pharaohs."

Rice dust

Some specialists in tropical medicine have suggested that any one of a large number of selective diseases may have affected all three of these men and caused their deaths. They noted evidence in other cases of death from inhalation of rice dust. One of them reported a case of a fungus carried in rice dust in Sri Lanka which had affected only fifty people in a large community. Since it seems to act in a selective fashion, this same fungus might be 600 an explanation of the deaths associated with the Egyptian tomb.

Blame the bats!

Now, more than fifty years after Lord Carnarvon fell victim to the "Curse of the Pharaohs," a Dublin medical specialist thinks he has found the answer to the King Tut mystery.

Dr. George Dean, Director of the Medico-Social Research Board in Dublin, Ireland, is convinced that the men all died from an infection from some fungus dust which they inhaled. He is sure that dust from bat droppings could cause this kind of infection. He had been involved in research in Rhodesia, where he had interviewed and examined many government officials and research specialists who had explored some remote caves in the Urungwe 700 ← district where the bat droppings were sometimes as deep as six feet. These men had contracted a fungus histoplasma from the dried bat dung dust.

So he believes that infection was introduced to the tomb by the bats which came in after the tomb was opened for exploration. He conceded that there is no way of ever knowing this with any degree of certainty. He does feel, however, that all three men did walk through underground corridors which were deeply crusted with large quantities of dried bat droppings. Were the bats, then, the instruments of 800 ← the "Curse of the Pharaohs"?

Experts disagree

Many Egyptologists find Dr. Dean's theory hard to accept. They point out examples of other anthropologists who have been exposed to similar circumstances and who have lived to a ripe old age. They argue that there could be many types of selective fungi which could have been involved.

Dr. Dean defends his position, however. He argues that it is soundly based on evidence from his research in Rhodesia. But many people do not believe his theory. The legendary "Curse of the Pharaohs" 900 → will continue to persist for many more years.

——STOP——ASK FOR YOUR TIME——

Record time immediately and answer the questions on content.

Time_____Sec.	RATE (from table on page 313):	R. _____
No. Correct:_____ (key on page 321)	COMPREHENSION (50% for each correct answer):	C. _____
V–1	EFFICIENCY (R ✕ C):	E. _____

Record on Progress Chart on page 299

ANSWER THESE QUESTIONS IMMEDIATELY (V–1)

1. (T – F) The "Curse of the Pharaohs" has finally been explained in a way that is generally accepted as a reasonable explanation.

2. (M. C.) Dr. Dean believed the cause of death was a fungus histoplasma developed from the inhalation of:
   _____(1) the damp stale air in the central tomb room.
   _____(2) the dust from the deposits of dry bat dung.
   __X__(3) the dust from ancient rice left in the tomb.
   _____(4) the dust from the walls of the tomb.

Exercise V–2

World between the Tides
by JOAN E. RAHN

─────── **WAIT FOR SIGNAL TO BEGIN READING** ───────

The sea has a split personality

At high tide it can be a powerful and often cruel giant that crashes on the rocks and beats to death the very life it holds.

At low tide it can be a meek and gentle soul, showing the tenderness of a mother caring for the creatures who depend on her for their existence.

As she withdraws from her assault at high tide, she exposes a world teeming with life in the sands and rocks of the beach.

It is this world that is studied at the Oregon Institute of Marine Biology, one of several marine 100 biology stations along the western coast of the United States. The station is a small one, and the neighboring fishing village of Charleston is but a tiny dot on a map of Oregon, but the abundance of plant and animal life in the intertidal zones of the area make it a marine biologist's paradise.

At high tide these rocky shores seem inhospitable and unlikely habitats for plants, for the algae at high tide are covered by water and only bare rocks are seen emerging from the ocean—rock that frequently may be inaccessible to humans. Furthermore, when the waves are high and violent, it seems 200 impossible that anything—plant or animal—could maintain a hold under the unmerciful pounding that may continue for hours.

Creatures between the tides

But when the tide is low a whole new world is revealed. Here the rocks are as luxuriant with vegetation as those a few feet above were barren, and the dividing line may be quite sharp. The slimy surface of the algae that covers the rocks in such profusion can make footing treacherous, and a newcomer is hard put to keep from slipping and catching a foot among the rocks. The bases of these algae 300 are a broadened holdfast, and secrete a cementing substance which glues the plant firmly to the rock. The attachment is so secure that none but the most violent action can separate a healthy alga from its footing as anyone who has tried to do so will testify. Indeed, it is sometimes easier to tear the stalk of the plant than to make a clean break between the holdfast and the rock. At low tide, deprived of the buoyancy of water, the algae lie draped over the rocks, for they have no sturdy supporting fibers as land plants do. 400

Most of the intertidal plants large enough to see with the naked eye are brown and red algae. Green algae are fewer in number, and only a few diatoms are large enough to be seen with the unaided eye. All algae, of course, contain the green pigment, chlorophyll, but the browns and reds receive their common names from the colors of the other pigments that they contain—fucoxanthin in the brown, phycoerythrin in the red, and phycocyanin in blue. Because of the varying proportions of these 500 pigments, brown algae may appear to be any shade from brown to olive to almost green. The red algae are red to brown in color—frequently a rusty red—but sometimes are even blue-green. The algae plants have no flowers—in fact, marine plants seldom flower—only the eelgrasses with their long thin leaves, grow and flower in salt water.

Strange animals

Marine animals, like mussels, which are frequently covered with barnacles, are welcomed by the less-than-surefooted human intruders, for their rough surfaces are a relief to have underfoot after walking on the slippery algae. (The barnacles are not quite so welcome, though, if you fall and cut yourself on them.)

600 Starfish, sea urchins, and anemones are some of the animals more obvious to the first glance. Many starfish have five or six arms, but larger ones have a multiple of these numbers—the big Pycnopodia has about 20! The beautiful purple of the sea urchins will never be forgotten by anyone who has seen them in their rocky niches. Anemones exposed by the receding tide retract their tentacles and are exceedingly unattractive, but those that are covered by the water remaining in a tidepool expand the tentacles with which they trap food, and then resemble a many-petalled flower.

The nudibranches, or sea slugs, range in color $\overset{700}{\leftarrow}$ from a drab tan to the orange and iridescent blue trimmings of Hermissenda. The bryozoans could easily be mistaken for plants; indeed their name means "moss animals."

Inspection of the intertidal zones

The biologist who would search out these treasures on a summer day must be prepared to brave the cold early morning hours. The summer tides which are the lowest, and therefore the best for collecting, occur on the Oregon coast about dawn, but meeting the tide often requires arising before the sun. Cold water welling up from the ocean bottom keeps the air cold and if there is a fog, as there so $\overset{800}{\leftarrow}$ often is, heavy clothing is in order.

Despite the fog, the low temperatures, and the care required in scrambling over the rocks, a visit to the intertidal zone is exciting, and well worth the effort. It can be fully enjoyed only through personal experience; for the breeze coming off the ocean, the sound of pounding waves with their fascinating beauty, and that pleasantly tired feeling that follows physical effort in the fresh air are all part of the story, and these can never be completely captured $\overset{900}{\rightarrow}$ in words and pictures.

——STOP——ASK FOR YOUR TIME——

Record time immediately and answer the questions on content.

Time_____Sec.	RATE (from table on page 313):	R. _____
No. Correct:_____ (key on page 329)	COMPREHENSION (50% for each correct answer):	C. _____
V–2	EFFICIENCY (R × C):	E. _____

Record on Progress Chart on page 299

ANSWER THESE QUESTIONS IMMEDIATELY (V–2)

1. (T – F) The sea has consistent and dependable moods with little difference shown in the changes of the tide.
2. (M. C.) When exploring this area between the tides, the most dangerous feature is:
   _____(1) the slimy algae that lie draped limply over the rocks.
   _____(2) the mussels with their rough surfaces.
   _____(3) the starfish and anemones with their grasping tentacles.
   _____(4) the dense fog with its heavy chill factor.

Exercise V–3

First Dogs of the Land
by RAYMOND A. LAJOIE

(Reprinted with permission from *Modern Maturity*.
Copyright 1976 by the American Association of Retired Persons.)

———————————— WAIT FOR SIGNAL TO BEGIN READING ————————————

Presidential dogs

Dogs, by an overwhelming majority, have been the favorite pets of America's Presidents and their families. Of the 37 Presidents from Washington to Ford, 29 have been dog owners.

Perhaps it all started when the Puritans on the Mayflower voyage to Plymouth in 1620 brought along one male and one female dog.

Almost all United States Presidential families have been fond of dogs and sometimes have owned several during their administration. The Ford's "First Dog" was Liberty, a golden retriever given to the President by his daughter, Susan.

The Nixons had three dogs: Vicky, a miniature poodle; Pasha, a Yorkshire terrier; and King, an Irish ⟵100 setter.

Meeting the famous guests

President Johnson had four dogs in the White House: two beagles, a collie, and a crossbreed named Yuki. He was especially fond of his four dogs and Yuki was his favorite. But Him and Her, the beagles, and Bianco, a white collie, also received a great deal of loving attention. "Probably every world leader of the time met the dogs," says Traphes Bryant, retired White House kennelman. "It was a common sight to see President Johnson and his dogs walking with a foreign visitor. When he would lose one, the ⟵200 President would become visibly upset."

Between world powers

President Kennedy had many dogs in the White House. Perhaps the best known were Charlie, a Welsh terrier, and Pushinka, offspring of a Russian canine space explorer. Soviet Premier Khrushchev sent Pushinka as a gift for Caroline Kennedy. In 1963, Pushinka and Charlie had four puppies, certainly a first event of its kind to take place between world powers.

Dwight D. Eisenhower was dogless in the immediate years prior to becoming President. But he had a Scottish terrier that traveled all over the world with him during World War II when he was Supreme ⟵300

Commander of the Allied Forces. It is interesting that the day after he was elected President he arranged for an addition to the Eisenhower household: another Scottie—a black one—called Skunk who was the President's pet for a long time.

Early dog lovers

George Washington, appropriately enough, was the first dog loving President. He bred foxhounds, an interest that coincided with his enthusiasm for fox hunting.

A future President once helped Washington with his dog breeding ventures. John Quincy Adams, who was then 18 and later to be the sixth President, cared 400→ for seven foxhounds when they were sent to Washington from France as gifts of the Marquis de Lafayette. Young Adams was acting as an assistant to his father, John Adams, who was then in service abroad as a member of the U.S. diplomatic corps.

An incident during the Revolutionary War reveals how General Washington felt about pet dogs. He recognized a stray as belonging to enemy General Howe and immediately had the animal returned to its owner.

Hounds and bird dogs were favorites of other Presidents: Thomas Jefferson, James Madison, James Monroe, William Harrison, John Tyler, James Polk, and Zachary Taylor.

500→ Jefferson, Madison, and Monroe, who had grown up with hunting dogs in their native Virginia, took their animals to Washington. Andrew Jackson had several well-trained gun dogs.

President Abraham Lincoln owned a crossbreed and was sufficiently fond of the dog to have its likeness reproduced by tintype, the forerunner of modern photography. Abe's love for dogs is immortalized in the famous statue of him as "The Hoosier Youth," erected in Fort Wayne, Indiana, which shows him stroking a hound at his side.

Changing breeds

By the time of Theodore Roosevelt's administration, other breeds had risen in Presidential 600→ popularity. The Roosevelt household overflowed with children and pets of all kinds, including several terriers.

The President and his six children owned a rat terrier, a bull terrier, several dogs of unknown ancestry, and a St. Bernard that responded to the name of Rollo. The Chief Executive also owned sporting and hound dogs and took a keen interest in the breeding and development of these animals.

Airedales were White House pets during the Harding and Wilson years and President and Mrs. Calvin Coolidge owned three dogs: a wirehaired fox terrier, sheepdog, and collie named, respectively, Peter Pan, Rob Roy, and Prudence Prim. Rob Roy liked cold coffee and President Coolidge often fed ⁷⁰⁰⟵ him from his own saucer, to the astonishment of White House guests.

Herbert Hoover had a number of dogs—a collie, German shepherds, an English setter, and Norwegian elkhound.

Fala, President Franklin Roosevelt's celebrated Scottie—and perhaps the most widely publicized of all White House pets—was given to him when four months old and was devoted to his master for the rest of Roosevelt's life. More often than not, news photographs of Roosevelt showed Fala somewhere in the foreground and he was referred to in at least one ⁸⁰⁰→ of the President's speeches. Fala sat in on numerous press conferences and was constantly at FDR's side.

The Truman family also loved dogs and Margaret has talked of them fondly in her writings about her father and her years in the White House.

From Washington's foxhounds to President Ford's golden retriever, Presidential dogs reflect the roles—whether hunting companions or house pets—that dogs play in their owners' lives. They also reflect an enthusiasm shared by most Americans.

One more thing: Not to upset the legions of cat lovers, as Margaret Truman has pointed out in her writings, many Presidential Families have had them, ⁹⁰⁰→ too!

——STOP——ASK FOR YOUR TIME——

Record time immediately and answer
the questions on content.

Time_____Sec.	RATE (from table on page 313):	R. _____
No. Correct:_____ (key on page 321)	COMPREHENSION (50% for each correct answer):	C. _____
V–3	EFFICIENCY (R X C):	E. _____

Record on Progress Chart on page 299

ANSWER THESE QUESTIONS IMMEDIATELY (V–3)

1. (T – F) Although many of the "First Dogs" were of well-known breeds, apparently there were also several of them who had mixed ancestry.
2. (M. C.) The first President to own a dog that was a gift from a foreign dignitary was:
    _____(1) Adams.
    _____(2) Johnson.
    _____(3) Kennedy.
    _____(4) Washington.

Exercise V–4

A Real Old-Fashioned Christmas
by DEREK GILL

(Reprinted with permission from *Modern Maturity*. Copyright 1975 [1980] by the
American Association of Retired Persons.)

—————————— **WAIT FOR SIGNAL TO BEGIN READING** ——————————

"And we wish you a real, old-fashioned Christmas!"

The cheerful greeting will be uttered and written countless times each year, summoning to mind the merriest montage of carols, roast turkey, mistletoe, eggnog, trees aglitter with lights and bulbs, and children hanging stockings over a cozy hearth.

Whose idea was it?

Certainly no one can claim it all for himself, but largely responsible for the deeply etched images of a real, old-fashioned Christmas is the Victorian novelist Charles Dickens. His stories of Scrooge and Mr. Pickwick consolidated traditions that might otherwise have been lost among the gloomy morals and mores of the time in which he lived. 100

Dickens himself introduced his unforgettable characters to America in 1868. Although he was then frail, and indeed within two years of his death, he electrified huge audiences with readings from his books.

On Christmas Eve of that year, Bostonians thronged a theater to hear the most popular novelist of his day. He charmed them by reading an abbreviated version of his classic "A Christmas Carol," which carries one of the best definitions extant of the spirit of Christmas.

Most of us recall how, at the outset of the story, miserly Scrooge's cheerful nephew enters the office 200 of his uncle to wish him a merry Christmas. The old man responds with a contemptuous "Bah! Humbug!" then goes on to protest that Christmas is "a time for paying bills without money; a time for finding yourself a year older and not an hour richer."

Disbelief

Scrooge's nephew says, "I've always thought of Christmas as a good time, a kind of forgiving, charitable, pleasant time; the only time I know of in the calendar of the year when men and women seem by one consent to open their shut-up hearts freely and to think of people below them as if they really 300 were fellow travelers to the grave. And therefore, Uncle Scrooge, though it has never put a scrap of gold or silver into my pocket, I believe it has done me good and I say God bless it!"

Although the character of Scrooge is deliberately over-drawn, his attitude was not uncommon. The "humbug" and frivolity of Christmas festivals were decried from the Victorian pulpits. Many of the best-loved carols were banned from the churches as being "pagan"—which is one reason why carolers took to the streets.

Answering the accusation that his stories paid 400 too little heed to the real spirit of Christmas, Dickens quietly responded, "It is good to be children sometimes and never better than at Christmas when its mighty Founder was a child Himself."

Bleak childhood

Paradoxically, Dickens' own childhood was bleak and cruel. Poverty stalked his own home and twice he saw his father sent to the dreaded debtors' prison of Marshalsea.

The wretchedness of Dickens' early years inspired him to contrast the greedy soul and miserable self-centeredness of Scrooge with the joy and deep caring home of Scrooge's ill-paid clerk, Bob Cratchit.

Although Dickens did not himself innovate 500 Christmas traditions and customs that are so much a part of our contemporary Christmas, he salvaged them and gave them his imprint.

Influence

The Christmas card was introduced by his artist friend, John Calcott Horsley. When Dickens started to send cards to his colleagues and friends, the idea became popular. It is appropriate that many of today's Christmas cards are pictures or close copies of illustrations in his books.

The Christmas tree was introduced to England by Prince Albert, who brought the custom from his native Germany. Dickens loved the idea, and the next year had a tree hauled into his own home. 600

Certainly Dickens' description of beloved Mr. Pickwick being kissed under the mistletoe at Dingley Dell popularized the bucolic custom of hanging the berried plant from a ceiling lamp or over a doorway.

Who of the millions who have read *Pickwick Papers* can forget the account of the rotund Mr. Pickwick at that Christmas party being "pulled this way and then that, and first kissed on the chin and then on the nose and then on the spectacles"?

And one still hears the peals of laughter raised on every side as the whole company "sat down by the huge fire of blazing logs to a substantial supper 700 and a mighty bowl of wassail . . . when up flew the bright sparks in myriads as the logs were stirred and the deep red blaze sent forth a rich glow that permeated the furthest corners of the room and cast its cheerful tint on every face."

When I visited Dickens' London home, my imagination was not hard tested to visualize him presiding over a groaning dining room table.

The author was one of the few geniuses recognized in his own time. His name was almost as well known as Queen Victoria's.

Death of Christmas

800 → When he died on June 9, 1870, a newspaper obituary told about a small, ragged child in Drury Lane saying, "Charles Dickens dead! Then will Father Christmas die, too?"

Far from it!

Father Christmas—or Santa Claus as he is more generally known in America—was given immortality by Dickens, and it can be safely assumed that so long as the benevolent old fellow has the strength to crack a whip over his reindeer, so long will we join the merry company of Mr. Pickwick, Bob Cratchit, Tiny Tim and a reformed Ebenezer Scrooge—and, 900 → of course, the author who created these immortals.

——STOP——ASK FOR YOUR TIME——

Record time immediately and answer the questions on content.

Time____Sec.	RATE (from table on page 313):	R. _____
No. Correct:_____ (key on page 329)	COMPREHENSION (50% for each correct answer):	C. _____
V–4	EFFICIENCY (R × C):	E. _____

Record on Progress Chart on page 299

ANSWER THESE QUESTIONS IMMEDIATELY (V–4)

1. (T – F) Charles Dickens was one of the few geniuses recognized in his own time.
2. (M. C.) Which of the following individuals mentioned in this article was not a fictitious character created by Charles Dickens:
   ____(1) John Calcott Horsley.
   ____(2) Mr. Pickwick.
   ____(3) Ebenezer Scrooge.
   ____(4) Bob Cratchit.

Exercise V–5

Safer Ways to Drive at Night

(Excerpted by permission from *Changing Times,* the Kiplinger magazine, March 1967 issue.
Copyright 1967 by the Kiplinger Washington Editors, Inc., 1729 H Street, N.W., Washington, D.C. 20006.)

─────── **WAIT FOR SIGNAL TO BEGIN READING** ───────

The mid-teen girl got a good grade in driver education, had no trouble passing the state driver's license test and enjoys driving in the daytime, but at night, she's terrified.

The older man, proud of his 50-year driving record, has several close calls at night and wisely decides to do his future motoring in daylight only.

The healthy, 40-year-old executive with a quarter of a million accident-free miles behind him begins to find himself tense in evening rush-hour traffic and exhausted when he reaches home.

The housewife who drives half a dozen errands a day through all kinds of traffic asks her husband to ←100 take over to deliver a few Girl Scouts to an evening meeting.

These drivers operate under widely varying conditions; yet, the same problem worries them all—the difficulty and danger of nighttime driving.

Night driving hazardous

They have cause to worry, for a recent national survey of traffic accidents showed that 25,800 traffic fatalities occurred at night. Barely more than half of our annual death toll, true, but remember that most driving is done during daylight. The death rate for night driving is more than *two and a half times greater* than the daylight death rate. 200←

What makes night driving so difficult? Reduced vision due to insufficient light is only one of the problems; for most of us, there are other notable nighttime impediments to good driving. They may arise from the car you drive, the road you ride on, or your own physical condition, and frequently, mishaps involve all three

The car you drive

Your windshield has been pock-marked by flying gravel, spattered with muddy or salted water, speckled with rain, dust or bugs, or smeared with a greasy wiping rag. Your night vision is impaired. Glare from street lights, electric signs, and oncoming headlights is an irritating product of a dirty windshield, but the broken-up picture you see is a worse 300← enemy. Filmed-over eyeglasses can sabotage you too; keep them polished.

A car with a dirty windshield will have headlights that are even dirtier. A spattery roadcoating on them robs you of road illumination you need and dims the marking of your car for oncoming traffic. Also, headlights must be aimed right—if too high, they blind oncoming drivers; if too low, they fail to pick out dangers in time for you to evade them.

At night, worn wipers can dangerously alter 400→ your view with streaks of water and dirt. The blades wear gradually; yours may be worse than you realize. Check the blades and if they're streaky, replace them now. Don't wait for a rainy night to get the message the hard way.

Sixteen one-hundredths of 1% of odorless, invisible carbon monoxide in the air you breathe can kill you in an hour and even tinier amounts can seriously affect your night vision before you realize you're being poisoned. Your car's exhaust system can be leaky without being noisy, so the only safe course is to check the muffler and pipes twice a year, 500→ oftener on older cars.

The roads you travel

Bumper-to-bumper driving in rush-hour traffic may not be as necessary as you think. If you experiment with leaving work 15 minutes earlier or later than usual, you may find traffic that's easier to live with. If a schedule change isn't practical, try lesser-known routes or a nearby new freeway. In many metropolitan areas it's possible to go a mile or two out of your way and still get home 15 minutes earlier—and on less gasoline—in traffic that is less dense.

When you have a choice of several routes for 600→ getting to a night meeting or party, choose the way that has good lighting, a minimum of intersections, little or no construction in progress, few schools or stadiums to attract crowds. Avoid large shopping centers and areas with drive-ins that teenagers frequent. Familiarize yourself with the special perils of roads you must travel at night—the spots that get slick in a new rain, ditches easily disguised by a little drifted snow, places where spasmodic splotches of bright neon confuse you, the fast-breaking curves and bridges at the bottoms of hills, chuckholes, dips, loose gravel, soft shoulders, places where rain water $\underset{\leftarrow}{700}$ collects.

You the driver

About a third of our auto accidents occur during the first four hours of dusk and darkness, the National Safety Council says. Peak traffic is one reason why this is the most dangerous driving period. Another is that drivers may be below par physically and mentally at this time of day.

You know how it is—a tough day at the office and you're fatigued, nervous, perhaps a bit short-tempered. Hundreds of others sharing the streets with you are in the same condition, which is hardly a situation conducive to safety.

Fatigue reduces your visual acuity. Your $\underset{\leftarrow}{800}$ reflexes slow as you tire and even your muscle coordination may be temporarily impaired; consequently, at these high speeds or in heavy traffic, these deficiencies can allow you to make a serious mistake. Also the fatigued worker who has smoked heavily and who stops for a quick one before starting the drive home is truly operating on only partial vision, especially if a few whiffs of carbon monoxide are added to the mix.

Finally, watch ahead for advance warning and information signs; then you'll avoid snap decisions that may force you into sudden, perhaps tragic, $\underset{\rightarrow}{900}$ maneuvers in the dark hours.

———STOP——ASK FOR YOUR TIME———

Record time immediately and answer the questions on content.

Time_____Sec.	RATE (from table on page 313):	R. _____
No. Correct:_____ (key on page 321)	COMPREHENSION (50% for each correct answer):	C. _____
V–5	EFFICIENCY (R × C):	E. _____

Record on Progress Chart on page 299

ANSWER THESE QUESTIONS IMMEDIATELY (V–5)

1. (T – F) For most of us there are problems other than reduced vision that impede good nighttime driving.
2. (M. C.) About a third of our auto accidents occur during:
   _____(1) the first four hours of dusk and darkness.
   _____(2) periods of fatigue and nervousness.
   _____(3) the rush hour and bumper-to-bumper traffic.
   _____(4) the "cocktail" hour.

Exercise V–6

Guidelines to Efficiency

(Reprinted from excerpts from the January 1974 issue of *The Royal Bank of Canada Monthly Letter* by permission of the editor.)

— WAIT FOR SIGNAL TO BEGIN READING —

A modern necessity

In a simpler world the pioneer could follow the lead of his instinct in tackling jobs, but in the complex life of today we need consciously to apply efficiency even in making a plan for doing the chores.

Efficiency gets things done in the smoothest way, with least wear and tear, and with the smallest expenditure of energy. This involves a certain amount of thinking. One must observe, apply knowledge and experience to the circumstances, and decide what to do and how to do it. An efficient person will use facts and skill: he needs also good judgment. 100

To the gifted craftsman, whatever his occupation, his work has dignity. There is a simple but pleasurable grace in the pursuit of everyday jobs as if they were the liberal arts.

Precision is vital in many manufactured articles, but the degree varies according to the requirements of the product. While a tolerance of an eighth of an inch may be allowable in fitting a wheel to a wheelbarrow, it would be grossly inefficient in an electronic device where tolerances are measured in thousandths of an inch.

The ingredients

Some ingredients of efficiency are: knowledge, time, energy and material. One of the most important 200 of these is time. Procrastination is the great enemy of efficient time use. Putting off necessary tasks causes additional labor, and reduces the time available for the development of new ideas.

The person who is striving for efficiency needs a good head of steam. No machine that is a hundred percent efficient has ever been invented, but engineers keep working on the problem of increasing the percentage of energy the machine uses effectively.

Here is an example from track sport, given to us by Walter B. Pitkin in "More Power to You." To some persons the act of running may seem to be a 300 simple activity: you merely move your legs faster than in walking. But one who races knows better. The old style called upon a runner to fling his advancing foot as far forward as possible. It came to earth somewhat in front of the runner's body, acting as a momentary brake on the body's forward motion.

Then runners learned to keep the body ahead of the advancing foot. This eliminates the waste of energy in lifting the runner over his advanced foot.

Economy of energy is illustrated in the kitchen, 400 where compact grouping of sink, stove, refrigerator, cupboards and counters reduces the amount of walking needed in preparing a meal, and in the workshop, where planned arrangement of tools reduces the waste of time and energy used in searching for them.

To continue to work in an efficient manner requires the worker to keep informed of what is happening in his profession or trade. An effective person does not allow changing circumstances to escape his notice, but makes an adjustment of thought and action to cope with the altered situations.

Facing difficulties

The person who works efficiently is in good 500 position to face difficulties with assurance. He has, in fact, an inclination to look for and to like difficult tasks, because it is in doing them that he shows his worth.

When difficulties thicken upon him, the efficient person has the tendency to persevere. He recognizes the problems and anxieties that may arise in a task, but does not dwell upon them. He knows that he is displaying the highest quality of efficiency when he tackles a job that is extremely tough and does it so that the result approaches perfection.

To such a person a check to progress is temporary. The measure of his efficiency is what 600 he succeeds in doing in spite of unfavorable circumstances rather than because of favorable circumstances. Great works of scholarship, of creative skill, and of technical complexity have been carried to conclusion under disadvantageous conditions.

The person who persists in trying, using the best means he knows of, is likely to attain efficiency even if he has but ordinary intellectual gifts. He is wiser and more competent today than he was yesterday, because he is constantly learning.

To the efficient person a mistake is part of 700 his learning process. He isn't always on top of the world: even great musicians and painters have their comparatively uninspired periods.

Every person who contributes anything significant to life is wrong some of the time. That is why pencils have erasers, but the eraser should not wear out before the lead.

Be confident

Having developed your plans with the greatest possible efficiency, whether they are plans for business expansion or solving a household problem, move with confidence. Knowledge that you have prepared efficiently raises your morale, and your cheerful, confident and zealous manner will inspire others with a sense of purpose, enthusiasm, and a feeling for success.

What then is our aim? To direct our expendi- 800 ⇆ ture of energy and time toward a purpose with the best principles to guide us. We will use patience and enthusiasm, tact and vigor, a single mind to the job in hand. We will have planned imaginatively, used careful coordination of resources, and acted with determination.

This may appear to be a large order, and in truth it is, but it is the only known way to move from mediocrity to excellence. Being efficient means the difference between wavering performance and fixed indubitable achievement. A person's efficiency 900 → is the secret of his value to the world.

——STOP——ASK FOR YOUR TIME——

Record time immediately and answer the questions on content.

Time_____Sec.	RATE (from table on page 313):	R. _____
No. Correct:_____ (key on page 329)	COMPREHENSION (50% for each correct answer):	C. _____
V–6	EFFICIENCY (R × C):	E. _____

Record on Progress Chart on page 299

ANSWER THESE QUESTIONS IMMEDIATELY (V–6)

1. (T – F) Efficient people always seek better ways of doing things.
2. (M. C.) The definition of efficiency most acceptable to this writer is:
    _____(1) thinking and thoughtful planning.
    _____(2) good use of knowledge, time, energy, and material.
    _____(3) precision and economy of material usage.
    _____(4) always putting your best foot forward.

Exercise V-7

Stones in Bloom

(Reprinted from the December 1980 issue of *Soviet Life* by permission of the editor.)

WAIT FOR SIGNAL TO BEGIN READING

Stony desert

One thousand refugees from the historical Western Armenian region of Sasun settled on the land of the present Talin region of the Armenian Soviet Socialist Republic from 1915 to 1920. They had escaped from a massacre of Armenians organized by the Turkish authorities.

"When the refugees built our village of Nerkin Sasunashen in 1922, there were only 28 families here," says Gekhaznik Shamoyan, chairman of a collective farm. "Now the population of the village is about 1,000 people."

Here is how writer Gevorg Emin describes these places: "Just imagine a desert paved with enormous stone slabs where only wormwood grows from soil $\leftarrow$100 which has been carried by the wind into the cracks between the stones."

The inhabitants of Nerkin Sasunashen village waged a real war against the cruel stone ruler that covered their land, and they won. The collective farm of the village is neither rich nor poor. There are hundreds of such average farms in Armenia. The farmers there sow oats and wheat, grow apricots, pears, peaches and apples. However, the main source of income is tobacco. The tobacco field covering an area of 20 hectares annually brings in an income of over 100,000 rubles. Every year the collective farm $\leftarrow$200 deposits from 200,000 to 250,000 rubles in its bank account. The collective farm owns about 2,000 sheep and nearly 500 head of cattle.

Need for specialists

"A big farm requires specialists and machinery," continued Gekhaznik Shamoyan. "Every year several people enroll at higher educational establishments in Yerevan. This year alone 12 graduates of our high school have entered agricultural, zoological-veterinary and pedagogical institutes. The farm grants some of them stipends which are bigger than usual. A specialist with a higher education is quite usual in the countryside today."

Not long ago the population migration to the towns was a serious problem in the republic. Rapidly $\leftarrow$300 developing industry required workers, and they were supplied at the expense of Armenian villages. This process affected Nerkin Sasunashen too—about 100 families moved from the village to Yerevan. But for several years now no one has left his or her native village. The farmers' income has increased in recent years. Besides the money they earn at the collective farm, they also get a considerable income from their household plots—up to 10,000 rubles a year on the average. Each family has a two-story stone cottage, $\rightarrow$400 color TV, refrigerator, garage and car. The state has built a day-care center for 75 children. The fee is 18 rubles a year.

Transportation and culture

Many cars and a new highway nearby that runs from Yerevan to Leninakan, the republic's second biggest city, have solved the problem of leisure activity. It is only an hour's drive to the capital, where there are theaters and museums. Nerkin Sasunashen itself has a house of culture with a movie house, a library and an excellent song and dance folk ensemble whose members live in the village.

"Some of those who left have already re- $\rightarrow$500 turned," says collective farmer Mariam Oganesyan, who is greatly respected by the villagers and has recently been elected to the Supreme Soviet of the Armenian SSR. "It is nice to see the closed-up and deserted houses come to life again. Movses Gevorkyan is a typical example. In Yerevan he was the director of a restaurant. However, in the end he gave up the job, returned to the village with his family and now lives in his father's house. The income of the collective farm has made it possible to change rural life and create the same amenities as in the cities.

$\rightarrow$600

Whims of the weather

The chief problem of Nerkin Sasunashen, as of any Armenian village, is the shortage of water for the fields. A major network of large and small canals was built in Armenia during the past decades, but sometimes there is still not enough water.

"We are dependent on the whims of the weather," says mechanic Arakel Shavarshyan. "This year, for instance, the crop of apricots and peaches was destroyed by spring frosts. However, that's a rare occurrence, only once in 30 or 40 years. But the hot, dry summer is always with us.''

A water reservoir with a capacity of 1.5 million 700← cubic meters is under construction in the Talin region at present. It is one of the 16 water reservoirs in the republic whose construction will really revolutionize Armenian agriculture. ''When we get water for the fields, the crops of wheat and tobacco will increase and the farmers' incomes with it by nearly one and a half times.''

Thanks to the efforts of the people, the stone-covered virgin land of the Talin area has become green, and orchards and new villages have appeared. You can go to any part of Armenia and determine at once where there is water and in what amount; 800← life in these places depends on it. The Armenian

climate is harsh, and not a single blade of grass can grow here without water. But with hard work and irrigation there is nothing that the industrious hands of a farmer who loves his land cannot do. It is not without reason that Armenian grapes and other fruits taste so good, for, as a poet once said, ''The bitter soil has for the first time been permeated not with blood, but with water, and it now gives us the 900→ sweetness that has accumulated in it over the ages.''

——STOP——ASK FOR YOUR TIME——

Record time immediately and answer
the questions on content.

Time_____Sec.	RATE (from table on page 313):	R. _____
No. Correct:_____ (key on page 321)	COMPREHENSION (50% for each correct answer):	C. _____
V–7	EFFICIENCY (R × C):	E. _____

Record on Progress Chart on page 299

ANSWER THESE QUESTIONS IMMEDIATELY (V–7)

1. (T – F) The arid, stony desert land in Armenia has forced most of the farmers to move to the cities to make a living.
2. (M. C.) The major problem in the Talin region is the limited supply of:
   _____(1) water.
   _____(2) transportation.
   _____(3) stones.
   _____(4) personal motivation.

Exercise V–8

Great Depths for More Gas

(Reprinted from the Fall 1974 issue of the *Texaco Star*
by permission of the editor.)

——————— WAIT FOR SIGNAL TO BEGIN READING ———————

Greeted by the barks of dogs and chirps of birds, dawn broke one day in May, 1974, over the rolling desert landscape of Pecos County in Southwest Texas. The only other sounds were from a distant drilling rig—a steady whirring of surface machinery revolving a drill bit, chewing through rock four miles below the barren plains.

There at Texaco's Spears Gas Unit Well Number 1, three miles west of the town of Fort Stockton, a massive rig, towering 175 feet above the Texas plains, was deepening the well from 22,575 to 22,830 feet in search of new reserves of natural gas. 100 ←

Dwindling production

Located in the gas- and oil-rich Gomez (Ellenburger) field, Spears Number 1 was first put into production on July 20, 1973, with a flow rate of 2.6 million cubic feet of gas a day. Within a year, daily production dwindled to less than one million cubic feet, far below the expected rate. Ways were sought to make the well more productive.

The top 600 feet of the Ellenburger rock formation, the sedimentary rock layer located at the bottom of this well and one in which natural gas is often found in abundance, were insufficiently porous to allow gas to escape into the well hole at adequate 200 ← rates. Treatment of the rock surrounding the well bottom with hydrochloric acid to increase its porosity failed to increase the flow of gas to acceptable levels.

Texaco decided to deepen the well when test drilling at offset wells one mile east and one mile north of Spears Number 1 indicated that additional gas-bearing layers of a more porous Ellenburger rock lay just below the top 600 feet of this formation.

At Spears Number 1, where a five-inch liner, or casing, had already been permanently cemented into the lower half of the well, there was a limitation 300 ← on the size of the drill bit and drill pipe that could be used.

Problems of efficiency

Finding a suitable drill bit that would fit in such a confined space and efficiently drill at such an extreme depth proved to be a problem. Conventional roller-bearing bits were ruled out because of their short life expectancy of 20 feet of penetration over a four-hour period. Their use would have required 13 extra round "trips," each taking 17 to 20 hours, in addition to approximately 100 hours increased drilling time.

400 → A trip "in" is the laborious, time-consuming, and costly procedure of connecting the sections of drill pipe together, into one continuous string, as they are lowered to the bottom of the well. A trip "out" is the reverse of this procedure.

During drilling, conventional bits tend to wear out rapidly, sometimes losing teeth in the hole. If not retrieved, these fragments can easily destroy a new bit.

The bit finally selected was one of industrial diamonds embedded in the face of a brass matrix. Valued at $3,000, this bit would make it possible not only to drill the entire 255 feet in one trip but 500 → to drill with a minimum of torque, or circular tension, on the more than four miles of drill pipe required. Excessive torque on such long lengths of drill pipe can cause the pipe to part.

A diamond bit chips the rock into fragments smaller than coffee grounds, which are easily removed from the hole by circulating fluid down through the center of the hollow drill string and up through the casing annulus, which is the narrow space located between the casing and the drill string. Coarse-toothed conventional bits produce much larger rock fragments, 600 → which are not readily removed by the fluid and can easily clog such a confined space.

Smooth drilling

After the drilling rig had been erected at the Spears Number 1 site, the wellhead over the old well was removed, and a blowout preventer system was installed.

An inexpensive, coarse-toothed mill bit was used to drill through five feet of cement that had been left in the bottom of the hole since the casing had been set, and to drill into the first foot of Ellenburger formation.

After the trip out had been made and the mill tooth bit removed, the new diamond bit was attached 700 → securely to the bottom of the drill string and lowered 22,581 feet into the well.

The drill string was then attached to the swivel, which not only holds the weight of the miles of drill pipe and allows it to be lowered as the bit digs deeper, but also allows the drill pipe to be rotated at the same time. The drill string was keyed to the rotary table on the rig floor. The rotation of this table turned the miles of drill pipe, thus revolving the diamond bit below.

After five days of continuous drilling with the same diamond bit, the remaining 249 feet of Ellen- 800 ← burger were at last penetrated, and the drill string was removed for the last time.

Increased flow

When the well was formally completed, tests revealed a flow rate of nearly 21 million cubic feet of gas a day, an increase of about 2,100 percent over the daily flow rate of less than a million cubic feet of gas before the Spears well was deepened.

Drilling for oil or gas is never a sure thing, but the four-mile-deep Spears well illustrates how it's worth taking a risk to provide the United States with 900 → the petroleum energy it needs.

——STOP——ASK FOR YOUR TIME——

Record time immediately and answer
the questions on content.

Time____Sec.	RATE (from table on page 313):	R. _____
No. Correct:_____ (key on page 329)	COMPREHENSION (50% for each correct answer):	C. _____
V–8	EFFICIENCY (R × C):	E. _____

Record on Progress Chart on page 299

ANSWER THESE QUESTIONS IMMEDIATELY (V–8)

1. (T – F) Industrial diamonds embedded in the face of a brass matrix were finally selected as the most efficient bit.
2. (M. C.) The additional depth added to the Spears Gas Unit Well Number 1 was approximately:
   ____(1) four miles.
   ____(2) 22,000 feet.
   ____(3) 175 feet.
   ____(4) 250 feet.

Exercise V–9

New Life in the Old Quarter
by DENNIS J. CIPNIC

(Reprinted from the Winter 1966–1967 issue of *Adventure Road* magazine
by permission of the editor.)

———————— WAIT FOR SIGNAL TO BEGIN READING ————————

The Quarter—a true renaissance

The Quarter, as it is locally known, is in the midst of a true renaissance—a sweeping awakening of all its faculties. The overhaul started with the establishment of the Vieux Carre Commission to enforce laws designed to preserve the historical color and charm of the 80 square blocks of the Quarter. Every building must look old, even if it's brand new and property owners cannot so much as change the color of paint on their shutters without the commission's approval. The laws forbid demolition by neglect and encourage restoration of old properties.

At the same time, a new residential atmosphere 100 came over the Vieux Carre. Artists, writers, scholars, architects, sculptors, all began moving in, which made it an "in" place, so they were soon followed by up and coming young-in-mind people from the business world and the professions. This started a trend toward restoring the Quarter's residential ascendancy which has now reached proportions of a land boom. Over half the buildings in the Vieux Carre are either restored, being restored, or in the planning stages. Property values have quadrupled in five years and hundreds of new air-conditioned apartments have been created inside 150-year-old town houses, which 200 on the outside, still look exactly as they once were.

These new inhabitants turned out to be "with-it" purchasers. Whereas, up until about two years ago, when the new influx reached appreciable proportions, the Quarter was hard put to support its traditional praline shops and antique stores. Now there has suddenly sprouted along the main thorough-fares of Bourbon, Royal, St. Peter and St. Ann Streets a new world of art galleries, boutiques, Mod clothiers, cafes, and import decorator shops. Antiques, wrought iron, hand-made candles, Hong Kong tailoring, paper flowers, painting of every description, the latest fashions from London—you name it, and you can 300 find it.

A new turn

New Orleans has always been a night town; the Quarter doesn't wake up till noon, and doesn't shut down again until 4 A.M. or so. The street life starts with a stroll around the art displays in Jackson Square and Pirate's Alley during the afternoon, some galleries and stores are open until midnight, dinner is best taken after eight, and the wail of the blues starts promptly at eight-thirty at Preservation Hall.

Preservation is the ground floor of a Quarter home on St. Peter Street which features bare benches, 400 old soda shop chairs, peeling walls, a church pew in the foyer, and some of the purest jazz extant. Several years ago it didn't exist; the Negro musicians who invented jazz as a musical form were still alive, many of them living a forgotten existence in Quarter tenements. Al and Sandra Jaffe, two young Philadelphians who came to New Orleans with the "New Wave" inhabitants, decided something needed to be done about this lamentable situation.

They opened the Hall, which features nothing but live music and soft drinks, brought the musicians 500 out of limbo, and started the re-birth of traditional jazz. Preservation is packed every night, at a dollar per customer. You can stay as long as you like for your dollar; the bands use no sheet music, so they never play the same number the same way twice in a row. The Hall has led to several imitations, one of them, Dixieland Hall, around the corner on Bourbon Street, being quite good in its own right.

Jazz in New Orleans

Jazz belongs to New Orleans. Basin Street, Rampart Street, Bourbon Street, Storeyville, Louis Armstrong, Jelly Roll Morton, they all blend together 600 to make quite a concoction. And with the new life which has come to the Quarter, New Orleans has inherited two new ingredients as well: Pete Fountain and Al Hirt. Both bearded, both native sons, both very popular international stars, they both have nightclubs on Bourbon Street where before stood only clipjoints.

Museums too have had a renaissance; a fine wax museum, in the true tradition of the famous Madame Tussaud's, is now open on Conti Street. There are several excellent period homes open as museums—one, a three story apartment in the oldest high rise condominium in the New World, the 700 Pontalba on Jackson Square, is exactly as it was in 1850. A fascinating colonial pharmacy is also in the

Quarter, as is the Mother Cabrini Doll Museum and several other special collections.

In many ways, New Orleans is a living museum as rows of antique shops on Royal Street have more treasures, free for the browsing, than many a fee-charging museum elsewhere. Raymond Weill's Stamp Shop, also on Royal, is world famed as headquarters of the finest rare stamps in existence, and some of his wares are always on display in the windows or inside the showcases. Within three blocks are at least $\overset{800}{\leftarrow}$ a dozen art galleries displaying works of every conceivable style, and one of them, also on Royal Street, features a rather interesting collection of archaeological antiquities from the middle Americas.

At night, along Bourbon Street, the barkers at clubs open the doors to give strollers a peek at the show which is just starting.

If you'd passed the buildings in New Orleans several years ago, you'd never have guessed that one of the most important acts in American history was consummated there: The Louisiana Purchase. Today these buildings stand, restored, bringing America's past to life, and $\overset{900}{\rightarrow}$ symbolizing the new life in the Old Quarter.

——STOP——ASK FOR YOUR TIME——

Record time immediately and answer
the questions on content.

Time_____Sec.	RATE (from table on page 313):	R. _____
No. Correct:_____ (key on page 321)	COMPREHENSION (50% for each correct answer):	C. _____
V–9	EFFICIENCY (R × C):	E. _____

Record on Progress Chart on page 299

ANSWER THESE QUESTIONS IMMEDIATELY (V–9)

1. (T – F) Buildings in the French Quarter have been restored and modernized inside, without destroying the historical color and charm.
2. (M. C.) "Preservation Hall" has been instrumental in bringing back the nearly forgotten:
    _____(1) lifelike wax museums.
    _____(2) praline shops.
    _____(3) traditional jazz music.
    _____(4) art galleries featuring paintings of Old New Orleans.

Exercise V–10

Nine Dishonest Sales Practices

(Reprinted from *The Willow-Haynes Report–Special Report*
by permission of the editor.)

—————————— **WAIT FOR SIGNAL TO BEGIN READING** ——————————

Land resale solicitation firms

High-pressure land salesmen offer to list the little land owner's installment-plan land for resale for a fee of anywhere from $100 to $200. There are many firms who are taking in hundreds of thousands of dollars every year, authorities estimate.

In most cases, there is no resale market whatever, and the land owner or the prospective buyer should be aware of certain practices.

1. Concealing or misrepresenting facts about value

Salesmen may present general facts about the area's population growth, industrial or residential development and real estate price levels as if they apply to your specific lot. You may be encouraged 100← to believe that your piece of land represents an investment which will increase in value as regional development occurs. A salesman may tell you that the developer will resell the lot if you require. This promise may not be kept.

2. Failure to honor refund promises or agreements

Some sales promotions conducted by mail or long distance telephone include the offer of a refund if the property has been misrepresented, or if the customer inspects the land within a certain period of time and decides not to buy. But when the customer requests the refund he may encounter arguments about 200← the terms of the agreement. The company may even accuse its salesman of having made a money-back guarantee without the consent or knowledge of the developer. Sometimes the promised refund is made, but only after a long delay.

3. Misrepresentation of facts about the subdivision

A salesman may offer false or incomplete information relating to either a distant subdivision or one which you visit. Misrepresentations often relate to matters such as the legal title, claims against it, latent dangers such as swamps or cliffs, unusual

300→ physical features such as poor drainage, restrictions on use, or lack of necessary facilities and utilities. Read the property report carefully with an eye to omissions, generalizations or unproved statements that may tend to mislead you.

4. Failure to develop the subdivision as planned

Many buyers rely upon the developer's contractual agreement or an oral promise to develop the subdivision in a certain way. The promised attractions that influenced your purchase—golf course, marina, swimming pool—may never materialize after you become an owner. If you are planning on immediate vacation use of the property or are working toward a specific retirement date, you may 400→ find that promised special features of the development are not available when you need them.

5. Failure to deliver deeds or title insurance policies

Documents relating to the sales transaction may not be delivered as promised. Most sales in the promotional land development industry are made by contract for a deed to be delivered when the purchaser makes his last payment under the terms of the contract. A dishonest developer may fail to deliver the deed or deliver it only after a long delay.

6. Abusive treatment and high-pressure salesmen

Hurrying the buyer into a purchase he may later 500→ regret is only one ploy of high-pressure salesmen. Abusive language is also used to embarrass customers who delay an immediate decision to buy.

7. Failure to make good on sales inducements

Free vacations, gifts, savings bonds, trading stamps and other promised inducements are used to lure people to sales presentations or to development sites. These promised treats may never materialize. Sometimes special conditions are attached to the lure or a customer is advised that gifts go only to lot purchasers. A "free vacation" may be the means of delivering the prospective buyer to a battery of high-pressure salesmen in a distant place.

8. "Bait and switch" tactics

600 ←

Lots are frequently advertised at extremely low prices. When a prospective buyer appears he is told that the low-priced lots are all sold and then is pressured to buy one that is much more expensive. If the cheaper lot is available, it may be located in an inaccessible location. If accessible, it may be much too small for a building lot or have other undesirable features.

The buyer may be lured to the property with a certificate entitling him to a "free" lot. Often the certificate bears a face value of $500 to $1,000. If the buyer attempts to cash it in, the amount is simply 700 ← included in the regular price—often inflated—of the lot he chooses.

Often this so-called "bait and switch" technique has a delayed fuse. Buyers who purchase an unseen lot for later retirement may be unpleasantly surprised when they visit the development. The lot they have paid for may be remote from other homes, shopping and medical facilities.

9. Failure to grant rights under the interstate land sales full disclosure act

800 → The purchaser may not be given a copy of the property report before he signs a sales contract. Some salesmen withhold this detailed statement until the customer chooses a specific lot. Sometimes the buyer receives the report in a mass of promotional materials and legal documents. Unaware that he has the report in his possession, he fails to read and understand it before signing a sales contract.

Where to complain

If you believe you have been cheated in a transaction, write to HUD/OILSR, 451 Seventh St. S.W., Washington, D.C. 20410. Set forth specific details of your complaint and include the name of the developer, name and location of the subdivision and copies 900 → of the contract or other documents you have signed.

——STOP——ASK FOR YOUR TIME——

Record time immediately and answer the questions on content.

Time_____Sec.	RATE (from table on page 313):	R. _____
No. Correct:_____ (key on page 329)	COMPREHENSION (50% for each correct answer):	C. _____
V–10	EFFICIENCY (R X C):	E. _____

Record on Progress Chart on page 299

ANSWER THESE QUESTIONS IMMEDIATELY (V–10)

1. (T – F) These dishonest sales practices are given to help buyers recognize misleading retail sales activities.
2. (M. C.) Which of the following was not discussed as a dishonest sales practice:
      _____(1) Distortion.
      _____(2) Delay.
      _____(3) Extortion.
      _____(4) Misrepresentation.

Exercise V–11

Sample the Walleyed Pike
by ANNA CIFELLI

— WAIT FOR SIGNAL TO BEGIN READING —

Well-known in the Twin Cities!

"Visitors who accidentally discover us act as if they had just caught a twenty-pound walleyed pike," says Arthur Palmer, owner of the Lowell Inn in Stillwater, Minnesota. Though the fifty-year-old landmark may not be as famous as Paul Bunyan, the reputation of its three dining rooms and twenty-one guest rooms is impressive. Palmer estimates that about one out of ten Minneapolis–St. Paul residents has eaten there at least once.

Many travelers consigned to business in the Twin Cities—headquarters for about a dozen Fortune 500 companies—also make the thirty-minute trip from downtown Minneapolis (Highway 35W north to Route 100← 36 eastbound). It's a pleasant drive, and the last stretch offers a glimpse of the St. Croix River valley— an opulent greenbelt in the summer, a blue-snow wonderland in a Minnesota winter.

No rustic pub in the country, the Lowell Inn is a stately three-story mansion, with large white columns and arched windows topped by yellow canopies. Hickory rockers line the shaded portico. Inside, there's a lobby with overstuffed chintz chairs and antiques arranged around a fireplace. A customer has the sense of stepping into the living room of a colonial manor. Off in one part of the 200← room, discreetly tucked away, is the cocktail lounge.

Three restaurants

The three restaurants, each with its own decorative scheme, all open off the lobby. The Matterhorn Room is a large and formal salon, dominated by weighty Swiss wood carvings. By contrast, the Garden Room seems cool and airy; one of its features is a trout pool stocked with a selection of very fresh entree possibilities.

The George Washington Room is a magnificent hall, sunlit on a clear day, and furnished with so pure an attention to authenticity that it almost seems an anachronism in an era of mass production. Around 300← the hall, which seats eighty-five people, are antique sideboards that display fine crystal pieces, Capo di Monte porcelain, and a collection of Dresden china. Tables are impeccably set with hand-crested Irish linen tablecloths and antique Sheffield silver, with Williamsburg ladder-back chairs to complete the picture of colonial comfort.

The food served at the Lowell Inn seems as authentic as the furnishings. "Though you might call it midwestern gourmet," says Palmer, "it's basic, honest food prepared by accenting, not disguising, natural flavors." The meal starts simply: fruit juice, 400→ soup (the kind varies from day to day; one might be Bisque du Pape, from a secret family recipe) or a fresh-fruit salad, distinguished by a light honey dressing. Next come hot homemade crescent rolls, crisp wafers, and anise-flavored Swiss pear bread, which is made from another family recipe, and really does have bits of pear among its ingredients.

Lunch

At lunch, there is a well-rounded assortment of a dozen or so entrees—sautéed chicken livers in a morel sauce (made with pure beef stock and morels, nutty-flavored mushrooms), a three-quarter-pound barley-fed pork steak, sweetbreads, or one of the fresh brook trout from the Garden Room's pool. If 500→ you've yet to taste the regional specialty, this is a good place to sample a fresh fillet of walleyed pike, breaded and panfried.

With the entree—honest food indeed—everyone gets healthy helpings of whipped potatoes and red cabbage, plus a choice of another vegetable. In the midwestern relish-tray tradition, there is also an offering of cottage cheese, chutney, and watermelon pickles. Desserts are rich and varied: pecan pie, blueberry cheesecake, a maple frango (homemade ice cream with a kick of Vermont maple syrup), a meringue filled with ice cream and crowned, in season, with strawberries or peaches—plus sundaes 600→ and parfaits. A selection of cheese, from Swiss Gruyere to Liederkranz, is also available.

For a more elaborate meal, try the Matterhorn. Like the price ($22.50), the Matterhorn's menu is fixed: escargots, Fondue Bourguignonne, a dessert of green grapes with sour cream and brown sugar, and a sampling of four Swiss wines. After that repast, the bill seems downright modest.

The inn's wine list is an oversized volume that might seem daunting to the most determined oenophile. No one can fault the variety: some sixty European and 245 California vintages. The prices range from $8 for a California Chardonnay to $600 for an 1806 Progue Marne.

700 ←

A family affair

Arthur Palmer and his wife, Maureen, keep watch over every detail at the Lowell Inn and its restaurants, buying food and furnishings from 2,150 purveyors around the world. The inn's special blend of coffee, for example, is the product of an old gentleman in Switzerland who grinds by hand coffee beans from Kenya. Corkscrews are supplied by Rolls-Royce.

Running the Lowell Inn is very much a family affair, with seven of the Palmer's nine children active in the business today. Palmer's mother, who ran it

800 → before him, was a member of her family's traveling theatrical company, and had married the group's pianist. During the Depression the company disbanded, and his parents began to operate the inn. After buying it, they gradually fashioned the place into a home for themselves and their paying guests. But the inn's history of hospitality predates even the Palmer family. Local legend says it was at an earlier structure on the same site that members of Company B of the First Minnesota Regiment took leave of their loved ones as they went off to the Civil War. Later it was the social center for Stillwater's lumber barons and

900 → their ladies.

——STOP——ASK FOR YOUR TIME——

Record time immediately and answer
the questions on content.

Time_____Sec.	RATE (from table on page 313):	R. _____
No. Correct:_____ (key on page 321)	COMPREHENSION (50% for each correct answer):	C. _____
V–11	EFFICIENCY (R × C):	E. _____

Record on Progress Chart on page 299

ANSWER THESE QUESTIONS IMMEDIATELY (V–11)

1. (T – F) The major food promoted on the menu of the three restaurants is panfried fillet of walleyed pike.
2. (M. C.) The Lowell Inn is:
   _____(1) an international inn near the Matterhorn.
   _____(2) a new lavishly furnished hotel in downtown Minneapolis.
   _____(3) a well-established family business in Stillwater, Minnesota.
   _____(4) one of a chain of fine-quality resort hotels.

Exercise V–12

The Rockies' Riotous Ski Festivals
by DON CANNALTE

(Reprinted from the January 1967 edition of the United Airlines' *Mainliner* magazine
by permission of the author.)

———— **WAIT FOR SIGNAL TO BEGIN READING** ————

Ever since the slumbering mining town of Aspen, Colorado awoke twenty years ago from a deep sleep, and went about the business of becoming America's most glamorous ski resort, its citizens have been toasting nature's blessings and their own ingenuity.

Every winter ski-hungry vacationers converge on the town, laying claim to most or all of more than 6,000 beds, cutting through powder snow and traffic down superb mountains, and generally adding to the crush of *après-ski* goers.

Aspenites respond to this fun-loving immigration with a twinkle in their business eye, and a bit of hi-jinks themselves. At no time does this happy wonderful town unveil its personality more than during Winterskol—Toast to Winter.

Winter carnivals are a good-times addition to any ski vacation for young or old, the family or the unattached, and there are many worth attending.

A welcome to ski-enthusiasts

The Colorado community of Breckenridge every February declares itself a "free sovereign and independent state" for one three-day weekend and holds its colorful Ullr Dag festival. Ullr, the mythical Nordic God of mountain sports and skiing, reigns over the festivities, which include races, parades, and the right to celebrate independence. A visa (costing 25 cents) is required to enter the Kingdom of Breckenridge.

Carnival-goers at Jackson Hole, Wyoming, must hug the sidewalks during the All-American Cutter Races, in which chariot-like cutters drawn by two-horse teams, race through the streets of Jackson. Winter sports connoisseurs also will be treated to Ski-Doo races and snowplaning on Jackson Lake.

At Leadville, Colorado, snowshoe baseball sets the tone for the town's annual frolic-filled Winter Carnival weekend. The feature at nearby Steamboat Springs (Ski Town, U.S.A.) is ski-joring, as men on skis rope themselves to horses which charge along the street toward the finish line.

A winter Mardi Gras

Perhaps none is more colorful and vibrant than Aspen's Winterskol, held in mid-January. Winterskol was born as an idea to stimulate community interest among the townspeople. The first Winterskol wasn't too elaborate, although Lana Turner showed up. There was a parade with most of the local residents participating, and few people watching, some ski races and a Winterskol Ball, held in a drafty cold hall with a roof that leaked.

There was a hockey game, although no rink, ski-joring down Main Street, and two of the saloons challenged each other to team racing with trays of beer. Lack of funds may have limited the activities but lively imaginations carried the day. One restaurant was decorated with underwear hung on a clothesline and strung above the bar.

Still, the festival was considered a success and was held again the next year, and Miss Turner liked the idea enough to return for the second year to stay a week.

The spirit, informality and many of the events of that first Winterskol have prevailed over the years (ski-joring was replaced by dog-joring in later years due to lack of open space), and this year's annual fun-filled carnival was no exception.

From a roaring Christmas tree bonfire, cheered by the blaze, everyone then gathered at the foot of Little Nell to watch 70 skiers weave a graceful abstract down Aspen Mountain. A hockey match and skating exhibitions at the Ice Palace completed the evening's scheduled events before everyone adjourned for socializing at his favorite *après-ski* warming hut.

There are bigger parades, but few are more colorful than the one concocted by Aspenites for Winterskol. Handsome, suntanned instructors from Aspen and Vail ski schools provided an impressive complement to the unfolding foolishness. A daring young acrobat did somersaults on a moving trampoline while wearing skis. A local haberdasher knitted the longest stocking cap (129 feet) on record and paraded it with the help of a dozen youngsters trailing behind. The festival theme "there is No Aspen" (the subject of an advertising campaign by rival

Steamboat Springs), allowed imaginations to dress up the float entries with a variety of merriment.

Fun for everyone

The fun carried into the afternoon with ski races by teams representing the various lodges and restaurants, dog-joring at the park and something called broomball at the Ice Palace. The social highlight of the festival, of course, was the Winterskol costume ball, featuring no less than 15 entertainment groups 700 and fireside dancing at the Four Seasons.

Action resumed the next morning on Aspen Mountain with the traditional and hilarious Saloon Slalom, entered by employees and proprietors of local bistros, races for the children (urged on by over-exuberant parents, the youngsters slalom down Little Nell, pausing to wolf down a piece of pie before crossing the finish line), and a sky diving–ski meet.

In the latter event, the contestants parachute to the top of the slope, don skis and schuss down the hill. The sky divers take the air drop in stride: the 800 fun begins if and when they get their skis on for most have never been on the boards before. Husky dogsled races along a 10-mile course fill out a busy day's activities.

Winterskol, like other winter carnivals, never really ends. It signals a season-long of pleasure for ski-addicts and general winter vacationers alike. It's a great way to take the pale out of winter and put a little "spring" in your life.

Winterskol in Aspen is a long and frolicsome holiday which involves every winter sports enthusiast —spectator and participant alike, and we're confident these ski festivities will continue having an 900 enthusiastic response.

——STOP——ASK FOR YOUR TIME——

Record the time immediately and answer the questions on content.

Time___Sec.	RATE (from table on page 313):	R. ___
No. Correct:___ (key on page 329)	COMPREHENSION (50% for each correct answer):	C. ___
V–12	EFFICIENCY (R × C):	E. ___

Record on Progress Chart on page 299

ANSWER THESE QUESTIONS IMMEDIATELY (V–12)

1. (T – F) All of the Rockies' riotous winter festivals are focused primarily on ski contests.
2. (M. C.) The most riotous of them all is the one held each January in:
   - ___(1) Aspen, Colorado.
   - ___(2) Breckenridge, Colorado.
   - ___(3) Jackson, Wyoming.
   - ___(4) Steamboat Springs, Colorado.

Exercise V–13

Think and Live
by GREGORY RAY

(Reprinted from the July 1974 issue of *Wyoming Wildlife*
by permission of the editor.)

―――――― WAIT FOR SIGNAL TO BEGIN READING ――――――

Safe boating is no accident

More than 1,700 men, women, and children throughout the United States will have a quiet summer this year. They won't be spending lazy afternoons fishing and basking in the sun while being gently rocked to sleep in their boats. Gone are their days of water skiing and swimming; for these are the 1,700 people that met a grim death in boating accidents last year.

It is hardly shocking to find that the number of casualties is roughly proportional to the number of boaters. But surprisingly few of all watercraft accidents are caused from collisions; rather they 100 are individual upsets most often a result of an overloaded boat combined with inclement weather.

Weather conditions are a major factor. Thunderstorms can engulf boats miles from the dock before the occupants hardly even notice a cloud in the sky. Such storms are common during summer and approach suddenly, bringing violent winds and often torrential downpours.

On these vast expanses of water, a boat can suddenly disappear from sight leaving little trace of a tragic accident. Often it takes weeks to recover the bodies of boating victims. Strong underwater currents, craggy ledges, weeds and tremendous water depths often made search operations either difficult or nearly 200 impossible.

Keep your cool

Capsizing a boat, particularly when a person is far from shore, can be not only a chilling experience, but also a terrifying one. This writer observed a group of Girl Scouts last summer purposely capsizing their canoes so they would know what to do if they overturned accidentally. While most of the girls remained relatively calm, some of the scouts panicked even though all the girls were carefully supervised and help was nearby. In addition, the young canoeists were wearing approved life jackets and the exercise was conducted on a small, shallow lake within 50 ft. 300 of shore.

But despite this, several of the girls were panic-stricken. As in so many incidents of this type, if a person maintains composure there is often a good chance of making it to shore safely. Unless a boat is completely submerged, it usually is advisable to hang onto the hull, since even capsized boats will usually have some buoyancy. In addition, if any portion of the hull is still showing, it will be easier to spot than a single person in the water—hence a good reason to stay with the boat.

Wear a preserver

Leaving a boat and heading for shore is often a deadly mistake without a life preserver. Land is almost always farther away than it appears and in the cold water so common for the large reservoirs, even excellent swimmers find it difficult treading water for several hundred yards. A number of reputedly good swimmers have died during the last five years attempting to make it from their boats to shore. Some of these people collapsed from fatigue, while others became entangled in weeds and were unable to free themselves.

In looking over the grim tales of boat-related drownings for the last several years, it appears many of the deaths could have been prevented had the boat occupants been wearing life preservers; yet last summer, 34 people were arrested for using their boats with either too few life preservers or no life preserver at all. The law requires one "personal flotation device" to be within ready access of every person on board a boat.

If tradition is any fortune teller, there will be more boat-related deaths during the July 4 week than any other time of year. This is why the National Safe Boating Council annually designates this period as National Safe Boating Week in hopes of focusing attention on safety.

Follow these easy rules

Though safe boating is largely common sense, unusual conditions prevailing on certain waters make it extremely important to pay particular attention to "basic" rules. Here are some that are continually violated and consequently result in a number of deaths each year: (1) Check the capacity plate on your boat. If it says the boat can carry six people, figure on four. Rough weather can easily swamp a

141

boat filled to capacity; (2) Head for shore immediately when dark clouds start gathering. Don't wait until it starts raining and blowing—it's too late then; 700 ← (3) If caught in a storm, immediately have everyone in the boat don a life preserver; (4) Carry plenty of extra gas. A boat that is left powerless in a storm can easily be capsized or washed onto rocks; (5) Be exceptionally careful when boating in the late fall and early spring. The cold weather during this time of year makes death from exposure a real threat, since even in 40 degree water a person may succumb in as little as half-an-hour; (6) Make sure every child on board is wearing a life jacket at all times. There are 800 ← several sizes available, so make sure the one your child is wearing fits properly.

Though this is by no means a complete list of boating tips, nearly all the boating deaths over the years could have been avoided had one or more of these simple rules been followed. More information can be obtained from the U.S. Coast Guard Auxiliary as well as the American Red Cross. These agencies both conduct courses not only to improve boating safety, but also boating skills as well.

Remember the slogan "Safe boating is no 900 → accident."

——STOP——ASK FOR YOUR TIME——

Record time immediately and answer
the questions on content.

Time____Sec.	RATE (from table on page 313):	R. _____
No. Correct:_____ (key on page 321)	COMPREHENSION (50% for each correct answer):	C. _____
V–13	EFFICIENCY (R × C):	E. _____

Record on Progress Chart on page 299

ANSWER THESE QUESTIONS IMMEDIATELY (V–13)

1. (T – F) Most watercraft accidents occur individually as a result of excessive speed and inclement weather.
2. (M. C.) All of the following were given as good safety rules for boating except:
    _____(1) head for shore if it starts to rain.
    _____(2) never stay with a capsized boat.
    _____(3) always keep a life preserver within easy reach.
    _____(4) always carry extra gas.

Exercise Exercise V–14

The Guns That Went West
by DICK KIRKPATRICK

(Adapted from the technical data by James E. Serven. Copyright 1966 by the National Wildlife Federation.
Reprinted from the October-November 1966 issue of *National Wildlife* magazine by permission of the editors.)

—————— WAIT FOR SIGNAL TO BEGIN READING ——————

A tradition of fine firearms

Through the middle of the Nineteenth Century, the first few cautious Americans began to penetrate the vast unknown wilderness west of the Missouri and Mississippi Rivers, pushing our young nation's territories toward the Pacific. Some, like Lewis and Clark who blazed the trail to the Northwest in 1804, went in large, well-organized groups. Others went into the vast unknown alone or in small groups—all of them necessarily living off the land, taking its fruits and its hazards as they found them.

One thing they all had in common: They carried the finest firearms they could find and afford, for the raw West was unforgiving of anything but the best in men or weapons. Hostile Indians, fearless grizzlies, stampeding bison, and a thousand lesser hazards demanded instant and accurate shooting, while months and years away from civilization demanded faultless dependability.

The men whose guns failed them were seldom seen again; the ones who came back told stories, not only of the unbelievable wonders they had seen, but also of the faithful firearms that saw them through their adventures. The builders of these successful guns prospered, and founded an industry as well as a tradition that survives to this day—a tradition of fine firearms in the hands of self-reliant men who built a nation. Even today, millions of westerners and other Americans still use sporting firearms for hunting and target shooting.

The development of American firearms parallels the "winning of the west" so closely that it is difficult for historians to decide which sparked the other. Indeed, the two complemented each other through their history.

Types of weapons used by pioneering Americans

The first party west, Lewis and Clark, carried Model 1803 flintlock rifles made at the Harpers Ferry Arsenal. They served adequately, certainly being superior to the military smooth-bore muskets of the period, and set a pattern for the next few years' military expeditions.

The Mountain Men needed absolute reliability, superior accuracy, and were willing to pay for the best. Many of the best of them—Jedediah Smith, Jim Bridger, Kit Carson, Jim Clymen, the Ashley-Henry expeditions, and the Fremont expeditions, bought sturdy .50 caliber percussion rifles from Jake and Sam Hawken of St. Louis, then the fitting-out and jumping-off place for hunters, trappers, and explorers. That they lived to become celebrated scouts and guides is a tribute to the reliability of the Hawken rifles.

Following the Mountain Men's trails—indeed, using them often as guides—came the military expeditions under Pike, Kearney, Cooke, and others, and the first wagon trains of pioneers. Like the military, the pioneers took the advice of the experienced hunters and trappers, and invested in good rifles.

Along with his rifle, the well-armed early westerner often carried a handgun. Most popular through the early years were the heavy but powerful percussion muzzle loaders, called "horse pistols" from the practice of holstering them on the saddle. Most prized among them was the .54 caliber dragoon model.

In the later 1840's, percussion six-shooters came onto the market, and were greeted with enthusiasm by the firepower-hungry pioneers and soldiers. The huge early Colt dragoon models quickly developed into lighter, more efficient handguns, the most popular being the .36 caliber 1851 Navy Colt. Only the later Peacemaker has been so immortalized in literature of the West.

Another handgun which enjoyed great popularity down through the middle century, though perhaps not with such legendary characters as Kit Carson and John Fremont, were the small percussion pocket pistols made by Henry Derringer and others.

Major trends in firearm development

The demand for more firepower produced developments in shoulder arms at the same pace, and the first major breakthrough was the breech-loading rifle—first developed as a carbine because of its convenience to a mounted rifleman. As cavalry and mounted infantry were sent west to fight the Indians and protect the settlers, they took with them the faster-firing breech loaders. The Hall, Sharps', Remington and Springfield carbines became the standard long guns and stories of their effectiveness helped advertise them across the West.

Military and civilian demand from the West had brought steady improvement in American firearms, but the War between the States brought almost feverish development of more efficient, 700 ← faster-firing guns of all kinds.

In 1866, the first breech-loading rifles with metallic cartridges reached the West, and spelled doom for the Indians. In their first full battle use, 27 Remington rollingblock rifles in the hands of experienced drovers turned away repeated charges of 3,000 Sioux. The favorite tactic of the Plains Indians, the massed charge, became obsolete and the end was soon in sight for the "wild" west.

One of the most widely used, but least glorified, of frontier guns was the double-barreled shotgun.

Many makes saw action; so many that no brand 800 → stands out among the others.

After the turn of the century, the Westerner left his rifle in its scabbard or over his mantel, and if he went armed at all, it was with a smaller pocket or belt pistol. The rugged big guns of the west disappeared into attics and scrap heaps, to remain until the post-World-War-II renaissance of interest in the frontier and its accoutrements put them in collectors' cases, often at prices that would have shocked their original purchasers.

And the principles that grew up with them— that of the armed American defending himself, his 900 → loved ones, and his property—live on today.

——STOP——ASK FOR YOUR TIME——

Record the time immediately and answer questions on content.

Time____Sec.	RATE (from table on page 313):	R. _____
No. Correct:_____ (key on page 329)	COMPREHENSION (50% for each correct answer):	C. _____
V–14	EFFICIENCY (R × C):	E. _____

Record on Progress Chart on page 299

ANSWER THESE QUESTIONS IMMEDIATELY (V–14)

1. (T – F) The Mountain Men demanded absolute reliability and superior accuracy from their weapons.
2. (M. C.) The major purpose of the development and improvement of these guns was:
   _____(1) to overcome the Indian tribes and gain property.
   _____(2) to kill wild game such as buffalo and bear.
   _____(3) to sell them for display as collectors' items.
   _____(4) to protect individuals from the dangers in their environment.

Exercise V–15

Ottawa
by ALLAN SEIDEN

(Reprinted from the May 1975 issue of *Travel*
by permission of the editor of Travel/Holiday, Travel Building, Floral Park, New York.)

———————————— **WAIT FOR SIGNAL TO BEGIN READING** ————————————

Mysterious image

As a child I'd spent many long weekends fishing the Rideau Lakes that seem to wind endlessly into one another just to the north of Kingston, Ontario. One of the adventures for me at the time was a trip through the locks of the Rideau Canal which ultimately led, I was told, to a place some hundred miles distant called Ottawa. Being a kid, the Indian sound of this city mixed with the near wilderness of these lakes to form a mysterious image that I was to find unrelated to the reality of Canada's national capital. But many years were to separate that mystery from 100 the day I arrived, to be confronted not by a frontier village, but the Gothic fantasy of Parliament Hill.

Ottawa is not an old city even by North American standards. Its name, derived from the Indian word to trade, *adawe,* speaks clearly of its early foundations, if not of its reason for being. By the 1820s, Canadian experience with the new Republic to the south had not always been peaceful. American attacks upon Canada—a mixture of military defense and more aggressive anti-British nationalism—had left the British with little reason to trust Canada's interior, 200 since it passed under American scrutiny and control for long stretches between Montreal and Kingston. This supply route was particularly vulnerable at Fort Ogdensburg, New York, where the St. Lawrence was commanded by American guns.

Planning the canal

Wishing to assure a totally internal supply route, a canal system was planned that would connect Kingston (and thereby Lake Ontario) with the St. Lawrence via the Rideau Lakes and the Ottawa River, which flowed into the Saint Lawrence near Montreal. In 1826, Lt. Col. John By of the Royal Engineers began the system of locks and canals that would not 300 only cut through the land, but would also climb and descend the hundreds of feet of varying elevations that blocked the way. It was several of the 47 locks built for this purpose that had loomed in my memory and were to appear again in the heart of Ottawa.

A settlement had been made on the banks of the Ottawa River in 1800 by a small group of farm families from New England. Trudging up the frozen river in midwinter, they established a community called Wright's Village. From Wright's Village the 400 Ottawa River continued hundreds of miles into the forested wilderness to the west. Nearby, the Gatineau River joined the Ottawa, its course leading into the northern wilderness. This access to vast timber resources was a source of income for the families of Wright's Village, and became a source of Ottawa's future growth and wealth. Just to the south a third river, the Rideau, joined the Ottawa in a plunge over twin falls. These heights presented the first obstacles in the construction of the Canal, which took six years to complete, cost the British Government a substantial 4 million dollars, and was complicated by several 500 malaria epidemics. When opened in 1832, the system wound nearly 127 miles by river, lake, canal and lock to its Kingston destination and provided not only the secure internal supply route first desired, but a route of commercial importance to the development of what was to become the city of Ottawa.

Planning the city

Not only did Lt. Col. By plan the Canal, he also helped in the planning of the city that developed at its entrance, and which at the time of its founding, was called Bytown. The Bytown Museum, built originally as the commissary during the Canal's 600 construction, is Ottawa's oldest building and houses a museum of the city's history.

By 1855, when Bytown had become Ottawa, it had also become a rail and logging center of significance. Access to wilderness timber was made easy by the region's broad rivers, which served not only as transportation and power for man, but also for logs which were floated to Ottawa by the millions. Though today most of the pulp and paper mills that once faced the Ottawa River are gone, the short cruise that takes you several miles downstream passes by jams of logs hugging the shore in large stockades, evidence 700 of continuing forest wealth.

The Queen's choice

It was not forestry, however, that was to direct Ottawa's history for long. In 1857, anxious to secure a permanent capital for the Canadian Provinces, Queen Victoria chose Ottawa because of its central location between the culturally French and English provinces. The selection was confirmed by the Canadians themselves in 1867, when the United Provinces secured independence and Ottawa was chosen as the national capital of the Dominion of Canada.

The Parliament buildings, symbolic of the significance of the national capital and the Canadian parliamentary system, were begun during this period, but little remains of the original buildings because a ⟵800 fire in 1916 totally destroyed all but the Parliamentary Library. Reconstruction began almost immediately and followed the original design with Gothic style turrets and gables, steep roofs and wrought-iron grillwork which dominate my memory of the city.

Ottawa is not a city tied to a past. It is a city ready to celebrate its past, present and future, and it happily invites guests to the party. In more than a symbolic sense Ottawa is celebrating its own coming of age and the coming of age of the nation for which 900→ it stands as a capital.

——STOP——ASK FOR YOUR TIME——

Record time immediately and answer
the questions on content.

Time_____Sec.	RATE (from table on page 313):	R. _____
No. Correct:_____ (key on page 321)	COMPREHENSION (50% for each correct answer):	C. _____
V–15	EFFICIENCY (R × C):	E. _____

Record on Progress Chart on page 299

ANSWER THESE QUESTIONS IMMEDIATELY (V–15)

1. (T – F) The city that developed from the early settlement of Wright's Village was originally called Bytown, after one of the men who planned the city.
2. (M. C.) The thing that most influenced Ottawa's history was the city's use as:
   _____(1) the first permanent capital of the Canadian Provinces.
   _____(2) the access route to rich timberlands.
   _____(3) a center for hydroelectric power.
   _____(4) a financial center for westward expansion.

Exercise V–16

The Gooney Bird Contest
by C. A. STEVENS

(Reprinted from the May/June 1979 issue of *Frontier* magazine
by permission of the editor.)

-------- WAIT FOR SIGNAL TO BEGIN READING --------

Which pilot?

In 1971 *Business and Commercial Aviation* magazine decided to find out who had spent the most time in a DC-3. A contest was started by Torch Lewis, who wrote a monthly column for the magazine called, "Greenhouse Patter." In March 1971, the contest was announced in this column with these simple rules:

1. You may report all logged hours in a DC-3, C47, R4D or any other legitimate configuration—both pilot and copilot time. Just stipulate the periods in each—World War II, prewar airline, FAA, postwar military, postwar civil and the like. Your word will be accepted as to amounts and places, ←100 but please document.
2. Mail your entry to DC-3, c/o *Business and Commercial Aviation*, One Park Ave., New York, New York.

The contest closed May 30, 1971, and the winner was to be announced and knighted at the Reading, Pennsylvania Air Show on June 11, 1971.

You weren't supposed to be bashful. If you had a friend you knew with scads of Gooney time you had to urge him to enter. Sorry, no DC-4-5-6-7-8-9-or-10 times were accepted, although Lewis said he'd give a premium to those with DC-1-2 and DC-2½ time. Does anyone know who was the pilot of ←200 the DC-2½? Old-timers will remember that as the Douglas used in the final evacuation of the Philippines in 1942—a DC-3 with a DC-2 wing on one side. The time trophy was to be given by Douglas Aircraft Company.

King of the Gooneys

Frontier Captain Bill McChrystal's cohorts encouraged him to enter the contest. He submitted documented DC-3 time totaling 17,111 hours—an equivalent of sitting in the nonpressurized, nonair-conditioned DC-3 day and night for almost two years.

On May 31, 1971, McChrystal was notified that he was the winner and was invited to attend the 22nd ←300 Reading Air Show June 11, 1971. Captain McChrystal had been declared the pilot with more DC-3 time than any other pilot in the world.

Torch Lewis, in his August 1971 column, described the trophy presentation to McChrystal as follows: "If there were two sets of dry eyes in the house amongst the standing and cheering crowd, they did not belong to Captain or Mrs. Bill McChrystal, who were standing to my left on the dais about to receive the trophy." The inscription on the trophy states: "In recognition of an intrepid aviator who has 400→ achieved masterful control of the Gooney Bird, world's most beloved aircraft."

How richly he deserved it! Seventeen thousand, one hundred eleven hours in a Gooney! His logbooks stood a foot high, and people came by in wonderment to scan them and congratulate Bill on a feat which may never be duplicated.

It started in 1938

Graduating as valedictorian from the University of Portland in 1936, Bill received a scholarship to Stanford University, where he attended law school for one year. His flying career began in 1938, at Thompson Flying Service in Salt Lake City, where he bought flying time. The man responsible for his 500→ enthusiasm to fly was none other than the late retired Pan American Captain Charlie Blair, actress Maureen O'Hara's husband.

In 1939 McChrystal was accepted for the civilian pilot training program sponsored by the government when war clouds began appearing on the horizon. He later qualified for pilot training with United Airlines. On December 6, 1941, the day before the Pearl Harbor attack, he was on his first flight as a copilot with United, a charter flight from San Francisco to Denver carrying Russian ambassador Maxim Litvinoff and his party.

During the war, McChrystal was assigned to 600→ the Air Transport Command, both in Alaska and the Asiatic-Pacific Theater, and was employed by Western Air Lines. After the war the native Salt Laker resigned his copilot job with Western to accept a job as captain with Challenger Airlines. In 1950 Challenger, Monarch and Arizona Airways merged and became Frontier Airlines.

An old friend

It has been some time since McChrystal has piloted a DC-3, but he hasn't forgotten his old friend. "The DC-3 was part of my life for 22 years," he says. "You can't live with a gal that long without having fond memories." Around 2,000 Gooneys are still flying throughout the world with small airlines 700 and corporations.

McChrystal's wife was a stewardess for United Airlines, graduating from the first class of nonnurses United hired. "And you know what," Bill says, "we only made one complete flight together." Now Bill and his first mate have their own crew of four—all girls.

McChrystal has retired from Frontier and in 1977 was elected as the first president of Frontier Airlines Retired Pilot's Association. The association now has a membership of 50 retired Frontier captains. These retired pilots have had DC-3 Gooney Birds strapped to their fannies for a combined total of over

800 750,000 hours, and that includes approximately 900,000 takeoffs and landings.

The retired veterans have flown all of the various types of aircraft that have been operated by Frontier, from DC-3s to Boeing 737 jets. Frontier's retired pilots each have at least 25,000 hours of flight time with a safety record of no fatalities or serious injuries to passengers or crew members—a remarkable record considering at least two-thirds of their flying time was conducted over rugged mountainous terrain.

I wouldn't be surprised either if a few Gooneys are still flying when all of our modern jets are in the 900 bone yard.

——STOP——ASK FOR YOUR TIME——

Record time immediately and answer
the questions on content.

Time_____Sec.	RATE (from table on page 313):	R. _____
No. Correct:_____ (key on page 329)	COMPREHENSION (50% for each correct answer):	C. _____
V–16	EFFICIENCY (R × C):	E. _____

Record on Progress Chart on page 299

ANSWER THESE QUESTIONS IMMEDIATELY (V–16)

1. (T – F) The famous Douglas DC-3 was known by veteran pilots as the Gooney Bird.
2. (M. C.) At the time of his selection as the winner of the contest, Bill McChrystal was a pilot employed by:
    _____(1) Western Air Lines.
    _____(2) Challenger Airlines.
    _____(3) Frontier Airlines.
    _____(4) United Airlines.

Exercise V-17

John Muir
by RUSSELL McKEE

(Reprinted from the November-December 1966 edition of the *Colorado Outdoors* magazine
by permission of the publications chief.)

—————— WAIT FOR SIGNAL TO BEGIN READING ——————

John Muir's early youth

Some say John Muir was the father of our national park system while others say he was America's first great conservationist. Still others bill him as founder, custodian and majordomo of the whole wilderness concept in American thinking. John Muir himself claimed he was, by profession, a tramp.

Who was this bearded, ascetic little man who lived most of his life alone in the wilderness, existing on tea and dry bread, that he could meet with presidents, and fire the imagination of a whole nation with his zeal for the delights of natural beauty?

Muir was born in Scotland in 1838, and emi-100 grated with his family to Kingston, Wisconsin, in 1849. There the Muir family hacked out a quarter-section homestead farm and young John got his first taste of American wilderness. He educated himself at night after working 16 hours in the fields, and at age 22 left home for study at the University of Wisconsin. He had a genius for mechanical inventions and contrived a working clock (though he had never seen the inside of one) and various other gadgets. After graduation from Wisconsin he was well on his way to a fortune in various manufacturing ventures, 200 when an accident blinded him for several weeks. During this time of worried convalescence, he determined to quit the cities and spend the rest of his life among the wild things he loved.

A cross-country walk

Accordingly, when he recovered, he walked cross-country from Kentucky to the Gulf Coast, went on to Cuba, and after various other rambles took passage from New York to San Francisco. Soon he found the luxuriant Central Valley and the high Sierras of California, always walking and living for the most part on a Spartan supply of tea and dry bread.

He rambled up and down the Sierras and other 300 parts of the West, carefully recording all he saw, and gradually began to write and lecture about the natural beauties he found in these mountain areas. One of the periodicals that printed his articles was the "Century Magazine," and in 1889, the editor, Robert

Underwood Johnson, traveled to California for a camping trip with Muir. Together, they saw the growing destruction of those forest areas by lumber, mining, and sheep grazing interests. Johnson suggested that Muir stump for establishment of what 400 would be called Yosemite National Park, a public area protected from exploitation. In the excited talk that followed, Muir saw that his life work could be the awakening of America to the preservation of its natural beauties. Johnson published Muir's articles on Yosemite and a bill was introduced into Congress immediately, but it failed to pass that year. However, the bill was entered again the following year, and on October 1, 1890, Yosemite National Park came into existence.

Muir stumped for more such areas and in 1892 helped found and was named president of the Sierra Club, still a powerful conservation organization. Through this club, he rallied new support for public 500 lands, and by 1893, the Federal government had set aside 13 million acres in western parks and forests. However, destruction on these lands continued despite Federal laws, and in 1896, Muir served as guide and adviser to a forestry commission of six men, who toured the West viewing the remaining natural areas and the devastation being wrecked on others. The commission reported to President Cleveland in 1897, who promptly created 13 new forest reservations in eight western states, urged repeal and modification of fraudulent timber and mining laws, called for scientific management of forests to maintain a permanent timber supply, and created two 600 new national parks—Grand Canyon and Mount Rainier. A total of 21 million acres was involved.

Roosevelt aids in the battle for conservation

By then the lumber, mining and stock grazing interests were thoroughly aroused, and through their lobbies were able to overturn in Congress much of this, but still the fight went on, and when Theodore Roosevelt entered the White House, public sentiment was swinging steadily in favor of more conservation. Roosevelt did much to stimulate the work that Muir had started, and even traveled west to camp with

Muir soon after taking office. The two men, virtually alone during this historic four-day outing, tramped 700 over part of Yosemite and talked about the tremendous problem of land preservation during this great period of national expansion. The effect this camping trip had on development of the national parks and forests now available in this country can hardly be estimated, but it is perhaps enough to note that 43 million acres of land were in national forest when Roosevelt became President; that another 151 million acres were added during his two terms of office; and that the number of national parks was doubled.

John Muir died in 1914, but in his honor a 800 lake, a Sequoia grove, a glacier, a mountain peak and a butterfly have been named. Trails, passes, peaks of land and promontories also bear his name. His stern Scottish father had taught him that all vanities and touches of pride were bad seeds to chew and John Muir would perhaps be embarrassed by the esteem in which his name is now held. Yet for all his modesty, John Muir was himself an able conservationist who shook a nation from its lethargy, and who preserved our country's natural gifts. We 900 can claim ourselves fortunate for his existence.

——STOP——ASK FOR YOUR TIME——

Record time immediately and answer questions on content.

Time_____Sec.

RATE (from table on page 313):

R. _____

No. Correct:_____
(key on page 321)

COMPREHENSION (50% for each correct answer):

C. _____

V–17

EFFICIENCY (R × C):

E. _____

Record on Progress Chart on page 299

ANSWER THESE QUESTIONS IMMEDIATELY (V–17)

1. (T – F) John Muir was a revered conservationist who stimulated American thinking about wilderness concepts.
2. (M. C.) One of Muir's staunchest supporters, Theodore Roosevelt, aided land preservation efforts by:
    _____(1) signing the bill which established Yosemite National Park.
    _____(2) creating 13 new forest reservations in eight western states.
    _____(3) doubling the number of national parks.
    _____(4) urging the repeal and modification of fraudulent timber laws.

Exercise V–18

Impeachment in American History
by HON. EARL F. LANDGREBE

(Reprinted from the July 18, 1974 issue of the *Congressional Record*.)

──────────── **WAIT FOR SIGNAL TO BEGIN READING** ────────────

The Johnson trial

The classic illustration of what American Presidents, while in office, have had to endure and which is most pertinent to our time is the almost successful impeachment and conviction of President Lincoln's successor, Andrew Johnson. His efforts to put into effect the more generous policies that Lincoln had advocated with respect to the South and other controversial matters brought him into sharp conflict with members of both the House and the Senate. Everything came to a head when he dismissed Secretary of War Edwin Stanton, who not only opposed the President but secretly acted as an informant for his bitterest opponents. Congress had 100 just passed a law designed to block such an action by an American President and reinstalled Stanton.

President Johnson in his defense claimed that his viewpoint would have been supported by every President from Washington to his own day. And he was right if John Adams' position was typical of other former Presidents. Long before the Johnson issue had arisen President Adams during a heated discussion remarked, "if the President of the United States has not enough authority to change his own secretaries, he is no longer fit for his office."

If President Johnson had meekly accepted such 200 a law as Congress had proposed it would have broken down the Madisonian concept of "checks and balances" in the interrelationship of the President and the Congress. The uniquely important office of the Presidency would have been degraded into some kind of political secretariat that could readily be made the tool of designing politicians.

Many Americans clamored for the impeachment of President Nixon as though it were a simple matter to accomplish with clear-cut procedures and would entail a minimum disturbance to either our national life or the structure of American government. They should have read the story of the whole sordid 300 business of the impeachment by the House of Representatives and attempted conviction by the Senate of President Andrew Johnson.

Dr. Ronis W. Konig, author of "The Chief Executive" states that President Johnson's trial by the Senate was presided over by a Chief Justice "who wanted to be president; having a craving for the office

that Lincoln once likened to insanity." In line of succession was the "president protempore" of the Senate whom the author describes as "vulgar and vituperative." The galleries were crowded with the senators, their wives and daughters, "blooming with 400 finery," scores of reporters and distinguished visitors from other countries, all of whom had competed furiously for the limited number of only one thousand passes per day for the eleven and one half weeks that the trial lasted.

The "radicals" secured an adjournment for ten days, despite the objection of the Chief Justice, to line up every possible vote against the President. The prosecutor at the trial before the Senate called President Johnson, "a traitor, a tyrant, a usurper and an apostate."

Those who voted "No" withstood incredible pressure with soldierly firmness, even though friends, 500 position and fortune were ready to be swept away, and were the heroes in these contemptible proceedings.

Our system of American government with its delicate balance of responsibility between the legislative and executive branches, fashioned with painstaking care through three-quarters of a century, was preserved and a fearsome threat to our representative democracy in America went down to defeat by only a single vote. If President Johnson had been successfully convicted, the door would have been left wide open for the dismissal of any President, on political rather than legal grounds. Professor Rexford G. Tugwell writes that the radicals in Congress were determined to reduce the Presidency 600 to "ministerial status."

Impeachment—a megaton bomb

The threat of impeachment and conviction has been likened to that of a megaton bomb—too frightening to contemplate except as a last and desperate expedient. Professor Clinton Rossiter regarded impeachment as "The extreme medicine of the Constitution, so brutally administered, in this one instance in which it was prescribed, as to provoke a revulsion." President Jefferson could not even envision a situation where it might lawfully be used.

Despite the ominous words of Professor Rossiter and the skepticism of President Jefferson the fact remains that impeachment is still an integral part of the Constitution of the United States. How then do $\overset{700}{\leftarrow}$ we account for the fact that no President of the United States has been impeached and convicted in almost two hundred years of our nation's history, in spite of several abortive attempts to apply impeachment and one unsuccessful effort to obtain conviction? One reason undoubtedly is because of the dire penalties entailed as set forth in the Articles of the American Constitution: Article I, Section 3 (7) which reads in part: "removal from Office, disqualification to hold and enjoy any Office of honor, Trust or Profit under the United States . . . the Party convicted shall never- $\overset{800}{\leftarrow}$ theless be liable and subject to Indictment, Trial, Judgment and Punishment, according to Law."

If the convicted President should happen to be a family man, the pall of disgrace would fall not only on himself but on his wife, his children and his grandchildren "to the third and fourth generation." It might well cut him off completely from the sources of livelihood for which he has spent the greater part of his lifetime in preparation. And who will aver that the nation that elected him will not itself be on $\overset{900}{\rightarrow}$ trial before the eyes of the whole world?

——STOP——ASK FOR YOUR TIME——

Record time immediately and answer
the questions on content.

Time____Sec.	RATE (from table on page 313):	R. _____
No. Correct:_____ (key on page 329)	COMPREHENSION (50% for each correct answer):	C. _____
V–18	EFFICIENCY (R × C):	E. _____

Record on Progress Chart on page 299

ANSWER THESE QUESTIONS IMMEDIATELY (V–18)

1. (T – F) The process of impeachment has clear-cut procedures that involve a minimum disturbance to the government.
2. (M. C.) Most of this article was related to the possible impeachment of which president?
   _____(1) Richard Nixon.
   _____(2) Andrew Johnson.
   _____(3) Lyndon Johnson.
   _____(4) Abraham Lincoln.

Exercise V–19

Sludge Slough
by R. C. BURKHOLDER

(Reprinted from the November 1973 issue of *Wyoming Wildlife* by permission of the editor.)

———————————— **WAIT FOR SIGNAL TO BEGIN READING** ————————————

Henry David Thoreau had his Walden Pond, John Muir had his High Sierras, Bob Marshall had his Wilderness Area, and I have Sludge Slough!

Sludge Slough is an environmental phenomenon —as world-famous for the study of *hydro*-ecological life cycles as McGruder's Gully is for the study of *terra*-ecological life cycles.

What makes Sludge Slough so captivatingly interesting, at least to the limonogol . . . limnygo . . . limnomol . . . fresh water expert, is the fact that the life cycle of Sludge Slough is much easier to research and study than the more complex life cycles found in other lesser-known bodies of water such as Lake Erie, the Salton Sea, and the Panama Canal. 100 In addition, each link in the food chain found in Sludge Slough is a rare, threatened, endangered, and/or picked-upon species.

Inasmuch as you are now goose-pimply with academic interest, let me briefly describe, in scientific detail, the hydro-ecological life cycle of Sludge Slough.

To begin with, all life cycles can be depicted as a closed circle, and the cycle of Sludge Slough has no beginning and no end, so let's start between the beginning and the end with the sludge of Sludge Slough.

A. Sludge

Sludge Slough is surrounded by, underlain with, 200 and wallows in the ickiest, gooiest, and muckiest sludge. There are two primary sources of this sludge: (1) deceased organic debris of every· imaginable kind, and (2) decomposed aluminum foil, snuff cans, beer bottles, old tires, and cardboard cartons.

At this point in the cycle, the sludge don't do nothin'; it just lays there—dead, lifeless phhht!— and smells a lot, but then, comes the spring and summer thunderstorms with the dark, billowing clouds scurrying across Sludge Slough. Thunder rumbles overhead and lightning flashes into the muck making complex electro-chemical reaction which takes place and, lo, we have life in Sludge Slough! 300 Honest . . . plain, ordinary, run-of-the-mill sludge is now . . . *bio-sludge!*

B. Bio-sludge

Bio-sludge consists of many, many billions and trillions of microscopic one-celled ugly little animals, plants, and combinations thereof which swim, crawl, slither, float, wiggle, hop, and squirm all over the place. This bio-sludge performs three bio-socio-ecoenvironmental functions: (1) it eats common sludge, (2) it chases other bio-sludge back and forth through the slough, and (3) it serves as the one and only food source for the *sludge guppy*.

C. Sludge guppy

Sludge guppies are tiny fish ranging in size 400 from 0.00085 mm to 0.00635 in. in length which feed exclusively on bio-sludge when they are not cannibalizing each other. Since the sludge guppy population is all-male in character, reproduction takes place through a process known as photosexo-frustration. Every evening individual sludge guppies turn green and go all to pieces, a reproductive technique which assures a goodly supply of sludge guppies for the *slough sludgeminnow*.

D. Slough sludgeminnow

The slough sludgeminnow can be readily identified by:

1. an invisible lateral line encircling the body from tail to anal fin,
2. dorsal fins located on the ventral side of the body,
3. one large greenish-blue eye and one small 500 yellowish-red eye, and
4. the fact that there are no other minnows in Sludge Slough.

Unlike other minnows found in Sludge Slough, the slough sludgeminnow does not form harems in the late summer, mate in the fall, and spawn in the spring. Slough sludgeminnows spawn first, then mate, forming up into large schools which are fed upon by the voracious *sludge sloughfish*.

E. Sludge sloughfish

The sludge sloughfish, although it ranges from 8″ to 45 pounds in size, is inedible, unpalatable, and as a sporting gamefish, the sludge sloughfish provides less thrills and excitement than an empty bottle of $\overset{600}{\leftarrow}$ Geritol on the end of a line. One avid sludge sloughfish fisherman stated on our official Sludge Slough Recreation User Questionnaire and Interview Form 146-c (6/73):

> Reeling in one of them there fish is like dragging a pair of shorts across the slough but it sure beats watching the chrome rust on my pickup every weekend!

The last link in the Sludge Slough life cycle/food chain—the *sludge sloughfish fisherman.*

F. Sludge sloughfish fisherman

The sludge sloughfish fisherman plays a very important role in the hydro-ecological life cycle of Sludge Slough, specifically, if the sludge sloughfish fisherman did not routinely provide source material $\overset{700}{\leftarrow}$ for sludge; i.e., trash and garbage such as aluminum foil, snuff cans, beer bottles, old tires and cardboard cartons; there would be no sludge and no Sludge Slough.

Recommendations

Naturally, we have developed some suggestions and recommendations for the administration (technical interference with) and management (scientific manipulation of) the hydro-ecological life cycle of Sludge Slough.

1. To assure an adequate supply of bio-sludge, we suggest that the U.S. Weather Bureau—in cooperation with the Environmental Protection Agency and General Services Administration—plan, program, and schedule lightning strikes into Sludge Slough on a year-round basis.

$\overset{800}{\rightarrow}$ 2. Assuming the recommendation above is initiated, we should have no difficulty in maintaining an acceptable population level of sludge guppies, slough sludgeminnows, and sludge sloughfish in their natural and pristine habitat.

3. However, consideration should be given to stocking Sludge Slough with barracuda, piranha, and shark just to see what happens to the natural and pristine habitat mentioned in item No. 2 above.

4. On second thought, forget it . . . we just received word that someone bought Sludge Slough and is planning to drain it, level it, and build a combination Museum of Natural History and Institute $\overset{900}{\rightarrow}$ for Ecological Studies on it!

——STOP——ASK FOR YOUR TIME——

Record time immediately and answer
the questions on content.

Time_____Sec.	RATE (from table on page 313):	R. _____
No. Correct:_____ (key on page 321)	COMPREHENSION (50% for each correct answer):	C. _____
V–19	EFFICIENCY (R × C):	E. _____

Record on Progress Chart on page 299

ANSWER THESE QUESTIONS IMMEDIATELY (V–19)

1. (T – F) The author recommended further funding for ecological research on the Sludge Slough.
2. (M. C.) This analysis of the hydro-ecological life cycle of Sludge Slough is:
    _____(1) an analytical analysis.
    _____(2) an ecological experiment.
    _____(3) a hydrological history.
    _____(4) a fictional fantasy.

Exercise V–20

Saving the Sea Floor
by PETE HOLMES

—————— WAIT FOR SIGNAL TO BEGIN READING ——————

In its short history, the federal marine-sanctuary program has suffered from bureaucratic foot-dragging, and has been threatened with assaults from Congress. The program has also been a rallying point for citizens concerned about ocean wildlife and habitat.

A brief history

In 1972, Congress passed the Marine Protections, Research, and Sanctuaries Act (MPRSA), laying out a three-pronged approach to curb degradation of U.S. ocean waters. Title I established procedures to be followed by the Environmental Protection Agency and, for some activities, by the Army Corps of Engineers, to control dumping of wastes into the sea. Title II directs the Commerce 100 Department's National Oceanic and Atmospheric Administration (NOAA), in cooperation with the Coast Guard, to run a comprehensive research program on ocean dumping.

The most innovative provision of the MPRSA, certainly the most controversial, is Title III, which authorizes NOAA's Marine Sanctuaries Program. Title III calls for the Secretary of Commerce, with Presidential approval, to designate marine sanctuaries "for the purpose of preserving or restoring such areas for their conservation, recreational, ecological or esthetic values." Sanctuaries may be designated as far seaward as the outer edge of the outer continental shelf, in coastal and tidal waters, or in the Great Lakes and their connecting waters. 200

Title III lets NOAA impose sanctuary-management plans that may supersede another federal agency's authority. Title III does what no law has done before: It provides for the regulation of *all* uses affecting a particular ecosystem. Marine sanctuaries are to be designated at the site of distinctive marine resources whose protection and use require comprehensive, geographically oriented planning and management.

Nominations for marine sanctuaries may come from any individual or organization. These proposals are reviewed by several federal agencies. Public hearings and workshops are held near the suggested sanctuary. An environmental impact statement is prepared prior to Presidential approval of the 300

designation. If the sanctuary is within a state's jurisdiction, approval from the governor is required. After designation, activities not compatible with the reasons for establishing the sanctuary are prohibited or restricted, but in general all other public uses are allowed.

Early sites

Two ocean sites were chosen in 1975 and were relatively noncontroversial. The Monitor Marine Sanctuary is an area one mile in diameter surrounding the wreck of the U.S.S. *Monitor* off Cape Hatteras, North Carolina. The 100-square-mile Key Largo Coral Reef Marine Sanctuary is adjacent to the John 400 Pennecamp Coral Reef State Park in the northern Florida Keys.

In 1977, the Office of Ocean Management (OOM) was established within the Office of Coastal Zone Management. In 1978, OOM studied sanctuary candidates off California and Alaska, the Flower Garden Banks in the Gulf of Mexico, and the Looe Key coral reefs off Florida. The first sanctuary proposal to conflict with offshore oil-and-gas development was the East and West Flower Garden Banks in the Gulf. Oil-and-gas exploration was just beginning; active leasing of additional tracts was in progress at the Interior Department. OOM's white paper on the Flower Gardens sanctuary drew immediate, 500 heavy criticism from Interior, and from Rep. John Breaux, then chairman of the House Oceanography Subcommittee of the Merchant Marine and Fisheries Committee.

The Office of Ocean Management was disbanded in late 1978, and the marine-sanctuary program was given a new director and moved to a new office with the already existing Estuarine Sanctuary Program. In 1979, this new office released the Draft Environmental Impact Statement (DEIS) for the Flower Garden Banks Marine Sanctuary. It was a significant retreat by NOAA from its original plan for Flower Gardens, and drew sharp criticism from conservationists.

Conflicting interests

Perhaps the most critical time for the marine-300 600 sanctuary program came in the midst of the Flower

Gardens debate, when Georges Bank, off Massachusetts, faced with its first oil-lease sale, was nominated for consideration as a marine sanctuary. New England fishermen insisted that President Carter call off the sale. Environmental attorneys hedged their bets with lawsuits that relied partially upon NOAA's marine-sanctuary authority to head off risky oil-and-gas development. In October 1979, however, NOAA administrator Richard Frank pulled the rug from under under the fishermen and environmentalists by cancelling sanctuary consideration for Georges Bank.

In 1980, reauthorization hearings for the by now controversial Sanctuaries Act were held by the two House subcommittees (Oceanography, and Fisheries 700 and Wildlife Conservation and the Environment, both of the House Committee on Merchant Marine and Fisheries). Titles I and II were topics for debate, but Title III drew the most fire, with a proposal, from Rep. Breaux, to scrap the entire sanctuary program. Another bill would have seriously restricted the sanctuary program. But both bills were withheld, thanks to support for the program from Rep. Gerry Studds, then chairman of the Oceanography Subcommittee. A Dear Colleague letter, from Rep.

Edward Stack of Florida, also was signed by several influential congressmen.

Public support

800 Public support for the marine-sanctuary program has been outstanding with Sanctuary nominations coming into Washington from all over the country. Sanctuary workshops recently held in California drew hundreds of enthusiastic participants. A marine-sanctuary coalition composed of national conservation organizations has reviewed every candidate considered by NOAA, and has helped with technical comments and political support.

Much needs to be done to establish the goals and intent of the six-year-old marine sanctuary program. The most difficult problem—which will require attention from senior NOAA officials and cooperation from other federal officials, particularly at Interior— will be overcoming the oil vs. environment debate 900 that now delays development of marine sanctuaries.

——STOP——ASK FOR YOUR TIME——

Record time immediately and answer
the questions on content.

Time_____Sec.	**RATE** (from table on page 313):	R. _____
No. Correct:_____ (key on page 329)	**COMPREHENSION** (50% for each correct answer):	C. _____
V–20	**EFFICIENCY** (R ✕ C):	E. _____

Record on Progress Chart on page 299

ANSWER THESE QUESTIONS IMMEDIATELY (V–20)

1. (T – F) The federal marine-sanctuary program has been popular and successful as a means of identifying and preserving many significant areas of sea habitat.
2. (M. C.) One of the major problems in the administration of the program has been:
   _____(1) the limited number of appropriate potential sites for consideration.
   _____(2) the conflict of interest with the offshore oil-and-gas development.
   _____(3) the autocratic administration by entrenched bureaucrats.
   _____(4) the lack of public support for the program since 1972.

SERIES VI

Exploratory Reading Exercises

Instructions

The Series VI exercises are designed to develop your ability to read continuously one long article and then to recite on the material at the end. This type of reading will be contrasted with that of the exercise in Series VII, where you read in smaller units and do a spaced recitation. Many students argue that they do not have time for the SQ4R method of study or for self-recitation. A comparison of your efficiency scores between these two types of exercises is one of the best objective answers to your own possible hesitancy to try these study techniques.

As in Series V exercises, you will find the length and the readability scores at the top of each article and you will find the numbers in the center margin that will help you to estimate your speed. Articles become progressively more difficult as you proceed through the series, and here again you are working toward increasing reading speed and reading level. In this case, however, you have more material and more ideas to retain, and you will be tested more thoroughly on the material read.

When given the signal to begin an article, you should read as rapidly as possible, concentrating on main ideas and watching for any clues to those ideas. When you finish reading, check your time immediately, and record your rate in the same manner as in Series V by using the table on page 315.

Then go on to the ten questions on the material, and answer them as accurately as possible. Answer the (T–F) and the (M.C.) questions as instructed before. In the Completion (C) questions, you are to fill in the word or words that will best complete the meaning of the sentence. After these are scored according to the keys on pages 322 and 330, you compute your comprehension by multiplying your number of correct answers by ten. Then compute your efficiency by multiplying the *rate* score by the *comprehension* score and record the *efficiency* score on the Progress Chart on page 299.

Suggestions

These are referred to as Exploratory Reading Exercises because they are designed to help polish tools of reading for new ideas, greater detail, or further understanding of materials with which you are already familiar. These may be materials already sorted by the Idea Reading approach and identified for a little more thorough reading. Materials identified by this type of reading for specific study purposes or for significant long-range use normally will be marked and set aside for study reading or critical reading.

Normally, this reading procedure will not result in long-range retention of details unless the content is closely related to personal needs and unless reading is reinforced by additional study skills focused on long-term comprehension.

For general reading about new ideas or new interests, this type of reading utilizes high-speed reading skills tempered with selective judgment to find materials appropriate for more careful study.

Your rate on these materials will depend on much more than the arrangement on paper, the content, or the instructor's motivation. You can control your rate and efficiency by your own personal motivation and attitude. What you already know about the topic, how you feel about the topic, and what previous associations you may have with the topic or the author will have a strong effect on your reading activity.

In this longer reading material, one criterion is especially important, however, and that is your ability to concentrate for an extended period of time without interruption. This will require effort on your part. You will have to avoid the tendencies to daydream, to let your attention be distracted by nearby audio or visual factors of passing interest. Perhaps you should review again the materials on pages 19–24 of this book regarding concentration and basic study skills. Content of these articles will cover a fairly wide range of material, some of which may be of immediate interest to you and some of which may not. For the purpose of these exercises, you should try to develop an inquiring mind and try to seek new ideas. You can apply a fairly rapid reading rate to such materials. You may be surprised to find out how much content you can pick up even at relatively high reading rates.

Thinking about the title, checking out your own knowledge of the topic, and posing questions to which you want to find answers will provide a mental setting in which you should achieve effective concentration and maximum reading efficiency.

Exercise VI–1

Noisy Chorus of the Sea
by WILLIAM N. TAVOLGA

(Reprinted from the April 1967 issue of *Natural History*
by permission of the editorial secretary.)

───────── WAIT FOR SIGNAL TO BEGIN READING ─────────

Some fishes gnash their teeth, others sound like foghorns—the porpoise whistles and squeals—crustaceans add to the clamor by clicking and rasping. Through use of the spectrograph, we now know more about the sounds of alarm, feeding, mating, and reconnaissance.

In recent years most people have come to realize that the sea is not the "silent world" of Jacques Cousteau's well-known book on undersea adventure. In reality, the oceans are at least as noisy as, *and often noisier than,* our average terrestrial environment. One of the reasons for this, as we shall see later, is the varied and large amount of sound ⤾100 contributed by water currents and marine animals. Another lies in the very nature of the medium, for water is a far better conductor of sound than air because it is about a thousand times denser; also it is virtually incompressible under normal circumstances. Consequently, more energy is required to start the movement of sound through water, but once started, this acoustic energy will be transmitted farther and much faster. The velocity of sound in air is about 330 meters per second (1,080 feet per second); in water it is almost 1,500 meters per second (4,920 ⤾200 feet), and these figures are significantly affected by changes in temperature and pressure. In the oceans, since salt water is denser than fresh, the velocity may go as high as 5,050 feet per second—almost five times greater than in air.

The transmission of sound through sea water is further enhanced because much of the sound is conserved by reflection. It is reflected from the surface of the water (up to 99.9 percent of the energy is reflected back); from the sea floor; and from the interfaces formed by layers of water that are at different temperatures.

One other fact must be considered for we are ⤾300 not aquatic beings. Even with Scuba gear we cannot match our air-adapted ears to underwater sounds, and it is difficult for us to conceive what the marine environment sounds like. We must, therefore, use artificial hearing aids, as it were, to translate for us.

Measuring the sound

In addition to the frequency of a sound, commonly called its pitch, we must know something of its intensity, or volume. This we express in units called decibels (abbreviated to dB). Decibels are actually logarithmic values, and it just happens that our sensory processes, including hearing, follow some ⤾400 approximation of a logarithmic law. Our perception is such that when one sound seems twice as loud as another, the actual difference may be very large or very small, depending on the absolute intensity of the two sounds. One decibel is close to the minimum difference that we can detect in the intensity of two sounds, but a one-decibel difference in a very soft tone is an extremely small difference in pressure, while at a loud tone it may be ten or a hundred times greater. A decibel, therefore, is a relative measure and is always given in reference to some preselected ⤾500 zero point.

If we measure the sound pressure in the sea, including noise produced by wave motion, by vertical and horizontal currents, by water friction against the sea floor, by the noise of boats and ships, and superimposed on all that, the noises of marine animals, the average level of ambient sea noise becomes about 10 or 15 decibels *above* the one-microbar reference level. This is comparable to a busy office with typewriters clattering, papers rustling, people walking and talking, telephones ringing, and the din of outdoor traffic.

The marine animals commonly recognized as ⤾600 sound-producers can be broadly divided into three groups. (1) The invertebrates include crustaceans (crab, shrimp, lobsters) as principal sonic forms; also some mollusks and a few other forms. (2) The vertebrate class of fishes includes many sonic species among the 20,000-odd known forms; perhaps a majority of these are at least potential sound-producers. (3) Virtually all known species of marine mammals are sound-producers, principally the cetaceans (whales, dolphins, porpoises).

The noisy crustaceans

Most crustaceans can produce various clicking or rasping sounds with their claws, mandibles, and other parts of their shell-encrusted bodies. The sounds often accompany normal locomotion; however ⤾700 there are many species that produce sounds at other times by specialized structures.

We can only guess at the functions of the crustacean sounds. Some may be related to territorial defense; others may serve as cues in reproductive behavior; in many cases they may be merely incidental to feeding. There has been virtually no experimental work in this area of invertebrate behavior, and the field is wide open for research.

Sounds from fishes

Marine fishes produce three general types of sounds: stridulations (rubbing or rasping), swim-bladder vibrations, and hydrodynamic disturbances.

The stridulations roughly compare to the sound of crickets rubbing their wings together. Such movement of one rough surface against another gives a $\overset{800}{\leftarrow}$ rasping noise, a series of short broad-band pulses. Many species of fish produce them when they gnash their teeth or rub patches of denticles in the pharynx. Usually the sounds come during feeding; other times during fright or serious difficulty, as when the fish is captured. There is some evidence that such seemingly incidental sounds are actually a primitive form of communication. For instance, a fish hearing these "feeding sounds" can associate them with the presence of food and respond accordingly.

The most efficient and highly evolved sonic mechanism in fishes is the swim-bladder. Originally, $\overset{900}{\leftarrow}$ this thin-walled, air-containing sac probably served to control the buoyancy of the fish. It now has several other functions. In many species it is equipped with a set of specialized muscles capable of vibrating at surprisingly high rates (up to at least 300 contractions per second in some species). For this drumming sound the entire swim-bladder with its enclosed air serves as an underwater loudspeaker of considerable efficiency. Prominent producers of such sound are members of the drumfish family (family Sciaenidae), including croakers, sea trout, and sea drum.

The biological significance of many of these sounds remains obscure. In a few cases, as with $\overset{1000}{\leftarrow}$ $\overset{1350}{\rightarrow}$ toadfish and drumfish, the drumming is clearly related to spawning behavior and comes only from males. In others, as with groupers and squirrelfish, the explanation is territorial behavior—a resident animal sounds off when approached by an intruder, but there are also puzzling areas. Alarm and fright

often evoke sounds; just as often, they halt the sonic activity.

The marine mammals

In contrast to fishes, cetaceans are warm-blooded, air-breathing mammals, and include a variety of forms, commonly called whales, dolphins, and porpoises. These produce sounds that fall into $\overset{1100}{\rightarrow}$ two general categories: (1) short, broad-band sound pulses, or clicks, and (2) sustained whistles, squeals, and other cries.

As far as is known, all the species of toothed whales produce the short, pulselike clicks. The clicks come from a specialized vibrating organ found within the complex of air chambers leading to the blowhole. It has been shown that these clicks are primarily intended to locate objects by means of the returning echoes. This highly efficient and accurate sonar system rivals that of bats. Echoes from the clicks give the marine animal much information about its $\overset{1200}{\rightarrow}$ environment, especially the location and type of food that it is hunting.

It is not really surprising that marine animals in general show so many adaptations that utilize the acoustic channel for various behavior patterns. The surprising aspect is that only recently have biologists come to appreciate this fact.

With underwater vision often masked by turbidity, with the chemical senses hampered by disturbing currents and slow diffusion rates, sound is therefore the most efficient long-range mechanism for supplying marine animals with necessary information about each other and the rest of their environment.

Meanwhile, technological advances over the past twenty years have given scientists an acoustic $\overset{1300}{\rightarrow}$ window into the ocean, and marine biology now can enlarge our meager knowledge of the behavior and distribution of marine life. This knowledge is essential and basic to all oceanographic studies, which are growing in importance as it becomes evident that future generations of man will depend increasingly on the seas for their food resources.

——STOP——ASK FOR YOUR TIME——

Record time immediately and answer
the questions on content.

Time_____Sec.	RATE (from table on page 315):	R. _____
No. Correct:_____ (key on page 322)	COMPREHENSION (10% for each correct answer):	C. _____
VI–1	EFFICIENCY (R $\times$ C):	E. _____

Record on Progress Chart on page 299

ANSWER THESE QUESTIONS IMMEDIATELY (VI–1)

1. (T – F) In reality the oceans are often noisier than our average terrestrial environment.

2. (T – F) Air is a better conductor of sound than water.

3. (T – F) More energy is required to start the movement of sound through water than through air.

4. (C   ) Measuring the intensity and volume of sound is expressed in units called _____.

5. (M. C.) Marine animals commonly recognized as sound producers are the marine mammals, the invertebrates including crustaceans, and the:

_____(1) vertebrate class of fishes.

_____(2) mollusk and shell fish.

_____(3) drumfish family.

_____(4) eels and squids.

6. (T – F) Movement of one rough surface against another, as when fish gnash their teeth, is called a hydrodynamic disturbance.

7. (C   ) The most efficient sonic mechanism in fishes is the _____.

8. (T – F) Scientists have discovered a specific biological significance in many of these fish sounds.

9. (T – F) An acoustical window to the sea becomes more important as it becomes evident that future generations of man will become increasingly dependent upon the sea for food resources.

10. (M. C.) Echoes from the "clicks" give the marine animal much information about:

_____(1) density of the water.

_____(2) its environment.

_____(3) location of nearby boats.

_____(4) changes in current.

Exercise VI-2

Letter to a Dead Teacher
by BEL KAUFMAN

(Reprinted from the March-April 1975 issue of *Today's Education*
by permission of the executive editor and the author.)

———— WAIT FOR SIGNAL TO BEGIN READING ————

Dear Mr. Stock:

You probably wouldn't remember me, even if you were alive. I sat in the third row back in your English 512 class in South Side High School in Newark, New Jersey. You gave me an *A* minus for being unprepared.

You had asked us to write a composition in class about one of Hardy's heroines (Was it Tess?), but I had neglected to read the book assigned. Caught off guard, writing frantically against the clock, I described a young woman, the room she sat in, the beam of light from the high window, her hands in her lap, her thoughts in her head. I anticipated failure, disgrace, worst of all—your disappointment. Instead, you gave me a minus for being unprepared and an *A* for something uniquely mine. Your scrawled comment in red ink on my paper read, "This isn't Hardy's character, but you've made yours very real."

Startled into gratitude, I became aware of my own possibilities. You *recognized* me.

I needed recognition, I was a shy, uneasy girl, too foreign, too intense. The English language, newly learned, lay clumsy on my tongue. Long sausage curls coiled down my shoulder blades—this, in the age of the shingle bob and the spit curl. Instead of the scarlet Cupid's bow mouth, I was allowed but a pale touch of Tangee lipstick. How I longed for spikedheels and gunmetal silk stockings. How I yearned for plucked eyebrows, flapping galoshes, a slicker with boys' initials painted on it, the boys themselves!

From the time I arrived in this country at 12 until skipping had brought me to the approximate age suitable for high school, I had been the oldest in the class, the last to be called, the least to be noticed. I was monitor of nothing.

I don't think you knew what you did for me, Mr. Stock. We teachers seldom know whom we influence or how or even why. It was not my defects you emphasized, but my worth. For the first time I realized that what I had made up inside my mind could be real to someone else. Great teaching has to do with that first time, that gasp of discovery: "Eureka!" "Oh, I get it! I see!"—a new planet in the sky or letters of the alphabet that suddenly form a word.

Other teachers dealt differently with us. One would silently, lips pursed, enter a meticulous zero into an ominous black notebook. Another, down the corridor from you, would review publicly and with exquisite sarcasm all our past misdeeds, of which the current one was the ultimate transgression.

Actually, I recall very few of my teachers. In Latin, the teacher made us sit quietly, hands on desk, eyes front. This was called "maintaining discipline." In history, our teacher perched on the windowsill, dangled his legs, and wooed us with false camaraderie.

You assumed one simple fact: If the lesson was interesting, we would be attentive. We were more than attentive. We hated to see the period end, for you knew when to ask the provocative, unexpected "Why?" which tumbled upside down our whole cluttered cart of preconceptions and set us thinking long after the dismissal bell. You did not try to charm or to beguile us. You never pretended to be a pal. You were a *teacher*. Your dignity was unassailable. Because you respected yourself and us, we were able to respect ourselves.

Another time you called my handwriting distinctive. Did you say *distinctive* or *distinguished*? I no longer remember. What matters is how much that meant to me. In my skipping of grades, I had skipped right over the Palmer Method of ovals and strokes; consequently, my handwriting was different. But *distinctive*—imagine that!

Somehow, you made everyone feel special. Once you quoted from Shakespeare: . . . who can say more than this rich praise—that you alone are you?" I knew you meant me. And so did each of the 34 others in the room.

When one of us returned after an absence, you would say, "We missed you." When one was unprepared, you would shake your head: "Too bad; we were hoping to know what *you* think." When one came late, you assumed there was good reason for it that need not be asked. You treated us as adults, your equals, and so—in your class—we were. "Don't be captious," you would say, taking it for granted that we either knew the word or would look it up in one of several dictionaries you always left scattered around the room. We looked it up. Because you knew we were fine people, punctual attenders, conscientious homework doers, honorable test takers, devoted scholars, and responsible citizens, we were. For you, we were! You were sincere, before the word became suspect; tolerant, before the word 800 became loaded. Kids know what is phony. Children and lovers always know. It was unthinkable to offer you anything shoddy or second-rate. I see only now that your demands on us were enormous.

I don't remember clearly what you looked like; you were short, I think, and roundish, but I recall the sound of laughter in the room. You were never one to buy a cheap laugh at the expense of someone else or to stoop to a gag, but—quick to see absurdity —you shared it with us.

And you shared with us your loves. "Listen 900 to this!" you would say, eagerly opening a book, unashamed to be moved by a poem, unafraid to use words like "magnificent."

Those were the days of the after-school clubs (We called it "enrichment"), school spirit, Field Day, and the senior yearbook with its photos of (except for one black girl) white, middle-class, alphabetized children with neatly brushed hair, over inscriptions such as: *Reading Maketh a Full Man* and *Future Plans: College and Professional School.*

Those were the days when teachers, especially to my European eyes, were creatures set apart. I recall my shock when I noticed one morning that my algebra teacher had a run in her stocking like 1000 any ordinary person. Those were the days of obedience as absolute as the silence, when a demerit for conduct could destroy us, when chewing gum in class was a serious infraction, when "Sez you!" to a teacher was unheard of insolence.

Those were the days of our innocence, and I recall them with nostalgia, especially now, especially as a teacher.

I wonder how you would fare in today's urban public high school, where teachers have become The *Enemy* and students—mostly angry Blacks and frustrated Puerto Ricans trained in failure from the 1100 day they were born—wage daily war against us. Are teachers like you really dead? I try to imagine you in a school I know, one of the worst in New York, where frightened teachers look the other way and helpless administrators send forth streams of directives advising them to lock their doors, hide their window poles, and hold on to their pocketbooks, because there are cops in the lobby, pot on the stairs, muggings in the halls, assaults in the lavatory, robbery at knife point, vandalism, arson, and worse.

You would have a rough time of it today, Mr. 1200 Stock, but I think you would be unafraid. You would not look the other way or talk only from the mouth out. You would treat each child as a human person. And you would still expect students to do their best—not Hardy's or anyone else's but their own— whatever that best might be.

Teachers like you are not dead as long as there are children who can one day say, "I had a teacher once. . . ." Perhaps at this very moment, someone, someplace, is saying this about one of us. That is our immortality.

1300 Dear Mr. Stock, I wanted to show you by recalling the past, how different schools are today, but I see this has turned out to be a love letter to you. Well, there are times when a love letter needs to be written, even if it is never mailed.

Your Unforgetting Forever Pupil,

Bel Kaufman

1350

——STOP——ASK FOR YOUR TIME——

Record time immediately and answer the questions on content.

Time_____Sec.	RATE (from table on page 315):	R. _____
No. Correct:_____ (key on page 330)	COMPREHENSION (10% for each correct answer):	C. _____
VI–2	EFFICIENCY (R × C):	E. _____

Record on Progress Chart on page 299

ANSWER THESE QUESTIONS IMMEDIATELY (VI–2)

1. (T – F) The writer of this letter remembers the teacher giving her an *A* minus for being unprepared.

2. (M. C.) She was impressed that the teacher:

 _____(1) complimented her.

 _____(2) recognized her.

 _____(3) scolded her.

 _____(4) promoted her.

3. (T – F) The writer remembers clearly all of the teachers she ever had.

4. (T – F) She resented the fact that Mr. Stock made such enormous demands on students in his classes.

5. (M. C.) Mr. Stock always impressed the writer most as being a:

 _____(1) friend.

 _____(2) charming person.

 _____(3) teacher.

 _____(4) disciplinarian.

6. (C   ) He once called her handwriting _____.

7. (C   ) She praised him because he seemed to make everyone in his class feel _____.

8. (T – F) With her European background, the writer always viewed the teachers as something special and extraordinary.

9. (T – F) The writer feels that Mr. Stock would have a very rough time in New York schools today.

10. (T – F) The writer concludes that teachers like Mr. Stock are really dead and gone in today's school system.

Exercise VI–3

How to Become a Millionaire
by ARNOLD TOLAR

(Reprinted from the December 1966 issue of *Moderator*
by permission of the editor.)

―――――――――― **WAIT FOR SIGNAL TO BEGIN READING** ――――――――――

At 38, John Diebold, the Automation man, is a millionaire. "Half the stuff in the *Wall Street Journal* isn't so," says John Diebold, the man who should know.

You get the feeling John knows which half.

There he is, the founder of automation in the entrepreneur outfit with the Snoopy face. Fantastic—the combination is shattering: there's the guy who wrote the book, *Automation* (1952), invented the word we have nightmares about, and he's this shy, yet almost impulsive, ex-merchant marine who might look good in a huge pinafore, but there he is hung out in his double-breasted Saville Row duds and he's 100 telling you how to become a millionaire.

It goes like this: You're a student, and in order to get started, you first should have a good liberal arts background, including a healthy injection of math. Instead of bothering with undergrad business courses, start sizing yourself up in terms of the crucial question: Am I a businessman or a managerial prospect? Try running your own campus enterprise and then try managing a going concern. Which do you like to do more?

Your big decision

Once you've answered that crucial question, you are ready to go management or go business. 200

If you go management, you will probably head for business or public administration graduate school where the training is not utterly essential. Diebold admits he scarcely knows how many degrees his men have, and notices only when he's sending out a recommendation letter for someone. Besides, business schools aren't exactly in bed with the computer age. "Business schools still teach you how to make decisions on too little information."

If you go business, you will probably go one of three routes: 1) start as an assistant to a top executive; 2) start with a small company, rise rapidly, and leapfrog to a top position with a large 300 concern; 3) start your own company. As you may have guessed, "business" means the hard-nosed entrepreneurial way. Don't go near it, says Diebold, if you don't like the heat in the kitchen or on the production line.

The vast majority of students, Diebold predicts, will go the managerial route when faced with the business vs. management choice. "The great development in the country is the professional manager." The professional manager is not driven by the profit motive, as is the businessman; feeling equally at home 400 in a profit or nonprofit institution. To illustrate that, the professional manager and the businessman are "worlds apart," Diebold tells this story about one great international management association, meeting in New York: only one of twelve businessmen he talked to in the city while the meeting was in session knew about it.

Be aggressive

You've chosen your route to take and now in choosing your company, don't look for starting salary: it's an illusion, especially given inflation. Says Diebold, "I took the lowest starting salary of all my Harvard Business School classmates—$300 a month" plus a future: The boss looked him over 500 closely. Diebold got a launching pad, and took off, later absorbing the boss's firm into the Diebold Group.

Also, be aggressive in looking over companies, visit brokerage houses and get their readings. Be tough with recruiters. Read a lot, especially biographies of contemporary businessmen and don't overlook sick companies. A bad balance sheet can indicate an opportunity. If you catch those companies at the right moment, you could help turn the tide and end up riding the crest. The good balance sheet is fine for finding "nice, secure jobs."

The main thing is not the job but the man. A 600 young man should spend most of his time understanding his options. "A job is mostly a man understanding himself." That's where the new technology comes in: Unless a young man is used to thinking like that, he's not going to be ready to make his way in the new management environment.

The main thing is to stay on top of the relevant information, and to use it properly. That's what automation is all about, says Mr. Automation.

Staying on top means, first, reading everything you can get your hands on. Diebold reads the

New York Times thoroughly, usually one other city newspaper, two news magazines, all the general 700 ← business magazines, including the *Economist* and The *Wall Street Journal* which are clipped for him. He even considers women's magazines important; you never know when you'll spot something relevant.

Once you get moving, though, the press isn't enough, for usually, if you read about a development in the press, it's too late, really. You've got to develop your own intelligence network so you find out ahead of time and can check for the real meaning of events. Was that promotion really a promotion? Did an announcement of success really signify failure? A young man must have the desire 800 ← to get behind the news, for if he doesn't, says Diebold, he's lost.

The language of the computer man sounds familiar when labeled intelligence network. The young executive with the desire to know what's really true is the one who's going to make the most of the new technology. Soon the machinery will enable the executive to know anything he wants—instantly, the premium then, being on asking the right questions. Since you can't just learn answers anymore, like absorbing the front page of the *Times,* you've got to learn how to ask questions which is what you do when you put together an intelligence network. 900 ←

By and large, management today is not asking the right questions; by getting the hang of it, you'll get a head start. Diebold has loads of fun with this in his speeches and articles such as the *Harvard Business Review* article, where Diebold lashes at conventional managers for "overemphasis on hardware and underemphasis on the design of comprehensive systems." More fundamentally, he writes, the contemporary corporate structure has gotten in the way of the cross-departmental responsibilities and vision needed by the modern executive who asks the right questions. "Executives 1000 are doing little more with ADP than adding speed and ← economy to tasks performed with earlier equipment." Diebold's favorite weapon is the word "change." "Technology means to business not only a change in how you do things but a change in what you do— a change in goals as well as in the route you take to reach goals."

So if you want to be an executive of the future, and make your million, you've got to ask fundamental questions about organizational goals. You must be a broadly educated man, free of 1100 → overspecialization, and continually learning. You must have an intimate knowledge of what people want, for "it is the human desires that shape the opportunities which spawn enterprise." This is crucial because automation means social change more than it means new machines.

Computers are remaking the business environment by removing the constraints on business structure, and making decentralization, for example, unnecessary. The future executive will be able to talk to a computer, literally, and it will feed back information on the total enterprise. Market intelligence, control information, strategy decisions already made, and feedback for change will all be made available instantly. A nearly infinite number 1200 → of options will be at your fingertips.

John Diebold, practicing what he preaches, is constantly asking new questions, seeking out new sources of information, and when you ask him what it's all about he probably will say, "I'm interested in the development of fluid computers which work either with liquid, or air, and animal languages." If that stumps you, don't stop him, or he'll be off on something else.

If you want to bat in Diebold's league you'd better get moving. The new technology creates a vacuum, and it's guys like Diebold who jump in there with solutions. There's a Charles Addams cartoon 1300 → on his office wall which goes like this: As two caterpillars are looking up at a butterfly, one says to the other, "You'll never catch me up in one of those things."

You can either get caught up in it, or like 1350 → millionaire John Diebold, you can go out after it.

——STOP——ASK FOR YOUR TIME——

Record time immediately and answer
the questions on content.

Time_____Sec.	RATE (from table on page 315):	R. _____
No. Correct:_____ (key on page 322)	COMPREHENSION (10% for each correct answer):	C. _____
VI–3	EFFICIENCY (R × C):	E. _____

Record on Progress Chart on page 299

ANSWER THESE QUESTIONS IMMEDIATELY (VI–3)

1. (C   ) John Diebold is known as the _____ Man.

2. (T – F) He recommends that young men try out small business ventures of their own on the college campus.

3. (C   ) The first step in becoming a millionaire is to get a good liberal arts background, including a healthy injection of _____.

4. (T – F) Diebold feels that undergraduate business courses are unessential.

5. (T – F) Mr. Diebold makes a point of knowing what college degrees his men have.

6. (T – F) Diebold predicted that most students go the business route when confronted with the business vs. the management choice.

7. (M. C.) In order to "stay on top," you must first:

_____(1) have a sound background in undergraduate business courses.

_____(2) read everything you can get your hands on.

_____(3) have essential training in public administration school.

_____(4) learn how to make quick decisions on a minimum of information.

8. (T – F) Diebold claims that management today is not asking the right questions.

9. (T – F) Having answers to all the questions asked by associates is considered one of the greatest attributes of success in management.

10. (M. C.) If you want to be an executive of the future, you must:

_____(1) develop a high degree of specialization.

_____(2) exercise great caution in data interpretation.

_____(3) ask questions about organizational goals and processes.

_____(4) memorize complex computer language.

Exercise VI–4

Anger

(Reprinted from the December 1966 *News Release* of the American Medical Association
by permission of the director of magazine relations.)

————————————— **WAIT FOR SIGNAL TO BEGIN READING** —————————————

Anger has been defined as a sudden violent displeasure, often accompanied by a compelling impulse to make some efforts to retaliate. Getting angry or mad, as we sometimes say, is rather a common occurrence with normal individuals. And after a sudden or violent show of deep wrath, perhaps we have tried to rationalize and ask ourselves what it was in our normal mental make-ups that could trigger such a quick change from mental tranquillity to seething anger and indignation. Why did we shout, swear, say harsh things or get involved in actions that we later deeply regretted? Why were we not able to control our emotions better? Is it helpful ↙100 or harmful to us physically, to get mad occasionally and to pop off, blow our stacks, vent our spleens so as to get the anger out of our systems? Do you feel that you get angry or irritated more often or more easily than your associates?

In universities and research foundations throughout the country, scientists have been making some interesting studies, tests and discoveries about anger in humans as well as in animals. Perhaps some of their findings may provide answers to a few of the questions you've pondered concerning anger and ↙200 what it may reveal with regard to your own personality.

If you seldom get angry, does that mean that you have a better-balanced personality than one who does? No, it is perfectly normal for a person to feel anger, resentment or indignation when faced with irritating or provoking situations. In psychiatric studies conducted at Columbia University, hundreds of people were given personality tests, and then purposely subjected to maddening situations of every variety. In virtually every case, well-balanced individuals had a stronger and more pronounced anger reaction than unbalanced or abnormal persons. And other psychiatric studies showed that one of ↘300 the outstanding symptoms of mental unbalance is emotional apathy and lack of concern or feeling. So, if you frequently get burned up or mad when people or circumstances rub you the wrong way, don't fret too much about it—psychologically it's a perfectly normal reaction.

Gripes and pet peeves

What about people who have a multitude of gripes and pet peeves, and are constantly being irritated by little things? Scientists have found that the more small pet peeves a person has—the more minor things he finds irritating—the more likely he ↘400 is to be neurotic. Any normal person will likely suddenly exhibit anger when someone deliberately steps on his toes, yet he isn't likely to be hypersensitive and doesn't have a long list of little gripes. Incidentally, Rockefeller Foundation studies show that neurotic people easily become irritated when they are kidded even lightly, while well-balanced individuals tend to take it in their stride and perhaps appreciate the attention shown them.

Anger studies conducted at Columbia University and Oregon State College show that the average man gets angry and really loses his temper on an average of about six times a week, whereas ↘500 the average woman gets angry enough to blow her top an average of only three times a week or only half as often as men. The study also showed that women got mad most frequently at other people (real or fancied slights, and assorted personal grievances). Men's tempers were more likely to flare up at inanimate objects (such as a flat tire, a missed train, a faulty razor, etc.).

People in some walks of life tend to have shorter tempers than others. Perhaps the most authoritative and widescale study of this matter has been conducted by the late Hulsey Cason, a ↘600 psychologist who surveyed the anger reactions of thousands of persons from all walks of life. He found men and women engaged in professional callings (doctors, lawyers, etc.) tended to be slowest to anger. Farmers and those engaged in related agricultural occupations, ranked next. Businessmen and skilled workers averaged more frequent anger flare-ups and office workers and laborers lost their tempers more often.

Little things make us angry

Studies show that the power of so-called little things to provoke hostility and resentment—to exasperate a man to the point where he gets hot under the collar—cannot be overestimated. This is due to the fact that (1) they occur most frequently, 700 (2) they don't seem little at the time, and (3) like the mosquito, they possess an ability to irritate that is far out of proportion to their size.

Can you usually tell by looking at a person whether he is angry or not? Studies conducted by psychologists at the University of Pennsylvania showed that—contrary to popular belief—anger is one of the hardest emotions to discern purely from facial expression. When pictures of extremely angry individuals were shown to hundreds of college students (including those majoring in psychology) only two percent were able to correctly identify the emo- 800 tion. Indeed, expressions of angry people were most typically misjudged as "bewildered," "pleased," "amazed," or "puzzled."

Barnard College studies show that there are three times a day when people are quickest to anger —during the half-hour period preceding breakfast, lunch, and dinner. The investigators found that almost half of the temper outbursts of the subjects studied occurred during those times. The moral is— don't bring up a controversial subject on an empty stomach because people are most irritable when they're hungry.

Do most people "feel better" after an anger experience and after they had calmed down? In the 900 Barnard College study, only 15 percent of the subjects reported that they actually felt better after an anger experience while two-thirds said it left them feeling irritable and fatigued.

Just what determines the after-effect of getting angry? Studies at the Institute of Psychoanalysis, Chicago, show that it depends largely on whether you give expression to your anger, or whether it is repressed. Tests show that when anger is continually bottled up and consistently denied means of expression it builds up severe tensions which can do actual physical harm.

What should you do when you get angry

Providing for safe and sane means of express- 1000 ing it, working it off, or getting it out of your system, calls for discretion. If you go around punching people in the nose who make you angry, you'll soon end up in trouble. If you blow your top whenever the boss or an associate says something that burns you up, you'll likely soon be out of a job and minus friends. And social relations will suffer if you are not mature enough to control your actions and too frequently allow yourself the luxury of telling off the offending person.

1100 If you desire to be known as a person with emotional maturity, then determine to be alert and on your guard so as to make a special effort to control your anger the next time you see that you are getting upset. Don't be afraid to laugh at yourself and try to put the incident that stirred your ire into its proper perspective.

Also, you can learn to talk to your friends about the anger-provoking incident once you have cooled down a bit, with the idea of getting the incident completely off your chest. It may surprise 1200 you to know that talking rationally with another is an effective escape valve for most resentments; besides, it provides a healthy release of anger-inspiring tensions.

And still another safe and sane means of letting off steam is work and exercise. Maybe a brisk walk, a short run or any reasonable exertion for that matter. The idea is to provide an outlet and to work off your resentments and get them out of your system before they have a chance to fester and build up harmful tension.

Try not to let trifles trip you

Take a positive approach to your angry out- 1300 bursts if they are excessive. Think about your own failures, weaknesses and mistakes before you become too inconsiderate of others.

Remember that things said and done in times of sudden anger have cost much in time, tears, and health.

The following old aphorism has much truth: "The things that burn you up can also burn you 1350 out."

——STOP——ASK FOR YOUR TIME——

Record time immediately and answer
the questions on content.

Time_____Sec.	RATE (from table on page 315):	R. _____
No. Correct:_____ (key on page 330)	COMPREHENSION (10% for each correct answer):	C. _____
VI–4	EFFICIENCY (R × C):	E. _____

Record on Progress Chart on page 299

ANSWER THESE QUESTIONS IMMEDIATELY (VI–4)

1. (C   ) _____ has been defined as a violent displeasure.

2. (T – F) It is not really normal for a person to feel anger when confronted with provoking situations.

3. (C   ) The hypersensitive person with a multitude of gripes is likely to be _____.

4. (T – F) An outstanding symptom of mental unbalance is emotional apathy.

5. (M. C.) Recent anger studies indicate that the average man gets angry about:

_____(1) six times a month.

_____(2) six times a week.

_____(3) once a day.

_____(4) once every other day.

6. (T – F) Women usually get angry more often than men.

7. (T – F) It's easy to tell, by looking at a person's facial expression, whether or not he is angry.

8. (M. C.) People are most susceptible to anger when they are:

_____(1) hungry.

_____(2) teased and taunted.

_____(3) depressed.

_____(4) fatigued.

9. (T – F) Most people do not feel any better after an angry outburst.

10. (T – F) Work and exercise are effective ways of letting off steam.

Exercise VI–5

Mother Nature's Boiler

(*Friends*, February 1974. Reprinted by permission of
Friends magazine, Ceco Publishing Company.)

──────────── WAIT FOR SIGNAL TO BEGIN READING ────────────

Are we sitting on the solution to the energy crisis? Not coal, oil, or gas, but the barely tapped sources of geothermal power?

This is not speculative. In seven countries, including our own, power is being produced in this fashion. Millions, watching the hourly eruptions of Old Faithful in Yellowstone National Park, have gotten a suggestion of the potential. But Old Faithful, glorious as she is, is a pigmy when measured against other geysers that have been harnessed.

Amazing source of power

Steam—dry steam, it is so superheated—is generated when moisture from the earth's surface seeps down to the molten core miles below. The [100] enormous pressure thus created must find an outlet (which must be upward), and it does, whether it be in our many hot springs or in the geysers of Yellowstone or those in Sonoma County in California.

In Sonoma County, the practicality of harnessing this power has been proven. But here there was an abundance of evidence, in the form of geysers, that the core of the earth was an unstoppable percolator. Elsewhere, exploratory drillings will be needed to determine if the solid rock layer can be tapped. The idea is to inject moisture into the earth [200] deep enough to be turned into steam. The heat to do this exists in the magma, or liquid ball of fire at the center of the earth.

The system employed in California is to preserve the natural geyser by tapping into its main channel beneath the surface. There are eight such wells now, furnishing steam to drive turbines that generate more than 300,000 kilowatts. After use, the steam is cooled into water and returned to the earth, ultimately to be converted back into steam for more power.

Fragments of earth

The steam leaves the wellheads at a tempera- [300] ture of about 350°F, but it is not pure steam. On its way, it has picked up fragments of earth. These are removed by whirlers to prevent damage to the turbines. The steam then is fed into the turbines.

Only tests will tell if such steam punctures can be made near such spas as those at Saratoga Springs, N.Y., Mt. Clemens, Mich., and the hot springs in Arkansas, West Virginia, Florida, and other states. One thing is certain: the center of the earth is a gigantic boiler, ready to make steam when man can [400] find a way to feed water to it.

Quite unnoticed by many, a kind of geothermal race among nations is on to find less costly ways of stoking the boiler with moisture. Near Mexicali, Mexico, a research and development program wound up last year with the completion of its first geothermal plant, rated at 75,000 kilowatts.

Geologists believe that the magma has a temperature of 3,000°F. It must be kept in mind, however, that the molten core of the earth also is a ball, and this source of potential energy is available in equal amounts to every nation on earth. It [500] took hundreds of millions of years for the surface to cool to an average depth of 20 miles; so the supply of geothermal energy can be described as being beyond the foresight of man, if not endless.

Only a waterfall, producing hydroelectric power, can generate energy more cheaply. But Mother Nature's boiler is constant, whereas rainfall can limit the productivity of a waterfall.

Noise level

The Geysers, as the group of vents about 90 miles northwest of San Francisco is known, commit one affront to ecology—noise. As the vents are approached, they take on the pitched roar of hundreds [600] of screeching 747s shattering the sky.

Closer to the power plants and well vents scattered over the steep slopes of an extinct volcano the steam shrieks from the earth with enough decibels to compel one to wear special earmuffs, to escape risk of being deafened.

The man who discovered The Geysers, explorer-scientist William Bell Elliott, thought he had come to the gates of hell. That was in 1847.

It was not until 1922 that the first attempt to harness the steam was made. Drillers were successful in tapping the source, but the project had to be [700] abandoned because the dirt and rocks in the steam made it a literal piece of sandpaper. It corroded everything it touched.

Use of stainless steel alloys

Scientists knew the potential, but they were helpless. Whistling Annie, one of the larger wells at the Geysers, raged uncontrolled as it spilled off 10 times the energy of Old Faithful.

Magma Power Company and Thermal Power Company, working jointly and joined later by Earth Energy, a subsidiary of Union Oil Company, had another go at it in 1956. By that time, they had stainless steel alloys—corrosion-resistant—on their side, and the economic feasibility of extracting preheated energy from the bowels of the earth was established.

800
←

The development goes on, headed toward an expected maximum of about one million kilowatts' capacity in the Big Sulphur Creek in Sonoma County.

Besides the United States and Mexico, the other nations in the geothermal rush are Italy, New Zealand, Iceland, the Soviet Union, and Japan. But this is a market no one can corner. To each its own. Simply find where moisture is reaching the stratum overlying the magma, and the kilowatts will catapult.

The first uses of steam

The geothermal field is one in which the U.S. cannot claim a "first." That must go to Italy and the town of Larderello, about 40 miles outside Florence.

900
←

The first written record of this steam field dates from the Romans of 21 centuries ago. The belching fumarole in Larderello inspired Dante to write his "Inferno." With another quill, Elliott might have been able to write similarly of Sonoma County in 1847.

For nearly 70 years, production of electric power generated by the magma-heated steam has been in progress. Near Larderello, Italy, however, the layer of magma is only two miles or so deep. Wells driven to 3,000 feet come close enough for industrial purposes.

1000
←

Italian geologists have estimated, on the basis of present energy, withdrawal from the geothermal areas attainable at that level can be sustained for more than 11,000 years.

Iceland, in 1925, began the use of geothermal steam in homes, and New Zealand has used such steam to generate electricity since the early '50s. The Mexican development, constructed by Toshiba Electric Company of Japan, has been estimated to be drawing less than one percent of its potential. Other taps are in the making.

1100
→

Russian geologists have discovered a great hot-water basin, larger than the Mediterranean Sea, lying beneath Siberia, as unlikely a spot for geothermal heat as one might imagine. The initial output is going into health spas, more experimental drilling, and heating for nearby towns.

Exploratory drilling has been been commenced also in Cameroon, Taiwan, the Dominican Republic, Ethiopia, Israel, Kenya, Nicaragua, Saint Lucia, Turkey, Czechoslovakia, Burundi, Chile, Costa Rica, El Salvador, Guatemala, Jordan, Morocco, Tunisia, Hungary, and the Philippines.

Until the actuality of the energy crisis was made clear in the U.S., development of geothermal power limped along at a dawdling rate, but now it is full speed ahead.

1200
→

In the Salton Sea area of southern California alone, covering only 12,000 acres, it has been calculated that 100 wells could be driven to produce more than a million kilowatts, or more than that of a baker's dozen of Coulee Dams. This evidence that geothermal power is adaptable to man's needs has been seen in this California area.

And there are fringe benefits. The minerals belched in the raw steam, for example, can be made into a brine that can be processed and sold by chemical companies.

1300
→

After desalination, which occurs naturally when steam reverts to water, the fluid would be useful to irrigate arid lands as it settles back to the magma stratum from which it came.

Where will it all end?

Just because man has never drilled 20 miles into the mantle of the earth doesn't say that he couldn't if he had to.

And it would be a good bet.

1350
→

When Mother Nature turns the boiler on, something's cooking.

————STOP————ASK FOR YOUR TIME————

Record time immediately and answer
the questions on content.

Time_____Sec.	RATE (from table on page 315):	R. _____
No. Correct:_____ (key on page 322)	COMPREHENSION (10% for each correct answer):	C. _____
VI–5	EFFICIENCY (R × C):	E. _____

Record on Progress Chart on page 299

ANSWER THESE QUESTIONS IMMEDIATELY (VI–5)

1. (T – F) Fragments of earth in the steam have delayed the development of methods to harness the thermal power.

2. (C   ) The liquid ball of fire at the core of the earth is called the _____.

3. (M. C.) Geologists believe that the earth's core has a temperature of:

_____(1) 2,000°F.

_____(2) 3,000°F.

_____(3) 4,000°F.

_____(4) 5,000°F.

4. (T – F) Geothermal power can generate energy more cheaply than waterfalls.

5. (T – F) William Bell Elliott discovered The Geysers near San Francisco in 1847.

6. (T – F) Any country with financial backing can control the market for geothermal energy.

7. (T – F) The U.S. was first in the world to harness the geothermal fields.

8. (C   ) One of the earliest countries to use geothermal steam in homes in 1925 was _____.

9. (M. C.) In Siberia, geologists have discovered a great hot-water basin larger than the:

_____(1) Mediterranean Sea.

_____(2) Dead Sea.

_____(3) Salton Sea.

_____(4) Adriatic Sea.

10. (T – F) The molten core of the earth is only about 20 miles below the surface in most parts of the world.

Exercise VI–6

Emotions within the Family

(Reprinted from the 1967 pamphlet of the Metropolitan Life Insurance Company
by permission of the publishers.)

———————— WAIT FOR SIGNAL TO BEGIN READING ————————

When we show our children our love and give them our sympathetic understanding, we help to give them a large measure of protection against many of the disturbing conditions so common among adults today. Children need to grow in an environment that provides not only physical nourishment but emotional support as well.

Love and closeness which a child experiences within the family are positive forces that help him to grow strong and self-confident. Faith in his parents, and in the security of his home, helps him to have faith in himself. When parents are reasonably well-adjusted and get along together, they are better 100 able to be sensitive to their children's needs. As they learn to deal maturely with their own problems, parents become freer to give their children emotional support. Of course, "maturing," a process that goes on all through our lives, frequently involves a good measure of self-discipline and self-control. It comes not only with experience but with our sincere efforts to understand ourselves and those around us and to use this understanding to make our lives and our relationships more satisfying.

Family living, of course, is never all sweetness and light, for it is subject to subtle pressures—job and money worries, illnesses, large and small emergencies. 200 And, try as we may, we sometimes cannot help taking out our tensions on the people nearest and dearest to us. Yet, most of us know that it is very disturbing to children when parents quarrel and argue in front of them. Although it would be unrealistic to expect that an argument would never occur in front of the children, it is wise to avoid airing grievances this way. Constantly quarreling before the children is not only very upsetting to them, but makes them unwilling participants in a conflict over which they 300 have no control.

Even the happiest married couple may sometimes give vent to anger and irritation, all a part of living, in the presence of the children. However, constructive efforts on the part of parents to cooperate and resolve their difficulties outweigh these occasional upsets. It is only when quarrels and bickering permeate the atmosphere that children are harmed. Continual conflicts within the family can threaten a child's security, make him fearful, and undermine his chances of developing healthy attitudes. A child's fears and insecurities may show up in so-called problem behavior—nail biting, bed wetting, bad 400 dreams, wakefulness, fear of the dark, perhaps even trouble with school work. Family tensions are certainly not the only source of nervous reactions among children, but they obviously have an influence.

While no parent and no family is perfect, it is worth every effort to make family life as peaceful and cooperative as possible. Problems have a way of shrinking, or even being prevented, when we take the time really to listen to and enjoy our children. Moments for relaxed, light-hearted companionship and sharing of interests may actually have to be squeezed into our busy days and weeks but the time 500 can and should be found, even if it's just a pleasant hour around the family dinner or breakfast table.

Lessons for us all

It is not wise—it's definitely unhealthy—to keep emotional tensions bottled up. Instead we should look for the most reasonable way to work them out. For some of us, just talking over our problems fully and freely with a sympathetic friend or adviser helps to clear the air. It can often help to relieve any feelings of guilt we have about our own disagreeable thoughts and feelings when we discover similar ones in others. This is one of the values of group 600 discussion and study groups—especially among parents. These sessions give people a chance to exchange ideas and viewpoints which can lead to keener insights and better understandings.

It is important to learn how to handle our emotional tensions—to know and to accept our physical and emotional limitations. All this is easier said than done, but understanding is the first step. As we reach a better understanding of the common emotional stresses and are able to recognize them instead of trying to ignore them, we shall begin to see a reduction in those illnesses that strike out at 700 us through our own inner conflicts.

We can all, in our own way, practice an important bit of preventive medicine by applying this knowledge to our children. Childhood is not the happy, carefree time of life we may like to imagine it on looking back. Most of us have forgotten or repressed many of our childhood tragedies because they were too painful for us to remember, but we can help our children by learning to become more sensitive to their needs and to see, insofar as it is possible, that they are free from excessive worry and tension. 800 ←

It is not emotions that are at fault when we refer to emotional problems. After all, an emotion, whether pleasant or unpleasant, is simply a person's response to his understanding and judgment of a fact or a situation as he sees it. It is not our job to help our children hide their feelings; it is our job to help them to express and use their emotions constructively.

When we're upset or angry, we can try to blow off steam or work off our feelings with physical exercise. Pitching into some activity, like working in the garden; taking a long walk; playing a game of 900 ← tennis or going in for some other sport not only helps to relieve anger but makes it easier to face and handle irritating problems more calmly. (Besides, getting some regular exercise is a great way to keep yourself in good physical condition.)

It helps to get it off your chest sometimes by confiding worries to a sympathetic friend. When what appears to be a serious problem starts to get you down, it's wise to discuss it with your family physician, or your clergyman, or with an understanding member of your own family. Often another person 1000 ← can help you to see your problem in a new light. This may be the first step toward a constructive solution. If your problems seem to be getting out of hand, your own doctor may want to recommend a specialist, or refer you to a guidance clinic or a family service agency.

Many of us get upset about circumstances which are beyond our control. Sometimes we even try to make people over to suit our own ideals and then feel frustrated or let down when we find that this 1100 → cannot be done. We can look for the best in others while realizing that nobody is faultless.

When you feel that you are going around in circles with a problem or a worry, try to divert yourself. As simple a thing as going to the movies, reading a story, or visiting a friend can help you out of a rut. And there's no harm in running away from a painful situation long enough to catch your breath and regain the composure you need to come back and face the problem. When possible and practical, a change of scene can give you a new perspective. 1200 → There are times when we all need to "escape"— even if it's just a letup from routine. Certainly everyone needs and should have a few hours to call his own, away from immediate cares and worries. For some of us this might well mean a few moments just to be alone.

If you should need medication, your physician may prescribe medicine which temporarily helps you to relax without affecting your mental agility. But avoid self-medication. There are different types of sedatives and tranquilizers available for various purposes. Only a doctor can usually know and prescribe the amount and type that's right for the individual person.

1300 → A person's physical condition affects his outlook on life. There are no simple solutions to the problems of life which cause undue stress and tension, but if you keep yourself physically fit, you will have more zest for living and be able to take 1350 → stress and handle everyday tensions more easily.

——STOP——ASK FOR YOUR TIME——

Record time immediately and answer
the questions on content.

Time_____Sec.	RATE (from table on page 315):	R. _____
No. Correct:_____ (key on page 330)	COMPREHENSION (10% for each correct answer):	C. _____
VI–6	EFFICIENCY (R × C):	E. _____

Record on Progress Chart on page 299

ANSWER THESE QUESTIONS IMMEDIATELY (VI–6)

1. (T – F) "Maturing" is a process that goes on all through our lives.

2. (C   ) Constant _____ between the parents is very upsetting to the children.

3. (M. C.) The first step in learning to handle our emotional tensions is that of:

_____(1) understanding.

_____(2) consultation with an expert.

_____(3) saying the opposite of what we feel.

_____(4) learning to keep them under control.

4. (T – F) It is probably wiser to keep our emotional tensions to ourselves and not share them with others.

5. (T – F) Childhood was a happy, carefree time of life for most of us.

6. (T – F) Expressing your emotions means that you have emotional problems.

7. (C   ) Our job is to help our children express their _____ constructively.

8. (T – F) When we're angry, a good means of outlet is physical exercise.

9. (M. C.) When we are confronted with a painful situation or problem, usually the best solution is to:

_____(1) consult an expert.

_____(2) escape—try to divert yourself.

_____(3) take tranquilizers.

_____(4) become involved in happy family relationships.

10. (T – F) A person's physical condition affects his outlook on life.

Exercise VI–7

Edison and Electricity

(Reprinted from a pamphlet of the same name
by permission of the General Electric Company.)

— WAIT FOR SIGNAL TO BEGIN READING —

New Year's Eve in Menlo Park

It was New Year's Eve, 1879. A strange air of expectancy and excitement gripped the New Jersey village of Menlo Park. Nearly 3,000 persons restlessly milled about the streets, and crowded close to the piazza of Mr. Edison's laboratory. Some had driven as far as 20 miles in carriages and wagons, but most had come by special trains run by the Pennsylvania Railroad for the occasion. They were there to witness the first public demonstration of Edison's wonderful new light.

As the early winter twilight deepened into darkness, the murmur of the throng was hushed in ⮐100 anticipation. Inside the laboratory, a deft stroke of a finger made 60 lamps, placed on poles up and down the snow-covered street, spring to light among the bare branches of the trees. A ripple of involuntary applause ran through the audience. One old farmer was heard to remark, "We-ell sir, it's a pretty fair sight, but danged if I kin see how ye git the red-hot hairpin in the bottle!"

In the days and weeks that followed, Menlo Park became a kind of Mecca for the intelligently interested and the merely curious. Farm folk and city folk, scientists and businessmen, came nightly in ⮐200 ever increasing numbers to see the "Edison lights."

An indifferent public

But widespread public acceptance of incandescent illumination was extremely slow—or so it seemed to the Edison group. For some time Menlo Park was the only place in the world where a complete incandescent system was on display. Relatively few, therefore, were able to see it in operation. Even the most glowing newspaper description could not arouse a general public interest in the new lighting.

Then too, there was opposition from gas and arc-light companies. As it became apparent that the new lamp threatened to displace the older illuminants ⮐300 this opposition increased. On at least two occasions attempts were made to discredit the new system while it was being demonstrated before municipal officials. A member of one such visiting party managed to short-circuit a part of the system at Menlo by means of a piece of wire running up a sleeve, over his shoulder, and down the other sleeve. Special watchers, appointed by Edison, caught the erstwhile saboteur in the act. When the fact leaked out that the man had an interest in a gas company, public ⮐400 sentiment in favor of the electric light was greatly enhanced.

Among the city officials who made the pilgrimage to Menlo Park was a delegation representing New York's Board of Aldermen. The outcome of their visit was an agreement by which Edison was to install a trial lighting system in an area on lower Manhattan—an area soon to become famous as Edison's "First District." The Edison Illuminating Company of New York was formed to do this job. The Wizard was now committed to making an historic step; his dream of "great cities alight from central stations" was coming ever closer to reality.

The task begins

500→ Putting the project on a profitable commercial footing proved to be a Herculean task—a far greater undertaking than the impatient New Yorkers realized. Plans for the installation were complete in essential detail, but devices had to be invented, developed, and built as the need for them arose. Necessity was the mother of these inventions —and Edison was the father.

Of necessity, Edison became a manufacturer. "There was nothing we could buy," he related, "or that anyone could make for us." So new companies were formed by Edison men to supply the new devices.

Since the Illuminating Company was reluctant ⮐600 to manufacture them, Edison formed a lamp company and began producing lamps in one of his old Menlo Park buildings. Although the first lamps cost about $1.25 to make, Edison offered to supply all the lamps required by the Illuminating Company at 40¢ *apiece!* He was sure that he could produce them at a profit by effecting economies in production methods and by mass production.

The lamp factory was moved to larger quarters in Harrison, New Jersey, in 1880, when about 30,000 lamps were produced, at a cost of nearly $1.10 each. As production rose in the next few years, costs went ⮐700 down. "The fourth year, I got the cost down to 37¢," related the inventor, "and with a 3¢ profit per lamp, made up in one year all the money I'd lost previously. I finally got it down to 22¢, sold them for 40¢, and they were made by the millions. Whereupon the Illuminating Company thought it a very lucrative business and bought us out," he recalled.

Jumbo and the Mary Ann

One of Edison's greatest triumphs in dealing with electrification of the First District was his development of a suitable generator. The project required electric current in undreamed of quantities. Existing generators were far too small and inefficient.

<u>800</u> ←

The Wizard began by studying the design of dynamos then in use. Then he proceeded to fashion one unlike any of the others. It had two huge parallel magnets which made it resemble the Roman numeral II, and earned it the nickname *Long-Waisted Mary Ann*. Though the design violated accepted principles, it worked. What's more, it was nearly 90 percent efficient.

The famous Jumbo dynamo was developed and exhibited at the Paris Electrical Exposition in 1881. The bipolar Mary Ann design was coupled with a huge 150-horsepower steam engine. Where previous generators had been driven by complicated belting and shafting, the Jumbo's engine was linked directly to the dynamo. Its size alone caused people to gape. It weighed 27 tons and was capable of lighting 1,200 incandescent lamps.

<u>900</u> ←

No one knew what to expect when the Jumbo was first tested one winter's night at Menlo Park. Heretofore the speed of stationary engines was rarely more than 60 revolutions per minute, but this machine was designed to turn up 700 rpm, and at a much higher steam pressure than most engines.

The shop in which the machine was set up stood on top of a shale hill. Edison amusingly recalled that at 300 revolutions "the whole hill shook under her," and at 700 rpm "you should have seen her run! Why, every time the connecting rod went up, she tried to lift the whole hill with her!"

<u>1000</u> ←

After this harrowing experience, the Jumbos were not run at more than 250 rpm, which was really all that Edison had wanted anyway.

"65" becomes a Mecca

Early in 1881, the Edison Electric Light Company leased an ornate brownstone mansion at 65 Fifth Avenue, New York, for an office. The house was an ideal place for showing off the lights in everyday operation, and also provided a headquarters from which Edison could closely supervise the many activities connected with the First District lighting installation.

<u>1100</u> →

For the next four years, "65" was a beehive of activity, day and night. Every day after dark, thousands of visitors came to see, to ask questions, and to marvel.

As they had at Menlo, Edison and his men worked with utter disregard of time. But all who worked at "65" remarked about the wonderful spirit of comradeship which existed there. They were all pioneers together, working for a common cause, all enthusiastic believers in the electric light. Edison himself was never closer to his men than during this period of their work together.

<u>1200</u> →

The year 1881 was one of tremendous strain and back-breaking toil for Edison. The host of new and important business interests had to be tended, and the First District installation demanded much of his time. Somehow he managed to keep up his research, taking out about 89 patents that year. In addition, he built experimentally the world's first fullsize electric railway at Menlo.

Success

By the end of the following year, the First District had become a profitable success. Edison had achieved his goal. He had subdivided electric current when others said it couldn't be done. He had invented a practical incandescent lamp where hundreds had failed and had made an efficient dynamo. He had planned, built and operated a complete electrical system powered from a central station.

<u>1300</u> →

<u>1350</u> →

——STOP——ASK FOR YOUR TIME——

Record time immediately and answer the questions on content.

Time_____Sec.	RATE (from table on page 315):	R. _____
No. Correct:_____ (key on page 322)	COMPREHENSION (10% for each correct answer):	C. _____
VI–7	EFFICIENCY (R × C):	E. _____

Record on Progress Chart on page 299

ANSWER THESE QUESTIONS IMMEDIATELY (VI–7)

1. (C   ) The occasion of all the excitement on New Year's Eve, 1879, at Menlo Park was the first public demonstration of Edison's new _____.

2. (T – F) The public accepted this new method of illumination very rapidly.

3. (C   ) Attempts to sabotage some of Edison's demonstrations were made by representatives of the _____ companies.

4. (T – F) The first installation of electric lights made necessary the invention of many additional control devices.

5. (T – F) Edison manufactured his first lamps at a great financial loss.

6. (M. C.) Edison did not develop a profit margin on the sale of his lamps until:

_____(1) the second year of manufacture.

_____(2) the fourth year of manufacture.

_____(3) the sixth year of manufacture.

_____(4) the tenth year of manufacture.

7. (M. C.) The Jumbo dynamo was designed to operate at how many revolutions per minute?

_____(1) 60

_____(2) 350

_____(3) 700

_____(4) 1,000

8. (T – F) The mansion at 65 Fifth Avenue was purchased as a home for Mr. Edison and his family.

9. (T – F) Edison was a rather autocratic supervisor and never got to know any of his men very well.

10. (T – F) By the end of 1882, Edison had achieved his goal of subdividing electric current.

Exercise VI–8

Crusader in the Pine Barrens
by GLEN EVANS

(Reprinted from the November 1974 issue of *Dynamic Maturity*
by permission of the editor and the author.)

———————— **WAIT FOR SIGNAL TO BEGIN READING** ————————

Elizabeth Woodford at age 59 has absolutely no problem in finding valuable and satisfying ways to use her time and talents. Quite the contrary. She calls herself "a sort of mishmash of a person—part naturalist, part botanist, part conservationist." She could add that she also is a top-notch nature photographer, a teacher, a writer, a rescuer of wild birds and animals, and a compelling lecturer. In addition to all this, she's a wife, mother, and grandmother.

The focal point for all of Elizabeth Woodford's activities and goals is her "home country," New Jersey's Pine Barrens, a wildland of swamps, lakes, and 100 pine woods that still cover around 1.3 million acres (more than 2,000 square miles)—a strange and peacefully quiet place to find in an industrial state. The term "barrens" is misleading, coming from the fact that the loose sandy soil isn't suited to conventional crop farming. But nature finds the Barrens ideal for many other things. This is an amazing land of pyxie moss, pitch pines, wild orchids, cranberries, sundews, bog asphodel, and at least 400 other varieties of plants. It is a region of more than 150 species of wildlife: Birds, deer, muskrats, raccoons, harmless snakes, frogs, rabbits, foxes, 200 flying squirrels, and even an occasional beaver lodge.

Living with nature

She and her husband Jim, a vocational agriculture instructor, are working to keep at least part of the Barrens that way—undeveloped and natural, preserving the unique and ecologically important character of this land. The Woodfords are part of that environment. They live in an unpretentious house beside Cedar Run Lake, near Medford Township, and use their 130 acres as a wildlife refuge and outdoor classroom to teach classes in Environmental Nature. Scattered around the grounds are the pens of an animal "orphanage" where orphaned and injured birds and animals are cared for until they 300 can be returned to their wild habitat. "We're careful not to make pets of them," says Mrs. Woodford. "They have to learn to take care of themselves, not depend on us, if they are to survive in the world."

"It's a wonderful place to live," Elizabeth Woodford told me when I interviewed her at her home. "But there's so much to do and to be done." As we talked, she sat bottle-feeding two tiny 8-day-old raccoons whose mother had been killed by a car. 400 Later she showed me her menagerie, which included as a permanent resident a large red-tailed hawk which can never fly again because one wing was shot away by a hunter's bullets. As "temporaries" there were a family of small-fry possums, a treeful of young raccoons, and a baby gray squirrel. These are only a few of the orphaned and wounded skunks, owls, fawns, foxes, and others that have received another chance at life in the Barrens through the ministrations of the Woodfords.

"But there's so much to be done," Elizabeth Woodford repeats. She was thinking of the inward 500 push of development. The Pine Barrens lie in south central New Jersey just a few miles east of one of America's major thoroughfares—the Jersey Turnpike—35 miles from the Philadelphia-Camden complex and only slightly more than 100 miles from New York.

The threats to the Pine Barrens come from many directions. As one of the largest tracts of "open," relatively unsettled areas in the industrial northeast, aviation planners see the Barrens as an ideal location for a gigantic jet airport. One such project, a supersonic jetport, was defeated by the active opposition of conservationists some years ago, but other proposals for air bases, and industrial 600 complexes keep popping up. The rivers and lakes among the piney woods, as well as the expanses of land, are attracting the attention of developers who have bought up large tracts to be bulldozed and shaped into "new towns."

As environmentalists see it, such large-scale "development" could bring ecological disaster to this unique wilderness. They point out that the natural balance of sandy soil, water, vegetation, and wildlife in the area is a very delicate one. Stripping away the pine woods, for example, could set in motion destructive forces, such as erosion, that would quickly 700 degrade the character of the land, lakes, and rivers, and would mean the doom of much of the wildlife which now thrives in the Barrens.

Getting the message across

A sturdy, brown-haired woman of extraordinary zeal, Elizabeth Woodford says, "It's through our various activities—all of them—that Jim and I hope to get the Barrens' story across."

These activities are numerous, indeed. For some time the Woodfords have been active in the movement, presently being conducted by the Jersey Shore Audubon Society, to set aside a major portion of the forest land as the Pine Barrens National Monument and Reserve. This plan would embrace the heart of the forest, nearly 550 square miles.

800 ←

Mrs. Woodford believes that if enough people could *see* what the Barrens are really like, and the kind of wildlife they support, they would understand why this unique area is worth saving. Toward this purpose she has become a skilled photographer and has taken thousands of beautiful color slides of the plant and animal life and the scenery of her beloved Barrens.

"In the beginning I pestered several camera shop owners for information," she says, "but mostly I learned by trial and error." She now expertly uses a fine Swiss camera and has an assortment of special 900 ← lenses and lighting equipment. But far more important than the camera is the "eye" she has developed for spotting natural subjects, be it a bird, flower, or scene, and the skill to dramatize it on film. Most of her photos are taken on hikes around the Barrens, and she points out that her subjects always are photographed in their natural setting, "as they are," a process that sometimes requires infinite patience to wait for just the right moment to snap the shutter.

These photographs—thousands of them—have become part of a series of 12 illustrated lectures 1000 ← that Mrs. Woodford has presented to conventions, schools, clubs, and study groups.

As if all this wasn't enough to keep her busy, Mrs. Woodford writes a weekly column, "Wild and Free," in the Burlington County *Times,* teaches an evening adult education class on the Pine Barrens at two separate county high schools, and conducts field trips and tours for groups at the Cedar Run Wildlife Sanctuary.

Then there are the many conservation and natural science groups in which she is active—among them the Medford, N.J., Conservation Commission, the Burlington County Natural Sciences Club, Phila- 1100 → delphia's Botanical Club, the New Jersey Audubon Society, and the Federation of Conservationists.

Elizabeth Woodford's crusade is no recent development. Even as a girl she carried home wounded wild animals and birds, and the natural sciences were her favorite subjects in school; she graduated from the Barnes Horticultural School in Merion, Pa. "I spent most of my spare time outdoors, in the company of my creature friends," she says. For almost 30 years now she has been spreading the message about the uniqueness and ecological importance of the Pine Barrens in every way that she can.

1200 →

As I was leaving the Pine Barrens, I thought about the chances of saving this land of pitch pine, sand, and tea-colored cedar water—of mysterious swamps and green shadows, curly fern grass and bright-colored tree frogs. I thought about what Elizabeth Woodford had told me about the delicate fabric of this land in which the strands of plant and animal life are interwoven and interdependent and can so easily be disrupted and destroyed by works of man. There's no doubt that the Pine Barrens are in jeopardy—just as are so many parts of our beautiful country. But I'm cheered by the fact that, like Elizabeth Woodford, there are people who have 1300 → no intention of abandoning their crusades. "There's simply too much important work remaining to be done," she says. "I plan to keep at it for many more years. We have the Pine Barrens today. But we want to save them for those who follow us 1350 → tomorrow."

——STOP——ASK FOR YOUR TIME——

Record time immediately and answer the questions on content.

Time_____Sec.	RATE (from table on page 315):	R. _____
No. Correct:_____ (key on page 330)	COMPREHENSION (10% for each correct answer):	C. _____
VI–8	EFFICIENCY (R × C):	E. _____

Record on Progress Chart on page 299

ANSWER THESE QUESTIONS IMMEDIATELY (VI–8)

1. (T – F) Elizabeth Woodford claims that she hasn't enough to do.

2. (T – F) The Woodfords keep many small animals around their home as pets.

3. (T – F) The Pine Barrens are located within fifty miles of a large city.

4. (C   ) The conservationists organized a few years ago to defeat a proposal to build a large _____.

5. (T – F) Mrs. Woodford uses many special lenses and lighting equipment for her nature photography.

6. (C   ) She believes the best way to convince people of the values of the Barrens is by showing them through _____.

7. (C   ) Which of the following was not mentioned among Mrs. Woodford's activities?

_____(1) Illustrated lectures series.

_____(2) Weekly newspaper column.

_____(3) T.V. series on wildlife.

_____(4) High school field trips.

8. (T – F) The author really was convinced that the Pine Barrens were in jeopardy.

9. (T – F) The Woodfords are not in favor of setting aside 550 square miles of their land as a Pine Barrens National Monument.

10. (M. C.) Mrs. Woodford has been an active ecologist for about _____ years.

_____(1) 50

_____(2) 30

_____(3) 10

_____(4)   5

Exercise VI–9

Malignant Neglect
by MARK WEXLER

(Reprinted from the August-September 1980 issue of *National Wildlife*
by permission of the editors—© 1980 by the National Wildlife Federation.)

—— **WAIT FOR SIGNAL TO BEGIN READING** ——

State of siege!

It looked like a truce had been declared in rural Jackson Township, New Jersey, earlier this year, but actually the community was in a state of siege. Residents were hanging tattered white flags from their doorsteps to signal tank trucks whenever their homes ran out of water. The trucks were deployed as an emergency measure after tests showed the town's underground water supplies had been poisoned by buried chemical wastes. "We moved here from New York City so the children could live in the country," said Susan McCarthy, a young housewife. "Now, we're afraid they might get cancer." 100 ←

Nine hundred miles away, in Memphis, Tennessee, Evonda Pounds feared for the safety of her children, too. Scientists could not explain why her neighbors had been hit by a rash of maladies, including 36 cases of cancer in 74 homes. The houses had been built atop an old industrial dump, but some officials seemed anxious to downplay the possibility of any connection.

Across the country, in Riverside, California, Rickie Clark was similarly plagued by a nagging question. It began when she learned that her daughters had been playing for months in the polluted runoff from a poisonous dump. "I keep wondering," said 200 ← Clark, "if my kids will be able to have normal kids of their own someday."

The fears and frustrations of these three mothers are not all that unusual these days. In recent years, thousands of Americans have been exposed to dangerous levels of poison from chemical wastes buried or dumped by companies that don't know what else to do with them. The scope of the problem is staggering, but the individuals affected by it often cannot get government or industry to take action. "When chemicals are spilled on, or buried in dry land," says attorney Ken Kamlet of the National Wildlife 300 ← Federation, "it can be difficult to prove that a health hazard exists. Local authorities may not have money for testing, the state may not have any waste program at all and federal funds may not be available unless there is evidence that a hazard definitely exists."

This year alone, some 60 million tons of hazardous wastes will be generated by 750,000 U.S. companies. Only about ten percent of those wastes will be disposed of properly, even though some of them are suspected of causing cancer and a variety 400 → of other ailments. Just as disturbing, no one knows the amount—or the location, for that matter—of all the dangerous wastes buried in years gone by.

These poisons are a legacy of America's synthetic life style, and they exist quite apart from the old-fashioned municipal "dumps" that have caused so many problems over the years. Some of them are by-products from the manufacture of such familiar consumer items as hair dye, paints, acrylic clothing and even toilet soap. Others, like polychlorinated ciphenyls (PCB's), asbestos, cadmium, mercury and lead have long been important industrial materials. Still others, like DDT, dieldrin and mirex, have been 500 → agricultural mainstays. Many of these substances were used in enormous quantities for decades before their hazards to human health were revealed. More recently, U.S. laws clamping down on air and water pollution only increased the flow of dangerous chemicals into the earth.

No firm plans

A year ago, *National Wildlife* reported that the U.S. did not have any firm plans for cleaning up its poisonous dumps. Since then, the Carter Administration has declared the problem a top priority but the overburdened U.S. Environmental Protection Agency (EPA) has barely begun to make the commitment stick. In 1976, Congress ordered 600 → the agency to develop a "national road map" showing where all the dangerous wastes are generated, and where they are being buried. Last spring, the EPA finally decided how to carry out that order.

The agency's new rules require all manufacturers to fill out a report every time a shipment of hazardous wastes leaves their facilities. That report must designate where the wastes are going, and verification must be filed with the EPA by the owner of the disposal site after the wastes are accepted. In addition, all disposal sites must be certified "safe" by the agency. According to the EPA, that means 700 → the sites must be lined with clay or some other impermeable material, and they must be located at least 500 feet from any water source. Owners of these sites must assume up to $5 million liability for any damages that might occur.

Underground movement

The EPA's new rules should bring about 70 percent of our annual production of toxic wastes under control, but it will be at least five more years before that happens. More ominously, little or nothing will be done about the enormous accumulations of chemical garbage already in the ground.

At least half of all Americans get their water [800] from underground aquifers, yet no one knows how badly many of these supplies have been poisoned. Once groundwater is tainted, it may stay that way for years to come. Not long ago, some residents near Pensacola, Florida, complained that their water "tasted bad." Officials traced the problem to fertilizer wastes buried 75 years earlier!

Prior to World War II, burial was considered a perfectly acceptable way to get rid of just about anything. But the chemical wastes produced during the postwar industrial boom presented a new problem as they did not easily decompose when they were buried. Eventually, the places where many of them [900] had been dumped were covered over and made into "landfills" out of sight, out of mind. Houses and schools were frequently built on top of them. It was only a matter of time before some of the poisons seeped down to contaminate groundwater.

Sometimes the toxins go up, not down. Two years ago, festering chemicals buried 30 years earlier began oozing out of the ground in the notorious Love Canal area near Niagara Falls, New York. The cost of cleaning up that neighborhood, and taking care of all the families there, will eventually run into the [1000] hundreds of millions of dollars. Who is responsible for paying those costs? In the past year, several bills have been introduced in Congress to cover the cleanup of all future "Love Canals," as well as any abandoned commercial waste-disposal facilities. These proposed "superfunds," which range from $500 million to $1.6 billion, would be contributed by both industry and government. At this writing, none of them is expected to pass this year.

New poisons

Meanwhile, new poisons are being generated all the time, and state officials are having trouble locating communities that will accept disposal facilities. [1100] "Everybody wants them removed from their neighborhoods, but nobody is willing to have them put down nearby," says EPA assistant administrator Eckardt C. Beck. In Minnesota, for example, state authorities received a large EPA grant to establish a "safe" landfill where chemical wastes manufactured all over the state would be taken. More than a dozen Minnesota communities were selected for this site, but at each of them, citizens voted down the plan. Finally, the state gave up and returned the grant money to the EPA.

Many companies have resorted to desperate measures to jettison their toxics. Some truck wastes [1200] thousands of miles to phantom dump sites. A number have even shipped poisons abroad. "Some of the stuff is being buried on plant property, some of it is being dumped in the woods!" says one North Carolina solid-waste official. "They're getting rid of it any way they can."

The problem is particularly acute in the Northeast, where a large percentage of the nation's hazardous wastes are generated. "The word is out that there are a lot of trees they can dump behind in New England," says Dennis Roberts, attorney general of Rhode Island. Adds New Hampshire's attorney general, Thomas Rath: "We're standing by while [1300] criminals haul poison into our state." Earlier this year, Rath's agents uncovered more than a half dozen illegal dumping grounds in just one small area. "God only knows what's being dumped in the woods!" he exclaims. But even when people do know, [1350] there frequently is not much they can do about it.

——STOP——ASK FOR YOUR TIME——

Record time immediately and answer
the questions on content.

Time_____Sec.	RATE (from table on page 315):	R. _____
No. Correct:_____ (key on page 322)	COMPREHENSION (10% for each correct answer):	C. _____
VI–9	EFFICIENCY (R × C):	E. _____

Record on Progress Chart on page 299

ANSWER THESE QUESTIONS IMMEDIATELY (VI–9)

1. (M. C.) In New Jersey, residents had to have water delivered to their homes because:

_____(1) water supplies had been poisoned by buried chemical waste.

_____(2) water supplies had been depleted because of recent drought.

_____(3) a main water line had broken.

_____(4) the water had not been properly purified.

2. (T – F) Government and industries are often slow to take action in the chemical waste problem.

3. (T – F) Many of the hazardous wastes people are exposed to are suspected of causing cancer.

4. (C   ) The governmental agency put in charge of the problem of cleaning up poisonous dumps is the

_____.

5. (T – F) Buried waste materials may not create problems until many years later.

6. (C   ) One problem is that many chemical wastes are buried but do not _____.

7. (M. C.) One of the most notorious toxic waste problems occurred in:

_____(1) Death Valley, California.

_____(2) Poison Spider, Texas.

_____(3) Toxin, Tennessee.

_____(4) Love Canal, New York.

8. (T – F) Because of the increased awareness by industries of the toxic waste problem, no new poisons are being created.

9. (T – F) Large grants of money have solved the toxic waste disposal problem in some states.

10. (T – F) The writer is optimistic that this problem may be corrected very soon and that people will feel more safe.

Exercise VI–10

Concepts of Communication

(Reprinted from Chapter IX, *Guidebook for Prospective Teachers*,
Ohio State University Press, 1948 by permission of the authors.)

―――― **WAIT FOR SIGNAL TO BEGIN READING** ――――

Communication

You can get a hint concerning the higher purposes of communication by looking at the word itself. Communication is much more closely related to the word community than it is to any of the instruments of communication which man has created, such as language, radio, and pictorial or dramatic art. This point suggests that you will miss the deeper meaning of communication if you allow yourself to think only of the machinery of communication. You might get a further hint if you really examine the meaning of the word *community*.

What is a community?

You probably think of houses and streets full 100 of people at first, but as you think of modern means of transportation you remember that many teachers teach in consolidated schools and have to think of their community in a broader sense. We have come to think of community boundaries more in terms of "time of travel" than in terms of linear distance. Modern research in aeronautics makes it possible to travel to any part of the world within a few days' time. The major cities of the world are connected by many air lines that make them only a few hours' flying time apart. Whether we wish it or not, we find 200 ourselves drawn into a world community.

Breadth of community

Our means of communication today enable us to hear people in distant lands as they speak, and our recent progress in television, such as Telstar, enables us to see events in other parts of the world as they happen. All this makes us realize that linear boundaries no longer define a community. We need to look for a better definition. To have a community there must be something in common. Above all there must be some common values and some common ways of living. One has a true 300 community only to the degree that men enjoy common understandings and work together for common ends. A world community can be achieved only as men of different races and nationalities come to some common understandings, recognize some common problems, and work together for some

common ends. The physical community must be supplemented by a community of mind and spirit. An insane asylum cannot become a community without becoming sane, for by community one always means a community of mind. One must have mind or spirit to build common understandings with others. Unless one can communicate his meaningful 400 experiences to others, he cannot enter a community of understanding with them.

Purpose of communication

The primary purpose of all communication, then, is to build increasingly more community of mind in the world. All the machinery of communication whose creation has been sponsored by a democratic state comes into its own, only when it is consciously employed to this end, namely, the end of building community of mind. It is in this enterprise that you must learn to take your central satisfactions. It is this purpose which must determine the quality of your employment. Perhaps it is desirable to take a more deliberate look at what all of this 500 means.

All communication, if it is really communication, brings about some community of mind. Even when a man swears at you or threatens you, he establishes a temporary community of mind. You share the thought that he has expressed and you have had a momentary meeting of minds. But such a getting together is very much like a meeting of the match and powder keg. Communication moves between two extremes. Sometimes it is used primarily to inflate the ego, and the speaker indulges himself 600 with the momentary sympathies of his audience; but unless all that is said has been designed to benefit the hearers as well as the speaker, the delightful meeting will result in a delayed explosion. Language, therefore, when used in the wrong spirit, brings community of mind into being for a moment in such a way as to make subsequent understanding almost impossible.

Severing communication channels

Of course civilized people do not, as a rule, swear at one another. They have more refined and more subtle ways of cutting people down to such a size that they can more conveniently see over their heads. Probably some of the members of this class <u>700</u> have such smooth techniques along this line that they can combine a word, an inflection, and a look so artfully that no one but the person for whom the remark is intended will object, but that one person may want to die or commit murder. It is psychologically necessary for some people who become the victims of certain attitudes to go around setting themselves up by cutting other people down. Even the best persons are a little guilty of this kind of behavior at times. The extent to which a person allows himself to indulge in this pastime determines in large measure the extent to which he can <u>800</u> communicate with others. He soon finds that the doors at every entrance are being quietly shut in his face, and that day by day he is standing more and more alone. An invisible wall builds itself around such a person. The lines of communication leading into and from the world in which he lives mysteriously disintegrate. No loud talk, no cursing of his luck or of others, and no grant of power can enable him to penetrate this spiritually suffocating barrier to communication which he has brought into being by his attitude. <u>900</u>

What, then, is this quality which communication must have in order that it may serve the larger purposes of deepening sympathies and broadening understandings? Perhaps the problem can best be approached by recalling that every man is different from every other man. Since each person differs from everyone else, if people associate it is as inevitable as night following day that they will differ with one another. However inevitable this situation may be, it is true that when people differ they often make that fact cause for offense. When people "beg to differ with you" in a cocky or belittling way, you are <u>1000</u> almost sure to take offense. Some take offense when differences are expressed respectfully or even with humility.

Odd, is it not, that one should feel called upon to apologize for the fact that he is different from one, that he differs with another. If persons take offense, even polite offense, because one grew up with red hair, another with black skin, one as a Republican,

and another as a Democrat, they are taking offense at differences rather than taking a sympathetic interest in differences with others. They are making it difficult <u>1100</u> to communicate with one another.

Scientific attitudes

A look at the method and spirit of science also gives a feeling for the spirit of communication which builds community of mind. Regardless of race, creed, language, or nationality, the true scientist is interested in, sympathetic to, and open-minded about, the sincere and honest opinions of any other scientist whose thinking comes within his field of work. Differences of opinion are exchanged, cross-fertilization takes place, and new ideas spring up where only old ones grew before. They build an even broader community of mind, and science grows apace. Tolerance and <u>1200</u> open-mindedness prevail in order that conflicting opinions can be exchanged and men may grow in wisdom.

The spirit, therefore, of your personal and private conversations as well as of your public or professional exchange of ideas may or may not be marked by democratic qualities. If, as a consequence of attempts at communication, more community of mind, more common understandings, have been brought into being, then may you be assured that human communication is serving a purpose which justifies the invention of ingenious devices for extending the blessings of communication among men.

Communication—a two-way road

<u>1300</u> As time passes you must rate yourself in two different roles. As the actor playing the active role of communicating, how well can you call this spirit of ethical community into being? As audience, how well can you foster this spirit in the way you participate in any enterprise of which you may be <u>1350</u> a part?

——STOP——ASK FOR YOUR TIME——

Record time immediately and answer
the questions on content.

Time_____Sec.

No. Correct:_____
(key on page 330)

VI–10

RATE (from table on page 315):

COMPREHENSION (10% for each correct answer):

EFFICIENCY (R × C):

R. _____

C. _____

E. _____

Record on Progress Chart on page 299

ANSWER THESE QUESTIONS IMMEDIATELY (VI–10)

1. (T – F) The primary purpose of communication is economic.

2. (　C　) These authors believe that basic to understanding communication is the understanding of the word _____.

3. (T – F) They state that community boundary lines today are thought of in terms of traveling time.

4. (T – F) The idea is presented that a community implies common standards of speech, religion, money, and politics.

5. (　C　) Basic to any community in the true sense, these authors believe there must exist a community of

_____.

6. (M. C.) These authors believe that civilized people put other people "in their place" by:

_____(1) tactful choice of words and speech inflection.

_____(2) swearing at them.

_____(3) exerting political pressure.

_____(4) use of police force.

7. (T – F) True communication necessitates a sympathetic interest in individual differences.

8. (M. C.) The characteristic of the scientific attitude which makes better communication possible is:

_____(1) the limited range of interest.

_____(2) the absorption in pure science.

_____(3) the mind open to new ideas.

_____(4) the technical level of vocabulary.

9. (T – F) Ideas do not always accompany the words that express them.

10. (T – F) The spirit essential to communication is the conviction that you have a good idea to which you must convert others.

Exercise VI–11

The Old Mint

(Reproduced from the government document entitled "The Old Mint.")

──────── **WAIT FOR SIGNAL TO BEGIN READING** ────────

There's gold! In California

When the rare yellow metal was found at Coloma (Sutter's Mill) by James W. Marshall in 1848 the cry of discovery ricocheted around the world.

The temptation of untold riches to be found in the land could not be denied. The California gold rush was on.

Prospectors swarmed into the territory and, by 1850, the gold mined in the hills had grown from a trickle to a deluge. The heavy outpour swamped the refining and coining facilities of the distant Philadelphia Mint. To continue to expose the precious cargo to the hazards of the time-consuming journey 100 intensified the dangers to the ponderous load.

The coinage situation in the West was in a chaotic state. Many different kinds circulated— French Louis-d'ors, Dutch guilders, Indian rupees, Mexican reals, English shillings, and our own American pieces. Even so, there was a scarcity and gold dust, while acceptable, was not a convenient medium of exchange. To remedy the difficulty, private mints sprang up which converted gold into coins— but this was not a solution.

In a four year period, 1848 to 1852, California had turned from a collection of sleepy Spanish villages into a restless, prospering territory that 200 led to statehood in 1850. The population had increased from 15,000 to about 250,000 and the mines had produced $200,000,000 worth of gold.

Then, concurring in a recommendation from President Millard Fillmore that a branch Mint be established in California, Congress acted on July 3, 1852, and authorized the construction of a United States Mint at San Francisco.

A small building, just 60 feet square, was erected on Commercial Street and the Mint started receiving deposits on April 3, 1854.

Obstacles connected with the supply of materials retarded and diminished the coinage operations during that year. However, $4,084,207, all in gold pieces, was coined between April and December, 300 1854, and gradually the coins there replaced the miscellaneous assortment in circulation.

Within ten years, it was apparent that the little Mint was sorely inadequate to meet the expanding coinage demands of the region. Again, a Mint with ample capacity to provide for the great mineral districts of the West was proposed. Not until 1872–1873, was the building completed and the work of fitting up the necessary machinery.

The new Mint at 5th and Mission was occupied in the summer of 1874, and was one of the best 400 appointed Mints in the world. It was first considered unnecessarily large but the Director stated, ". . . in fitting it up with a refining and coining capacity equal to the present demand it has been found necessary to occupy the entire building.

"The San Francisco Call," in its November 1, 1874, issue, described the Mint as a noble, substantial structure and reported: "The fire department will have little trouble quenching any conflagration that may arise within its walls, and unless an earthquake gives it a subterranean quietus, it bids fair to stand up for centuries."

The Mint was destined to live up to this early 500 assessment of its sturdy construction. The first critical test of survival was the holocaust that was the San Francisco earthquake and fire of April 18, 1906.

The disaster devastated the City of San Francisco. The city's water pipes broke under the onslaught of the violent quakes and fires raged unchecked throughout the area.

Just three weeks before the calamity, the Mint had completed a private water supply system of hydrants and hoses on each floor. Two wells located in the inner court supplied sufficient water for Mint employees and U.S. soldiers to fight a seven hour 600 battle against the towering flames that licked at the iron shuttered windows.

The intense heat melted the glass in the windows and flying embers ignited a dozen small fires on the roof and in the courtyard where lumber and timber were stacked.

Fifty employees of the Mint whose own homes were in the path of the fire made it to work that day. Family worries competed with their devotion to the mint. Duty won out. They remained to man the water hose. The Mint and its contents were saved. The destruction of the city gas works, however, 700 forced a halt to the melting, annealing and assaying operations fueled by gas.

Left standing virtually alone amid the rubble of the disaster with $200,000,000 in gold in its vaults, the Mint was the only financial institution in the city able to open its doors for business.

The subtreasury had been destroyed, bank buildings lay in ruins; the banking system ground to a dead stop.

An orderly flow of money in and out of the city was vital to its survival and to the well-being of the people. Only the Mint was in a position to begin accepting and administering the relief funds that poured in and, until the banks could once again ⤺800 operate, the Mint handled all remittances to and from the city and disbursements within the city as well.

San Francisco didn't take long to restore and revitalize itself and the Mint was there as the city grew and prospered anew.

The commercial demands of the nation also increased and further expansion of minting facilities was necessary. In the summer of 1937 San Francisco personnel made another move; this time into an imposing marble edifice some distance from the principal business center where the old building is located.

Known as the San Francisco Assay Office, today it manufactures one-cent pieces for general ⤺900 circulation bearing the famous "S" mintmark. It also produces the proof and uncirculated coin sets for sale to the public. In 1971, it added the 40% silver proof and uncirculated specimens of the Eisenhower dollar coin to its special coin programs.

After minting operations were transferred from Mission Street to the new location at 155 Hermann Street, the Old Mint was occupied by other government agencies until 1968.

Then the Old Mint was finally vacated and declared surplus to government needs. Empty and swiftly deteriorating, the unsightly building became the center of swirling controversy between agitators ⤺1000 for its demolition to make way for a high rise and instigators for its preservation and restoration as an architectural, cultural, and historical landmark.

In the spring of 1972, President Nixon intervened to save the old building from its uncertain fate. He announced the transfer of the building from the General Services Administration to the Department of the Treasury's Bureau of the Mint for restoration and continued use by the government and the enjoyment of the public.

In a sudden burst of activity, workmen began arriving at the old, deserted building to accomplish 1100→ the restoration. A short year later, in April 1973, the Mint's Special Coins and Medals and Computer employees were able to move their mushrooming operations into the commodious rooms in the rear of the building, newly renovated and equipped to speed the processing of millions of mail orders received yearly from the public for the special coins and medals produced by the Mint.

The move back to the Old Mint adds another historical highlight to the continuing story of the building's existence. It is the first public building to open in compliance with Public Law 92-362, 1200→ providing for the adaptive use of surplus historic structures.

Preservation for its own sake is rarely enough. Unless historic buildings can also be made to serve a useful purpose, the danger is always present they will be destroyed as obsolete and a part of our nation's past will be lost forever.

The interior of the Old Mint has been completely rehabilitated to lead this double life and the exterior restoration is expected to be completed soon.

In the meantime, the museum rooms authentically restored to their original 1874 appearance are open to the public. And exhibits of historical and educational significance will continue to be developed.

1300→ Now teeming with new and useful life, the beauty of its past preserved, the welcome mat is out once again. The old building that has survived time, earthquake, fire and abandonment, and that has played such a crucial role in the growth of California 1350→ and the West has re-opened for visitors.

——STOP——ASK FOR YOUR TIME——

Record time immediately and answer the questions on content.

Time_____Sec.	RATE (from table on page 315):	R. _____
No. Correct:_____ (key on page 322)	COMPREHENSION (10% for each correct answer):	C. _____
VI–11	EFFICIENCY (R × C):	E. _____

Record on Progress Chart on page 299

ANSWER THESE QUESTIONS IMMEDIATELY (VI–11)

1. (C   ) The early day gold mined in California was sent to the U.S. at _____.

2. (T – F) Gold dust was the only acceptable medium of exchange in California until the new mint issued coins in 1854.

3. (M. C.) The new and enlarged building, which is now called the Old Mint, was first occupied in:

_____(1) 1854.

_____(2) 1864.

_____(3) 1874.

_____(4) 1906.

4. (T – F) The San Francisco earthquake and fire devastated the mint building.

5. (T – F) Immediately after the fire, the public banking system in San Francisco ceased to function.

6. (T – F) In 1968 the Old Mint was officially vacated and declared surplus property.

7. (M. C.) Since 1937 the basic product of the Mint has been coined in the:

_____(1) Mission Street Federal Building.

_____(2) G.S.A. Headquarters Building.

_____(3) San Francisco Post Office Annex.

_____(4) San Francisco Assay Office.

8. (T – F) Restoration of the Old Mint building was not begun until 1975.

9. (C   ) Several rooms have been restored to their original appearance and will serve as a _____.

10. (T – F) Mail orders for special coins and medals produced by the mint are now being handled in the restored building.

Exercise VI–12

Communication and Propaganda

(Reprinted from Chapter IX, *Guidebook for Prospective Teachers,*
Ohio State University Press, 1948 by permission of the authors.)

——————— **WAIT FOR SIGNAL TO BEGIN READING** ———————

Communicating with others

Can you imagine yourself living under conditions such that it would be impossible to communicate with other people? You could not get in touch with anyone by using the telephone, telegraph, or letter; you could not turn on a radio and hear other people; you could not attend a motion picture or look at a television screen; you could not get in touch with anyone by writing, talking, painting, reading, or playing any musical instrument. Without some means of communication you would be living in complete isolation. You would be unable to transmit your ideas to other people and unable to $\overset{100}{\leftarrow}$ receive any ideas from anyone else.

Methods of evaluating communications

In this modern world we are constantly subjected to a barrage of information and misinformation, persuasion, deception, and variations of opinion. In our democracy we prize freedom of speech and freedom of the press. This means that we place on the individual a tremendous responsibility for evaluating the ideas which are relayed to him through the radio, press, movies, newspapers, magazines, and personal contacts. Americans are readers of many kinds of material.

As a citizen you have a responsibility for deciding what to believe and what not to believe; $\overset{200}{\leftarrow}$ what to read and what not to read; what sources are representing special interests and what sources are striving to be fair. This is a process of evaluation which you will have to continue for life. Teachers have a very important task of helping young people to develop some standards for evaluating the material which they receive from the various media of communication.

One of the purposes of education is to develop individuals who will maintain suspended judgments until all available evidence is collected, act intelligently in terms of available information, and evaluate their activity in terms of other evidence that becomes $\overset{300}{\leftarrow}$ available. Schools should help to give students a range of knowledge that will enlarge the outlook of their minds. But schools must recognize that there are groups which do not wish to encourage the development of that kind of a thinking citizen. Many groups use methods of mass communication to get individuals to make conclusions on partial, cross-sectional, or distorted information. They are desirous of leading people into attitudes which will make them jump to conclusions without paying much attention to available evidence. These attempts to lead people to emotional thinking are usually called $\overset{400}{\rightarrow}$ *propaganda.* This threat to clear thinking is used on a large scale in the world today. It may not always be "anti-something," but it may be used to lead you to the support of some cause by painting a rosy picture of all the nice aspects of it. A thinking person should beware of communication channels that appeal to his emotions and that encourage him to act quickly without giving careful consideration to the matter at hand. Propaganda can often be detected by some general techniques which are commonly used to mislead your thinking.

$\overset{500}{\rightarrow}$ *Name calling*—Bad names are given to those the propagandist would have us condemn; good names to those he would have us favor. Examples are "progressive teacher," "Communist," "bureaucrat," "Conservative," "Jew," "Fraternity Man," "Socialist," "regular fellow," etc.

Glittering generalities—We are told that "the American system is threatened" and are lured with such attractive phrases as "social justice," "the more abundant life," "economic freedom," "the welfare of the common man," etc. These vague terms may have different meanings to everyone, and we frequently put our own meanings into the mouth of the speaker rather than try to decide what he really $\overset{600}{\rightarrow}$ means by seeing how his actions define his terms.

Flag waving—The propagandist associates his cause with the American flag, the Christian religion, or with some person of great prestige. He attempts to make you feel that loyalty to your God and your country dictates that you agree with him.

Slogans—The propagandist finds some catchy phrase which may stick in one's mind. Then he tries to get it generally accepted without an analysis of its meaning. Examples are "democratic way of life," "it's Luckies 2 to 1," "The skin you love to touch," "For men of distinction," "good to the last drop," $\overset{700}{\rightarrow}$ etc. Applying the question, *why, what,* or *how* to some of these slogans may help you see how superficial many of them are.

Repetition and fabrication—The propagandist loves to take an incident and magnify its importance. He is similar to the old gossip who likes to make the story just a little better before she passes it on. By repeating it over and over he attempts to make you accept its validity. You may protect yourself from this to some extent by trying to get at the source of some of your information which you question.

Bandwagon technique—You are led to believe ←800 you should do something because "everybody's doing it," "it's smart to be seen at the Cliff Cafe," etc. Campaign managers and advertisers know the human tendency to follow the crowd and will invariably predict victory for their candidate or widespread use of their product. Here again you need to question, "Who is everybody?" "Why is it smart?"

Suppression and distortion of facts—Many of the socioeconomic cartoons lead to considerable distortion of the facts. Many of our labor journal cartoonists would have everyone believe that employers and capitalists are all bloated bigots with tall silk hats. Each political party has cartoonists ←900 who try to make the other party look ridiculous. Pictures showing only a limited view of a situation are often used to distort reality. The things that are omitted in a news report may be just the things that you need to know to reach a wise decision. By withholding the whole truth from you, you may be led to reach a decision which the propagandist favors.

Ambush and showmanship—Wealthy interests and pressure groups sometimes use the ambush method of winning public opinion. They may use pressures to get their employees or their debtors to promote their ideas. They may organize "front" ←1000 organizations which take on an attractive name and carry on the publicity. They may give large sums to philanthropic institutions and then make the institution fight their battles. Oratory many times appeals to the emotions and does not present any facts. In case of doubt, you might try to discover who is financing the group or speaker in question.

These and many other methods may be used to lure the gullible thinker into false and sometimes dangerous conclusions. The tenseness of our international situation and the war of ideologies now 1100→ going on make it important for you to consider carefully the ideas to which you are exposed.

One of the most important factors influencing the communication of ideas is the reader's understanding. Dr. Edgar Dale has suggested several questions which might be asked in an effort to evaluate your own ability as a reader. Although these questions apply to reading of newspapers primarily, you can frame some parallel questions to apply to magazines, radio programs, movies, speakers, etc.

1. Am I familiar with a number of newspapers, not only the good ones but the poor ones as well?
1200→ 2. Do I plan my reading in terms of (a) time spent, (b) material read, and (c) the order and speed in which the material is read?
3. Have I examined all parts of the material to find out what's in it?
4. Can I find desired information quickly by using the index, summary, etc.?
5. Am I familiar with the way a typical news story is constructed?
6. Do I get the most out of the big news stories by following them day by day as they develop?
7. Am I able to read, understand, and criticize the editorials in daily newspapers?
300→ 8. Do I have an efficient speed and comprehension in reading?
9. Am I familiar with some important factors which influence the nature and accuracy of news: (a) the reader, (b) ownership of the paper, (c) political affiliations, (d) the reporter, (e) the editor, (f) the make-up editor, (g) space restrictions, 1350→ and (h) advertising?

——STOP——ASK FOR YOUR TIME——

Record time immediately and answer the questions on content.

Time_____Sec.	RATE (from table on page 315):	R. _____
No. Correct:_____ (key on page 330)	COMPREHENSION (10% for each correct answer):	C. _____
VI–12	EFFICIENCY (R ✕ C):	E. _____

Record on Progress Chart on page 299

ANSWER THESE QUESTIONS IMMEDIATELY (VI–12)

1. (C   ) In a democracy the evaluation of ideas presented to the public is the responsibility of the _____ _____.

2. (T – F) Teachers should evaluate all materials presented to students to protect them from misunderstanding the ideas.

3. (T – F) Some people do not believe that students should be taught to analyze and evaluate the material they read.

4. (C   ) Attempts to lead people to emotional thinking are called _____.

5. (M. C.) The technique which appeals to one's own definition of terms such as ''economic freedom'' and ''American way of life'' is called the technique of:

_____(1) repetition.

_____(2) suppression of facts.

_____(3) flag waving.

_____(4) glittering generalities.

6. (T – F) The author suggests that you apply the questions *why, what,* and *how* to any slogan approach.

7. (T – F) The ''bandwagon'' technique is described as that which uses a popular ''name brand'' to gain attention.

8. (T – F) Socioeconomic cartoons usually present an accurate view of a situation.

9. (T – F) The "ambush" technique implies the use of some ''front'' organization to expound the ideas.

10. (M. C.) According to the author, one of the most important factors influencing the written communication of ideas is:

_____(1) the reader's understanding.

_____(2) the political affiliation of the writer.

_____(3) the size and style of type used by the publisher.

_____(4) the newspaper that carries the story.

Exercise VI-13

Stress—and Your Health

(Reprinted from the 1967 pamphlet of the Metropolitan Life Insurance Company
by permission of the publishers.)

——— **WAIT FOR SIGNAL TO BEGIN READING** ———

What is stress?

Stress is commonly defined as intense exertion —strain and effort—the wear and tear of life. A mother in childbirth and her baby being born, a child on that first day of school—or a student facing an important examination—is sure to experience some stress.

The athlete striving to win a race—the circus performer walking a tightrope—the artist trying to produce his best work—all are under stress. A working man with a sick wife, trying to double as father and mother to his family, is under considerable stress as well as the mother who works to support 100 her children and comes home to a housewife's job at night is also under stress.

A businessman who worries continually about office problems while he's at home, or about home problems while he's at the office, is under stress.

There are varying degrees and different forms of stress—mental, emotional, physical—all having some impact—sometimes good, sometimes harmful —upon health. Stress can often be the spice of life or, depending upon circumstances and a person's capacities and reactions, it may have damaging side effects which may lead to disease, cause us to age prematurely, or sometimes even shorten life. 200

A key to health

Through all normal living and our daily activities, our body cells are continuously being worn out and replaced with new ones. In a medical sense, stress has been defined as the rate of all wear and tear caused by life. All emotions—love as well as hate, for example, and also physical exertion— swimming, golf, or just a brisk walk—involve stress. This type of stress is good for us because the thing that's important is not the stress itself but its effects.

Whether or not the strain caused by our experiences can make our bodies become susceptible 300 to diseases—or perhaps even to accidents—depends to a great extent on our adaptability to these experiences.

Authorities believe that by understanding our individual reactions—and having some knowledge of our limitations—we can help to prevent excessive stress.

Hormones— the body's chemical messengers

The "attack" on the body which can cause stress might be invasion by disease or it might be an injury, or even an emotional crisis. If the trouble is a burned finger, the sudden injury sets off an "alarm reaction" within the body. First the nervous system 400 sends out an SOS and among the physical forces alerted are the body's "chemical messengers"—the hormones—which are quickly sent into action. The tiny pituitary gland, located under the brain, dispatches a special hormone—a substance called ACTH. This pituitary hormone signals the adrenal glands, situated just above the kidneys which, in turn, send out other hormones (corticosteroids) thus putting the body in a state of preparedness to handle the emergency. In response to the "alarm signals," special hormones rush to the injured area where they steady the work of the healing processes, helping 500 to speed up or slow down activity as needed. The pituitary and adrenal glands balance the body's chemistry by helping to coordinate and regulate the functions of other organs in the body. With their help, disease can be resisted or an injury healed without overly disturbing the working order of the rest of the system.

Strong emotions, too, such as fear cause bodily changes because emotions, in general, are meant to make us act. When fear occurs, nerve impulses and hormones (adrenalin) speed through the system causing the heart to beat rapidly. Blood vessels of the stomach and intestines contract, shunting the 600 blood to muscles for quick action; breathing speeds up, and other changes occur which help to pitch us to a point where we can meet an emergency or go through a difficult situation.

Because we can't and wouldn't want to live like vegetables—without feeling or responsiveness— normal emotional stress is useful in many ways.

In contrast to healthy stress, however, intense and persistent anger, fear, frustration or worry, which we may bottle up inside ourselves, can threaten health.

Mind + body = psychosomatic

One of the advances of modern medicine is the increasing recognition of the importance of emotions in influencing body health. This view recognizes that $\overset{700}{\leftarrow}$ mind and body work together as one (not as separate units), with the body reacting upon the mind, and the mind upon the body.

The knowledge that illnesses must be considered and treated in relation to the whole person forms the basis for psychosomatic medicine (psyche, mind + soma, body). Much has been written about this concept, but much has been misunderstood; so let's examine a few popular misconceptions.

After listening sympathetically to a neighbor's detailed account of her latest symptoms, a Mrs. R. said: "Just you forget about it, my dear; it's probably only psychosomatic—you know—when you imagine $\overset{800}{\leftarrow}$ you're sick."

Mrs. R. meant to reassure her neighbor, but she fell into the all-too-common error of thinking that psychosomatic illnesses are not real ones. People feel pain just as intensely whether the cause is physical or emotional, and failure to seek professional advice at the first warning sign of trouble can and often does lead only to more serious difficulty later on.

When Mr. J. was told that his wife's illness was emotional in origin, he said to himself, "Well, that's a relief, anyhow. If it's only psychosomatic, it can't do her any real harm."

Like Mr. J., many people have the mistaken $\overset{900}{\leftarrow}$ idea that a psychosomatic illness is one that is purely imaginary, that if the patient would only forget about his ailment, it would quietly and quickly disappear.

Many people think that since psychosomatic has something to do with the mind or the emotions, such illnesses cannot cause any physical damage. In order to see why these notions are untrue, let us look first at some of the common effects of emotions on the body—not in illness, but in everyday situations.

Physicians base their knowledge—that emotions play an important part in many types of $\overset{1000}{\leftarrow}$ physical illness—on facts with which we are all familiar. All of us have experienced some of the effects of emotions on bodily functions. Most of us can recall blushing when embarrassed or having a tight feeling in the chest or a weight in the pit of the stomach before an examination or having our heart pound and our hands perspire when excited or afraid. These are normal reactions of the body to specific situations, and are beyond the control of our will power; they generally disappear quickly once the cause is removed.

$\overset{1100}{\rightarrow}$ Knowing how these normal emotions influence body functions, we are better able to understand how strong and persistent emotional conflicts may, over a period of time, disturb the working of body organs, such as the heart or the stomach. It is believed that in some cases they can eventually result in actual change in the organ itself.

Prolonged emotional tensions are thought to play a prominent role in certain kinds of heart and circulatory disorders, especially high blood pressure; digestive ailments, such as peptic ulcer and colitis; headache and joint and muscular pains; skin disorders; and some allergies.

What's to be done?

$\overset{1200}{\rightarrow}$ First, and always in discovering the causes of illnesses in which there are emotional factors, a complete physical checkup must be made. It is most important for the patient to have confidence in his doctor so that he will feel free to express troublesome thoughts without fear of being ridiculed or belittled. The physician needs to know about the life of his patient and his responses to various situations. With this knowledge, he can help him to become aware of how fears and worries may have caused or contributed to the illness.

Because of knowledge about the emotional $\overset{1300}{\rightarrow}$ factors involved in many types of illness, there is less reason than ever for neglecting to consult a physician at the first warning sign of trouble. Many ailments of a psychosomatic nature can now be treated with greater hope of success than ever before, if brought $\overset{1350}{\rightarrow}$ to the early attention of the family physician.

——STOP——ASK FOR YOUR TIME——

Record time immediately and answer the questions on content.

Time_____Sec.	RATE (from table on page 315):	R. _____
No. Correct:_____ (key on page 322)	COMPREHENSION (10% for each correct answer):	C. _____
VI–13	EFFICIENCY (R $\times$ C):	E. _____

Record on Progress Chart on page 299

ANSWER THESE QUESTIONS IMMEDIATELY (VI–13)

1. (T – F) Stress is usually thought of as intense exertion—strain and effort—the wear and tear of life.

2. (C   ) The different forms of stress are mental, emotional, and _____.

3. (M. C.) Whether or not the strain caused by our experiences can make our bodies susceptible to diseases depends chiefly upon:

_____(1) bodily resistance to invading viruses.

_____(2) ability to handle daily living without stress.

_____(3) adaptability to these experiences.

_____(4) symptoms of heart palpitation and severe headache.

4. (T – F) The hormone dispatched by the pituitary gland is a substance called ACTH.

5. (T – F) Fortunately for us, strong emotions cannot precipitate bodily changes.

6. (T – F) The mind and the body function as separate units in maintaining bodily health.

7. (T – F) Because a psychosomatic illness is purely imaginary, if the patient would forget his ailment, it would go away.

8. (T – F) Normal reactions of the body to specific situations are beyond the control of our will power.

9. (M. C.) To discover the cause of an illness *the first thing* to do is to:

_____(1) have a session with your psychologist.

_____(2) investigate past life experiences.

_____(3) resolve any internal conflicts.

_____(4) have a complete physical checkup.

10. (C   ) Many ailments of a _____ nature can now be treated with greater chances of success than previously thought.

Exercise VI–14

Student Travel: The High-Risk Route
by WILLIAM A. SIEVERT

(Reprinted from the November 11, 1974 issue of the *Chronicle of Higher Education*
by permission of the editor.)

—————— WAIT FOR SIGNAL TO BEGIN READING ——————

News items

"A Boston University student is seen hitchhiking near the campus. A few days later her body is found in a field in New Hampshire."

"Near Ypsilanti, three Eastern Michigan University students are slain by a fourth student who had offered each of them a ride. Two University of Michigan students and two nonstudents are also murdered before a 20-year-old killer is apprehended."

"In Santa Cruz, Cal., four female student hitchhikers—two from the University of California at Santa Cruz and two from Cabrillo Junior College—are raped and murdered by a former mental patient."

Thumbing

The uplifted thumb has become almost as big 100 an institution on American college campuses as blue jeans.

Unfortunately, as the popularity of hitchhiking has increased among students, so have the risks. So much so, in fact, that many campus security forces and student groups alike have been developing new strategies to deal with the dangers of thumbing.

For the most part, student organizations are lobbying for safety controls on hitchhiking while campus and passing out a companion brochure called informational campaigns to convince students not to hitchhike at all.

"Hitchhiking is certainly one of the greatest concerns of college security officers, a concern based 200 on the high incidence of crime reported," according to John W. Powell, executive secretary of the International Association of College and University Security Officers.

Mr. Powell says that the number of hitchhiking-related rapes, robberies, injuries—and occasional deaths—has continued to rise, despite the efforts of campus authorities to warn students. "The current emphasis of campus security people everywhere is on educating students to the dangers," he says.

Education is really about all campus police can do. Donald Ryan, security officer at Boston University, says, "There's not much we can do.

300 You can't enforce laws against hitchhiking any more than you can against jaywalking."

Adds Melvin Fuller of the Eastern Michigan University security force. "A person hitchhiking is usually standing on city streets, not on campus where we have our authority."

Nonetheless, Mr. Fuller says that "whenever our officers go to the dorm for talks, the dangers of hitchhiking are brought up."

At the University of California at Santa Cruz, security chief John C. Barber admits, "We realize it is futile to say, 'Don't hitchhike,' in an area like ours where everything is casual and friendly. We still urge students not to hitchhike, but we say—if you do, 400 at least follow a few tips."

Four hitchhiking students were among those killed in a highly publicized series of nine murders in the Santa Cruz area in 1972 and '73. Edward Kemper, 28, who picked up the students in a car with a university parking sticker (his mother worked on the campus), later was convicted of the slayings.

"Not a Victim"

Since then, says Mr. Barber, the university has been showing a film made at the Santa Barbara campus and passing out a companion brochure called "Not a Victim" to offer students specific precautions they can take:

—Ride with a friend.
500 —Look into the back seat before entering a car.
—Check out the driver's appearance and clothing.
—Make mental notes of the car's description and license number.

In addition, Mr. Barber urges students to make sure the car has an inside door handle on the passenger's side; Kemper's did not.

Boston University's Mr. Ryan says he reminds students that it is not only the hitchhiker who is in danger by accepting a ride from a stranger. "It works both ways," he says. "The driver can find himself in trouble, too."

"Anyone can resemble a student, carry books 600 under his arms; a driver feels sorry for him, gives him a ride, and gets robbed. It happens all the time."

In 1967, during the period when three students

—all thought to be hitchhikers—were murdered in separate incidents by a fourth student, Eastern Michigan's security force began taking out advertisements in the student newspaper urging people not to thumb rides.

"Every time we have a problem, we advertise again. We have to keep harping on it," Mr. Fuller says. "But people are quick to forget."

At least some students are not forgetting and are launching programs they hope will protect hitchers around their campuses.   700 ←

Two of the more advanced of these programs are located in Colorado university towns—Fort Collins and Greeley.

With the approval of the city council of Fort Collins, students at Colorado State University are operating the "Community Carpool" project. This year-old program licenses both drivers and hitchhikers.

Hitchhikers register with the carpool committee for 25 cents, providing identification and their home addresses. Upon registering, the hitchhikers are issued official, brightly colored hitching cards.

"The hitchhiker holds up the card instead of his thumb and shows it to the driver before entering a car," explains Steve Smith of the Colorado Student 800 ← Lobby and the Colorado State student association.

Similarly, drivers who register with the committee are issued windshield stickers that are easily visible from the curb.

The Fort Collins streets department has cooperated with the program by erecting more than 40 signs designating certain corners as "safe turn-out" points.

The turn-out points provide students with convenient locations for seeking rides and offer drivers safe areas to pick up passengers without blocking traffic.

Last spring, students at the University of Northern Colorado at Greeley started a similar program.

Clarifying a "confusing" law

Mr. Smith says that the Colorado Student Lobby will be seeking legislation this winter to 900 ← expand the two programs statewide. The lobby also is working toward companion legislation that would legalize hitchhiking throughout the state—or at least clarify what the lobby considers to be the "confusing" law currently on the books.

The California state legislature this year turned down an even tougher proposal to license hitchhikers. Under the California plan, introduced by Assemblyman John F. Dunlap with the support of some student groups no person would be issued a permit if he had criminal action pending against him, if he was on parole or probation, or even if he 1000 ← had an outstanding traffic violation.·

The California Student Lobby had not yet decided whether to support the highly restrictive bill when it was killed. The lobby expects one or more similar, but perhaps milder, bills to be introduced next year.

From Brandeis to San Francisco State University, more colleges are establishing designated hitchhiking stands on their campuses or at the edges. Many institutions first set up such stands in campus parking lots during last winter's energy crisis, when car-pools and group travel were being encouraged.

The stands allow hitchhikers to seek rides in 1100 → groups and seem to provide more protection because they are located on college property rather than on public streets.

"Share-a-ride" stops

California State College at Hayward, for instance, has "Share-a-Ride" stops at its campus entrances to encourage students to give one another lifts up and down the large hill on which the classroom buildings are located.

The University of California at Santa Cruz operates a free bus and tram service from its classroom complexes to the campus gate a mile and a half away. In the evenings, the trams are used for a "Dial-a-Ride" service. Students call the service, 1200 → and a university-sponsored tram or bus picks them up and takes them wherever they want to go around the five-square-mile wooded campus.

Similarly, telephone "ride-wanted" switchboards are rapidly replacing bulletin-board listings as a means of coordinating long-distance travel.

Campus discussions

At Ohio State University, student groups—particularly those in dormitories—have sponsored seminars featuring both campus and city police discussing the problems associated with hitchhiking.

On several occasions, policewomen have visited the Ohio State campus to lecture to women's groups. At Santa Cruz, a special program provides instructions for women on how to protect themselves.

Other campuses concentrate on radio and 1300 → newspaper advertising or posters to remind students of the dangers of thumbing.

One of the more visual posters has been created by Syracuse University's "Eyes and Ears" student marshal program.

The poster depicts a pretty country meadow with a human body lying in it. A white sheet covers 1350 → the body—except for one huge extended thumb.

——STOP——ASK FOR YOUR TIME——

Record time immediately on next page and answer the questions on content.

ANSWER THESE QUESTIONS IMMEDIATELY (VI–14)

1. (T – F) Campus police at many colleges are urging students to refrain from hitchhiking.

2. (M. C.) The major effort of campus police to reduce the crime associated with hitchhiking is to:

_____(1) patrol the areas where students often thumb rides.

_____(2) post warnings against picking up hitchhikers.

_____(3) provide educational programs about dangers of hitchhiking.

_____(4) penalize all students who are caught hitchhiking on campus.

3. (M. C.) "Not a Victim" is:

_____(1) a film used in college classes on safety.

_____(2) a T.V. documentary on dangers of hitchhiking.

_____(3) a book about a happy hitchhiker who got in with the wrong crowd.

_____(4) a brochure about precautions to keep hitchhikers out of trouble.

4. (T – F) Edward Kemper was the victim of an escaped mental patient who picked him up.

5. (C) Two of the most advanced programs for protection of student hitchhikers are in colleges in the state of _____ .

6. (T – F) The "Community Carpool" program licenses both drivers and hitchhikers.

7. (C) In the Fort Collins area, the local street department posts signs designating certain areas as safe _____ points.

8. (T – F) At the time this article was written, the California legislature had recently passed a tough law to require registration of all hitchhikers.

9. (T – F) In some places "ride-wanted" switchboards are replacing bulletin-board listings in promoting contacts between drivers and students.

10. (T – F) This writer seems to feel that the potential dangers of hitchhiking have been greatly overpublicized.

213

Exercise VI–15

Bridge over Time
by GREGORY RAY

(Reprinted from the July 1974 issue of *Wyoming Wildlife*
by permission of the editor.)

—————————— WAIT FOR SIGNAL TO BEGIN READING ——————————

To many travelers, Wyoming looks like nothing more than an arid plateau; yet with every passing car, countless natural wonders are overlooked. Many of these are only a few miles from the major interstate highways and most are marked by a small highway sign.

Such is the case of a modest announcement on the north side of the road near the westbound lane of Interstate Highway 25. Without fanfare it says merely, "natural bridge."

Following the arrow on the off-ramp sign takes motorists four-and-three-quarter miles south on a small road marked "Converse County 13." It's a pleasant drive through the country. Birds fluttering 100 effortlessly through the air and the gentle aroma of summer make it an exceptionally enjoyable side trip from the four-lane asphalt interstate.

Nearing the mountains, the road winds slowly through rolling hills and then veers to the left through a gate and down into a canyon.

Crossing a creek, there is still no sign of a natural bridge; however, a tremendous abandoned building towers above the trees and stands as a silent eulogy of an early-day attempt to build an electrical generation station on the stream to run water pumps for irrigating the land above the canyon. 200

Beyond this concrete and steel mastodon is a grassy area spotted with picnic tables and outdoor fireplaces. Here, sheltered by a large, red sandstone amphitheater, the creek flows sleepily through this quiet valley and under Ayers Natural Bridge.

It's not a huge natural bridge and perhaps is more impressive for its pastoral beauty than its sheer size, though it spans 90 feet at the base and leaves a gapping 20-foot-high archway that is penetrated by the rich, blue sky.

The unusual rock of this area reveals in layers the geological history of these formations. The bridge was formed through the eons of time after the land 300 rose above the vast seas that once covered Wyoming. In terms of geologic time, this natural wonder is relatively new—probably created some 50–100,000 years ago, though an exact determination of this has not been made.

The bridge itself is part of the Casper Sandstone Formation laid down during the Pennsylvanian age more than 280 million years ago. The rock was pierced by the slow sculpturing of La Prele Creek after a narrow neck of sandstone was isolated by the meandering stream. Time eventually eroded this 400 middle-paleozoic rock to what it is today.

The forces of wind and rain also smoothed the rock amphitheater walls that gently caress the small secluded valley that contains the Ayers Natural Bridge Park.

Land donated

Though now a small and well-maintained park of approximately 15 acres, this scenic area was privately owned until 1920, when, partly due to local interest in the bridge, Andrew Clement Ayers, then owner of the land, donated the site as a Converse County free park.

So keen was local interest in the natural bridge and other natural features of the area that residents 500 of the town of Douglas donated their labor to help build an access road to the site.

Nestled among the abundant shade trees and lush grass are picnic and camping facilities—35 cookout grills, four large sheltered picnic tables, 30 fireplaces, and 40 open-air picnic tables as well as a small camping area.

Despite a lack of national publicity or, for that matter, any highway advertising, there are a surprising number of people visiting the park each year. It is estimated somewhere between 25,000 and 30,000 people view the bridge annually. In addition to this, the registration book at the park 600 entrance literally shows entries of visitors from all over the world.

Because of this annual influx of tourists, the park was doubled in size about six years ago. Popularity of the park varies according to the season, however. Springtime traditionally brings the fewest numbers of people to view the stone attraction, while July is one of the most popular times for this side excursion.

Over the years the park has become a favorite spot for hunters during the fall months. The campground facilities can accommodate 20–30 groups, though due to its popularity, there is a three-day camping limit in the park.

Officially the area opens April 1 and closes $\overset{700}{\leftarrow}$ November 1, but weather and water conditions can affect this. During the spring when heavy runoff occurs, there occasionally is danger of flooding, since La Prele Reservoir is located only about a mile-and-a-half up the canyon. If this happens, the park is closed briefly until the possibility of stream overflow has passed.

In early spring and late fall when the weather is highly unpredictable, an occasional snow storm will necessitate either a late opening or an early closing of the park, though during many years the area has been kept open year round.

Best time to visit

It would be difficult to judge the most spec- $\overset{800}{\leftarrow}$ tacular time of year to visit this site. The saturated green of spring and early summer make this area extremely scenic. Spring is also the time of year that La Prele Creek is liveliest. Awakening from the long winter, both the aquatic wildlife and the water itself seem eager for summer to make an official appearance. As if emphasizing this, a local resident pulled a 5-pound rainbow trout from the creek this spring.

In the fall, the turning leaves of this small deciduous-covered valley make it spectacular. The frenzied activities of summer diminish to a sleepy $\overset{900}{\leftarrow}$ pace. The stream flows casually through the bridge and the lazy days of summer gradually relinquish to the cool breezes of approaching winter.

Throughout the year, however, the unique features of the park make it a delightful side trip. In addition to the bridge itself, and the large, red sandstone formation surrounding the area, there is also a mica-speckled crystal cave in the park that is open to the public. Although this cavern is relatively small compared with others in the United States, it adds an additional dimension to this geologically fascinating area.

As if this weren't enough to entice even the $\overset{1000}{\leftarrow}$ most skeptical sightseer or amateur geologist to the area, colorful lichen formations are found dotting the rocks atop the sandstone bluffs surrounding the park, giving one the impression such colorful green,

yellow, and orange accents were left behind after a careless artist dripped the hues from his pallet.

The climb up to the top of the amphitheater is steep and there is no trail. However, from the edge of this sandstone cliff there is a magnificent view of the natural bridge and the park as well as the $\overset{1100}{\rightarrow}$ surrounding sagebrush landscape. From here the park stands out as an oasis in an otherwise subdued horizon.

The graceful elbows in the stream, framed delicately by the natural bridge archway, disappear quietly into infinity, while the steep canyon walls focus attention on the valley floor where a small walkway crosses the creek leading visitors over to the far side of the sandy riverbank.

Sources of water

There is approximately a mile of stream that wanders through the park. Beyond this, on both the upstream and downstream ends, is private land. La Prele Creek is not the only source of water for the $\overset{1200}{\rightarrow}$ area, however; several natural springs, in addition to two wells, give park visitors an opportunity to savor the natural underground liquid that has over the years been a selling point for several prominent brewers of hops and barley.

Despite the conveniences of the park, there are no concession stands to mar the natural beauty of the area. An attempt to maintain the scenic wonders of Ayers Natural Bridge in pristine condition is performed by a caretaker now residing at the park year round. Though park officials have had little trouble with vandalism, they wish to preserve this sandstone monument to perpetuity.

$\overset{1300}{\rightarrow}$ This unique rock edifice was formed by an ancient sculptor over millions of years ago. While it has little of the fame of such huge national parks as Yellowstone and Yosemite, it contains a variety of scenic wonders not found elsewhere and is well worth a five-mile side trip from the interstate $\overset{1350}{\rightarrow}$ highway.

——STOP——ASK FOR YOUR TIME——

Record time immediately and answer
the questions on content.

Time_____Sec.   RATE (from table on page 315):   R. _____

No. Correct:_____   COMPREHENSION (10% for each correct answer):   C. _____
(key on page 322)

VI–15   EFFICIENCY (R × C):   E. _____

Record on Progress Chart on page 299

ANSWER THESE QUESTIONS IMMEDIATELY (VI–15)

1. (T – F) In the park is an early-day attempt to build an electrical generation station.

2. (M. C.) The Ayers Natural Bridge Park is impressive for its:

_____(1) sheer size.

_____(2) historical past.

_____(3) tremendous towers.

_____(4) pastoral beauty.

3. (C   ) The bridge is part of the Casper _____ formation.

4. (T – F) Douglas Creek sculptured the red sandstone rock bridge.

5. (T – F) The maintained park is approximately 15 acres.

6. (T – F) Camping facilities are not available in the park.

7. (M. C.) The most popular visitor time for this stone attraction is:

_____(1) July.

_____(2) September.

_____(3) November.

_____(4) January.

8. (T – F) The opening and closing dates, weather permitting, are April 1 to November 1.

9. (C   ) In addition to the stream and two wells, there are several natural _____ in the park.

10. (T – F) There is one concession store in the park.

Exercise VI–16

A Scrambler's Gamble in Pay TV
by GEOFFREY COLVIN

———————————— WAIT FOR SIGNAL TO BEGIN READING ————————————

At age 50, Oak Industries seems affected by the same mysterious force that sometimes causes executives of similar vintage to chuck the Brooks Brothers suits, quit the company, and take up hang gliding. The results have been exhilarating. Until about five years ago Oak, based in Crystal Lake, Illinois, was a gray, chalk-striped manufacturer of components and electronic materials—respectable but heavily soporific items like controls for gas ranges— and hardware for the cable-TV industry. It has since moved to Rancho Bernardo, California—and jumped into show biz as an operator of pay television systems. Now Oak finds itself, through several ventures, in the vanguard of the video revolution. . . .

Oak's new growth isn't so much a sharp break with its past as an adventurous extension of one of its traditional businesses, guided altogether soberly by Everitt A. "Nick" Carter, 63, a mechanical engineer who has been Oak's chief executive since 1959. For 15 years Oak has been making converter boxes, which sit on the tops of televisions in homes that get cable TV; the boxes convert the frequency of the cable signal to a lower frequency the set can handle. The enterprise didn't amount to much until recently, but Oak's early start helped it achieve two advances in converter technology that have done a lot for the cable industry and proved crucial to Oak's own fortunes.

In 1971 Oak figured out a way to scramble one or more of the channels sent over a cable system. The signal could be viewed only after a serviceman had gone to the cable subscriber's home and adjusted the converter box. The development of scrambling technology by Oak and others helped cable take off in the seventies by making it easier for cable operators to offer subscribers some things they badly wanted, like recent movies, for an extra fee. . . .

Direct to Miss Smith

As useful as this kind of scrambling was to the growth of cable, it isn't very efficient. Sending servicemen to thousands of homes is expensive. Then, if a subscriber doesn't pay his bill, the serviceman faces the unenviable chore of going back to the subscriber's home to make the premium channel unviewable. Meanwhile many cable subscribers who don't take the premium channel have found that, with the help of instructions passed along through a sort of viewer's underground, they can themselves adjust the box to get the extra channel —without paying, of course.

Oak solved all these problems—and took a giant step toward becoming a pay-TV operator itself—with the development in 1973 of a converter box that was, in the jargon of the trade, "addressable." That meant the cable operator could send messages from the system's origination point (called the head-end) to any *one* of the thousands of boxes in the system. If, for example, Miss Smith on Maple Street calls the local cable system and says she would like to start receiving HBO at an extra charge of $10 a month, the cable operator simply tells the equipment at the head-end to start sending Miss Smith's converter box the electronic instructions to unscramble HBO. If Miss Smith doesn't pay her bill, it's equally simple to cut HBO off. And because the box's ability to unscramble is activated by an electronic impulse from the head-end rather than by a serviceman with a pair of pliers, stealing the signal becomes far more difficult.

In addition to cutting costs, addressability holds promise of attracting such a flood of money that it makes cable operators' heads swim. In an addressable cable system, subscribers can also be charged for individual programs. The dizzying result: extra revenues of millions of dollars in just one night. With an addressable system, the cable operator can—as he never could before—offer big attractions such as heavyweight title bouts and charge what the market will bear.

For all addressability's allures, though, the demand for Oak's new box was, until recently, tepid. Cable operators had millions of boxes in place and didn't cotton to the idea of junking them for an unproved system. But addressability caught the eye of A. Jerrold Perenchio, now 50, a former fight promoter who staged the Bobby Riggs-Billie Jean King tennis match, once tried to take over Columbia Pictures, and is a partner of Norman Lear, the producer of such TV hits as *All in the Family*. Perenchio came to Oak when he was attempting to get into the untried business of subscriptions TV, often called STV, and soon they were partners.

STV operators begin by taking over a TV station and sending out over the air the kinds of programs cable operators offer on premium channels. STV sellers scramble the station's signal, just as cable operators scramble their premium channels. To get the programs, the viewer must lease a descrambler from the operator. Oak had no trouble adapting its ⬅800 addressability system and scrambling technology to STV.

As it happened, Nick Carter had already decided that Oak needed to expand beyond components and electronic materials, where he foresaw puny profit potential. Perenchio's idea fit with Carter's plan.

The combination of Oak technology with Perenchio's programming and promotional savvy made perfect sense, but tensions over who was in charge doomed the marriage from the start. Oak says Perenchio immediately sold enough shares in his half of the partnership to assure himself a profit no matter what happened. The move was within his rights but struck Oak officials as evincing a certain lack of faith. ⬅900 Ditto when according to Oak, he secretly called in consultants to evaluate Oak's descrambler box. . . .

The tense alliance finally ended when Oak bought out Perenchio's original 49% interest in the venture for $55 million. . . .

A lovely business

Return on equity looks at least as ravishing because STV requires so little investment. Cable systems have to string miles of cable at a cost that sometimes tops $100,000 a mile in cities, while STV goes through the air. It has only to buy or lease an existing TV station—a doggy one will do—and ⬇1000 then install boxes in subscribers' homes. Since the Los Angeles operation turned the corner, Oak has gone into Chicago, Miami, Fort Lauderdale, Dallas, and Phoenix, and is moving soon into Houston. . . .

Oak succeeds in part because it's usually the first STV operator in each market it enters and is also more enthusiastic than most about exploiting addressability's pay-per-view capability. Last December, for example, when Oak's stations

broadcast a Rolling Stones concert live, 146,000 subscribers paid $10 each to watch. . . .

Oak sweetens its STV take by making the decoder boxes itself. It sells its boxes to its wholly 1100➡ owned STV ventures, which can take a 10% investment tax credit, based on the regular retail price of about $150. But the boxes cost Oak considerably less to make, so the tax credit is effectively higher. While Oak is its own biggest customer, it also sells the boxes to other STV operators with addressable systems. . . .

When, or if, cable comes

All together, Oak's STV operations—nonexistent five and a half years ago—bring in 24% of company revenues and 30% of operating profits. Lately, STV has started looking even better. Conventional wisdom when STV started held that it 1200➡ would wither when cable inevitably came to town, offering an array of channels for about the same price. But things are not developing as expected. . . .

Oak may have other, so far untested, advantages in the battle with cable. Its engineers are working on splitting the STV signal in half to provide two channels where today there is only one, thus doubling the attractiveness of STV. And because its ventures pay back their investments so quickly— before cable arrives—they could, if necessary, cut prices fiercely and still make money.

Still, no one supposes that STV will ever supplant cable or even come close. That's just fine with 1300➡ Oak. The reason: it stands to profit as cable prospers because the addressable box, forsaken for years, has recently become the hottest product in the cable industry. . . . The box's cost has come down, reliability has improved, and many conventional 1350➡ boxes are fully depreciated and ripe for replacement.

——STOP——ASK FOR YOUR TIME——

Record time immediately and answer
the questions on content.

Time_____Sec.	RATE (from table on page 315):	R. _____
No. Correct:_____ (key on page 330)	COMPREHENSION (10% for each correct answer):	C. _____
VI–16	EFFICIENCY (R × C):	E. _____

Record on Progress Chart on page 299

ANSWER THESE QUESTIONS IMMEDIATELY (VI–16)

1. (T – F) Oak Industries is a very old and conservative company.

2. (M. C.) Oak was one of the pioneers in the technology of:

_____(1) cable TV.

_____(2) video games.

_____(3) gambling.

_____(4) hang gliding.

3. (T – F) The cable TV converter boxes were very useful but not very efficient.

4. (C   ) Solutions to many problems came with the development of a new box that was _____.

5. (T – F) Oak's new box was an immediate success.

6. (C   ) Broadcasting scrambled signals and then leasing out descrambling units known as _____ TV.

7. (T – F) Perenchio lost money in the Oak deal.

8. (T – F) If cable comes, STV stations can still be profitable.

9. (M. C.) The key man in Oak's development was:

_____(1) Rancho Bernardo.

_____(2) ''Nick'' Carter.

_____(3) A. J. Perenchio.

_____(4) T.V. Scrambler.

10. (T – F) Oak achieved success by taking an early gamble in the video revolution.

Exercise VI–17

Wooded Wonderland
by ROGER HART

(Reprinted from the November 1973 issue of *Natural History*
by permission of the editorial secretary.)

──────────── **WAIT FOR SIGNAL TO BEGIN READING** ────────────

Exploring with Peter

I'd spent an hour searching for Peter because I wanted him to take me to his favorite places. Finally he came whipping along the road on his bike. He took me to his favorite spot and showed me the remains of a model landscape, all but destroyed by yesterday's rain, which his sister and he had built out of shale and twigs.

Chattering away, he hurried me along to his fishing place, convincing me it was *the* fishing place and that no one else knew about it.

Days like this with eight-year-old Peter were part of two years of field investigation into the ex-100 ploration and experience of the landscape by children as they develop from birth to eleven years of age. Ironically, more is known about the relationship of baboons to their habitat than of the activities of children to their outdoor environment. It was important that I spend an extended period of time with a group of children living in a small, distinct environmental unit, so that I could monitor their movements and behavior and obtain reliable data. I selected Wilmington, Vermont, for the study because it not only met these specifications but also incorporated many 200 characteristics of an urban environment.

Children need to explore

For their social and emotional development children need a physical environment that they can comprehend and within which they feel competent and secure. They also have an urge to explore the landscape; this is related to their need to experience the diversity and extent of the components of their environment and to see these as part of a whole.

The need to feel effective as an agent of change is another strong factor in the healthy development of a child. Compared to the complex and ever changing world of people, the natural environment 300 remains relatively stable. A child can immediately see the transformations that he has effected. I have observed that children from about the age of three freely and frequently modify the environment if there are suitable areas available.

Children will not manipulate or modify an overtly cared for and guarded landscape. Manicured lawns, miniature trimmed trees, and the absence of dirt piles, surface water, and large trees all convey a strong message to a child—"do not touch." This is the situation in most new suburban housing tracts. In this respect the children of impoverished inner-city 400 areas have a richer environment in abandoned lots containing piles of dirt, scrap wood, and other materials suitable for modifying the physical landscape, although such areas lack the special qualities—trees, water, varied topography—that natural elements possess.

The range a child is allowed to travel without accompaniment is limited by parents for a variety of reasons: inferior ability to deal with traffic and the desire to avoid unfavorable social influences are among the most common. Also, because children have to squeeze much of their play into short periods of time defined by institutional and family schedules, 500 they must play within their neighborhood. In this defined space, a child must find a landscape sufficiently rich to satisfy the desire for free exploration, discovery, collection, and creation.

Children's needs for a variety of experiences are usually thought of as being provided for by such institutions as playgrounds, organized sports, schools, camps, and clubs. Such solutions, however, lead to more compartmentalization, segregation, and specialization of children. Their desires for play are not sufficiently regular or planned to enable them to prestructure all activities with their friends. Many of a child's most exciting games or projects happen by chance.

Social development may be fostered if children 600 have free access to areas where they can meet casually and engage spontaneously in cooperative activities such as building complex stream systems in the sand.

Children also need places where they can be alone; I have watched children many times playing alone in the dirt or by a small pool of water. Freedom from interruption and interference by adults is important; time to reflect on experience and develop a personal ordering of his world is essential to a child. By experiencing and re-creating the world in this way, a child can develop the individuality 700 that is needed for healthy relations with others.

Importance of a physical environment

The physical environment also plays an important role in supporting a child's emotional security and developing a sense of personal identity. Children who encounter frequent changes of residence or who live in neighborhoods that suffer from heavy wrecking and building activity will find it difficult to construct a stable image of the environment. Continuity of experience is most important. I have observed, for example, that a child can develop such a strong attachment to a tree that its removal, if necessary, must be carried out with care and understanding. It is an indication of the need to give order to the world that a child's most frequently observed creative activity out of doors involves the building of miniature 800 landscapes—cities, houses, garages, and airports.

Using the natural environment

The natural environment offers a wealth of play potential for young children, with trees and small patches of water the most valued elements. One tree can engage a child for days at a time or, periodically, over a span of years. Manufacturers of playground equipment have found it impossible to recreate such richness. The children of Wilmington demonstrated to me that there are countless routes up "a good 900 climbing tree"; many notches, cracks, or rough spots can be used, depending upon the child's desire for challenge at any time. Any kind of bush or tree allows children to exercise great creativity in the construction of houses, forts, tents, and imaginative laboratories. A mature tree is excellent, of course, for hanging a rope swing and has the added attraction of a host of insects.

Children do not need large wooded areas; in fact, many play only on the fringes of woods. But the pressures of land use and an unwillingness to recognize the importance of natural elements have 1000 1350 made them scarce in most urban areas. Natural elements are systematically removed from suburban areas and urban playgrounds in the name of esthetics, durability, and safety.

Adventure playgrounds

One solution to the lack of suitable natural areas for city children are "adventure playgrounds," in which they are given the opportunity and the materials to dig tunnels, plant gardens, and build places by themselves. These playgrounds try to create in microcosm the qualities of a town most valued by children, with trees, varied topography, earth, and building materials as essential elements. Adventure playgrounds were introduced in Denmark during 1100 World War II and caught on in England during the 1950s, but the concept has been slow to take hold in the United States. A major criticism by adults is that these areas are ugly, but the inclusion of trees could do much to alleviate this problem. It is doubtful, however, that such playgrounds could be created in sufficient numbers to be freely accessible to younger school-age children for they require the expense of a permanent and competent supervisor. Small natural areas, or "minicommons," spaced every few blocks and unsupervised except for the 1200 care of trees, could provide a supplement to larger, more widely spaced adventure playgrounds.

One hundred and forty years ago Friedrich Froebel, the German educational philosopher, introduced the concept of kindergarten into education. His ideas anticipated later findings in stating that a child is by nature a doer, and therefore learning is secondary to activity, out of which it grows. Froebel also emphasized the importance of experiencing the harmony of the natural world in the development of the child. Many kindergartens and schools still lack these qualities, but the city designer also has a responsibility in this matter. For the richer and 1300 fuller development of metropolitan children, more minicommon lands, featuring an abundance of trees, water, and soil, should be made as accessible as the wooded adventureland available to children in Wilmington, Vermont. Children do not need to be taught how to explore and learn; they will do so naturally given an environment that will allow it to happen.

——STOP——ASK FOR YOUR TIME——

Record time immediately and answer
the questions on content.

Time_____Sec.	RATE (from table on page 315):	R. _____
No. Correct:_____ (key on page 322)	COMPREHENSION (10% for each correct answer):	C. _____
VI–17	EFFICIENCY (R × C):	E. _____

Record on Progress Chart on page 299

ANSWER THESE QUESTIONS IMMEDIATELY (VI–17)

1. (T – F) The author studied children from birth to eleven years old.

2. (M. C.) The children studied in this article lived in:

_____(1) Atlanta, Georgia.

_____(2) Wilmington, Vermont.

_____(3) Spokane, Washington.

_____(4) San Jose, California.

3. (T – F) Children usually will not manipulate an overtly cared for and guarded landscape.

4. (C   ) A child needs to feel that he can modify his _____.

5. (M. C.) According to this writer, the range a child is allowed to travel is limited for all of the following reasons *except:*

_____(1) Children have an inferior ability to deal with traffic.

_____(2) Parents desire their children to avoid unfavorable social influences.

_____(3) Police do not understand a child's need to play freely.

_____(4) Children must squeeze much of their play into short periods as defined by schedules of home and school.

6. (T – F) Children's needs are adequately met by playgrounds, sports, camps, and clubs.

7. (T – F) Children need some places where they can be alone.

8. (T – F) A child's most frequently observed creative activity out-of-doors involves the cutting down of trees.

9. (T – F) Children need to be taught how to explore and learn in a natural environment.

10. (C   ) Friedrich Froebel, the German educational philosopher who introduced the concept of the kindergarten, believed that learning was secondary to _____.

Exercise VI–18

The Pompidou Art Center
by THOMAS W. TRASKA

(Reprinted from the February 1980 issue of *Travel/Holiday*
by permission of the editor and the author.)

──────── **WAIT FOR SIGNAL TO BEGIN READING** ────────

Fifty million visitors

During the first six months after its much pub-licized opening, the Centre d'Art et de Culture de Georges Pompidou attracted almost three million visitors—more than the Louvre and Napoleon's Tomb combined. Soon nicknamed "le Pompidou," or simply "le Beaubourg," after the neighborhood above which it rises, the Center logged more than six million visitors after one year—more than the Eiffel Tower. Upon celebrating two and one-half years of ever accelerating admission, the Beaubourg announced the arrival of its 50 millionth visitor. Celebrating its third anniversary, le Beaubourg is the number one attraction in a city of countless 100 legendary landmarks.

Needless to say, there are good reasons why thousands of visitors flock daily to the eighteenth-century neighborhood between Les Halles and Le Marais to stream through the vast glass cube which opened to notoriety on February 1, 1977. This is not an ordinary museum; in fact, it is not, strictly speaking, just a museum at all.

It has been reviled as "a warehouse," an "art refinery" and an "eyesore" by some and praised as a "temple of artistic creation" and a "giant happening" by others. The taxi driver who left me off on rue de Renard by the colorful wall of yellow, 200 red, blue, green, silver and white pipes and conduits, which carry air conditioning, heating, water, electricity and supplies throughout the structure, simply called it "une grande faute"—a great mistake.

Whatever the reaction, the reaction is strong. You cannot visit the Beaubourg without being caught up in its myriad activities and impressed by its en-ergetic view of art. The goal of its planners was not only to conserve the great art of the twentieth century but also to "animate" it. In this it is a success.

Here you can brush up on any of 40 languages 300 on cassette tapes in the language lab; attend a sym-phony where the hall itself becomes an instrument as its wall panels are electronically manipulated to change the sounds; chip a chunk off a two-ton chocolate sculpture; visit the atelier of Constantin Brancusi; watch the genealogy, life and death of an automobile; chart the geography of color; follow a publicity campaign; roam through a collection of one million books, periodicals and slides on art and design; contemplate landmarks of modern art; or trace the development of ordinary household utensils. Children may browse through a library where "no 400 adults are allowed" or crawl into a snakelike sculpture covering about an acre of space.

The restaurant on the top floor is not only one of the most interesting places in all of Paris to meet Parisians and visitors but it also offers spectacular views of the city from its rooftop terraces.

Marvel or monstrosity

What is the idea behind this mammoth and unorthodox organism of glass and girders, of pipes and ducts and moveable walls that rises so conspicuously on the Beaubourg Plateau in the Fourth Arrondissement—one of Paris' most ancient neighborhoods?

According to Robert Bordaz, President of the 500 Centre Georges Pompidou, "The creation of the Center is a singular adventure. For the first time, cultural activities which were heretofore dispersed are brought together in order to offer the visitor a comprehensive image of contemporary creation."

Judging by the multiplicity of activities and tremendous popularity of the Beaubourg, that idea has been brought to life.

For the design of the Center, an international competition was held in 1970. Architects from all over the world submitted 681 projects representing 49 countries. After much deliberation, an interna-tional jury awarded the highest honors to the project 600 by Renzo Piano from Italy and Richard Rogers from England. In March of 1972, excavation at the site of the future Center began, following this winning design. Upon completion, the total cost of the building came to approximately $200 million, making it one of the world's most expensive buildings. And the annual operating budget of well over $20 million makes it one of the world's best endowed art centers. What has all this talent, money and notoriety brought about?

The enormous structure of the Pompidou Center houses four principal departments of activities within its variable and flowing spaces on six floors.

Le Musee National d'Art Moderne

Formerly Director of Stockholm's *Moderna* 700 ⟵
Museet, Pontus Hulten directs the National Museum of Modern Art, whose collections were moved from the museum on l'avenue du President Wilson. Mr. Hulten describes the new location as "a place allowing better overall knowledge of art in this century from 1905 to the present, offering a spirit of openness, curiosity, participation and communication as well as reflection."

The 1,100 works of art in the National Museum form a nucleus of the Beaubourg and the focal point of interest for the foreign visitor. Located on the fourth and fifth floors, the works are arranged chronologically beginning with the work of "les Fauves" 800 ⟵ such as Derain, Vlamnick, Braque, Dufy and Matisse up to the contemporary "Pop Art" of Jasper Johns, Claes Oldenburg, Andy Warhol and Jim Dine. From 1905 to the present, the collection ranges over Surrealists such as Dali, Ernst, Magritte, Masson, Miro and Calder; Italian Futurists like Severini, Russolo, Carra, Magnelli and De Chirico; and "les Naifs" such as Leger, Klee, Picasso and Chagall.

A strength of the collection is its German Expressionist group of Kirchner, Nolde, Kandinsky, Pechstein, Macke, Kupka and Malevitch.

Although the Center was intended as a showcase of contemporary French art, the museum seems to 900 ⟵ lean heavily on the American "Pop Artists" and American Abstract Impressionists such as Jackson Pollock, Mark Rothko and Ad Reinhardt—a tendency initially criticized in the French press.

Between 1971 and 1976 almost 1,500 drawings were placed in the Modern's collection of graphic art and include works of Picasso, Picabia, Malevitch, Masson and Matisse among others.

The modern museum also maintains a schedule of new and changing exhibits.

Le Centre de Creation Industrielle

The center for Industrial Creation (CCI) is concerned mainly with providing information and resources for analysis and research to the professional designer. For example, its Product 1000 ⟵ 1350 ⟶ Information service provides data on every type of product found in the environment. Of interest to the visitor are the CCI's innovative exhibits touching on all aspects of our visual environment. Exhibits have ranged from "The City and the Child" and "The Advertising Campaign" to "The World of Railroad Stations."

Bibliothèque Publique d'Information

The Public Information Library, occupying sections of the first, second and third floors, was conceived as a living encyclopedia oriented toward the general reader and not the specialist. The separate catalogues, organized alphabetically by title and author, subject and genre, make it easy to 1100 ⟶ locate any of the approximately one million items accessible to the public.

Visitors from almost anywhere may assuage their homesickness by consulting the extensive collection of French and foreign periodicals, newspapers and publications in literature, music and art, and the comprehensive survey of international news displayed in the library.

For a respite from the pace of the city or from a rigorous siege of sightseeing, visitors are welcome to listen to records from the large collection on file, to look at slides on any number of topics or to brush up on their French or any of 40 foreign languages 1200 ⟶ in the language laboratory. The library also mounts changing exhibits.

L'Institute de Recherche et de Coordination Acoustique/Musique

Between the Beaubourg building itself and the fifteenth-century flamboyant Gothic style Church of Saint Merri is the immense subterranean "laboratory" of the IRCAM or Center for Acoustical and Musical Research headed by Pierre Boúlez. Here musicians may translate scores into the most sophisticated space age computer language. Theoreticians may attempt to create sounds that have never been heard outside of their own imaginations. Engineers may experiment with the effects of varying shapes of a room on a loudspeaker.

1300 ⟶ The center of this vast underground network of soundproof areas and elaborate techniques is an experimental hall with room for an audience of 400 people—L'Espace de Projection. Acoustically and visually, the Espace de Projection of adjustable acoustics is a marvel. The public is invited to hear the latest productions of this research center at various concerts.

——STOP——ASK FOR YOUR TIME——

Record time immediately and answer
the questions on content.

Time_____Sec.   RATE (from table on page 315):   R. _____

No. Correct:_____   COMPREHENSION (10% for each correct answer):   C. _____
(key on page 330)

VI–18   EFFICIENCY (R × C):   E. _____

Record on Progress Chart on page 299

ANSWER THESE QUESTIONS IMMEDIATELY (VI-18)

1. (C   ) The Pompidou Art Center is considered as one of the most popular attractions in Paris because of its large number of _____.

2. (T – F) One of the goals of the planners of the Center was to animate twentieth-century art.

3. (T – F) The Art Center is generally recognized as an artistic masterpiece.

4. (T – F) The Pompidou Art Center is located in one of the newest and most modern areas of Paris.

5. (M. C.) The organization of the Center is:

_____(1) an unidentified number of special attractions.

_____(2) one massive, integrated complex.

_____(3) four major departments of activities.

_____(4) six floors of separate collections.

6. (T – F) The Museum of Modern Art tends to emphasize primarily French pop artists and abstract impressionists.

7. (C   ) Many of the exhibits in the Center for Industrial Creation are provided for analysis and research of the professional _____.

8. (T – F) The Public Information Library is generally of more interest to the specialists in art and music.

9. (T – F) The experimental hall in the Center for acoustical and musical research is an acoustic wonder.

10. (M. C.) According to this article, Georges Pompidou was:

_____(1) the philanthropist who provided funds for the building.

_____(2) the mayor of Le Beaubourg.

_____(3) the first director of the museum.

_____(4) not identified in any specific way.

Exercise VI–19

Vitamin C and Other Good Things for Your Gums

by LAURIE LUCAS

(Reprinted by permission from *Prevention,* August, 1980,
Copyright by Rodale Press, Emmaus, Pennsylvania.)

— WAIT FOR SIGNAL TO BEGIN READING —

Periodontal problems

Karen, a 48-year-old housewife, felt sure her oral hygiene was superb and her mouth was in tiptop shape. After all, didn't she brush her teeth twice a day, floss after each meal and get regular dental checkups? In fact, until a year ago, Karen wasn't even certain what a periodontist was. Alas, she learned in a big hurry.

But not until she noticed blood trickling from her gums when she cleaned her teeth or bit into corn on the cob. The resulting treatments, she recalls, were "the most painful and expensive ordeals I ever endured in my life." The therapy not only cost 10← more than $2,000, but cost her four teeth in hopes of salvaging the remaining 28.

Unfortunately, Karen's problem is hardly unique. It is an all-too-common one, shared by about 100 million Americans suffering from periodontal disease. The word "periodontal" refers to the gums and other tissues supporting the teeth. Also known as pyorrhea, the insidious deterioration of the gums and underlying jawbone is marked by inflammation and infection, eventually causing the teeth to loosen and fall out.

Oral specialists almost universally indict plaque—an invisible coating of food debris, dead cells and bacteria—as the most typical cause of periodontal 200← disease. If this gummy slime is not removed by constant brushing and flossing, the germs continue to proliferate and the tissue around the tooth breaks down, causing pockets of inflamed gums. As these pockets deepen, the gums recede and the bone in which the teeth are anchored begins to shrink and disappear.

Surgery

To halt the disease's progress, periodontal surgery is often employed to trim away unhealthy tissue, sculpture the bone around the teeth and reattach the gums by stitching them in place. In more severe cases, bone cells from other mouth areas may be grafted or transplanted. 300←

Although most investigators believe that bacteria cause periodontal disease, a growing number of researchers now suspect that nutrition serves a "modifying" or "secondary" role. Recent scientific reports indicate that sound nutritional habits may change both the susceptibility to and the severity of periodontal disease. After a three-year review of current data, Thomas Grow, Ph.D., who teaches biochemistry at the University of Florida College of Dentistry in Gainesville, concluded that although periodontal disease can't be prevented or cured solely by dietary means, "to ignore the nutritional considerations of these disease processes is a serious mistake."

400→ Within the last couple years, moreover, three impressive studies have strengthened earlier clinical findings demonstrating a relationship between vitamin C and periodontal health. Perhaps most exciting is a project by Henry Mallek, D.M.D., Ph.D., who discovered that vitamin C supplementation fortified the gums' protective barrier against periodontal disease.

Vitamin C plays a role

Dr. Mallek now teaches periodontics at the University of Detroit's School of Dentistry in Michigan. But for his thesis two years ago at MIT, he measured the ascorbic acid (vitamin C) levels of gingival (gum) tissue in teens and young adults before and after 500→vitamin C supplementation. Dr. Mallek selected 18 patients aged 17 to 24 with "little" or "slight" periodontal disease and divided them into two groups. Every day for a month the 11 members of the experimental group received 1,000 milligrams of vitamin C, while the 7 members of the control group received no extra nutrients. At the trial's end, measurements indicated higher ascorbic acid levels—15 to 20 times higher in some subjects—in the supplemented group's gums.

One researcher who believes that subclinical vitamin C deficiency may be more common than is generally recognized is Olav Alvares, D.D.S., Ph.D. 600→Inflamed and bleeding gums could develop as a consequence of subclinical ascorbic acid deficiency, claims Dr. Alvares, an associate professor of oral biology at the University of Washington in Seattle.

To study the connection between vitamin C deficiency and susceptibility to periodontal disease, the investigator used two groups of monkeys. The four control animals were fed a nutritionally adequate diet and ascorbic acid supplements. The six experimental monkeys received diets deficient in vitamin C and no extra nutrient boosts.

After researchers induced periodontal disease during the study's 23rd week, Dr. Alvares noted a "greater inflammatory response" in the experimental group. "Because of their ascorbic acid deficiency," he told *Prevention*, "we think their susceptibility 700 to periodontitis may be related to their white blood cells' impaired ability to ingest bacteria." Dr. Alvares also suggests that when oral specialists are unsuccessful in halting the progression of a patient's gum disease, the dietary intake should be evaluated. "Somehow," he contends, "in some cases patients still develop periodontal disease despite the dentist's efforts to minimize plaque accumulation."

Joseph Aleo, D.D.S., Ph.D., is in favor of reexamining the vitamin C nutritional requirement to prevent periodontal disease. His new laboratory research in Philadelphia suggests that ascorbic acid offers protection against this destructive gum condition 800 if cells are treated two to five days before exposure to endotoxin, a bacterial product that is one of the prime causes of periodontal disease. Dr. Aleo, associate dean and professor of pathology at Temple University's Dental School, told *Prevention* that adding ascorbic acid to a culture medium protected the fibroblasts (cells that produce connective tissue to support the teeth) against the endotoxin. Five days prior treatment with vitamin C, notes Dr. Aleo, afforded almost "complete resistance" to the endotoxin challenge.

Folate cuts inflammation

Other nutrients, however, are no slouches when it comes to fighting the ravages of gum disease. Some 900 investigators now think that folate, one of the B vitamins, reduces gingival exudate (fluid flowing from the infected and inflamed gums), an observation that suggests improvement in gum tissue health. In a more recent survey, Richard I. Vogel, D.M.D., of the New Jersey Dental School in Newark, demonstrated that folate may also help protect the gums of women taking oral contraceptives. Pill users receiving four milligrams of folate daily had significantly less gingival inflammation after 60 days than others who took no extra folate.

Dental research teams have approached the problem of periodontal disease from yet another perspective: tooth loss due to shrinking jawbone in- 1000 duced by a calcium deficient diet. In a well-known

study, Lennart Krook, D.V.M., Ph.D., and several associates fed 10 people with advanced periodontal disease 500 milligrams of calcium twice a day over a six-month period. At the experiment's conclusion, the investigators recorded remarkable improvements and even reversals in the disease process such as reduced inflammation and pocket depth along the root and decreased tooth mobility. Indeed, with the extra calcium in the diet, the shrunken jawbones began reforming and laying down new bony growth.

Phosphorus-calcium ratio is key

1100 Investigators in California have targeted another important dietary variable: the ratio of the mineral phosphorus to calcium. With a coworker, Kenneth E. Wical, D.D.S., chairman of the removable prosthodontics department at Loma Linda University's School of Dentistry, found that as phosphorus levels rise, increasing the phosphorus to calcium ratio, jawbone resorption (or shrinkage) seems to accelerate. They suggest that calcium and vitamin D supplementation will help strengthen the jawbone's resistance to mechanical and biochemical stress in patients with severe bone loss and an unbalanced phosphorus to calcium ratio.

Michael Alfano, D.M.D., Ph.D., is among a new breed of specialists who recognize the "modu- 1200 lating" role of nutrition in periodontal disease. For patients with severe jawbone loss, he recommends along with more traditional therapies a shift away from high meat diets toward low-fat dairy products rich in calcium.

"There's 20 times more phosphorus than calcium in beef," says Dr. Alfano, who directs the Oral Research Program at the Fairleigh Dickinson University School of Dentistry in Hackensack, New Jersey.

One doctor who remains dubious is Paul Keyes, D.D.S., a clinical investigator for the National Institute of Dental Research in Bethesda, Maryland. Claims Dr. Keyes: "A calcium deficiency would affect the whole body. The amount lost from the 1300 jawbone (in periodontal disease) is trivial when compared to the body's reserves."

Dr. Keyes recommends an old-fashioned kind of therapy as a gum disease preventative: salt and baking soda. "I've never seen a serious periodontal problem in people who brush regularly with these antibacterial agents," he contends. Of course, patients 1350 don't swallow the mixture.

——STOP——ASK FOR YOUR TIME——

Record time immediately and answer
the questions on content.

Time_____Sec.   RATE (from table on page 315):   R. _____

No. Correct:_____   COMPREHENSION (10% for each correct answer):   C. _____
(key on page 322)

VI–19   EFFICIENCY (R × C):   E. _____

Record on Progress Chart on page 299

ANSWER THESE QUESTIONS IMMEDIATELY (VI–19)

1. (T – F) If a person brushes and flosses his teeth well and gets regular dental checkups, he will not get periodontal disease.

2. (C   ) The typical cause of periodontal disease is _____.

3. (T – F) In some severe cases of periodontal disease, bone surgery is essential.

4. (T – F) Most experts agree that the primary cause of this disease is poor nutritional habits.

5. (M. C.) The gum's protective barrier against periodontal disease can be strengthened most effectively by:

   _____(1) supplements of vitamin C.

   _____(2) eating lots of apples.

   _____(3) eating lots of fresh vegetables.

   _____(4) supplements of vitamin E.

6. (T – F) The research monkeys' susceptibility to periodontal disease may have been related to the inability of their white blood cells to overcome bacteria.

7. (M. C.) Another nutrient that helps fight gingival inflammation is:

   _____(1) folate.

   _____(2) zinc.

   _____(3) endotoxin.

   _____(4) iron.

8. (C   ) Nutritional research indicates that one factor in the disease may be the balance between phosphorus

   and _____.

9. (T – F) People who eat a high meat diet have a higher incidence of shrinking jawbones than those who eat a low-fat dairy products diet.

10. (T – F) Serious periodontal problems are seen in people who brush regularly with salt and baking soda.

Exercise VI–20

Moon Rockets and Mud Hens
by GARY SOUCIE

(Reprinted from the January 1975 issue of *National Parks & Conservation
Magazine* [now *National Parks* magazine] by permission of the editor.
Copyright © 1974 by National Parks and Conservation Association.)

─────────── **WAIT FOR SIGNAL TO BEGIN READING** ───────────

Coexistence

Even in a land as noted for its natural, social, and political improbabilities as Florida, Merritt Island National Wildlife Refuge stands out. Imagine a refuge where the wildlife shares its habitat with rocket launch pads, a four-mile-long runway for the space shuttle orbiter, and the world's largest building—the Vehicle Assembly Building, where Saturn V moon rockets are assembled. The refuge shares common boundaries and 140,393 acres on the north end of Merritt Island with the National Aeronautics and Space Administration's Kennedy Space Center.

Lest you think the national wildlife refuge is just a token public relations ploy by NASA, be $\overset{100}{\leftarrow}$ advised that Merritt Island is the major waterfowl wintering area in Florida, that the Audubon Christmas Bird Count consistently ranks the island at or near the top for national wildlife refuges, and that the refuge is the nesting or breeding habitat for a number of rare and endangered species, among them the southern bald eagle, dusky seaside sparrow, brown pelican, Florida round-tailed muskrat, American alligator, green turtle, and the Florida manatee.

At the behest of the Bureau of Sport Fisheries and Wildlife (now the Fish and Wildlife Service), the Merritt Island refuge was originally established in 1963 on 25,300 acres of the space center. Nine $\overset{200}{\leftarrow}$ years later NASA initiated action to include the entire space facility within the refuge. Apparently troubles in other Florida wildlife habitat—namely alligator poaching and planned jetport development in the Everglades—convinced Dr. Kurt H. Debus, the space center's director and a dedicated preservationist, to turn over the remaining space center land to the refuge.

Merritt Island's wildlife apparently gets along just fine with the space program. In the ponds around launch pads 39A and 39B, where the Apollo moonshots and Skylab launches took place, tens of thousands of ducks and wading birds and pelicans $\overset{300}{\leftarrow}$ congregate, apparently quite used to the bustle of work crews and heavy machinery. During an actual launch, of course, the birds are alarmed into flight, but as soon as the rocket has cleared the area, they quickly settle down again.

Study of ecosystem

Under NASA grants, researchers from Florida Technological University (FTU) and the Florida Institute of Technology are studying the Merritt Island ecosystem and are preparing a study entitled "Ecological Effects and Environmental Fate of Solid Fuel Rocket Exhaust" for the space shuttle program.

FTU biologists, in their first year of study, $\overset{400}{\rightarrow}$ cataloged 537 species of plants in 313 genera; thirty plant communities in six major classes of plant associations ranging from mangrove marshes to scrub flatwoods; thirty-one species of frogs; three species of toads; twenty species of snakes, including the eastern diamondback rattler, cottonmouth water moccasin, and the black racer; six species of lizards; eleven species of turtles; and two thousand individual alligators. Merritt Island is one of the only four major rookeries of the declining loggerhead turtle in North America, the others being Cape Romain, South Carolina; Jekyll Island, Georgia; and Hutchinson's Island, Florida.

Mammals too!

$\overset{500}{\rightarrow}$ A mammal catalog will take longer but will include at least white-tailed deer, feral hogs, armadillos, bobcats, otters, raccoons, spotted skunks, the rare round-tailed muskrat, and many small rodents.

Prior to these studies, the Fish and Wildlife Service and the Indian River Audubon Society had identified 251 species of birds that regularly use the refuge (a third of which nest there, including twenty pairs of eagles and two thousand royal terns), and another thirty-one species that are classed as accidental visitors.

During the winter of 1973 Merritt Island refuge was visited by some 100,000 ducks of two dozen species and about 125,000 coots (also called mud $\overset{600}{\rightarrow}$ hens). Especially notable among the winter residents are large numbers of warblers and other passerines, including a small but stable nesting population of dusky seaside sparrows, and an extraordinary population of Louisiana herons.

Unique partnership

The relationship between NASA and the wildlife agency is unique in American conservation; the strange partners seem to get along as well as the wildlife and the rockets. Refuge manager Robert G. Yoder says, "Working relations between the refuge and NASA are excellent, considering the two parties: one of them with the primary purpose of launching rockets and the other with a major objective of wildlife conservation. It is a unique relationship and $\overset{700}{\leftarrow}$ one which we feel is mutually beneficial." Space center director Dr. Debus says, "The harmonious relations we enjoy with the Bureau of Sport Fisheries and Wildlife have worked to our mutual advantage. The Bureau's effective administration of areas not required for launch operations assures us that the great natural assets of the center will be preserved for the benefit of the public."

Administration of Merritt Island is not quite an equal partnership, however. NASA maintains primary jurisdiction, although land management outside the areas specifically devoted to rocket assembly and launching and other space program operations has $\overset{800}{\leftarrow}$ been delegated to the Fish and Wildlife Service. The NASA-Interior agreement under which the refuge exists is essentially a special use permit by NASA "on a basis of noninterference with the space program." The agreement reserves to NASA "the right to site any future space program facility at any location on the permitted area . . . , to make any use of said land which may be necessary in connection with the space program of the United States . . . ," and the right to terminate the permit "in the event NASA determines the termination of the permit is necessary in the interest of the national space program, the national $\overset{900}{\leftarrow}$ defense, or the public welfare." The major space program incursion into the refuge since the signing of the agreement on June 2, 1972, has been the siting of the space shuttle runway, the northern end of which is just behind refuge headquarters. This situation is hardly ideal for a wildlife refuge; but until the space center came along, Merritt Island was privately owned and partially under development, and it is doubtful the refuge could have been established without NASA. The space agency's property investment on Merritt Island is around $72 million, a bit steep for $\overset{1000}{\leftarrow}$ the refuge program budget.

Security area

About a third of the refuge/space center is fenced off as security area and closed to general public use. The reason, according to Gordon L. Harris, the space center's chief of public affairs, is "to protect the public from the rockets and the rockets from the public." During launch operations and any other time a rocket is on the pad, somewhat more of the refuge is closed to the public, because the explosive potential of a staged Saturn V rocket is equivalent to that of $\overset{1100}{\rightarrow}$ one million pounds of TNT, or about fifty times that of the Hiroshima A-bomb.

Despite these drawbacks, Merritt Island National Wildlife Refuge provides a good habitat for many diverse creatures. NASA and the space program seem to be the least of the refuge's problems. The major ecosystem changes on the island occurred before NASA's arrival—road building, mosquito control, some residential development, and the dredging of the Intercoastal Waterway. Brevard County wanted to site a waste incineration plant just outside the refuge/space center boundary on the extreme southwestern end of the complex and dump the ash on federal land. NASA said no—not because $\overset{1200}{\rightarrow}$ of any interference with the space program but because of the proposed incinerator's proximity to bald eagle and peregrine falcon nests. As a legacy of the pre-refuge days when the Corps of Engineers was NASA's land-managing agency, the wildlife agency has commercial orange groves and twenty-six commercial bee-keeping special use permits.

Publicity releases from NASA and the aerospace industry, in defending the space program against public attack and congressional budget-cutting, are fond of citing such space program spin-offs as teflon-coated frying pans; but Merritt Island National Wildlife Refuge may turn out to be one of the most $\overset{1300}{\rightarrow}$ impressive accomplishments of man's ventures into outer space, unless an expanded space program gobbles up the whole refuge. However, that does not seem likely with Dr. Debus in charge of the Kennedy Space Center and with conservation on the rise in a Congress grown somewhat disenchanted $\overset{1350}{\rightarrow}$ with the space program.

——STOP——ASK FOR YOUR TIME——
Record time immediately and answer
the questions on content.

Time_____Sec.	RATE (from table on page 315):	R. _____
No. Correct:_____ (key on page 330)	COMPREHENSION (10% for each correct answer):	C. _____
VI–20	EFFICIENCY (R × C):	E. _____

Record on Progress Chart on page 299

ANSWER THESE QUESTIONS IMMEDIATELY (VI–20)

1. (M. C.) The Merritt Island National Wildlife Refuge shares its habitat with rocket launch pads, a runway, and the world's largest building, the:

    _____(1) NASA Headquarters Building.

    _____(2) Sears Tower.

    _____(3) Empire State Building.

    _____(4) Vehicle Assembly Building.

2. (T – F) The Christmas Bird Count consistently ranks the island at or near the top for national wildlife refuges.

3. (C   ) The ecosystem studies on Merritt Island have been financed by _____.

4. (T – F) Merritt Island is one of only four major rookeries of the declining loggerhead turtle in North America.

5. (M. C.) The reason for fencing around a large part of the area is to protect the security of the:

    _____(1) endangered species.

    _____(2) mud hens and ducks.

    _____(3) space shuttle launch pad.

    _____(4) rockets and the public.

6. (T – F) Administration of Merritt Island is not an equal partnership.

7. (T – F) The explosive lift-off power of the rockets is a constant threat to the mud hens in the sanctuary.

8. (T – F) During launch operations and when rockets are on the pad the whole refuge is closed to the public.

9. (T – F) NASA refused to let Brevard County site a waste incineration plant just because the ash might interfere with the space center program.

10. (C   ) Expansion development and long-term plans for this wildlife refuge have been largely dependent on preservationist Dr. Kurt H. Debus, the director of the _____ .

Study Reading Exercises

Instructions

You know very well that some of your reading requires concentrated attention to details with emphasis on long-term retention for examinations or other later application.

These study exercises provide practice in a self-recitation type of reading. They are designed to help you understand some of the principles of self-recitation and spaced review. In a limited sense they provide a practical illustration of the fact that it is easier to remember soon after reading than it is after an interval of time occupied by other reading or other activities. In actual practice, however, you will need to make up your own questions for the periods of self-recitation.

Here the stress is still on increasing the reading speed and the reading level, but involved also is a stress on a study technique that will help improve long-range retention of material read. Here you expose yourself to ideas not only by reading about them, but by pausing frequently to think about them and to apply them to practical questions on the material. You should find that this technique helps to break the monotony of reading and to enable you to read with less tension and less fatigue because you bring into use more than one type of study approach.

These exercises are matched with those in Series VI for length, difficulty, and type of questions asked. Comparisons of your reading rate and reading efficiency scores on these drills with the comparable exercises in Series VI will give you some measure of your progress in mastering this technique of self-recitation as you read.

General directions on these exercises are the same as for those in Series VI except that you do not check your time until you have finished the tenth question in the exercise. You then compute your *rate, comprehension, and efficiency* as before, using the keys on pages 322 and 330. Then record your scores on the progress charts for study reading on page 299.

Suggestions

Although standardized exercises measuring efficiency in higher level study skills have not yet been devised, this series of exercises on a study type of reading provides a unique type of reading activity designed to combine some of the best features of developmental reading skills and higher level study skills. Your use of them will expose you to a practical application of some of the study skills that were discussed in detail on pages 19 to 24 of this book. Perhaps a rereading of that material would help you to develop a better understanding of what you are doing in this Series.

This system of reading provides an automatic break every few hundred words, so that you may stop and think about the material read and answer questions about it. This break gives your eyes a chance to rest and to come back to more effective reading on the next unit. The alternating pattern of thinking, reading, thinking, writing, thinking, reading, and so on helps to keep you more alert and to avoid many outside distractions and daydreaming.

The efficiency scores you attain on this series will be a good indication of your success in mastering some basic techniques of self-recitation and applying them to your reading activities.

Nothing in this series will keep you from going back to reread in order to answer questions. There is nothing to keep you from going ahead and reading the questions first, then coming back to read the material. Either of these approaches takes extra time, however, and will keep your rate and efficiency scores down. Hard work and deep concentration should enable you to read materials at a maximum short-term reading rate and to achieve enough short-term retention to handle the questions adequately.

Note that asking and answering questions at intervals do provide additional study skill application to reinforce those ideas that you picked up in rapid reading and to plant them more firmly in your mind. This process reduces the dependence on high levels of initial comprehension and frees you to function at a more rapid rate of initial study reading—in short periods interrupted by the self-recitation activity.

Efficient reading in study situations is not merely word-by-word reading at any rate. Good study habits require other thought processes to back up the reading process and reinforce it.

Good reading habits cannot be defined in terms of rate and comprehension alone. They are characterized by an open mind, a wide range of flexibility in reading rate, a judgment as to relative importance of material being read, and a deep understanding of oneself as related to the reading project at hand. Reading rate as a reading tool is only part of the repertoire of a good reader.

Exercise VII–1

Szzzzzzz
by TIM BRITT

(Reprinted from the May 1967 issue of *Wyoming Wildlife*
by permission of the editor.)

———————————————— **WAIT FOR SIGNAL TO BEGIN READING** ————————————————

One warm afternoon while working in eastern Wyoming, I dove to a nearby windmill to fill a water jug. As I slid out of the station wagon and my foot touched the ground, I heard it. Quickly, but quietly, I pulled my foot back into the vehicle and reached over the front seat for my .22 rifle. Taking but a second to eliminate the problem, I sat there and trembled for a few minutes.

It's not that snakes, even poisonous rattlesnakes, bother me so much, but I like to meet them on my own terms. Actually I think snakes are interesting critters, but again, I would rather be interested in them, than have them interested in me.

Many people have a tremendous, unreasonable fear of snakes, such as one timid lady who turns her head whenever a snake is shown on television. The nearest I have ever come to losing my life was when I was about twelve and brought a garter snake into the kitchen. Mom didn't limit use of the broom to the snake; she used it on me, too.

The prairie rattlesnake, *Crotalus viridis,* rarely found at elevations above 8,500 feet, inhabits rocky open regions, grassy prairies, canyons, and agricultural areas. Like many other reptiles, they are cold-blooded and derive their warmth from their environment. This is why it is quite common to see them basking on rocks, gravel roads, and other denuded areas, especially during the cool morning and evening hours. Prairie rattlers differ from other poisonous snakes in that they appear to be most active during the daylight hours while most poisonous snakes are nocturnal.

Warm-blooded animals are the preferred food of rattlesnakes. They feed to a great extent on field mice, small rabbits, gophers, prairie dogs, and occasionally birds.

Colorings of the Crotalus viridis

The ground color, or background color, of the prairie rattler varies from a light gray to "viridis," the species name for green in Latin. Actually, the most common color is a mottled grayish-green, with dark blotches, resembling solid figure-eights located down the center of the back from immediately behind the head all the way to the rattles. There may be from 33 to 55 of these blotches and they are normally outlined with white.

1. (T – F) The prairie rattlesnake is also known as the *Crotalus viridis*.
2. (T – F) The prairie rattlesnake is most commonly found in elevations above 8,500 feet.
3. (T – F) Most poisonous snakes are active during the daylight hours.

The prairie rattler is a common species

The prairie rattler, a species which inhabits a wide range over the western portion of North America, is one of the most widespread rattlesnakes in the United States.

When born, rattlesnakes with only a blunt "pre-button" at the tip of their tails, first shed their skin a few hours after birth and the rest of the first segment, or button is formed. Each time the snake sheds its skin a new segment is added to the rattle. This occurs two to four times annually. A snake's age cannot be determined by counting the segments of the rattle and attributing one year for each segment. If the button is on the rattle, a snake's approximate age can be estimated. Simply count the segments of the rattle and divide by three, the average number of times a rattlesnake sheds its skin per year.

This system can only be used when the button is intact at the tip of the rattle. Since the terminal rattles often wear away until finally they are lost, a string of nine rattles is unusual. The average lifespan of Wyoming rattlesnakes is seven or eight years, although some rattlers have been known to live up to twenty-five years. A twenty-year-old rattler would have 60 segments in its rattle at the three segments per year rate. Obviously, the rattles wear away, or are broken off much too rapidly to permit age estimation by this method except in the case of young snakes. The rattles are brittle and hollow and the segments fit together loosely; when the snake vibrates its tail the segments rub together and produce the "buzzing" or "rattling" sounds.

Prairie rattlesnakes vary in length 700 ←

The stories involving five- and six-foot rattlesnakes usually refer to one of the diamondback species or the timber rattler, for the prairie rattlesnake varies only from two to four feet when mature.

Despite the terrible and frightening stories told around campfires on dark nights, the chances of being fatally bitten by a snake are more remote than being struck by lightning. More persons die annually from the sting of bees, hornets, scorpions, and wasps and from spider bites than from snakebite. According to a national survey, conducted by Dr. Henry M. Parrish, the danger of suffering from the bite of a 800 ← poisonous snake while hunting or fishing is very low. Of all the snakebite cases in the United States only about five percent involved hunters and fishermen. The same survey showed that about fifty persons in this country die from snakebite each year. Most of the fatal snakebites in this country result from imprudent handling of poisonous snakes. Statistics show that the greatest share of the victims are less than twenty years of age. Bites are usually sustained on the hands, arms, legs, and feet.

A poisonous snake doesn't always coil before it strikes. Rattlesnakes cannot strike more than two- 900 ← thirds or three-fourths of their body length unless they have a firm backing or they are striking downward from an incline. A rattlesnake does not always rattle before striking, however, and this warning should not be counted on by the outdoorsman.

4. (M. C.) The snake sheds its skin as often as:
———(1) once a month.
———(2) once a year.
———(3) once every season.
———(4) two to four times annually.
5. (　C　) If the ————— is present on the rattle, a snake's approximate age can be estimated.
6. (T – F) The prairie rattlesnake varies from two to four feet in length when mature.
7. (　C　) In this country about ——— persons die each year from snakebite.

Rattlesnake venom, yellowish in appearance and slightly thicker than water, is a completely tasteless and odorless substance, which disintegrates rapidly upon contact with the air. This fact casts a shadow of doubt on the validity of the old story about the fang stuck in a boot. As folklore has it, a man was fatally struck on the foot by a rattler about 20 feet long, or some such length. Years later the man's son, putting on his father's boots, immediately died 1100 → from venom still in the fang, which had become embedded in the boot when the father was bitten.

The power of the strike embeds the fangs into the flesh of the victim and the muscles around the poison glands force the venom from the glands through the ducts and fangs into the wound. The action is similar to that which takes place in a hypodermic needle and syringe. The amount of poison ejected at any one time varies from part of a drop to two cubic centimeters, depending upon the 1200 → size of the snake and the amount of time which has elapsed since the last venom ejection.

The prime reason everyone should know the poisonous snakes of their region, their habits, distribution, and abundance is that it will ease the mind of the individual in his outdoor pursuits. Most people have heard so many fantastic stories involving snakes that they have developed a fear, rather than a respect for snakes. In most cases snakes, even rattlers, are beneficial and of direct economic value. In instances where poisonous snakes present special hazards around campgrounds, fishing areas, and other recreational sites, perhaps their destruction is justified.

1300 → 8. (M. C.) The color of rattlesnake venom is:
———(1) slightly yellowish.
———(2) deep gray.
———(3) milky white.
———(4) mottled brown.
9. (T – F) The action of the rattlesnake bite is likened to that of the hypodermic needle and syringe.
10. (T – F) The author urges one to kill every 1350 → rattlesnake he sees.

——STOP——ASK FOR YOUR TIME——

Record time immediately.

Time———Sec.	RATE (from table on page 315):	R. ———
No. Correct:——— (key on page 322)	COMPREHENSION (10% for each correct answer):	C. ———
VII–1	EFFICIENCY (R × C):	E. ———

Record on Progress Chart on page 299

Exercise VII–2

Stress: The Teen-age Brand
by DIANE EICHER

(Reprinted from the May 18, 1982 edition of the *Denver Post* by permission of the editor.)

—————— WAIT FOR SIGNAL TO BEGIN READING ——————

Feeling

They know the feelings: the sweaty palms, the headaches, the hands that shake and the face that blushes.

And they offer reasons for why it happens. Their parents are divorcing. Or a best friend is pressuring them to steal, or ditch school, or perhaps experiment with drugs. Maybe schoolwork is piling up, or their parents announce the family will be moving to a faraway place, which means a new school, new friends.

They're clear, all right, these teen-agers at Mrachek Middle School in Aurora, in talking about life's problems. But many of them seem surprised to hear that there's a catchword to describe it all. It's $\overset{100}{\longleftarrow}$ something they've heard their parents talk about.

Stress

It now comes in a teen-age variety!

And there are programs popping up to help stressed teens deal with what ails them. The Mental Health Association of Colorado, Inc. began a stress management program called TEANS—Teaching Early Adolescents New Skills—this school year, and Mrachek eighth graders recently participated in a TEANS session.

TEANS is being used in Aurora and Jefferson County Public Schools and in Adams County Schools. Trained volunteers present two one-hour programs during which the teens themselves offer input on specific stressful situations. $\overset{200}{\longleftarrow}$

And teens do talk readily about what's upsetting them. But it isn't just idle talk, or the product of dramatic, overactive adolescent minds. In fact, the major health problem of youths today is "generalized nervousness," according to a 1982 report on "Adolescent Health in Colorado" released by the Colorado Department of Health.

1. (M. C.) TEANS is an abbreviation for:

    _____(1) Teenagers Energy and Needs Study.

    _____(2) Teaching Early Adolescents New Skills.

    _____(3) Temporary Emergency Action Now Support.

    _____(4) The Early and Necessary Skills.

2. (T – F) The major health problem of youths today is generalized nervousness. $\overset{300}{\longleftarrow}$

Negative solutions

The report found that suicide is one of the top three causes of teen-age death, along with accidents and violence.

TEANS volunteers are attuned to those facts. During the program, they ask students to describe their symptoms of stress and to provide a list of possible solutions to problems. "Running away" and even "suicide" are among the more oft-mentioned solutions, but volunteers work with students to help them realize those are negative ways of dealing with stress.

The volunteers encourage students to come up with positive methods of coping with their stress, like $\overset{400}{\longrightarrow}$ talking to a counselor, exercise and meditative periods.

Causes are complex

At Mracheck last week, seven students offered insight on what they consider stressful. Parents divorcing was the first topic that came up, something four of the seven had experienced. They discussed stepparents, live-in boyfriends or girlfriends and the other residue of a family break-up.

"When your parents get divorced, you don't know what's going to happen . . . you're so confused, you wonder where your Dad is going," said Amy, remembering back to 10 years ago when her parents divorced.

Another stress-causer mentioned was peer pressure, "like when kids ask you to ditch," said $\overset{500}{\longrightarrow}$ Rich. "Yeah, and you're not cool if you don't do it," agreed Denine Cheeks.

Selena said she bent under the peer pressure once, "ditched, got caught, and I'll never do it again." And Amy said she recently skipped classes—by herself, "because I felt like I hated school"—and sat in Aurora Mall, just thinking. But the guilt—and stress—of that situation got the better of her, she says, and she confessed to her mother.

There is also peer pressure to drink and to use drugs, agreed the students.

3. (C) The most often mentioned negative $\overset{600}{\longrightarrow}$ solutions of stress from teen-agers are "running away" and _____.

4. (T – F) TEANS has found that peer pressure really isn't a major source of stress.

Pressures within the school

Another cause of upset mentioned by the students is school—homework, teachers and even the school building itself. Mracheck is an "open" school, with classrooms opening at the back into a common area, and the noise level is noticeably high.

"And if you tell the teachers you can't hear, they say, 'If you'd keep your mouth shut, you'd hear better,' " Selena said.

The students seemed to feel that parents—and sometimes teachers—have forgotten the problems as- ←700 sociated with adolescence, and a prime complaint is that no one will listen to them. For that reason, "escaping" to a friend's house—for dinner or to spend the night—seems to be a popular way of dealing with stress. Michele said she deals with upset by "going to places that make you feel good—made-up places," or, in other words, spending time in her room, thinking.

Caring in the home

Some of the teens say they send signals to their parents, to make them aware of the stress youths are facing, but the adults still don't take notice. ←800

"When I get in trouble, I want my mom to care," said Dom. "I would like her to make me feel guilty, or something."

Mike said a source of stress in his life is "when parents compare you to an older brother or sister" and cannot understand "why you can't be just like 'em."

5. (T – F) The noise level of Mracheck is a cause of stress to these teen-agers.

6. (C) Some students reduce stress by going to a friend's house for dinner or overnight visits to _____ pressures at home.

7. (M. C.) A prime complaint of students is that ←900 the common problems of adolescents are not recognized or have been forgotten by their:

      _____(1) peers.
      _____(2) brothers and sisters.
      _____(3) parents and teachers.
      _____(4) best friends.

Success of TEANS

Reports from the TEANS program, which began in 1981 with a grant from the Frost Foundation, indicate it is successful, said Pat Cary, volunteer coordinator for the Mental Health Association. While this program is targeted at early teens, one Mracheck

teacher said she believes "stress management in kindergarten would be good . . . these kids need it. A lot are looking for some help." She listed 1000→ mood swings—from depression to giddiness—and students who are easily angered among the manifestations of stress.

A fellow teacher said she tries to help stressed students by emphasizing the importance of a sense of humor about life and by offering suggestions on "how they might come out of a situation being a stronger individual."

Pat Cary said the TEANS program was begun because teen-agers don't have many sources to help them deal with stress and upset, which seems to be occurring today at an earlier age. She said she recently heard of a fourth grader who had developed 1100→ migraine headaches, apparently stress-induced.

For some of the students, the program helps them realize there is help out there, and they aren't alone in their worries, said Chris Rich, the mental health association's director of communications.

"One volunteer team was confronted by a seventh grade boy with tears in his eyes. His parents were filing for divorce that afternoon and he hadn't wanted to tell anyone," said Rich. "His teacher later told the team the boy hadn't talked for several months, had been very depressed, and that no one had been able to discover the cause."

1200→ Teen-agers identify many causes of stress in their lives most of which they feel are beyond their control. Many of these relate to the home situation such as divorce or death in the family, moving to new locations and having to make friends and conflicts with parents or siblings. Other pressures come from the school—lunchroom, playground, tests, teachers and homework. Many pressures come from interpersonal relationships with friends or enemies or from peer group pressure about drugs, liquor or other attitudes and activities. TEANS is helping many of them to realize that there are people who care.

1300→ 8. (T – F) One Mracheck teacher believes that stress management in kindergarten classes would not be good.

9. (T – F) TEANS was developed because stress and upset are occurring at an earlier age.

10. (T – F) The program helps some students to realize there is help available and that 1350→ they are not alone in their worries.

——STOP——ASK FOR YOUR TIME——
Record time immediately.

Time_____Sec.   RATE (from table on page 315):   R. _____

No. Correct:_____   COMPREHENSION (10% for each correct answer):   C. _____
(key on page 330)

VII–2   EFFICIENCY (R × C):   E. _____

Record on Progress Chart on page 299

Exercise VII–3

You and Your Depression
by STEPHANIE TATE

(Reprinted from an original article of the Uniwyo Reading Research Center
by permission of the director.)

—————————— **WAIT FOR SIGNAL TO BEGIN READING** ——————————

Depression has been well-known and has been described unmistakably from at least the time of Hippocrates, who called it melancholia. It is one emotional problem from which most people seem to suffer at one time or another. There are times when everyone feels dejected, gloomy, and listless. Bad moods can sneak up on you no matter who you are, where you live, or what your occupation is. A great deal of Abraham Lincoln's adult life is said to have been spent in depression, and Winston Churchill called the blues his "black dog." Many different people have many different names for it, but the $\overset{100}{\leftarrow}$ dejection of spirits is a common occurrence.

1. (C) Depression has been well known since the time of Hippocrates, who called it _____.

2. (T – F) Only certain types and classes of people are subject to depression.

Causes of depression

Depression can be caused by any number of circumstances. A physical problem or chemical changes in the body can trigger depression. The death of a loved one, some kind of trouble at home, dissension at work, or disappointment in a love affair also can work to bring on the blues. Often a supposedly forgotten event from the past can come $\overset{200}{\leftarrow}$ flooding back into your memory, encouraging a depressed mood.

Depression affects people in their adult years more frequently than those in their younger years. Young adult men seem to react with depression more commonly than young women, whereas toward middle age, women are more frequently affected.

The emotional problem of depression can have many physical side effects, brought about by the state of the mind, even though it is not an illness in itself. You may experience a general slowing down of physical and mental activity, and a loss of appetite and loss of weight while feeling dejected and discouraged. $\overset{300}{\leftarrow}$ You may lose interest in your surroundings and life may appear to be a hopeless burden.

3. (T – F) Physical side effects usually accompany depression.

4. (M. C.) Depression most frequently affects:
_____(1) male children.
_____(2) young adult males.
_____(3) female children.
_____(4) young adult females.

You can help yourself

As long as your depression remains in this state, there are ways in which you can help yourself to get over your sadness.

1. Alter some common day-to-day routines that you have, such as changing your time and place for $\overset{400}{\rightarrow}$ lunch. Go to work along a different route, or do something new with your spare time. If possible take a vacation to a place you have always desired to see. Lean away from the old and commonplace events toward the new and exciting.

2. Think of and list the accomplishments which you have made in both your personal and professional lives, then go back over them and consider the state of your mind beforehand—were you confident or sad and downcast? Remember that you can only do as much as you think you can.

3. Attempt to occupy yourself with some kind of $\overset{500}{\rightarrow}$ physical exertion. Set up a series of exercises to do with a friend, or invite an acquaintance to play tennis, giving you an opportunity to learn more about them. Keeping active with others often helps to take our minds off troublesome matters.

4. Build up confidence in yourself by focusing on things that you do especially well, and then pursue them. There is something that we all do exceptionally well, so don't be afraid to hunt for it.

5. Remember that there are others who would appreciate and who need your attention and concern. Transferring your concentration to $\overset{600}{\rightarrow}$ someone who is lonely or ill will not only help them to cope with their lives, but it will give you a feeling of satisfaction, importance, and well-being. There is nothing so rewarding as the knowledge that you have helped another person.

6. Discussing your situation with someone who cares is a good way to get your troubles off of your chest, and getting everything out into the open will almost always make you feel better. There *are* people who care. Try sharing your blues with

a member of your family, a close friend, or clergyman. Also, most communities now have telephone "hotlines" which you can call any time 700← of the day or night and speak anonymously with someone who wants to listen and help you. These people are there for just that reason, so don't have any qualms about calling them.

7. Enroll in some kind of a special interest class, learning to do something you've always wanted to, such as karate, guitar, astrology, or gardening. While expanding your knowledge and having fun, you can also strike up new friendships with fellow classmates. It is also worth considering attending classes at a nearby college or university to obtain that level of education or that degree that you 800← have always wanted. It is a challenge, but you must convince yourself that you are fully capable of meeting it.

5. (T – F) Helping others who are in need may be good for you when you are depressed.
6. (T – F) Stable behavior in sticking to old, familiar routines is essential in trying to combat periods of depression.

Severe depression

The occasion may sometimes arise when facing your persistently deep depression alone seems impossible. As your condition worsens, you may experience even more physical difficulties, such as lowered blood pressure and loss of muscle tone, as 900← well as sadness of facial expression, constipation, and insomnia. Unhappiness; the attitude of uncertainty, doubt, and defeat; and thoughts of suicide are common occurrences in severe depression. When you reach this state, completely submerged in your own problems, do not hesitate to seek professional help. Your local Mental Health Association can direct you as to where to find good professional assistance, taking into consideration your needs and problems and your financial condition.

Danger signals

In order to enable a person to distinguish between normal, temporary depression and a problem needing professional help, the National Association for Mental Health has listed 10 danger signals to 1000← watch for concerning the severity of your depression. You should seek help if:

1. You suffer a loss of self-esteem and continually question your personal worth.

2. You experience extreme dependency.
3. You tend to completely withdraw from people, because you feel immense fear of being rejected.
4. You lose your ability to concentrate on normal, everyday functions, such as writing, reading, and conversation.
5. You possess feelings of guilt and self-blame.
6. You threaten or attempt to commit suicide.
7. Changes occur in physical activities such as eating, sleeping, and sex.
1100→ 8. You find yourself reacting to other people's words and deeds with extreme irritability and sensitivity.
9. You feel hopeless and filled with despair, and the feeling persistently increases.
10. You find difficulty in coping with your emotions, and you misdirect your anger because of it.

7. (C   ) Thoughts of suicide are common in cases of _____ depression.
8. (T – F) The ten symptoms listed are normal and do not require professional help.

The National Association for Mental Health stresses that an individual should only become concerned if the danger signals persist without specific 1200→ cause, for some signals may be reactions to tension, disappointment, or loss, which will soon pass. Do not, however, fear to seek professional help. When you are plagued with a physical disorder you desire as well as require treatment, and so you should for severe depression, also. The important thing to remember is that depression is not only a normal occurrence, but that it is one of the easiest conditions to treat and cure. Do not be afraid if your emotions seem to become confused and in conflict. Confront them, help yourself to banish them, and obtain assistance if you find that you need it.

1300→ 9. (T – F) Many symptoms of depression may be based on temporary conditions which will change soon.
10. (M. C.) In cases of severe depression, the National Association for Mental Health encourages:
_____(1) withdrawal from the situation.
_____(2) intensive self-analysis.
_____(3) obtaining professional help.
1350→ _____(4) waiting for new changes.

——STOP——ASK FOR YOUR TIME——
Record time immediately.

Time_____Sec.   RATE (from table on page 315):   R. _____

No. Correct:_____   COMPREHENSION (10% for each correct answer):   C. _____
(key on page 322)

VII–3   EFFICIENCY (R × C):   E. _____

Record on Progress Chart on page 299

Exercise VII–4

Science and People

(Reprinted from the February 1975 issue of *The Royal Bank of Canada Monthly Letter* by permission of the editor.)

──────────── WAIT FOR SIGNAL TO BEGIN READING ────────────

Research is work

Some persons are challenged by the mysteries of the moon and stars; others by the mysteries of living things, including themselves. Seldom do we find a person who is not, at some time or another, interested in one of these mysteries, who does not feel the challenge of the unknown.

Nonscientists tend to believe that a laboratory is swarming with eye-popping discoveries every week, but no knowledge is gained and no theory is developed without a great deal of labor. Both the "pure" scientist and the "applied" scientist work arduously.

Theoretical research seeks to know things 100 better; applied research seeks to learn how to do things better. In one case knowledge is sought for her own sake; in the other case the desire is to find ways of applying a newly discovered fact or theory to solution of practical problems.

Research workers in pure science are vastly enlarging our field of knowledge. In John Milton's memorable words they are "still searching what we know not by what we know, still closing up truth to truth as we find it."

Asking questions

Aristotle, son of a physician at the court of King Philip of Macedon, organized the first scientific inquiry in the world. He was so curious about nature that he had a thousand men collecting material for 200 his natural history.

A good scientist has a tidy mind that keeps thoughts and facts in their proper place; ability to discriminate so as to discern what evidence should be accepted and to discard what is irrelevant, paying attention to small details in research to prevent something vital from slipping away unnoticed; ability to recover quickly after work has been interrupted, keeping an eye on what neighbors are doing in the way of finding out and doing new things.

The most valuable of all the perceptions we 300 use in scientific research is the perception of cause and effect. Too often we say "in the beginning" and imagine that we have pinned down a vital point from which everything else follows, but before long we find ourselves asking: "What was there before the beginning to make it possible for the beginning to begin?"

Insofar as science accepts the principle of 400 causality, and inasmuch as the universe cannot be self-caused, we are led inevitably to the conclusion that there must be a causal factor not comprised within our present view of the universe. Thomas Aquinas put this principle in a nutshell: "No thing is its own cause, for then it would precede itself, which is impossible."

1. (C) The most valuable perception in scientific research is the perception of _____ and effect.

2. (M. C.) John Milton's memorable words:
   ____(1) "Still searching what we know not by what we know, still closing up truth to truth as we find it."
   ____(2) "What was there before the beginning to make it possible for the beginning to begin."
   ____(3) "No thing is its own cause, for then it would precede itself, which is impossible."
   ____(4) "Necessity is the mother of invention."

3. (T – F) Thomas Aquinas stated this principle: "No thing is its own cause, for then it would precede itself, which is impossible.

Science and progress

Science is one field in which progress should be measured and given credit. Therefore, we should not withhold praise from famous men and women of the past because their concepts have been outdated: our important duty is to improve on what they did.

Newton has been acknowledged as the greatest scientist in history: he discovered the law of 600 gravitation, the laws of motion, the principles of optics, the composite nature of light, and with Leibnitz he invented the calculus.

There is not, however, any concept of Newtonian physics, believed at one time to be the whole truth, that has not been displaced. As Professor Alfred North Whitehead remarked: "The Newtonian ideas are still useful, as useful as they ever were, but they are no longer true in the sense in which I was taught they were true."

Icarus, whose airplane wings fell off and dropped him into the sea when the heat of the sun melted the wax that fastened them together, performed a useful service.

700 ←

The first crude microscope was focused on the hidden minutiae of life by the Dutch microscopist Leeuwenhoek, in the 17th century. Three men, Professor E. Burton of Toronto University, James Hillier, and Albert Prebus, produced the electron microscope in 1936, opening up a whole new world to investigation. Roger Bacon discovered the explosive possibilities in a combination of saltpeter, sulphur, and charcoal and produced gunpowder in the 13th century. The present century saw the birth of the atom bomb.

4. (T – F) The concepts in Newtonian physics have not been displaced.

5. (T – F) Icarus had the wax melt on his airplane wings. 800 ←

6. (C   ) The first crude Dutch-developed microscope was in the _____ century.

7. (T – F) Roger Bacon produced the electron microscope.

Important advances

Nobody can deny that science and invention have raised mankind to a higher level than the one occupied a hundred years ago. They have increased the output of work per man-hour, so that we are able to cope in some measure with the increased demands of a greatly enlarged population. Science has developed new products that cater to our comfort while increasing the number of occupations at which men and women may work.

900 ←

Two of the greatest advances of our age are the production of drugs like penicillin, insulin, and sulpha, which have prolonged our lives by many years, and labor-saving machinery which has made work easier and provided more leisure.

Science has given nutrition, literacy, and health to people in the developed nations, and they are being extended, though slowly, to the developing peoples of the world.

Science and technology change not only our material environment but our institutions, and this is a good reason for everyone to keep up with what is happening, to learn about, or try to anticipate, the 1000 ← social implications of scientific discoveries and attainments. Every newly discovered process and every invention has brought with it unpredictable uses, created new obstacles to be overcome, and uncovered new problems and frustrations to be resolved.

The discoveries of science cannot be put to practical use without the services of the technologist who makes inventions by interpreting something, adding or taking away, or dividing or multiplying something. Every invention that proves useful stimulates further scientific studies which lead to improvements and to more inventions.

Nearly everyone has said at least once: "Necessity is the mother of invention," but it remained for Herbert A. Leggett, Vice-President of the Valley National Bank in Arizona, to say in one of his monthly letters: "We live in an era when invention is the mother of the unnecessary." 1100 ←

Automation is the technological revolution of the second-half of the 20th century, just as mass production was of the first-half. The late Norbert Wiener, distinguished mathematician of Massachusetts Institute of Technology, did much of the conceptual thinking that underlies the new technology. He predicted that automation will lead to "the human use of human beings"; that we shall experience a phasing-out of the type of factory labor which 1200 → involves repetitive tasks. This will release men and women to use their specifically human qualities— their ability to think, to analyze, to synthesize, to decide and act purposefully—instead of wasting their talents on the dreary work that machines can do better.

These are fragments extracted from the scoresheet of science, typical of thousands of discoveries and developments that have contributed, alone or with improvement, to the advancement of human beings in peace and war.

8. (M. C.) The article mentioned two great advances of our age:

_____(1) soil conservation and medicine.

1300 →

_____(2) production of drugs and labor-saving machinery.

_____(3) electronic discharge and technological revolution.

_____(4) biological sciences and academic interests.

9. (T – F) Medical science is the technological revolution of the second-half of the 20th century.

10. (T – F) Norbert Wiener predicted that automation will lead to "the human use of human beings." 1350 →

——STOP——ASK FOR YOUR TIME——

Record time immediately.

Time_____Sec.

No. Correct:_____
(key on page 330)

VII–4

RATE (from table on page 315):

COMPREHENSION (10% for each correct answer):

EFFICIENCY (R × C):

R. _____

C. _____

E. _____

Record on Progress Chart on page 299

Exercise VII–5

Gardens under Glass
by LILLIAN STROHM

──── **WAIT FOR SIGNAL TO BEGIN READING** ────

More than a century ago, smoke belching from the factories of London led to the development of the miniature greenhouses now found in so many American homes, offices, and classrooms. Today, the glassed-in gardens are called "terrariums." Back in 1800s, though, they were called "Wardian cases," after Dr. Nathaniel Ward, an English surgeon and amateur horticulturalist.

Ward was dismayed to find that the bog ferns in his London garden were being killed by industrial pollution. Then, while inspecting a moth chrysalis he had covered with soil in a sealed glass jar, Ward found bog ferns actually thriving in their protected 100← environment. After experimenting with other plants in similar containers, he arrived at a remarkable conclusion. If plants had light, still air, and the proper amount of moisture, they could live encapsulated for years without care.

Subsequently, practical application of that discovery made it possible for countries to exchange plants that previously could not stand long ocean voyages. Sealed in glass cases, Shanghai sent new tea plants to India; Brazilian rubber trees were introduced into Ceylon; and botanical gardens exchanged rare and exotic plants from all parts of the world. More recently, ecology-minded home owners have found that modern Wardian cases can be made into tables 200← or hung from the ceiling in clear bowls of everything from antique bottles, old fishbowls, and brandy snifters to Steuben crystal cracker jars and various commercial plastic containers.

Used as classroom projects, terrariums demonstrate how a closed ecological system works. Energy supplied by sun or artificial light triggers the plants to use carbon dioxide from the air, plus water and plants food from the soil to produce plant sugars, a process called photosynthesis. The plant sugars take oxygen from the air and give off carbon dioxide, which is recycled back into the terrarium to make 300← more plant sugar, a process called respiration.

1. (T – F) Using a terrarium Shanghai sent tea plants to India.
2. (C   ) In the 1800s, glassed-in gardens were called _____ cases.

3. (M. C.) The process by which plant sugars take oxygen from the air and give off carbon dioxide is called:
   _____(1) resorcinol.
   _____(2) respiration.
   _____(3) photosynthesis.
   _____(4) photolysis.

The container

The possibilities are almost unlimited, from a traditional New England berry-bowl made with moss, tiny ferns, and creeping partridgeberry to a grouping of tropical plants, a woodland scene, or a 400→ cultivated garden. Here are some pointers on setting up your own "Wardian case."

A glass container is preferable to plastic for creating a suitable micro-climate for house plants. Plastic has a tendency to retain water droplets instead of dropping them back into the soil. Clear glass is better than tinted because it will transmit all available light. A glass bowl with an opening large enough to accommodate your hand is as easy to plant as a rectangular aquarium tank and the lustrous glass is equally decorative on a table or hanging from a bracket. Clear glass strips leaded together make a beautiful container to use with antique furnishings, and a 20-inch glass globe on a metal 500→ stand blends with modern furnishings.

The garden

Plants grouped in a terrarium should provide a contrast in color, form, texture, and growth habit; yet they need to be compatible enough to thrive in the same light, temperature, soil condition, and heavy humidity.

The woodland garden reproduces a natural scene in miniature by using native plants and rocks. Hemlock, spruce and laurel seedlings, wintergreen, club mosses, rattlesnake plantain, and partridgeberry are recommended for woodland scenes. Flowering plants might be violets, hepatica, bloodroot, or wild 600→ strawberries; lichens and fungi give color and contrast, but they need to be watched for mold.

The bog garden needs acid soil and a cool location. Carnivorous plants that catch and eat flies and insects include: purple pitcher-plant, sundew, huntsman, born venus flytrap. Other bog plants are sheep laurel, swamp blueberry seedlings, and cranberry.

The cultivated garden is easiest for a city dweller to create since these plants come from a florist or department store. Among the most popular plants are:

Filtonia, a wild plant from Peruvian jungles, has pink or white veins. The *Club moss* or *rainbow moss* is difficult to grow outside a terrarium. *Hoya* $\overset{700}{\leftarrow}$ *wax plant* has fragrant pink flowers. *Pittosporum,* of Japanese origin, is a shiny evergreen that can be trimmed into any shape. *Podocarpus,* an evergreen, will stay compact if pruned regularly.

The genus *Begonia* includes more than 1,000 species; for terrariums, the dwarf varieties are required. *Croton* is a tropical plant that needs bright light for best color. *Maranta* from Africa has beautifully marked leaves in shades of green, white, and pink. For ground cover, use *baby tears, philodendron, grape ivy,* or *moneywort.*

4. (T – F) Tinted glass will transmit light better than clear glass.
5. (T – F) Most materials for cultivated gardens $\overset{800}{\leftarrow}$ can be purchased from a florist.

The planting

First, wash the container in hot soapy water, rinse it thoroughly, and allow it to dry completely for 12 hours. To hide soil and roots, line container with sheet moss up to one-fourth the height of the container, placing top of moss toward glass. Then, add two inches of white pebbles for soil drainage, and spread a thin layer of hardwood charcoal bits over the pebbles to absorb chemical salts and decay gases. Next, use a layer of sphagnum moss to prevent the soil from washing into the drainage pebbles, or use $\overset{900}{\leftarrow}$ a layer of nylon net which serves the same purpose and will not decay. Now, add soil mix to fill the container one-fourth to one-third full. If you make your own mix, you will need one-third pasteurized garden loam, one-third builders' sand, and one-third milled sphagnum moss (moist but not soggy).

To make a bottle garden, the same materials are used but special tools are needed. A funnel made of rolled paper should reach almost to the bottom of the bottle to pour in the growing medium. A wire coat hanger can be fashioned into a plant placer by using straight wire with an open loop on one end. $\overset{1000}{\leftarrow}$ Plant roots are washed then lowered into the bottle with this positioner.

Long tweezers made from split bamboo are needed to hold the plant in the bottle until the soil is tamped down with a cork attached to the end of a dowel.

To water a bottle terrarium, run the water down the inside of the glass, using a kitchen basket. The water level can reach the top of the drainage pebbles. Usually, no ventilation is needed. When $\overset{1100}{\rightarrow}$ plants need trimming, a razor blade taped to a dowel makes clean cuts.

6. (T – F) Washed containers should be slightly damp for ideal planting.
7. (T – F) No special tools are needed for bottle gardens.
8. (T – F) To water a bottle terrarium, water is run down the inside of the glass.

The growing

Most gardens encased in glass do best with filtered light, not direct sun. If artificial light is used, special fluorescent tubes developed to simulate actual sunlight rays are more effective than regular tubes. A standard amount of light is 20 watts for every square foot of growing space.

Although sealed terrariums are possible, some $\overset{1200}{\rightarrow}$ ventilation is usually needed to keep the glass from fogging and obscuring the plants inside. Inserting a small pebble between the lid and container is one easy way to ventilate. Use very little fertilizer to encourage slow growth and trim back plants that become overgrown. Mold is the most common terrarium plant disease. Remove all infected plants and treat the garden with a fungicide spray. Too much water, not enough light, or poor ventilation will encourage mold.

One final thing: *talk* to the plants in your terrarium. If you do, they will grow better— especially $\overset{1300}{\rightarrow}$ if you remove the lid first. For as you talk, you will breathe carbon dioxide into the container, and green plants thrive on carbon dioxide.

9. (M. C.) Standard wattage for light per square foot of growing space is:
      ——(1) 100
      ——(2) 80
      ——(3) 40
      ——(4) 20
10. (C) $\overset{1350}{\rightarrow}$ The most common terrarium plant disease is ————————.

——STOP——ASK FOR YOUR TIME——

Record time immediately.

Time————Sec.

No. Correct:————
(key on page 322)

VII–5

RATE (from table on page 315):

COMPREHENSION (10% for each correct answer):

EFFICIENCY (R × C):

R. ————

C. ————

E. ————

Record on Progress Chart on page 299

Exercise VII–6

Totems under Siege
by ALEXANDER K. CIESIESKI

―――――――――― **WAIT FOR SIGNAL TO BEGIN READING** ――――――――――

With its teeth bared menacingly, the larger of the two figures has a fanciful likeness of a giant rock oyster. It was painstakingly carved into the base of an enormous totem pole during the mid-1800s by the Tlingit Indians of the Pacific Northwest. A smaller figure, on the right, represents an Indian fisherman. Together, the two objects portray the Tlingit legend of an angler who hooked a devilfish under a rock, only to have it tear loose. Against the better advice of his companions, the fisherman tried to capture his prey by reaching into a crevice, where the oyster seized him by the wrist. Despite heroic attempts to $\overset{100}{\longleftarrow}$ rescue him—or so the story goes—the poor fellow drowned in the rising tide.

For decades, this famous arrangement stood in the Tlingit village of Cape Fox, Alaska. Then, in 1938, it was moved south to Saxman Totem Park near Ketchikan at the base of the Alaskan panhandle. Weathering has produced some definite decay in these figures, but they are among the healthier remaining specimens of Alaska's "endangered totems," some of which were carved more than a century ago.

Today, totem carving is almost a lost art. And ironically, the same damp coastal climate that favors $\overset{200}{\longleftarrow}$ the growth of the western red cedars used for totems also provides excellent conditions for decay fungi that can destroy a pole in 50 years. Consequently, the few remaining totem poles of British Columbia and the Alaskan panhandle are under attack from wood rot and fungi. "Without protective measures, this unique heritage is doomed to slow deterioration," warns Dr. Joe W. Clark, wood products pathologist at the U.S. Agriculture Department's Forest Products Laboratory in Madison, Wisconsin.

1. (T – F) The Indian fisherman in the legend had been seized by a devilfish.
2. (M. C.) The paired totem arrangement is now $\overset{300}{\longleftarrow}$ located at:
   _____(1) Tlingit, Alaska.
   _____(2) Cape Fox Village.
   _____(3) Ketchikan Park.
   _____(4) Saxman Totem Park.
3. (C   ) Decay fungi can destroy a totem in about _____ years.

The makers of the Alaskan totems, the Tlingit and Haida Indians, were fishermen and hunters in a land of dense rain forests, rugged mountains, and countless streams. Although their territory was more than 1,000 miles long, it was only 100 miles wide. Here, the golden age of totem carving flourished from 1830 to 1880, occasioned primarily by two $\overset{400}{\longrightarrow}$ factors. The first and most obvious of these was the increased availability of iron tools. Secondly, and perhaps most important, a bourgeois class of Indian trappers emerged during the 1800s and commissioned craftsmen to create hundreds of totem masterpieces.

Interestingly enough, hardly any surviving totem poles stand today in the places where they were originally erected. Many were removed quite early from their original settings by private collectors and museums. By 1900, only about 600 remained. Some 40 years later, many of these had been all but destroyed by decay. Fortunately, the U.S. Forest Service and Indian Service transferred about 100 $\overset{500}{\longrightarrow}$ poles from abandoned Indian villages to present-day totem parks.

In the late 1960s, Dr. Clark was working on a wood-bridge decay survey in Alaska when he was approached by Indians who wanted to prevent further deterioration of the poles in their totem parks. Surveying the condition of the poles, Dr. Clark found about one-fifth contained such serious internal decay that they were in danger of breakage or collapse. The outlook for many of the other totems, however, was—and still is—much brighter. "There are techniques we can use to slow the rate of deteriorations," Dr. Clark said, "Exterior decay— $\overset{600}{\longrightarrow}$ due to surface-invading fungi—can be controlled fairly easily by application of colorless wood preservatives."

It is much more difficult, though, to control interior decay. Seventeen of the poles at Sitka National Historic Park on Baranof Island have been treated by a double diffusion preservative process, Clark reports. Each totem was immersed in two preservative solutions.

"There's no doubt most of the remaining totem poles could be preserved for additional years of outdoor exhibition," Clark emphasizes. "It's a question of how practical it is to do it. Hopefully, all of the relatively sound poles will be treated with effective preservatives to halt any decay present and to prevent 700 new infections. However, funds for such work must be obtained and a systematic program must be organized if such procedures are to be effective. Some of the poles are too badly deteriorated to be maintained outdoors and should be moved to sheltered exhibit areas.''

4. (T – F) Most of the totems were carved between 1830 and 1880.

5. (C) _____ decay is the most difficult type to control.

6. (T – F) Many of the totems should be moved to indoor display areas for preservation.

Prior to 1900, totem maintenance was never part of the Indian tradition. Most totem poles lasted 800 satisfactorily for 50 years or longer. The expense and labor required to lower a large pole, repair it, and re-erect it was such that the same effort could be better used to create a new pole. And, restoring the pole of an ancestor brought little additional honor.

The totem pole is distinguished by its two-dimensional aspect, its use of distortions for special effect, and its usual symmetrical arrangement of figures and motifs. The style is uniquely symbolic of its abstract treatment of the subject and its emphasis on the subject's salient features. Thus, a woman is dis- 900 tinguished from a man only by a labret, a spoon-like ornament inserted in a slit in her lower lip.

Never a religiously significant idol, the totem pole generally represents images and symbols derived from legends and folk tales of the Northwest coastal Indians. Their world was full of wonders; nature dominated by supernatural powers; all creatures were in part spirit; and some animals were thought to have supernatural powers.

7. (T – F) Restoration of old totem poles is an ancient Indian tradition.

8. (M. C.) Totem poles are used primarily to preserve:
_____(1) legends and folk tales. ← 1000
_____(2) family traditions.
_____(3) religious idols.
_____(4) historical events.

Some of the stories most commonly depicted on totem poles are those of Yethl, or Raven, creator of the world. The Tlingit and Haida believed it was he who freed the sun, moon, and stars from original captivity, released day light, caused the tidal waves of the sea, carried water to form lakes and rivers, and brought fire for mankind's use from a remote island. Although recognized as the great benefactor of man, he was pictured with something less than admirable traits: buffon, trickster, and philanderer.

1100 → Another rather frequent subject of "totemic" art is the story of Fog Woman. Associated with the run of fish when the mouths of streams are enveloped by low-lying fogs, she put all varieties of salmon in the Alaskan waters. When Raven fell in love with her, there were no salmon and he had to live on a meager diet of sculpins and cod. Once rich and secure, Raven became ungrateful and unfaithful to his wife. Abused and struck by Raven, Fog Woman started running toward the creek. Raven tried to catch her, but she slipped through his fingers like fog 1200 → and disappeared forever in the water. Fog Woman's daughters live at the head of every stream and to catch their glimpse is the last joy of a salmon on its final journey to die in the place of its birth.

Considering the unique and valuable role of the Alaskan totem parks in art and nature conservation, a visit to a site where totem poles were originally erected is still a highly moving experience. The villagers have long gone and the forest has reclaimed the clearing. The remains of fallen totem poles, too decayed to be moved decades ago, give 1300 → birth to new trees sprouting out of moss-covered trunks. Left in place, the old totem pole serves as a reminder to the modern-day visitor that nature is in a state of constant renewal.

9. (T – F) All totem carvings of Raven reflect deep respect.

10. (T – F) Fog Woman is portrayed as a 1350 → benefactor of the salmon.

——STOP——ASK FOR YOUR TIME——

Record time immediately.

Time_____Sec. RATE (from table on page 315): R. _____

No. Correct:_____ COMPREHENSION (10% for each correct answer): C. _____
(key on page 330)

VII–6 EFFICIENCY (R × C): E. _____

Record on Progress Chart on page 299

Exercise VII–7

The Lady at the Bell
by LON GARRISON

(Reprinted from the May-June 1967 issue of *Conservation Volunteer*
by permission of the editor.)

──────── **WAIT FOR SIGNAL TO BEGIN READING** ────────

In spite of their massive size and ancient hardware, the front doors of Philadelphia's Independence Hall swing easily and noiselessly. All of which added to the mystery, if it could be called that, of The Lady at the Bell.

She was just one of more than 2¾ million visitors who came to the Shrine in one recent year, and so "average" that after the incident no two observers were able to agree on her description. Just one of more than 2¾ million visitors? Not quite, for hers wasn't an "average" visit.

She pushed the big door open, one sunny afternoon last fall, and slipped quietly inside. Pausing 100 only long enough to let her eyes adjust to the darker interior, she walked straight to the Liberty Bell in the Tower Room at the end of the hall. Obviously acting from deep conviction, and a complete lack of self-consciousness, she dropped to her knees to offer a silent prayer. When she arose she leaned over, kissed the Bell, then walked out.

No flashbulbs popped. There was no fanfare, no publicity.

In her own way, The Lady at the Bell had chosen this as a fitting place to express to her Creator some significant personal message; then 200 she disappeared.

It is difficult for me to tell this story without developing a lump in my throat. But it has become a favorite because it illustrates a belief I've long held: the history of our land is important to our people because history belongs to the people.

A deep feeling for history

History is one of those good intangibles that spans everything from Federal preservation of major shrines of American history to individual concern for the events of local—or sometimes only family— significance. Occasionally these interests merge in surprising but understandable ways, as we realize anew the deep patriotism abroad in our land, and 300 the thoughtful respect our people have for historic places.

Throughout these United States, at different levels of time, I have seen the recognition of the worth of local history. The outcry appears to come from the same deep emotion—a determination that the symbols, the places, the concepts that shaped today's circumstances will be retained for patriotic reasons.

1. (C) The author stated that "History belongs to the _____."
2. (T – F) The Lady at the Bell arrived at Independence Hall accompanied by a great deal of fanfare and publicity.

This is indeed a very deep wellspring of endeavor and pride. And, along with it is a surprising ingenuity in developing combinations of uses, of ways of finance, of preservation, and of restoration techniques.

Through most of my working years, having had some association with American events and memorialized landmarks, I have always approached these responsibilities with considerable humility, because I recognize that I come upon the scene only lately. Every historical park represents a chain that leads from the original event on through the subsequent recognition and labor of unselfish people with a vision, a gleam to follow, that saved these places for 500 Americans of today and for future generations.

Historic preservation

This very real and personal concern for history, so prevalent today, has united like-minded people across America into the National Trust for Historic Preservation. Historic preservation has been tied to urban renewal. The recent Historic Preservation Act, Public Law 89–665, establishes grants-in-aid programs. The whole preservation movement is today stronger, better organized, and more hopeful of success than ever before!

The President announced the creation of the 17-member National Historic Preservation Advisory Commission whose responsibilities, explicitly defined by the Act, include:

*Advising the President and the Congress on 600 historic preservation.

*Recommending measures to coordinate all public and private historic preservation programs.

*Advising on information programs about these activities.

*Encouraging public interest and participation in historic preservation efforts through the National Trust for Historic Preservation and other private agencies.

*Recommending studies dealing with adequacy of laws, regulations and statutes at all levels of government.

*Recommending studies dealing with the effects of tax policies on the general problems of historic preservation.

*Providing advice to states and local governments to aid them in drafting historic preservation legislation.

*Encouraging training and education in the field of historic preservation through private and public institutions.

3. (T – F) Urban renewal has been associated with 700 historic preservation.

4. (M. C.) The National Historic Preservation Advisory Commission has:
_____(1) 17 members.
_____(2) 10 members.
_____(3) 82 members.
_____(4) 50 members.

5. (T – F) One of the duties of the Advisory Commission is to encourage training in the field of historic preservation.

I see in the Historic Preservation Act signposts to two general fields of endeavor. The governmental sector of concern runs from the Department of the Interior to the individual state governments.

The extensive, privately owned and operated historic properties constitute the second field of endeavor. They, too, can qualify for assistance, but 800 through the independent National Trust for Historic Preservation, not through a governmental bureau.

Effectiveness of the historic preservation

A major thrust of the Historic Preservation Act is this grants-in-aid program. Here one fact is being overlooked. The Act did not appropriate any funds, but only authorizes Congress to make future appropriations for this purpose. Future appropriations will have to be considered in relation to the total appropriation needs of the Nation.

A common aspect of the program, for both the governmental and private preservation efforts, is that these funds will be made for planning acquisition 900 and restoration, but not for operation.

This exception—that funds cannot be used for operation—gets to the heart of one of the major concerns of all historic preservation programs: what can be done with historic properties? How many historic houses can the Federal Government, a State, a County, a Town, or a privately financed society afford to restore and operate?

This very practical problem arises when any property is being studied for the degree of restoration. Does every historic house get the years of painstaking research and careful craftsmanship that has gone into Independence Hall? Or is it possible to restore only 1000 the exterior in some cases, or only one room of the interior and how can the rest of the building be used?

6. (T – F) The Historic Preservation Act appropriates money for their grants-in-aid program.

7. (M. C.) One exception of the preservation program is that the funds cannot be used for:
_____(1) acquisition.
_____(2) planning.
_____(3) operation.
_____(4) restoration.

Ingenuity in the use of restored structures

In many situations it is possible to establish standards for exterior restoration—creating or retaining a delightful and charmingly authentic community atmosphere. The best sites and buildings 1100 may be house museums, but the others can be restored outside and fitted for the utilitarian modern life of the community by contemporary use of the interiors.

Historic Districts are particularly good in preserving the flavor of a town's early history, its heritage, its character, without going overboard on the costs of total restoration, and without getting visitors intoxicated—or bored—on history.

Too many historic properties are actually dull for lack of attractive presentations of their "story." Too many are just bricks, mortar and fine furniture— these things do not speak for themselves; they need 1200 interpretation. This is the special art of park interpretive people, with their professional knowledge and standards.

There is no question that historians of today and of the future will laud the efforts being made today to preserve their historic scene.

The interweaving of life's personal values for an anonymous Lady at the Bell led to her identification of a Shrine of Liberty—Independence Hall—as a proper place for prayer. This was obviously a place for one of life's deeply expressive moments, yet this woman had an affection and friendship reaction to this major symbol of America that is deeply revealing.

1300
8. (T – F) Historic Districts are particularly good in preserving the flavor of a town's early history and heritage.

9. (C) Many historic properties, dull for lack of an attractive presentation, need interpretation to tell their _____.

10. (T – F) Historians of the future will decry our 1350 failures to preserve their historic scene.

——STOP——ASK FOR YOUR TIME——
Record time immediately.

Time_____Sec.

RATE (from table on page 315):

R. _____

No. Correct:_____
(key on page 322)

COMPREHENSION (10% for each correct answer):

C. _____

VII–7

EFFICIENCY (R × C):

E. _____

Exercise VII–8

Winning Isn't Enough
by PAUL H. GNADT

(Reprinted from the December 1973 issue of *Listen* by permission of the editor.)

———————— WAIT FOR SIGNAL TO BEGIN READING ————————

The generation gap was obvious. He was 62, gray, and the shadow of retirement was creeping closer. They were young, restless with energy, the first payroll dollar far from the bank and farther from their thoughts. Yet they listened.

He was speaking about integrity, honesty, and sincerity, highlighting his reasons with rhyme. Strange ingredients at a basketball camp for boys in seventh through twelfth grades who traveled across the country to perfect their passing, dribbling, and shooting under the experienced eyes of college and prep coaches. But the basketballs lay bounceless, and 250 pairs of sneakers were silenced in attention 100 as if what their awed owners were hearing was gospel from a living legend. It was. He is.

John Wooden, head coach of the University of California at Los Angeles basketball teams since 1948, winner of seven straight NCAA championships (nine of the last ten), and currently fast breaking through opponents and the record book with a 75-plus game victory streak, was telling the attentive athletes that "winning the game isn't important."

Important to John Wooden is that while playing the game you try your best. "Try your best and you'll never lose," he declares. "You may be outscored, but you'll know you did the best you 200 could do." And that, according to the mentor whose 37-year coaching career totals 807 victories against only 196 losses, is success.

1. (T – F) John Wooden is now a living legend.
2. (T – F) John Wooden says "winning is important."

A life's philosophy

He continued to talk about building the foundations for success. The verbal blueprint included words like industriousness, enthusiasm, cooperation, alertness, and self-control. Additional support is supplied by skill, confidence, faith, patience, reliability, and sincerity. The completed structure is known as John Wooden's "Pyramid of Success."

Without notes he went on for twenty minutes. 300 They listened. John Wooden knows the pyramid. He lives it every day.

Living every day began in 1910 at Hall, Indiana, near Monrovia. Four Wooden brothers and their father, Joshua, formed the first of many quintets meaningful to John. The family farmed sixty acres, and there were plenty of chores for the boys to share. Joshua had a tremendous influence on his sons. He was hardworking, honest, and fair. He always made his boys' best interest his primary concern. He read the Bible daily and 400 encouraged the boys to read along. Today, next to photos of his grandchildren and memorabilia of seasons past, a Bible occupies a permanent and prominent place on Wooden's UCLA office desk.

The love that existed in the Wooden father-son relationship is best evidenced by the grade-school graduation gift John received from his dad. It was a piece of paper with this handwritten creed for John to live by:

1. Be true to yourself.
2. Make each day your masterpiece.
3. Help others.
4. Drink deeply from good books, especially the Bible.
5. Make friendship a fine art.
6. Build a shelter against a rainy day.
7. Pray for guidance, count and give 500 thanks for your blessings every day.

Long since worn out and transferred by typewriter to a small card, it travels in Wooden's wallet next to the torn pieces of a $2 bill Joshua gave to John on his first birthday in 1911. "There is no doubt that the father-son relationship between me and my players is a direct result of the love and guidance my father gave me," says a thankful Wooden.

Joshua believed in mixing work and fun; so in the classic tradition, he nailed a bottomless tomato 600 basket up on the hayloft wall for his sons to use. A few years later it was replaced by an iron ring, but progress with the ball wasn't as swift. Old rags stuffed inside a pair of Mrs. Wooden's black cotton hose substituted as the basketball.

3. (T – F) The University of California constructed the "Pyramid of Success."
4. (C) A _____ occupies a permanent place on Wooden's office desk.
5. (T – F) Joshua had little influence on John's values.

Success at basketball

Scrappy and tireless, John Wooden earned "all-state" basketball recognition for three years at Martinsville High, and was recruited by two colleges within Indiana—namely, Ball State and Notre Dame. ⁷⁰⁰ The opportunity that basketball gave Wooden to attend college became important since the family was forced to give up the farm prior to John's starting high school.

To everyone's surprise, John chose to attend Purdue University in West Lafayette, attracted by the basketball team's reputation and their fast-break style of play under Coach Ward (Piggie) Lambert.

Learning that if a student made the dean's list he received free tuition, Wooden studied especially hard.

He received some honors for hustling on the basketball court also, namely "All-American" for three consecutive years of varsity competition with recognition as "College Player of the Year" while a ⁸⁰⁰ senior. This resulted in a call from the U.S. Military Academy at West Point, which at that time was allowed to recruit top collegiate athletes for another four years of eligibility while studying for graduate degrees.

Wooden was ready to turn in his civvies and join the Long Gray Line when a feminine voice called a halt. Nellie Riley had been waiting back in Martinsville for John to graduate so they could be married. She wasn't about to postpone the wedding another four years while John dribbled along the banks of the Hudson. ⁹⁰⁰

Simultaneously, Wooden made another decision that would ultimately affect the lives of many people in general and the game of basketball in particular. George Halas, one of the founders of the National Football League, also had a basketball team for which he asked Wooden to play after graduation from Purdue. John's performance attracted the attention of the original New York Celtics, who offered him $5,000 for his services. When John discussed the offer with Piggie Lambert, the Purdue coach asked John why he had studied so hard and if he was ever going to use the knowledge he gained. ¹⁰⁰⁰ Convinced that coaching was the direction to follow, John turned down the professional offer and accepted a job in Dayton, Kentucky, as high school athletic director, coach, and teacher.

6. (T – F) Although offered a professional basketball contract, Wooden never played professional basketball.

7. (M. C.) Wooden attended college at:
———(1) Notre Dame.
———(2) Ball State.
———(3) Purdue.
———(4) UCLA.

Wooden goes West

The acorn, however small, was now planted in the Midwest. Two unusual events would occur before its branches of influence and success would spread west to UCLA.

The first happened after the Woodens had ¹¹⁰⁰ moved to South Bend, Indiana, where John coached at Central High. The attack on Pearl Harbor prompted John to enlist in the Navy, where he was trained as a fitness officer and assigned to a ship in the Pacific. Returning to South Bend following his discharge, Wooden continued coaching; but he soon became disenchanted with the city. Eager to coach on the college level, he accepted the post at Indiana State University in Terre Haute. Two years produced a 47–14 record and a trip to the NAIA tournament for second place. John had always hoped to return ¹²⁰⁰ to the Big Ten Conference as a coach, and the possibility became reality when Minnesota was one of two big-time schools to call with a firm offer. The other was UCLA. By prearrangement, on a specified evening Minnesota was to call for John's decision at 6 P.M.; UCLA, an hour later. A Minnesota snowstorm prevented the Minnesota athletic director from getting to a phone. When UCLA dialed on time, Wooden was headed for Westwood.

Wooden always carries a small cross in his pocket. He clutches it during times of tension. It reminds him to take care and beware of his reactions ¹³⁰⁰ under pressure.

8. (M. C.) His first college coaching job was at:
———(1) Purdue.
———(2) Minnesota.
———(3) Ball State.
———(4) Indiana State.

9. (T – F) Wooden was offered coaching positions at both Minnesota and UCLA at the very same time.

10. (C) Wooden always carries a small ——— ¹³⁵⁰ in his pocket.

———STOP——ASK FOR YOUR TIME———

Record time immediately.

Time———Sec.

No. Correct:———
(key on page 330)

VII–8

RATE (from table on page 315):

COMPREHENSION (10% for each correct answer):

EFFICIENCY (R × C):

R. ———

C. ———

E. ———

Record on Progress Chart on page 299

256

Exercise VII–9

The White Monster
by FRANK L. REMINGTON

(Reprinted from the February 1963 issue of *The Lion* by permission of the editors.)

—— WAIT FOR SIGNAL TO BEGIN READING ——

A warning that came too late

One winter day several years ago four veteran skiers climbed a snow-laden slope in California's Sierra Nevada Mountains. Suddenly one of the men looked up to see a mass of snow roaring down upon them. "Look out! Avalanche!" he screamed. The snowslide thundered onward engulfing them in a furious white tide.

Although entombed under the snow, two of the sportsmen were able to carve an air space around their faces. The third skier, unconscious, was buried under four feet of snow, his face downward and one leg and a ski twisted under him.

Fortunately, the fourth man, his head barely 100 out of the snow, spotted another group of skiers and shouted for help. The rescuers, digging more than an hour to extricate them, saved the skiers who doubtless would have perished in a short time had they not been sighted.

Avalanches, or giant snowslides, are nothing more than large masses of snow and ice in swift motion down a mountainside. Indeed, avalanches, one of the most treacherous forces of nature, rank with earthquakes, tornadoes, and floods as great natural destroying forces. They are little recognized as killers because they usually occur in remote mountain areas where they seldom threaten man 200 or his property.

There are two fundamental causes of avalanches: terrain and climate. Acting together, plenty of snow and a mountain for it to slide on can produce an avalanche without any other assistance. If a slope is not at least of 25 degrees steepness, however, there is small chance of an avalanche. The shape of the slope, too, somewhat governs its snowslide potential. As a rule, convex slopes pose a greater avalanche hazard than concave ones because snow settling on a bulging surface builds up more instability.

Whether a snowbank can maintain its position 300 on a slope is determined by the weight of the snow and the angle of the slope. If these combined factors equal or exceed the snow's cohesiveness, they can precipitate a snowslide.

Each winter hundreds, perhaps thousands, of avalanches cascade down the slopes of remote mountains.

The greatest avalanche disaster in United States history took place on a railroad, in March 1910, when a single slide swept three snowbound trains in Washington's Cascade Mountains to the bottom of the canyon. The resulting fatalities and over a million dollars in property damage forced the railroad to 400 build a tunnel which bypassed the slide area.

Avalanches in the U.S. reach only minor proportions compared to the devastating sizes they attain in other countries. Thousands of persons have been swept to their deaths and whole villages whisked away by giant waves of onrushing whiteness.

1. (T – F) Avalanches seldom pose a serious threat to individual lives or property.

2. (C) Avalanches are usually caused by the terrain or the —————————.

3. (T – F) The greatest avalanche in U.S. history took place in a small mining town.

Avalanche tragedies

Indeed, only last year, in January, one of 500 history's worst avalanches occurred on Mount Huascaran, which rises 22,205 feet high in northern Peru. Rocketing down the mountainous slopes, the ponderous mass of ice, snow, rocks, trees, and mud traveled nine miles before it lost momentum. By that time it had entombed almost 4,000 residents of the two villages of Huarascucho and Ranrahirca. Very few villagers survived the icy wave which was 40 feet high and 1,000 yards wide.

Villagers who live in the Alpine valleys of Austria and Switzerland expect avalanches each year. Often these snow inundations occur at the same place and on the same date each year. Past 600 experience has taught residents to erect houses and barns in strategic positions. Frequently they build massive stone bastions, not to stop the white terror, but to divert its course. In the U.S., too, snow sheds and diversion walls are erected as an effective protective measure to confine a slide to a certain path or turn it away from the object to be protected.

Perhaps the most bizarre avalanche disaster occurred almost a century and a half ago when a group of adventurers attempted to scale the Alpine peak of Mt. Blanc on the French-Italian border. 700 Walking over a glacier, the party suddenly was swept

400 yards down the slope in a tobogganing mass of snow. Although several escaped, most of the climbers were dashed to death in the deluge and their remains later recovered.

Three of the bodies, however, fell into a vast glacier fissure and were entombed beneath an ocean of ice and snow. Forty-one years later, the slow-moving glacier disgorged the bodies in Chamonix, six miles away. One survivor of the party, now a wrinkled old man, identified the perfectly preserved and youthful-appearing remains.

Forest Service

The U.S. Forest Service's avalanche study commenced in 1937 when a solitary forest ranger was sent to Alta, Utah, in the Wasatch mountain ⁸⁰⁰⇐ range, about 30 miles from Salt Lake City. He spent his full time observing snow and studying avalanches. From this pioneer work grew the Forest Service's present avalanche control program.

Over a period of years the Forest Service studies have revealed and interpreted many of the snow's secrets. Today the Forest Service Snow Ranger's chief duty is to recognize the development of a hazardous avalanche situation in time to do something about it. In fighting avalanches the Snow Rangers observe the snow and weather conditions continuously so that danger can be immediately ⁹⁰⁰⇐ recognized. In this work they consider 10 factors, all of which influence avalanche hazard: (1) depth of old snow; (2) old snow surface; (3) new snow depth; (4) new snow type; (5) new snow weight; (6) rate of accumulation; (7) wind force; (8) wind direction; (9) temperature development; (10) snow settlement.

4. (C   ) An icy wave of snow, rocks, and ice entombed nearly _____ residents in two Peruvian villages.

5. (T – F) One avalanche on Mt. Blanc perfectly preserved the bodies of three victims for forty-one years.

6. (M. C.) The U.S. Forest Service's avalanche study was established in:
   _____(1) 1925.
   _____(2) 1937.
   _____(3) 1949.
   _____(4) 1958.

   1000 ⇐

7. (T – F) The two primary forces influencing avalanches are wind force and direction.

Avalanche control techniques benefit not only winter sports areas but mountain highways and power and pipe lines at high altitudes. Some states like Colorado, where sliding snows present a constant winter hazard to motorists, have established their own highway avalanche protection services.

A person in the path of one of these tides of destruction, which often exceed a speed of 100 miles an hour, can do practically nothing to save himself. ¹¹⁰⁰→ Some fortunate ones have managed to stay atop the onrushing whiteness and ride it down the slope. Experienced mountaineers caught in a slide try to flop on their backs and make swimming motions with their arms and legs, attempting to maneuver to the edge of the avalanche. A victim buried in a mammoth slide has about as much chance for survival as a snowflake on a hot stove.

How to locate avalanche victims

One method involves a line of men advancing across the surface, probing the drift with long iron rods equipped with special hooks to catch in clothing. The other way makes use of specially trained ¹²⁰⁰→ German shepherd dogs. These canines locate an entombed person by scent much quicker than probing with a pole, provided the victim is not more than 12 feet under the snow.

Today many ski enthusiasts equip themselves with an avalanche string, a thin red rope about 25 yards long which is slung around the waist and dragged along.

Most persons who have witnessed an avalanche agree that it's a beautiful and spectacular sight to see—provided they're not in its path.

8. (T – F) The state of Colorado has its own highway avalanche protection service as a safety measure.

1300 → 9. (M. C.) Specially trained German shepherd dogs can detect entombed persons providing they:
   _____(1) aren't under more than 12 feet.
   _____(2) leave some marks.
   _____(3) cling to the avalanche string.
   _____(4) are able to signal.

10. (T – F) The avalanche string, a flexible rope, is about 25 yards long.

1350 →

——STOP——ASK FOR YOUR TIME——

Record time immediately.

Time_____Sec.

No. Correct:_____
(key on page 322)

VII–9

RATE (from table on page 315):

COMPREHENSION (10% for each correct answer):

EFFICIENCY (R × C):

R. _____

C. _____

E. _____

Record on Progress Chart on page 299

Exercise VII-10

How to Manage Killer Smoke
by WALTER McQUADE

——————— **WAIT FOR SIGNAL TO BEGIN READING** ———————

One of the haunting horrors of conflagrations in such "fireproof" multistory structures as the MGM Grand Hotel in Las Vegas last November and Stouffer's Inn in Harrison, New York, last December is the distance from the flames of so many victims, their relative uninvolvement. At the MGM Grand, a fire in the wall of a ground floor delicatessen apparently crawled above the false ceiling and flung a sudden ball of flame across the casino's gaming room, destroying everything in its path, including 12 people. But upstairs in the tower and in the hotel offices were found 68 more dead, while another 4 ←100 had died jumping from the tower. At Stouffer's Inn, a blaze swept through the corporate meeting rooms killing 24 executives of the Nestle Co. and Arrow Electronics. Many bodies were badly scorched, yet most fatalities were attributed to asphyxiation.

Like plastic bombs

Professional fire fighters are not surprised at the toll of remote deaths. To explain it they reverse an adage: "Where there's fire, there's smoke." Coroners say smoke inhalation, not flames, kills at least 80 of every 100 victims of fires.

Smoke used to be defined as visible suspended particulates of combustion, and its danger, besides confusion, was carbon monoxide poisoning. But ⇄200 that definition is no longer adequate in this era of ubiquitous polymer plastics and other poured and woven synthetics. The interiors of even fire-resistant structures are often veritable plastic bombs waiting to be ignited. When they are, clouds of toxic smoke— some of it invisible—are released, much denser and deadlier than smoke from natural substances. An extreme example is recalled by Dr. Victor H. Esch, chief surgeon of the District of Columbia Fire Department. In 1973 a fire started in a plastic wastebasket in the rear lavatory of a Boeing 707 near Paris, and the plane immediately made an ←300 emergency landing. "The inflight cabin interior fire did not involve the aircraft's fuel," says Esch, "but it was fed by the interior's materials, and 123 people died from inhaling toxic fumes and smoke."

Sprinkler systems can help by drenching fires. But sprinklers are sprung only after the fact of fire, so they do not preclude smoke. The task of controlling smoke is now being attacked by a handful of technical specialists banded into an iconoclastic trade organization called the Smoke Control Association. One city that has followed their recommendations for building code changes is 400→ Atlanta, and Denver is in the process. The Veterans Administration in Washington, proprietor of many hospitals across the country, is also urgently interested.

1. (T – F) Coroners say most victims of fires are killed by smoke inhalation.
2. (C   ) Toxic smoke is a product of materials made from _____.
3. (T – F) Sprinkler systems are sound protection from smoke danger.

Principles behind smoke control

There are two main principles behind smoke control in buildings. The first: smoke from a localized fire, especially in a tall, fireproof building, must be vented vigorously before it begins tearing at the 500→ throats of trapped people. According to Robert E. Taylor of Cleveland, president of the Smoke Control Association, when a fire breaks out in a skyscraper, the air conditioning usually is turned off at once, lest the fire follow the ducts. Taylor advocates leaving it on in almost all cases, but adjusting the air flow of the ducts in the zone of the fire to shunt the smoke outdoors.

The other part of smoke control is slightly more intricate. It calls for positive pressurization of air in areas around the fire to discourage the smoke from 600→ infiltrating escape routes. An example is the increasing of pressure in the wells of fire stairs, which can be done simply with fans that force in more air. The pressure differential can be very low, hardly noticeable to anyone without instruments. If the pressure were too high, of course, the fire doors to the stairwells might become difficult to open.

The eeriest terror

Corridors can be pressurized too, to keep them clear of smoke. This is already done in many multistory apartment houses; the hallways are fanned to pressure higher than the apartments to prevent cooking odors from leaking out of kitchens into the halls. This practice, Taylor says, has localized $\overset{700}{\longleftarrow}$ many a blaze in apartment houses of reinforced concrete or steel frame construction. A fire in such an apartment devours the furniture and fabrics, bursts the windows with its heat—giving the smoke an outlet—then burns itself out. In one apartment fire Taylor studied, even the wooden door to the hall had been consumed, yet only a few smoke smudges marred the corridor ceiling.

Probably the eeriest terror in multistory buildings, especially those with sealed windows, is the gaping elevator shafts, which sometimes behave like gigantic chimneys, sucking smoke and heat upward. When the MGM Grand conflagration was brought $\overset{800}{\longleftarrow}$ under control the Vegas firemen found three of the hotel's elevators jammed in the shafts. Heat had melted the hoist cables.

But elevator shafts also can be pressurized. The proposed Denver code insists they be, and also demands pressurized nooks in each floor's elevator lobby into which people confined to wheelchairs can roll to await elevators and directions from a public-address system (another code requirement). It can all be done in smaller buildings too. In one Marriott Hotel in Beachwood, Ohio, about the size of the fatal Stouffer's in New York State, the local fire inspector, well versed in smoke control, has persuaded $\overset{900}{\longleftarrow}$ the owner to install the whole gamut of mechanical smoke control equipment—pressurizing not only corridors and fire stairs, but the elevators too.

4. (T – F) Pressurized corridors suck the air away from the fire area.
5. (T – F) Gaping elevator shafts sometimes act as gigantic chimneys.
6. (M. C.) A proposed Denver code demands pressurized areas for people in wheelchairs located:
    ——(1) on the roof.
    ——(2) near the elevators.
    ——(3) near the stairwells.
    ——(4) beside each fire escape.

Cost of smoke control

The cost of smoke control is not high, considering its protective potential. Taylor, who is also $\overset{1000\ 1350}{\longleftarrow\ \longrightarrow}$ coordinator of codes and standards at Republic Steel Corporation (whose headquarters he has pressurized), figures that a complete smoke system for a new 36-story office building of 750,000 square feet

would cost about a dollar per square foot more than the usual basic $60 to $75 construction cost per square foot. The 57-story IDS Center in Minneapolis, designed by architects Philip Johnson and John Burgee, was completed in 1972 before the beginnings of smoke control in the U.S. When the management added pressurized fire stairs in 1976, $\overset{1100}{\longrightarrow}$ the cost of the retrofit came to only $59,500. Some insurance companies reward safety systems with premium reductions. When consultant Taylor's tennis-swimming-ice-skating club in Shaker Heights added a restaurant wing, he helped design a system combining sprinklers, smoke control, and alarms. Insurance savings paid for it within 18 months.

In contrast, omitting smoke control may ultimately prove expensive to building owners. A man and wife who said they had to grope down through a smoke-ridden fire staircase at the MGM Grand have sued for millions in damages, and they are not the only claimants. Medical experts such $\overset{1200}{\longrightarrow}$ as Dr. Esch believe that even if smoke inhalation is not immediately fatal, it may cause long-term problems for the lungs and heart. Among firemen the rate of lung cancer is high, and Esch believes that this has more to do with repeated exposure to toxic fumes than with smoking cigarettes.

7. (C) Considering the potential of smoke control, the cost is relatively ——— ———.
8. (T – F) The cost of providing pressurized smoke safety systems is prohibitive for most small apartment houses.
9. (M. C.) Smoke inhalation may cause long-term damage to the:
    ——(1) eyes.
    ——(2) digestive tract.
    ——(3) nervous system.
    ——(4) lungs and heart.

$\overset{1300}{\longrightarrow}$

The lifesaving fans

The fireman is an ultimate beneficiary of smoke control systems. . . . Fire marshal Leonard J. Billings . . . said . . . "Those fans would suck all the smoke out. It's not putting out a fire that's so hard, it's finding it in all that damned smoke."

10. (T – F) Fans help firemen locate the fire.

——STOP——ASK FOR YOUR TIME——

Record time immediately.

Time——Sec.	RATE (from table on page 315):	R. ———
No. Correct:——— (key on page 330)	COMPREHENSION (10% for each correct answer):	C. ———
VII–10	EFFICIENCY (R × C):	E. ———

Record on Progress Chart on page 299

Exercise VII–11

Making a Drama out of Shopping
by WALTER McQUADE

(Reprinted from the March 24, 1980 issue of *Fortune*
by permission of the editor—© 1980 Time Inc. All rights reserved.)

──────── **WAIT FOR SIGNAL TO BEGIN READING** ────────

Joining an illustrious chain

When Federated Department Stores in 1956 added Burdines to its lustrous chain (which includes Bullock's, I. Magnin, Rich's, Filene's), the old Florida institution consisted of just four stores—none of them dazzlers. Today there are seventeen Burdines strategically positioned throughout prospering south Florida. Surely the most original in design—and most exuberant in ambience—is the store that opened last summer in Boca Raton, a very well-heeled community situated between Miami and Palm Beach along the Gold Coast. The Boca Burdines may well be a pacesetter for department store branches across the country.

Traditionally, a store is appraised in the trade $\xleftarrow{100}$ by its annual sales per square foot, a figure usually hard to dig out of the proprietors. Federated stores, for instance, are estimated to sell $95 to $100 per square foot nationwide. By this retailing yardstick, the Boca experiment has easily passed the tough test of customer approval. Though less than a year old, the store is chalking up sales of more than $100 per square foot on an annual basis—a satisfying record for a fledgling branch. By fall, Boca should have moved about $17 million in wares, from men's jockey shorts to those $8,000 Oriental $\xleftarrow{200}$ folding screens bought to shield the glass walls of lavish vacation condominiums along the nearby beaches. And when the rest of the million-square-foot regional shopping center now rising beside the store is completed and occupied, that gross should surge higher. Burdines' principal rival, Jordan Marsh, owned by Allied Stores Corp., will be competing at the other end of the enclosed mall, but Federated won't mind. It owns the whole shopping center.

1. (M. C.) Boca Burdines is a:
   _____(1) grocery store.
   _____(2) sports shop.
   _____(3) flower shop.
   _____(4) department store.

2. (T – F) A store is usually appraised in the trade $\xrightarrow{300}$ by its annual sales per square foot.

3. (C) Boca Burdines is located in _____.

Superstore

From the beginning, the Boca store was envisioned as a laboratory for new merchandising methods—and as a bellwether for ten or more new stores Burdines plans to build in this decade. The chain's management asked a New York City firm of designers and architects, the Walker Group, to stand back from day-to-day assignments and produce a theoretical store of the future. Its leading partner, architect Kenneth Walker, soon dubbed the project "superstore." Following a free swinging approach $\xrightarrow{400}$ that combined the flair of a modern world's fair with sales techniques as fundamental as a medieval farmers' market, the firm first produced a large-scale model. Walker and his colleagues then collaborated with Reynolds, Smith & Hills, a Tampa architectural firm, in putting superstore ideas to work in the Boca design.

This is hardly the first department store to take an imaginative approach to merchandising. In recent years, many stores have turned into theaters of a sort to lure shoppers with the goal to outdramatize the mushrooming discount houses and other competitors. Utilizing a full repertoire of sales techniques, from $\xrightarrow{500}$ disco music to visual surprises, the store will try to transport customers into a stylish environment uniquely appealing to the kind of clientele it has selected as its own. The subliminal message is that only this particular store can provide the style befitting these particular customers. Witness the insistent young-couple merchandising of Federated's fabled New York store, Bloomingdale's, a legendary success in the trade.

4. (T – F) Boca Burdines was the first department store to approach merchandising in an imaginative way.

5. (T – F) The goal of the superstore is to out-dramatize the discount stores and other competitors.

An atrium for all seasons $\xrightarrow{600}$

To ensure a faithful following, abundant aisles of fully stocked counters and columns of newspaper advertising proclaiming good values are no longer enough. The focus is on what the shopper wants to become, and the sales pitch requires the liveliest and most flexible stage set possible on which to present a constantly changing show. Burdines cleverly uses architecture to do this.

The basic, two-story structure, composed of industrial materials, is practical and economical. Look up at the roof and you see typical aircraft-hangar constructions, beautifully detailed, with plenty of room left up there to insert an entire new floor of ←700 selling space, which would add 50 percent to the capacity of the branch. There is no basement level, because this is flat Florida, where the water level is just three feet down in the sand.

The president of the Burdines chain, John W. Burden, III, thinks the store's most appealing single quality is its feeling of expansiveness. The spacious atmosphere is produced by means of a central atrium reaching from the ground floor up through a penthouse on the roof, where walls of translucent plastic flood the core of the building with that wonderfully confident Florida daylight.

Dominating, but not completely filling, the ←800 atrium is a tall, steel framework. Into its matrix can be fitted large panels, which function not only as sign boards for special sales, but also as racks for blown-up photographs celebrating the way of life in the Boca Raton area. Enlarged photographs of the store's sun-and-sea surroundings show the people who live there as they would like to see themselves: happy, healthy, youthful, outdoorsy, well-dressed, witty—credit card America. The displays can be changed with the season or the specials on sale. Within this central framework of this stagestruck department store run the escalators, and hanging from ←900 one side near ground level is a bank of closed-circuit TV monitors that offer views of special events taking place elsewhere in the store.

The ground floor is laid out in a labyrinthian pattern that makes the casual customer linger in each department. Instead of the old-fashioned aisles which lead straight from one section to another, these run on the bias. Some older department stores have also employed this scheme to encourage impulse buying, but the result is often confusion for the customer who is looking for something specific. What the traditional stores lack is that central skylit atrium as a point of ←1000 orientation.

6. (T – F) One disadvantage of Burdines is that it has limited room for expansion.

7. (C) One of the most interesting features and the focal point of attention in this store is the _____.

8. (M. C.) To ensure a faithful following, Burdines cleverly uses:
    _____(1) fully stocked counters.
    _____(2) architecture.
    _____(3) sales pitches.
    _____(4) lots of advertising.

Many separate showcase departments

Despite the enticements that help suspend reality, Boca customers aren't likely to get completely lost in a shopping reverie. Each department is identified emphatically—sometimes with big neon lettering—and designed as a separate showplace. A 1100→ school bus signals the children's section, for example.

The sell is soft, with theatrical touches. In the juniors' department, clothing is displayed on mannequins seated in a diner. Parked on the carpet outside, and filled with more mannequins, is an automobile from the glamorous 1950s, an Edsel convertible, no less. Clothing manufacturers these days seem to assume that adolescent girls possess a nostalgia for the 1950s they never knew.

The spreading superstore

Word of the Boca blockbuster has spread throughout the merchandising world and is bringing the Walker Company other assignments from as 1200→ far away as South Africa. Burdines itself has incorporated some of the ideas from the superstore model in the Palm Beach store it opened several months ago, and three more Burdines now on the drawing boards will be superstores.

Richard H. Gundy, a Burdines regional vice president, expresses the pull of the Boca store: ''It's exciting, but still calm and comfortable. Even before Christmas, it didn't seem jammed. What it does is make shopping less boring.'' A recent Burdines customer had a giddier reaction. She had driven twenty miles from home nearer an older Burdines to 1300→ browse at Boca. ''This store is me,'' she said, and took out her credit card.

9. (T – F) Burdines is an exciting place in which to shop, but it is still calm and comfortable.

10. (T – F) The writer seems concerned that these unique arrangements and dramatic and colorful features may confuse some 1350→ shoppers.

——STOP——ASK FOR YOUR TIME——
Record time immediately.

Time_____Sec.   RATE (from table on page 315):   R. _____

No. Correct:_____   COMPREHENSION (10% for each correct answer):   C. _____
(key on page 322)

VII–11   EFFICIENCY (R × C):   E. _____

Record on Progress Chart on page 299

Exercise VII–12

High Soars the Eagle
by DICK KIRKPATRICK

———— **WAIT FOR SIGNAL TO BEGIN READING** ————

Our national bird

When the Continental Congress chose the "American Eagle" as our national bird on June 20, 1782, their choice seemed a logical one. The native bald eagle is a strikingly handsome, regal-looking bird, and the eagle has been a symbol of freedom, valor, and strength dating back beyond the earliest historical records.

Surprisingly, his nomination met some stout resistance among the founding fathers—and an occasional detractor still takes a pot shot at his selection.

Despite all resistance, and against the arguments that the bald eagle is a thief (he is), a timid coward (sometimes), a carrion eater (partly right), 100 and a bully (right again), he became our national symbol.

The most dedicated eagle detractor, however, can not deny that he is a fine-looking bird. The dark-brown body and darker brown wings contrast sharply with the pure-white head and tail feathers, which glisten in the sunlight in flight and stand out strongly against the dark browns and greens of his native forest backgrounds. A large adult female bald eagle can weigh over 14 pounds with a flat-stretched wing-span of over 90 inches and a body length of over a yard. The adult eagle has few, if any, enemies other than man, and can prey on almost any animal in sight at one stage of 200 its life or another. Though their primary and favorite food is fish, eagles commonly kill and eat other birds and small mammals—chiefly rabbits and other small rodents—with occasional spectacular attacks on much larger animals.

1. (M. C.) The eagle's detractors have described him as:
   ____(1) a thief and a bully.
   ____(2) a symbol of the feudal system.
   ____(3) a homely, timid-looking bird.
   ____(4) an appropriate choice as national bird.
2. (T – F) An adult female bald eagle may have a wing span of over 7 feet. 300
3. (C) The primary and favorite food of the eagle is _____.

Symbol of might or overrated bully?

These are the source of many eagle legends, and the reason for much of the bird's reputation as a varmint. There are records of eagle attacks on almost every species of animal—even humans—and one impressive account of three bald eagles cooperating in bringing down, killing, and feeding on a three-quarters-grown pronghorn antelope.

There is record of a near-successful attack on a two-year-old Hereford heifer, and many records—mostly exaggerated—of attacks on human children 400 (including one ridiculous tale of an eight-year-old boy being lifted 75 feet and carried 200 feet). There are, however, authenticated records of attacks on children—logical in view of records involving larger animals where the eagle attempts to kill but not to carry off its victim.

The term "carrion-eater" is probably another unearned libel on the eagle's reputation, depending on your definition of the word "carrion." Like any predator, the eagle takes its food in the easiest way possible, certainly welcoming the windfall of a dead fish washed up on shore. Since most estimates of 500 the eagle's diet are made from analysis of stomach contents, it's hard to estimate the original freshness of partly digested findings. Such washed-up spawners are the main food of the northern bald eagle during the salmon spawning season.

Whatever the circumstances, the strike of the bald eagle can be a fearsome thing. He will follow and attack a diving duck under water, strike and kill a big Canadian goose in midair, and pick a mountain goat kid off a lofty crag. Even in his most unpopular hunting activity—robbing the smaller osprey of his hard-caught fish dinner—he is impressive.

Another shortcoming of the bald eagle, often 600 pointed out by scientists brave and agile enough to reach an occasional aerie, is the bird's apparent reluctance to defend his own nest. Though occasional individuals will attack an intruder, there are few records of their actually striking him. By far the more usual conduct is for the eagle to retire to a safe distance, perhaps crying out, but offering no resistance. Against other predators and the annoyances of smaller birds, however, the eagle will defend itself, and will sometimes put up a fierce struggle when cornered or trapped. At the same time, many eagles have been observed under attack by smaller birds and seen to retire in order with a dignified 700 indifference. In general, however, in his conduct under pressure, the bald eagle is regarded by many authorities as a plain coward.

One really impressive feature on the eagle's side, however, is his nest-building capacity. Building in tall trees near water when possible, and returning to the same nest year after year, a pair will add another foot to the nest's height each season until it attains enormous proportions. Construction is mainly of sticks, branches and other available structural members in a sort of rampart, filled on the inside with smaller materials, then lined in the center with 800 softer stuffs. The sheer bulk of the nest accounts for one of the eagle's few natural hazards—weather. High winds and structural failure can bring down the massive nest before the eggs are hatched or while the eaglets are still unable to fly.

4. (T – F) Records show that an eagle will not attack a human child.

5. (M. C.) Because the eagle sometimes feeds on dead fish washed ashore he has been termed a:
——(1) scavenger.
——(2) spawner.
——(3) coward.
——(4) carrion-eater.

6. (T – F) Despite other shortcomings, a bald 900 eagle usually will defend his own nest against attack.

7. (T – F) One feature in the eagle's favor is his nest-building capacity.

Preservation of population

At the time of that debate by the Continental Congress, the bald eagle ranged over the entire North American continent, though most commonly around bodies of water that assured a good supply of fish. Since that time, however, man's depredations, both from hunting and from civilization's many changes in habitat, have greatly reduced their numbers. One new hazard is that of indirect poisoning through pesticides. However, the bird is not thought to be in danger of extinction anywhere. In 1000

June of 1940, the "American Eagle" came under government protection under the Bald Eagle Act, though the then-Territory of Alaska was not included. The 34 years of bounty hunting in that territory are believed to have resulted in the killing of at least 100,000 eagles. After years of debate and the passage of much conflicting legislation, the Alaskan Territorial Legislature repealed its eagle bounty law on March 2, 1953. The birds may still be killed when "committing damage to fishes, other wildlife, domestic birds and animals." With the end 1100 of bounty hunting, which had become an important source of income to many Alaskans, it is expected that the eagle population may return to "normal" within a few years.

Since the bald eagle is not a prolific breeder, it is hoped that protection throughout the continent will enable the population to achieve and maintain a balance. It may even increase, though not to a point of becoming an important predator again. A pair of eagles normally only produces two eggs—sometimes as many as three. They often manage to raise only one eaglet to maturity. The eggs have been described 1200 as "ridiculously small for so large a bird"; consequently the eaglet takes quite a long time to develop into a self-sufficient individual. Often they mate and nest while still in their juvenile plumage. Even so, their slow rate of reproduction caused Alaskan ornithologists to fear that even inefficient bounty hunting could render them practically extinct.

Whatever his shortcomings, the loss of our bald eagle population would be a tragedy. Despite his detractors, he will remain our national bird, and the general public, ignoring his shortcomings and those detractions, will probably continue to regard him as an excellent choice.

1300 8. (C) The Bald Eagle Act of 1940 provided protection for "American Eagles" everywhere in the United States except
_____.

9. (T – F) Because the bald eagle is a prolific breeder, there is little chance of population depletion.

10. (T – F) A pair of eagles normally produces 1350 two eggs, often raising only one eaglet to maturity.

——STOP——ASK FOR YOUR TIME——

Record time immediately.

Time_____Sec.

No. Correct:_____
(key on page 330)

VII–12

RATE (from table on page 315):

COMPREHENSION (10% for each correct answer):

EFFICIENCY (R × C):

R. _____

C. _____

E. _____

Exercise VII–13

Free and Responsible People

(Excerpted from an article in the November 1975 issue of *The Royal Bank of Canada Monthly Letter* by permission of the editor.)

— WAIT FOR SIGNAL TO BEGIN READING —

Everyone has the right to think and act and believe as he will, but also the responsibility to give an accounting sometime, somewhere, for what he chooses to think and believe and do.

The freedom one enjoys in a democratic country is not a matter of making absolutely free choice, but choice conditioned by a duty to act according to the trust reposed in one by fellow citizens. The foundation of a good nation is the sense of mutuality its people have.

Some pursue liberty in a frantic way, as if liberation from restrictions and laws were the greatest good in life. The legal basis of freedom is obedience 100 to certain social and moral laws—a person may be free and yet under constraint; he can be both disciplined and free. "Doing your own thing" is not necessarily an evidence of freedom: it may be sparked by pride, or a feeling of incapacity to measure up in the customary environment.

The idea of freedom is not an abstraction—we have freedom *from* and freedom *to*. The good society gives its people the opportunity to realize ever greater human and spiritual values. Like other moral virtues, freedom can only be maintained by carrying 200 out its duties.

A list of the liberties enjoyed by citizens would include religious liberty, political liberty, and the civil liberties: personal freedom, freedom of expression, and freedom of assembly and association. Every freedom has its correlative responsibility.

Whatever a person's position in society, laborer or executive, voter or politician, he has a duty to do his best. There are some who feel that if they obey the law they have done all their duty, but duty is not bounded by statutes. The sense of duty covers all cases of right doing where there is no law to 300 compel you to do it.

Duty is not a spectral figure, solemn and grim, stalking us and making notes of our delinquency. It is more like a guide, leading us to justify our existence by making the world a little better than we found it. If we had a hundred space platforms orbiting the earth, the human story would still be told in terms of individuals discharging their duty responsibly.

1. (C) The article stresses that freedom must be accompanied by _____.

2. (T – F) Duty is involved only where legal requirements exist.

Duty in a society

400 There are in this world hundreds of things which are right but which cannot be legislated for— things that will never be done unless someone is prepared to do them for no reward except a feeling that he is contributing what is expected of him to society.

If a person is to walk with his head held high, he must make his contribution in duty done, fairness, sympathy, and good taste. He may stand aloof from another person or crusade that displeases him, but he should not therefore feel called upon to make life uncomfortable for people who differ from him.

500 Acceptance of social responsibility means among other things not leaving others to do what we should share in doing. The world is so complex that we must inevitably owe much to our neighbors, but as far as possible every person should stand on his own feet.

Noblesse oblige is a beautiful concept which denotes the moral obligation to display honorable and charitable conduct. Human life depends upon a sense of obligation on the part of those people who are in a position to help others. Whether one be a capitalist, a worker, or a manager, he has this obligation to society.

600 Entry into the group called "noble" is open to citizens of all classes. It requires only that we possess and practice traits that are common among those who are noble. This brings into being a new sort of aristocracy, made up of men and women from all levels and walks of life: sympathetic, enthusiastic, of clear vision and free thought, dedicated to greatness and bigness of service to mankind.

3. (T – F) Nobility is restricted to those in the upper classes.

4. (C) *Noblesse oblige* denotes a _____ obligation to others.

Increasing pressures

700 In the last quarter of this century communities have had to take into account many features that did

265

not trouble them in the first quarter—the proliferation of services combined with an unprecedented industrial growth; an urban concentration creating many new needs at the municipal level; urgent need to control air and water pollution; to conserve oil, coal, and natural gas and find substitutes; to develop low-cost housing, efficient urban transportation, and recreational facilities such as parks, green belts, and libraries.

All these involve responsible thought and work. Just as in family life, life in the community requires $\overset{800}{\leftarrow}$ a mixture of dependence, sympathy, persuasion, and compulsion, and those who expect to reap the benefits of community life must undergo the fatigue of supporting it.

5. (T – F) Enjoying the benefits of a community requires some investment of work.

Living responsibility

What is it to live effectively responsible? It is to establish ourselves in the central undertaking of human life, in mutually fulfilling relationship with fellow humans. We need to remain human. Machines were introduced to be the extension of people's hands, but men are in danger of becoming an extension of the machine, functional robots, doing even good deeds mechanically.

Human beings are more and more refusing to $\overset{900}{\leftarrow}$ be regarded as statistics. B. R. Sen, Director-General of the Food and Agriculture Organization of the United Nations, said: "What the world needs most today is not merely a wider exchange of material benefits, essential though it is, but also a conscious dedication to the right of man to grow to his full stature, regardless of the place of his birth, the color of his skin, or of the faiths and beliefs he might cherish."

6. (M. C.) In all responsibilities, the article stresses the importance of remaining:
——(1) independent.
——(2) active.
——(3) human.
——(4) adaptable.

7. (M. C.) The authority quoted was an officer of $\overset{1000}{\leftarrow}$ $\overset{1350}{\rightarrow}$ the:
——(1) United States.
——(2) United Kingdom.
——(3) United Nations.
——(4) Canadian government.

Act with sensibility

Liberty and duty are twinned with right reason, but shouldering responsibility does not mean carrying all the world's problems. The Golden Rule does not prescribe that a person shall take no care for his own interests and his own welfare. The person who wishes to remain free must continue to carry a very substantial load of personal responsibility for his own well-being.

Sir John Lubbock, writer of scientific works, $\overset{1100}{\rightarrow}$ member of Parliament, and compiler of the first list of *The Hundred Best Books,* said: "We must be careful not to undermine independence in our anxiety to relieve distress. There is always the difficulty that whatever is done for men takes from them a great stimulus to work, and weakens the feeling of independence, and all creatures which depend on others tend to become mere parasites."

People need to be concerned about filling their role, about developing the "let's do something about it" attitude. Do-Democracy is democracy based on genuine participation through which a person answers $\overset{200}{\rightarrow}$ positively the question: "What duty do I owe to my country, to my neighbors, to my friends?" He will thus make history something more than a period to be lived through. He will be actively engaged in making history.

Acceptance of responsibility leads in business to the use of power and authority justly and sympathetically; in society it leads to a cooperative effort to improve the living conditions of all people wherever they live, and in personal life to the greatest fulfillment of an individual's capacity, large or small as it may be.

To act in that way is to assume responsibility $\overset{1300}{\rightarrow}$ as a free human being and as a part of the universe.

8. (T – F) The article cautions the reader not to get carried away with good works.
9. (T – F) Sensible people become actively engaged in making history.
10. (T – F) The use of power and authority violates the principles of freedom and responsibility.

——STOP——ASK FOR YOUR TIME——

Record time immediately.

Time——Sec.

No. Correct:——
(key on page 322)

VII–13

RATE (from table on page 315):

COMPREHENSION (10% for each correct answer):

EFFICIENCY (R × C):

R. ————

C. —— ——

E. ————

Record on Progress Chart on page 299

266

Exercise VII–14

Missing Matter
by STEPHEN P. MARAN

(Excerpted from an article in the January 1976 issue of *National History*
by permission of the editorial secretary.)

—————— WAIT FOR SIGNAL TO BEGIN READING ——————

Studies with a space telescope show that iron and certain other common elements are in short supply in the thin gas that pervades our galaxy. Theorists disagree on where the missing atoms are, but suggest various possibilities: they may have condensed into microscopic dust grains, they may have accumulated into icy baseballs floating between the stars, or they may have become concentrated in the heads of interstellar comets.

In 1904, a German astronomer, Johannes Franz Hartmann, at the Potsdam Observatory, discovered a curious effect in the spectrum of the star Mintaka, located in Orion's belt. He reported that *"the calcium line does not share in the periodic* [100] *displacements of the lines caused by the orbital motion of the star."* Hartmann stressed the importance of this result by publishing these words in italics in *The Astrophysical Journal.* Hartmann concluded that the calcium vapor responsible for the spectral line must be located somewhere in space between the earth and Orion.

1. (M. C.) Hartmann concluded that the calcium he had observed was:
  _____(1) on the star Mintaka.
  _____(2) in the earth's atmosphere.
  _____(3) in the space between earth and Orion.
  _____(4) in his telescope lens.

Interstellar gas

Since 1904, astronomers have found other [200] elements in space in addition to calcium, and have thereby identified a complex distribution of interstellar gas. With optical and radio telescopes, they have determined the spatial properties of this gas.

The importance of interstellar gas has grown over the years as new concepts of the origin of stars were formulated and it became clear to most scientists that stars are born by condensation from the clouds of the interstellar medium. At the same time it was accepted that much of the material of the stars is recycled back into space through the steady emanation of particles from the outer layers [300] of stars. If the stars are formed from the interstellar gas, however, then their chemical composition should resemble that of the gas. Unfortunately, some

of the key elements in the interstellar gas cannot be detected by the conventional techniques of ground-based astronomy. Their identifying spectral lines are in the ultraviolet wave-lengths that are absorbed in the earth's atmosphere and thus cannot reach the observatories below.

It first became possible to attack this problem in recent years when ultraviolet instruments were launched for brief intervals of observation on rockets that attain high altitude in the atmosphere. But the [400] greatest progress has come since August 21, 1972, when NASA launched the *Copernicus* satellite, one of the Orbiting Astronomical Laboratories, carrying a 32-inch ultraviolet telescope. The satellite attained a virtually circular orbit at about 460 miles above the surface of the earth. At that altitude, *Copernicus* is outside the great bulk of our atmosphere and can observe the ultraviolet light from a great many celestial objects. Its onboard telescope was specially equipped by Princeton University astronomers to investigate the interstellar gas.

Among the key results of the *Copernicus'* observations was the discovery that the amounts of [500] at least ten elements are significantly smaller in the interstellar gas than in the stars. The measurements were made relative to hydrogen, known to be the most common substance in the stars and consequently used as a convenient standard of comparison when measuring the trace amounts in which most other elements are present in the universe. The "missing" matter in the interstellar gas includes carbon, nitrogen, oxygen, and iron. Estimates of the underabundance of iron, for example, range anywhere from a factor of 5 to a factor of 100. Where has all the iron gone?

2. (T – F) Interstellar gas is detected by ultraviolet wave-lengths

[600] 3. (C) The most common substance found in the stars and therefore used for measurement comparisons is _____.

4. (M. C.) *Copernicus* was:
  _____(1) an Orbiting Astronomical Laboratory.
  _____(2) a NASA Space Flight.
  _____(3) a Princeton University telescope.
  _____(4) a Mars-bound space ship.

Dust grains

Astrophysicists believe that the missing matter is, in fact, present in the interstellar space but that it exists in a physical condition that does not allow it to absorb light in the spectral lines observed by *Copernicus*. The most obvious idea is that much of the gas has cooled and condensed into a solid state. Indeed, the presence of tiny solid particles in space 700 ← has been recognized since the 1930s. Although these "interstellar dust grains" do not produce spectral lines, they are responsible for a general diminuation of starlight received on the earth—an effect that tends to block out more shorter, blue wavelengths than longer, red wavelengths. The situation is somewhat analogous to the reddening effect a large city's smog layer has on sunlight. This has led astronomers occasionally to refer to the dust grains of space as "interstellar smog."

5. (T – F) Interstellar dust grains produce definite spectral lines.
6. (T – F) Existence of tiny solid particles in 800 space has been known since the 1930s.
7. (T – F) Interstellar smog is caused by the disturbance of space ships and astronaut activities.

Dust balls

According to George B. Field, who directs the Center for Astrophysics in Cambridge, Massachusetts, the iron and other substances that are depleted in the interstellar gas are simply stored in solid form in the dust balls.

Field believes that the respective amounts of missing elements are precisely what you would expect from such a condensation process, and he has designed a model dust grain to account for the observations.

His picture is consistent with radio astronomy observations that have revealed clouds of hydroxyl 900 ← gas in our galaxy and with other studies made by the Princeton astronomers. Field goes on to compare his interstellar grain model to a microscopic world. "The interior of the grain, like that of the earth, is composed of iron and silicates. Its outer envelope, like the oceans of the earth, is water. The whole is immersed in a gaseous atmosphere, bathed in ultraviolet light and cosmic radiation."

8. (C) The outer element of Field's model is an envelope of _____.

Comets

1000 → Other scientists, however, disagree. They do not believe that all of the missing material can be stored in interstellar grains, and they suggest further the build-up of solid, icy structures much larger than a single microscopic grain. The theoretical dimensions of these icy objects range from those of a baseball to the size of a comet. Objects of this type would not contribute to the interstellar dimming and reddening of starlight in the manner of widely diffused dust, nor would they be observable from the earth by any known method. In fact, even the comets of our own solar system generally are 1100 → invisible from earth except when they come close enough to pass within the orbit of Jupiter.

The obvious objection to these theories is that they predict the existence of things in space which we cannot hope to record or measure, and which can only be checked by additional theoretical calculations. On the other hand, we do find comets in the solar system and they do appear to contain such materials as dust grains, ice balls, and molecules that include hydroxyl and possibly even molecular hydrogen.

Since there are comets in our solar system, presumably they also exist elsewhere in space. The 1200 → question is, "How many comets does each star have?" Are there enough in our galaxy to explain the great amount of missing interstellar matter?

It seems likely that the so-called missing elements are not truly lost, but can be accounted for by one or another version of these theories, or by a combination of them. Certainly some of the unaccounted-for material must be located in dust grains, while some of it may exist in the form of larger objects, including comets. The medium of interstellar space gives rise to the stars, and they, in 1300 → turn, enrich that same medium with their own gaseous and particulate emissions. The life cycle of the galaxy must thus include "gas to gas" in addition to "dust to dust."

9. (T – F) Comets appear to hold ice and dust grains.
10. (T – F) All of the missing material is probably 1350 → scattered around in tiny dust grains.

——STOP——ASK FOR YOUR TIME——

Record time immediately.

Time_____Sec.

No. Correct:_____
(key on page 330)

VII–14

RATE (from table on page 315):

COMPREHENSION (10% for each correct answer):

EFFICIENCY (R × C):

R. _____

C. _____

E. _____

Record on Progress Chart on page 299

Exercise VII–15

Bill of Rights
by THOMAS I. EMERSON

(Reprinted with permission from *Public Affairs Pamphlet*, No. 489,
Copyright © 1964 by the Public Affairs Committee, Inc.)

──────── **WAIT FOR SIGNAL TO BEGIN READING** ────────

The Bill of Rights embodies the ground rules of our democratic society. It guarantees the citizen basic rights that the government may not infringe, imposes obligations upon the government, and establishes the fundamental principles by which we as a people attempt to live together and govern ourselves. The provisions of the Bill of Rights are set forth in the United States Constitution and it is the special, though by no means the exclusive, responsibility of the courts to see that they are enforced.

The United States Constitution as originally drafted and ratified by the states in 1789 contained only a few provisions that guaranteed the basic rights 100 of the individual. But the citizens of the thirteen states who were called upon to ratify the Constitution forced the leaders in most of the state constitutional conventions to promise that a Bill of Rights would be added. That promise was fulfilled in 1791 when the first ten amendments were approved by the First Congress and quickly ratified by the states. These ten amendments are often referred to as the Bill of Rights. However, all provisions of the Constitution that guarantee individual rights, whether adopted before or after the first ten amendments, are usually 200 thought of as constituting the American Bill of Rights.

Origin for the Bill of Rights

Most of the provisions of the Bill of Rights had their origin in hard-fought struggles for human rights in England and in the colonies. The due process clause derives from the Magna Carta, the prohibition against infliction of "cruel and unusual punishments" from the English Bill of Rights, and the First Amendment protection of freedom of expression from both English and American pre-Revolutionary experience with suppression of political opposition. Other provisions have their roots in later periods of our history. The equal protection clause of the 300 Fourteenth Amendment, for instance, embodies a concept of human equality that grew out of the abolitionist struggle to eliminate slavery and the "badges of servitude" in America.

The growth of legal doctrine relating to the Bill of Rights dates primarily from the 1920s. Not until after World War I did the Supreme Court turn its attention from restricting governmental power over business enterprise to protecting the rights of individual citizens. The greatest expansion in interpretation of the Bill of Rights took place from 1954 to 1968, when Earl Warren was Chief Justice. 400 Since then, under Chief Justice Warren E. Burger, such expansion has slowed considerably.

1. (T – F) The 1789 U.S. Constitution had few provisions to guarantee the basic rights of the individual.
2. (M. C.) The due process clause is derived from the:
   _____(1) English Bill of Rights.
   _____(2) Pentagon Papers.
   _____(3) Declaration of Independence.
   _____(4) Magna Carta.
3. (T – F) The greatest expansion in interpretation of the Bill of Rights took place from 1850–1900.

The role of the Supreme Court

There has been a great deal of controversy over the approach the Supreme Court should take 500 in interpreting the Bill of Rights. Some people argue for "strict construction," others for "liberal construction." These terms are somewhat misleading. Actually, a "strict construction" of the Bill of Rights, which was designed to *limit* the power of government, could result in an interpretation that would restrict government authority and expand the rights guaranteed to the individual.

The real issue is whether the Supreme Court should construe the constitutional guarantees narrowly, confining them to the specific areas that the framers had in mind in drafting them, or whether it should apply them broadly to meet the problems of contemporary society.

600 The process of constitutional interpretation is not a sterile and legalistic construction of the literal words of the text. Most of the provisions of the Bill of Rights are couched in broad language, intended to express a fundamental principle, and do not contain specific instructions for dealing with a particular problem. But the specific abuse against which the provision was originally directed can be

considered only one manifestation of a wider problem that may change in form but not in essence.

Function of the Bill of Rights

The primary function of the Bill of Rights is to protect "minority members" of society. They may be in such a position because they are poor or ←700 powerless, because they hold unorthodox ideas, because they belong to a minority religious, racial, political, or cultural group, or simply because they are opposing whatever "establishment" has power over them. The power structure, by definition, controls the major institutions. Those who wield the power are interested in getting results and tend to override or ignore the abstract rights of individuals who stand in their way. Protection of the minority right has been entrusted, in great part, to the one institution that stands somewhat apart from the battle, manned by persons trained in the application ←800 of general principles, and authorized to act as the conscience of the community.

It must be remembered that the Supreme Court and the courts generally are not the only source of protection for the guarantees of the Bill of Rights. Other institutions, such as our churches and schools, play an important part. A nation beset by many problems and torn by dissension finds it difficult to maintain a healthy Bill of Rights. Nevertheless, courts remain the frontline defense of the Bill of Rights and must carry out that task in a generous, positive, and even aggressive manner.   900 ←

4. (C) A _____ construction of the Bill of Rights would restrict government authority and expand individual rights.
5. (T – F) The author feels a real issue is how the people construe the constitutional rights guaranteed to the individual.
6. (T – F) The primary function of the Bill of Rights is to protect minority members of society.
7. (T – F) A troubled nation experiences difficulty in maintaining a healthy Bill of Rights.

Challenge of modern times

Few nations today have an effective Bill of Rights. Protection of the rights of the individual does not seem to be a natural tendency of a man ←1000

as a member of an organized society. It requires a conscious and deliberate effort over a long period of time.

The United States has been fortunate. A comprehensive system of individual rights was adopted at its founding and embodied in a written constitution. For a century and a half a natural balance of forces kept the ideas and practices of the system alive and relatively healthy. There were, of course, serious gaps and lapses—as in the case of black citizens or in many a police station; and 1100→ in such times of crisis as the Civil War, the growth of the labor movement, World War I, and the McCarthy era. Despite such lapses, the tradition of individual rights in this country has persisted and grown stronger.

In the last fifty years there has been a remarkable expansion of the legal doctrines that give substance to the Bill of Rights. At the same time, we face a very serious challenge to the existence of that system of individual rights.

Now we have learned that, left in purely negative form, the Bill of Rights is not always capable of achieving its goals: the equal protection clause has 1200→ not succeeded in producing equality between the races; justice for the poor is not attainable through hands-off policies; and freedom of expression cannot be realized where the media of communication are controlled by a single economic interest. The system of individual rights today needs affirmative support. This support must come through governmental processes. Thus we are faced with the paradox of using governmental power to aid individuals in realizing their rights while curtailing governmental power when it seeks to restrict those rights.

8. (T – F) Owing to social lapses and gaps, the tradition of individual rights has 1300→ diminished and grown weaker.
9. (M. C.) According to the article, in the last fifty years considerable expansion to the Bill of Rights has stressed:
    ____(1) political freedom.
    ____(2) rights of women.
    ____(3) legal doctrines.
    ____(4) freedom of expression.
10. (C) The system of individual rights today 1350→ must secure some _____ support.

——STOP——ASK FOR YOUR TIME——

Record time immediately.

Exercise VII–16

Cooper Mansion May Fall
by RICK HEADLEE

(Reprinted from the February 26, 1981 issue of *Wyoming Frontier Review* by permission of the editor.)

—————— **WAIT FOR SIGNAL TO BEGIN READING** ——————

Spectacular building

Since it was constructed in 1921 the Cooper Mansion has been one of the most spectacular buildings in Laramie. Only the large 19th century home of banker Edward Ivinson, now occupied by the Laramie Plains Museum, competes for highest honors.

The Cooper Mansion sits isolated amid a ring of tall cottonwoods near the corner of 15th Street and Grand Avenue, Laramie's busiest intersection. Until 1962 the old Wyoming Territorial Hospital stood as a kind of companion to the Cooper Mansion, east across 15th Street. But University of Wyoming expansion brought about demolition of the handsome brick hospital; now a 12-story dormitory occupies the site. ← 100

If university plans proceed undeterred, the Cooper Mansion soon will fall.

1. (T – F) The Cooper Mansion is the most spectacular building in Laramie, Wyoming, and has no competitors.

Style and structure

Like any true masterpiece of the baroque mode, the composition of the Cooper Mansion depends on the play of light to reveal its form. On all sides asymmetrical, the ''Mission Style'' design is characterized by the lively push and pull of advancing solids and receding voids.

The white stuccoed surface, affixed to exterior walls of brick four feet thick, provides a neutral ← 200 surface for a daily duet of light and shadow to dance across rows of columns, through upper and lower arcades, from carved *vigas* at top to red brick patios below. Over banks of upper and lower level French windows and doors, several shapes of roofs clad in red tile project as fixed awnings.

On the south face, a weave of massive cypress beams creates an arbor serving as central focus to the side. The forward thrusting beams of the arbor terminate in curvilinear carved ends. The whole arbor rests at front on four fat Tuscan columns.

A ''port-cochere,'' or covered carriage stop, on ← 300 the west side of the Cooper Mansion also has a roof of cypress beams comprising a large arbor. A second level balcony cantilevers on large curved brackets to allow occupants to oversee the arrival of guests. Like *vigas* on the southwestern pueblo, on the south and west sides rafter ends pierce through the stuccoed walls to end with elaborately carved ends.

On the south side a second level, three-arched arcade beneath a steeply pitched roof enjoys continual summer shade, making an effective summer air conditioner for the rooms behind.

400 → In winter months the lower sun penetrates through the arches to allow the second level interior to receive direct solar gain. On the north side a similar lower level arcade opens onto a large brick patio.

The Cooper Mansion was built for entertaining. Inside is an entryway of several marble arches, with stone veneers duplicating impressively the vestibule of an Italian Renaissance palace.

All floors have mahogany parquetry inlaid around the periphery with fret-work designs done in cherry, maple, almond, oak and birch. The eastern tower on the upper level has servants' quarters, while the western tower has three suites of rooms for 500 → members of the Cooper family. A grand staircase rises from the Renaissance entryway to the owners' suites above. A humbler stairs for the servants leads from quarters to the large kitchen below.

2. (T – F) The Cooper Mansion was built mainly for entertaining many guests.

3. (T – F) The house includes quarters for servants.

Family ownership

In 1921, a brother and sister from England had the mansion built as their home. Nearly half a century earlier their father, Frank Cooper, had come to Wyoming and established a large cattle ranch west of Laramie.

Eton graduate and English lord, Frank Cooper 600 → maintained also a ranch in Africa, but in Wyoming he seems to have found his creative matrix. Unlike so many other wealthy foreign born landowners in Wyoming during the 19th century, Frank Cooper engaged actively in expanding and diversifying the regional economy.

Where Sir Moreton Frewen, an Englishman compatriot living in Cheyenne, failed to develop an effective means for freezing slaughtered beef and transporting them by rail, Frank Cooper succeeded. By the Laramie River he built a large underground warehouse, to which he brought ice in winter. A stockyard and slaughterhouse established nearby delivered carcasses to the cold chamber.

700 → Cooper also invented an ice car to transport the beef far east and west of Laramie. Primarily

the enterprise shipped west, hence its name "The Marsh and Cooper Pacific Express." The business established Laramie as the cold storage center on the Union Pacific line, a role the town still maintains.

About 1895 Frank Cooper returned to England, where he began his own family. In 1904 he sold his ranch west of Laramie, but wisely retained the mineral rights. Discovery of vast oil deposits on the old Cooper Ranch in 1917 brought his children to Wyoming to monitor production and collect royalties. United States law required the children to 800← maintain a permanent residence in the United States, so they commissioned Laramie architect Wilbur Hitchcock to design a fine home east of town near the old Territorial Hospital.

4. (T – F) A brother and a sister from Africa had the Cooper Mansion built.
5. (C) These siblings came to the United States when _____ was discovered on the land their father owned.
6. (T – F) The Coopers' father had been successful both as an early cattle rancher and local businessman.

Colonel Richard Cooper, son of Frank Cooper, lived intermittently at the mansion. He befriended 900← author Ernest Hemingway, and together they traveled about the world, especially to Africa to hunt on the Cooper ranch. In 1943 Colonel Cooper married a woman from Idaho.

Barbara Cooper, the Colonel's sister, remained in Laramie and seldom went abroad. However, during World War II she returned to England and served as a London fire marshal. Although she never married, Barbara supported many young adults during their years as students at the University of Wyoming. In 1971 she died at her home in Laramie, leaving one niece as sole heir to the Cooper family estate.

7. (M. C.) Through the years, Barbara Cooper 1000← was:

_____(1) confined to the mansion and to the caring for her invalid brother until his death.
_____(2) married and raised a large family in the house.
_____(3) interested in young people and supported many students during their college years.
_____(4) a prominent social leader and used the house extensively as a social headquarters for the leaders of the city.

8. (T – F) Neither of the Cooper children were ever married.

Sale to University Foundation

In 1980 the University Foundation, a private nonprofit organization, purchased the Cooper Mansion and the full city block of undeveloped 1100→ lands lying west of it. The University of Wyoming administration then announced plans to solicit funds from the Wyoming State Legislature to acquire the property from the University Foundation.

Immediately, citizens concerned about the Cooper Mansion inquired of the university's plans for it. To their dismay the citizens learned the university expects to demolish the Cooper Mansion and build a new commerce and industry building in its place. A group, the Wyoming Architectural Heritage Foundation, took leadership in the effort to dissuade the university from destroying Laramie's major landmark.

Attempts to preserve building

1200→ The Heritage Foundation urged the university to consider locating the new academic facility on the remaining three-quarters of a block. In December, 1980, the consulting committee to the State Historic Preservation Office approved the Cooper Mansion nomination to the National Register. In a surprise and unprecedented move the Commissioners of the Wyoming Recreation Commission overruled the consulting committee by ordering the mansion nomination tabled. A petition campaign conducted by the Heritage Foundation indicates many people in Laramie and Cheyenne wish the mansion preserved.

Local effort to save the fine old mansion continues unabated. The Wyoming Architectural Heritage Foundation is continuing efforts to save this unique building.

1300→ 9. (M. C.) According to the writer, the University of Wyoming administration planned to:

_____(1) move the building.
_____(2) remodel the building.
_____(3) tear the building down.
_____(4) raise money for its restoration.

10. (C) The action of the Wyoming Recreation Commission caused the nomination to 1350→ the National Register to be _____.

———STOP———ASK FOR YOUR TIME———
Record time immediately.

Time_____Sec.   **RATE (from table on page 315):**   R. _____

No. Correct:_____   **COMPREHENSION (10% for each correct answer):**   C. _____
(key on page 330)

VII–16   **EFFICIENCY (R × C):**   E. _____

Record on Progress Chart on page 299

Exercise VII–17

How to Produce an Idea
by HELEN ROWAN

(Reprinted from *Think* magazine, Copyright 1962,
by permission of International Business Machines Corporation.)

─────────── **WAIT FOR SIGNAL TO BEGIN READING** ───────────

Degrees of creativity

The six-year-old child who succeeds in repairing his broken tricycle bell has a creative experience, New York University psychologist Morris I. Stein is fond of pointing out, but no one would claim that the repaired bell constitutes a "creative product" in the generally accepted meaning of the term.

It is possible, in other words, to differentiate roughly between individual creativity and social creativity. If you have an idea, it may be creative in comparison to all the other ideas you have ever had, which certainly represents individual creativity, or it may be creative in comparison to all the ideas *everyone* has ever had; this represents social creativity of the highest order.

In short, the basic difference may be one of *degree* rather than kind. The highly creative person may be so because of the kind of problem he sets for himself and the quality of his response to it, but his creative process is not necessarily very different from what everyone goes through, or at least can go through.

It is necessary to bear this in mind because of the aura of mystery which has surrounded the creative process—a mystery which has been augmented rather than dissipated by the numerous accounts left by the geniuses of history. Almost to a man—ancient or modern, writers, artists, musicians, scientists—they have gladly committed to paper accounts of how they did what they did and how they felt while they were doing it. The trouble with this kind of evidence, fascinating as it is, is that it is impressionistic, imprecise, and incomplete. Furthermore, one aspect has tended to overshadow all others in the public mind; this has to do with the role of "inspiration" in the creative process.

It is true that most highly creative individuals, even those as different in temperament and field as Samuel Coleridge and Bertrand Russell, do report flashes of insight, of sudden "knowing," but when these bursts of inspiration are seen in the context of the entire process of which they are a part, they take on different significance.

1. (C) The basic difference between social and individual creativity may be one of _____ rather than of kind.

2. (T – F) The child who successfully repairs a broken tricycle bell has produced a "creative product" in the generally accepted meaning of the term.

The four stages

To most people who have studied the problem, it seems apparent that the creative process occurs in four (or five, as some would have it) stages, while others say that what knowledge we have of the various stages is of little help because it is sheerly descriptive.

But for whatever it is worth, many participants and observers have described the stages of the creative experience in the following terms:

Preparation.
Incubation.
Illumination.
Verification.

Some break the preparatory stage into two parts, saying that in a sense one's entire life—the gaining of experience, education, the mastery of a medium, whether it be pigments or words or mathematical symbols—is preparation for the act of creating. Then next (or first) comes the stage of intensive preparation. The individual works, consciously and hard, on whatever problem he is trying to solve. This preparation involves enormous effort and eventually, in many cases, great frustration, with accompanying tension and anxiety.

3. (M. C.) The four stages of the creative process as described by many participants and observers are:
_____(1) preparation, incubation, illumination, variation.
_____(2) preparation, incubation, illumination, verification.
_____(3) preparation, experimentation, incubation, verification.
_____(4) preparation, incubation, experimentation, variation.

4. (T – F) Some people say that the preparatory stage may be divided into two parts, claiming that one's lifetime experiences, which are preparation for the act of creating, prelude the stage of intensive preparation.

The creator withdraws

Then the creator often withdraws from the problem, perhaps for a very short time, perhaps for a long period. There is no certain knowledge of what occurs during this period, but some psychologists believe that the subconscious is at work. Some believe that the period of incubation frees the individual of previous fixations, and that he is then able to see the problem with new eyes when he returns to it, while others would add to this⁷⁰⁰ hypothesis the idea that during the withdrawal period the creator is receiving helpful cues from his environment and experience.

Whatever it is that happens, next comes the moment everyone yearns for: the burst of insight, an experience of the "Aha" or "Eureka!" type that we all have had in some degree. But when considered in the light of all that has gone before, it loses some of its mystery. Remember that the individual has already established an outside criterion against which he may check his idea or insight; he has been desperately looking for something; he sees it, recognizes it,⁸⁰⁰ and cries, "Eureka!" (To give a homely example that has nothing to do with creativity, set yourself the task of finding a red-headed man who is speaking German and wearing green socks, and when you see him, you, too, will have an "Aha" experience.)

Following the illumination comes the period of verification or completion, in which time the individual applies all his skills and craft and intelligence to make solid the original insight and finish the creation.

A distinctive characteristic of highly creative individuals seems to be their ability to maintain an exceedingly delicate balance between the most⁹⁰⁰ intense effort, on the one hand, and suspension of conscious effort on the other. Even though few would go as far as Edison did in saying that genius is only one percent inspiration, the other 99 percent being perspiration, all genuinely creative people do show that "transcendent capacity for taking trouble" that Carlyle said made genius. But other kinds of traits seem to be just as essential to their creativity. Many observers have mentioned the attitude of playfulness highly creative individuals reveal—the ability to get both enjoyment and amusement from juggling ideas or paints or words or whatever. They also show a¹⁰⁰⁰ certain kind of restraint: they are not driven to pursue their purposes implacably and directly at all times, nor to force a solution arbitrarily, but they seem to trust themselves to recognize *the* right solution when it emerges, and have enough confidence to wait for it.

5. (T – F) The period of withdrawal from the problem that a creator often experiences is referred to as the incubation stage.

6. (C) The stage of the creative process in which the creator experiences a burst of insight and recognizes his goal is called the stage of _____.

7. (M. C.) The stage of verification is the period of time in which the creative individual:

    ____(1) withdraws from the problem to gain a more objective view.

    ____(2) establishes some outside criterion by which to obtain insight.

    ____(3) recognizes the ultimate creation he has desperately been seeking.

    ____(4) applies his skills, craft, and intelligence to stabilize the original insight.

8. (T – F) A distinctive characteristic of highly creative individuals seems to be their inability to maintain a balance between the most intense effort and the suspension of conscious effort.

9. (T – F) Creative individuals are driven to pursue their purposes implacably and directly at all times, showing little or no restraint.

No how-to-do-it books

The "how-to-do-it handbook of creativity" has never been written and probably never could—or should be. Nevertheless, it seems possible that all of us might increase somewhat the degree of creativity we show in our daily lives by making deliberate attempts to develop the kinds of attitudes, habits, and modes of operation that mark highly creative individuals. There is pretty general agreement that conscious effort alone cannot produce a creative achievement, but conscious effort may put us in a position where creative achievement is more likely.

10. (T – F) The author feels that all might increase the degree of creativity shown in their daily lives by attempting to develop the kinds of attitudes, habits, and modes of operation that are characteristic of highly creative individuals.

——STOP——ASK FOR YOUR TIME——

Record time immediately.

Time_____Sec.

No. Correct:_____
(key on page 322)

VII–17

RATE (from table on page 315):

COMPREHENSION (10% for each correct answer):

EFFICIENCY (R × C):

R. _____

C. _____

E. _____

Record on Progress Chart on page 299

Exercise VII–18

It Must Never Happen Again
by ROMAN RUDENKO

(Reprinted from the October 1976 issue of *Soviet Life* by permission of the editor.)

─── **WAIT FOR SIGNAL TO BEGIN READING** ───

Thirty years ago!

The Nuremberg Trial of the major Nazi war criminals was the logical outcome of the Second World War. After the countries of the anti-Hitler coalition routed Hitler Germany, for the complete triumph of justice it was necessary to punish the leaders of the Third Reich, those who made the gravest atrocities against humanity their state policy. To prosecute and punish the major Nazi war criminals, by agreement between the governments of the USSR, the USA, Great Britain and France, an international military tribunal was set up which 19 states joined. Though it consisted of four members and their 100 four assistants, it can be said without exaggeration that the Nazi criminals were tried by peoples of the world on behalf of the millions they had exterminated.

Almost the entire fascist leadership was put in the dock, except Hitler, Goebbels and Himmler, who had poisoned themselves with calcium cyanide; Gustav Krupp, who was paralyzed; Robert Ley, who hanged himself in his prison cell; and Martin Bormann, who went into hiding and was tried in absentia.

The peoples of the world saw the trial of the former rulers of Nazi Germany as a historically important and just act of retribution. For the 200 advocates of peace and democracy it was the continuation of postwar international cooperation in the struggle against aggression and fascism.

The attitude of Germans toward the trial is worthy of note. The U.S. information office published polls showing that the overwhelming majority of Germans, about 80 percent, regarded the Nuremberg Trial as just and the guilt of the defendants as indisputable.

1. (T – F) The whole leadership of the fascist party was tried at Nuremberg.
2. (T – F) The attitude of the Germans toward the trial was one of hostility.
3. (T – F) The Nazi criminals were tried on behalf 300 of the millions they had exterminated.

The International Military Tribunal was in session for more than 10 months. In conditions of the greatest publicity it examined some 4,000 official documents from the archives of Nazi General Headquarters, the German Ministry of Foreign Affairs, as well as the personal archives of Goering, Himmler, Ribbentrop and Rosenberg. The Tribunal heard more than 100 witnesses for the defense and for the prosecution, strictly and objectively assessed all the evidence, scrupulously examined the crimes of each defendant and on October 1, 1946, passed sentence.

400 Anybody who studies the materials of the Nuremberg Trial without bias agrees that it was conducted in an atmosphere of the strictest legality and that in no case was there any evidence that the rights of defendants were to any degree restricted or impaired or that the defendants were prevented from defending themselves against the accusations brought against them. The faultless legal development of the trial and the irreproachable legal substantiation of the judgment gave the Nuremberg Trial enormous validity.

Excerpts from German documents reveal the monstrous plans of the German fascists. Even before 500 attacking the Soviet Union, their plan was to starve out the population of occupied regions. The records of the conference on May 2, 1941, to consider the Barbarossa Plan—the code name for the plan of attack on the USSR—read that "the war should be extended only when . . . the Wehrmacht is supplied with foodstuffs at the expense of Russia. No doubt, this will entail the death of dozens of millions from hunger."

Obergruppenfuhrer SS Erich Bach-Zelewski, under oath, testified to the Tribunal that early in 1941, at a conference in Weselsburg, Himmler declared: "The aim of the crusade to Russia is to exterminate 600 30 million of the Slavic population."

This was not Himmler's personal declaration, Bach-Zelewski said, but a manifestation of the "Third Reich's policy, of Nazi ideology and the logical consequence of the entire National Socialist outlook."

In Oswiecim at least 2.5 million people were killed in gas chambers and no less than 500,000 died from hunger and disease.

The Nuremberg Trial exposed for the whole world to see the essence of German fascism, the criminal role of the German monopolies and brass hats in unleashing the Second World War. It revealed crimes unprecedented in their fanatical cruelty and scope, and unmasked the humanity-hating Nazi ideology.

4. (C) The original intention of the Third $\xleftarrow{700}$ Reich's eastward expansion was to exterminate a vast number of the _____ _____ population.

5. (T – F) Many critics feel that the Nuremberg Trial lacked legality and validity.

Tribunal judgment

In full conformity with the irrefutable proofs, the Tribunal recorded in its Judgment: The war crimes were committed on a scale unprecedented in history. These were committed in all countries occupied by Germany and were accompanied by cruelty and terror on a scope hard to imagine. . . . In the war with the Soviet Union the plunder of territory and the brutal treatment of the civilian population was worked out $\xleftarrow{800}$ to the most minute detail even before the offensive was launched. . . . Prisoners of war were subjected to brutal treatment, torture and murder. . . . Public and personal property was systematically plundered. . . . Towns, settlements and villages were purposelessly destroyed, without any military need.

German industrial and financial magnates took an active part in the Nazi plot against peace. There would have been no Third Reich without their capital investments and political backing. Without them the plans of criminal aggression could not have been carried out.

6. (M. C.) The trial showed that the war crimes were:

——(1) accidental. $\xleftarrow{900}$
——(2) premeditated.
——(3) trivial.
——(4) inconsequential.

7. (T – F) The aggressive atrocities of the Nazi campaign had strong support from many German capitalists.

Intolerable fascism

The Nuremberg Trial showed that fascism cannot be tolerated in any form, either as a state system, a political trend or as an ideology. It is an international crime threatening humanity whenever and wherever it appears.

Never has any trial united all the progressive elements of the world so unanimously in their desire to put an end to aggression and racism. It reflected the wrath and indignation of the people over Nazi atrocities and the conviction that those guilty should $\xleftarrow{1000}$ be punished so that such crimes are never repeated.

At the Nuremberg Trial it was established that the roots of the Nazi plot against peace go deep into the past. Early in the twenties the program of the Nazi party contained the seed from which the Second World War grew.

From Himmler's statements relating to October 1943 you can judge the ultimate goals of Hitler Germany in the war: ''. . . the war is being waged to blaze the trail to the East and to make Germany a world empire.'' This was not Himmler's personal view, but the intent of German fascism to dominate the world, as confirmed by many documents, in particular, the directive Oberkommando der Wehrmacht No. 32, which contained the plans of Nazi conspirators against Britain and the USA, their designs for the seizure of Egypt, Syria, Iran and Iraq. $\xrightarrow{1100}$

8. (C) The intent of German fascism was to make Germany a world _____.

9. (T – F) The Nuremberg Trial demonstrated the desire of many people to put an end to racism and aggression.

Gravest international crime

The International Military Tribunal acknowledged aggression as the gravest of international crimes. For the first time heads of state guilty of preparing, unleashing and conducting aggressive wars were tried as ordinary criminals, and the principle was applied that the official position as a head of state or acting under orders of the government will not be considered grounds to free them from responsibility or to mitigate their punishment. The principles of the Charter and the Judgment of the Tribunal, affirmed by the resolutions of the UN General Assembly, proved a substantial contribution to international law now in force and became its generally recognized norms. $\xrightarrow{1200}$

Today the records of the Nuremberg Trial serve as a warning: Fascism succeeded once in cheating the masses of people and involving the world in a dreadful catastrophe. It must never happen again! $\xrightarrow{1300}$

10. (M. C.) What must never happen again is the:

——(1) leadership of Hitler.
——(2) power and aggression of fascism.
——(3) Nuremberg Trial.
——(4) capitalistic development of Germany. $\xrightarrow{1350}$

——STOP——ASK FOR YOUR TIME——

Record time immediately.

Time_____Sec.   RATE (from table on page 315):   R. _____

No. Correct:_____   COMPREHENSION (10% for each correct answer):   C. _____
(key on page 330)

VII–18   EFFICIENCY (R × C):   E. _____

Record on Progress Chart on page 299

Exercise VII–19

Planet at Risk
by GUS SPETH

(Reprinted from the September 1980 issue of *The Living Wilderness* by permission of the editor—Copyright 1980 by the Wilderness Society.)

— **WAIT FOR SIGNAL TO BEGIN READING** —

It is becoming increasingly evident that there must be decisive global action, and soon, if the world is to cope successfully with the grave population, natural resource and environmental trends that are threatening the ability of our planet to sustain life as we have known it.

President Carter initiated an attempt, the first by any government, to make long-term quantitative projections regarding these trends. The result, the Global 2000 Report offers sobering confirmation of the dire prospect if the nations of the world fail to achieve a change of direction.

The picture painted by the report is one of a planet with more than 6 billion human beings by the year 2000—50 percent more than now; with growing numbers of people suffering hunger and privation; with mounting losses of croplands, grasslands and forests; with accelerating degradation of air and water; and with plant and animal species vanishing at a rate without precedent, carrying with them unassessed potentials for the future good of mankind in food, fuel, medicinal and other substances.

Even now, 800 million people live in conditions of abject poverty, their lives dominated by hunger, ill health and the absence of hope, and the earth's carrying capacity—the ability of biological systems to meet basic human needs—is rapidly eroding.

One of the most troubling of the Global 2000 Report's findings is the negative effect of rapid population growth and poverty on the productivity of renewable natural resource systems. We have become accustomed in recent years to warnings about the need to conserve nonrenewable resources, but the Global 2000 Report underscores the serious stresses that threaten the world's renewable resources, such as croplands, forests and fisheries, as well.

1. (T – F) The negative effect of rapid population growth and poverty on the productivity of renewable resource systems is one of the report's most troubling findings.

2. (M. C.) The report states that by the year 2000 the world population will be:
   _____(1)   6 billion.
   _____(2)   60 billion.
   _____(3)   800 million.
   _____(4)   200 million.

3. (C   ) The U.S. government study to deal with threatening population, natural resource and environmental trends is presented in the _____ Report.

Deforestation

At the present rate, according to the report, by 2000 some 40 percent of the remaining forest cover in the less developed countries will be gone. Most of this staggering loss will be in what biologically is the richest part of our planet—the humid tropical forests of Africa, Asia and South America. An estimate prepared for our study suggests that by 2000 between half a million and 2 million plant and animal species could be extinguished—a third to half of them in the vanishing tropical forests.

Deforestation will also destabilize water flows, leading to siltation of streams, reservoirs and irrigation works; depletion of ground water; intensified flooding and aggravated water shortages. In South Africa and Southeast Asia a billion people live in heavily farmed alluvial basins and valleys that depend for their water on forested mountain watersheds. By 2000, at the present rate, forests in these regions will shrink by half, seriously impacting food production.

The Global 2000 conclusions are not predictions of what *will* occur, but projections of what *could* occur if we do not respond. The projections should serve as effective warnings that vigorous, determined new initiatives will be required worldwide to meet human needs while protecting and restoring the earth's capacity to support life. If there was doubt before, there should be little doubt now—the nations of the world, industrialized and less developed alike, must act in concert to secure sustainable economic development, to control population growth and to protect the earth's resources and environment before the trends depicted in the Global 2000 Report become realities.

4. (T – F) According to the report, much of the rich forest cover in many parts of Europe will be lost.

5. (C   ) Water shortages and flooding could be anticipated results from severe _____.

6. (T – F) The report's conclusions are predictions of what could happen if present patterns continue.

Implication of the report

The humanitarian reasons for action by our own nation are strong enough by themselves, but we must be aware of the report's implications for our security ← 700 as well. Secretary Muskie said, "It is in our interest to do all we can now to counter the conditions that are likely to drive people to desperation later. . . . We would rather send technicians abroad to help grow crops than send soldiers to fight the wars that can result when people are hungry and susceptible to exploitation by others."

Will the world respond to the warnings delineated in the Global 2000 Report? I am optimistic that as people here and abroad come to realize the full dimensions of the challenge before us, a positive and ultimately powerful response will be forthcoming. ← 800

We already have made a good start in addressing many global problems. Our government has contributed importantly to a series of United Nations conferences on population, food and hunger, the human environment and other issues. A federal interagency task force recently studied and reported on tropical deforestation. The United States recently took an important initiative on long-range economic analysis and planning. Our country is a world leader in wildlife conservation, wilderness preservation and the assessment of environmental effects of governmental actions.

Other nations have also begun to respond to the problems noted in the Global 2000 Report. They are ← 900 beginning to replant deforested areas, conserve energy, make family planning measures widely available, take actions to reduce soil losses and desertification, explore alternatives to oil use and reduce the use of harmful pesticides.

7. (T – F) The author of this article is optimistic that the people of the world will respond positively toward the problems outlined in the report.

8. (T – F) President Carter's actions in 1978 and 1979 are the only significant expressions of the United States' leadership in wildlife conservation and wilderness preservation.

Coping with global demands

In bringing about needed changes, the United ← 1000 1350 → States has both the ability and the obligation to continue its strong leadership role. Even though many of the problems identified in the report seem remote from us, they are not, and we must turn our attention, ingenuity and generosity increasingly to them. We must cope with these global demands in part by laying a sound foundation at home. For example, by relying increasingly on energy conservation and renewable resources here at home, the United States is enhancing its ability to provide leadership abroad as countries search for sustainable 1100 → energy futures. We must also move to protect our domestic agricultural base, for if we continue to lose productive farmland at current rates, our position as a major food exporter—and our ability to feed people of other nations—will be jeopardized.

To provide the basis for a strengthened, sustained response to the problems identified in the Global 2000 Report, President Carter created a Presidential Task Force on Global Resources and Environment. In developing our follow-up to the Global 2000 Report, the task force will have a number of other studies and reports to draw upon: the World Conservation Strategy announced earlier 1200 → this year by the International Union for Conservation of Nature and Natural Resources; the UN Environment Programme and the World Wildlife Fund; the work of the World Bank under the able leadership of Robert McNamara; the papers of the Worldwatch Institute, which first brought many of these issues to wide public attention; and the contributions of many other national and international organizations, both governmental and nongovernmental. I look forward to working with all of these groups in forging a strong, effective response to the Global 2000 Report.

9. (T – F) The United States has so much 1300 → farmland that it will be able to continue supporting people of other countries for years.

10. (M. C.) To develop a plan of action, President Carter created a:
    ——(1) Presidential Task Force on Global Resources and Environment.
    ——(2) World Conservation Strategy Task Force.
    ——(3) International Union for Conservation of Nature and Natural Resources.
    ——(4) World Wildlife Preservation and Protection Fund.

——STOP——ASK FOR YOUR TIME——
Record time immediately.

Time____Sec.

No. Correct:____
(key on page 322)

VII–19

RATE (from table on page 315):

COMPREHENSION (10% for each correct answer):

EFFICIENCY (R × C):

R. _____

C. _____

E. _____

Exercise VII–20

Challenge to Selective Admission
by DONNA MARTINEZ

(Reprinted from an original article of the Uniwyo Reading Research Center
by permission of the director.)

———————————— **WAIT FOR SIGNAL TO BEGIN READING** ————————————

Freedom of choice in education

Were you ever encouraged to work hard so you could be accepted by the best schools when you successfully graduated from high school? Did you ever contemplate the fundamental characteristics that determined which institutions were recognized as most outstanding in the hierarchy in American higher education? With all the emphasis on freedom, equality, and nondiscrimination should not every individual have the opportunity for admission to a sound post-secondary educational system in this country which prides itself on having the most accessible higher education system in the world? Since the Morrill Act in 1862, over one hundred and twenty ¹⁰⁰ years ago, all of the states have established and expanded one or more open-access institutions where over fifty percent of high school graduates matriculate each year. With the proliferation of many public community colleges and the substantial resources of many kinds of financial aid now available to needy students, the real question of access is not who goes to college, but which college one goes to.

Institutions are by no means equal, however, and the student's future may depend as much on the nature of the institution attended as on attendance or nonattendance. In American higher education, some ²⁰⁰ types of institutions are convenient and interesting to some particular groups of individuals while others are remote and relatively inaccessible for a wide variety of reasons, many of which are practically indiscernable.

While most people are familiar with the hierarchy in private schools, where a few prestigious institutions occupy the top positions, they are not always conscious that a similar hierarchy exists within many of the public systems as well. While the private schools are well recognized for their selective recruitment, widely publicized standards of excellence, and various formal and informal procedures for selective admission, the public institutions are less obvious in proclaiming their ³⁰⁰ position on the hierarchy and often defend that they are really "open to any high school graduate." But if they have no acknowledged plan of selective admission, they often have a well developed and conscious plan of selective retention which serves to enhance and maintain their hierarchical position.

1. (T – F) Public universities always provide equal access to all high school graduates.
2. (T – F) Hierarchies exist in public institutions as well as in well-known private schools.

Equality of resources

The resources available in any public institution ⁴⁰⁰ are closely correlated with its position in this hierarchy. For example, the expenditures for educational and general purposes in the most selective public universities averaged over three times as high per student as those in the least selective four-year colleges or in the two-year colleges.

Students who gain entry into the more selective universities usually are exposed to the advantages of much richer resources, superior libraries, better equipment, finer buildings, better paid faculty members, and better residential facilities, whereas students who attend the less selective colleges usually miss the advantages of residential living and have reduced chances of completing their degree program.

⁵⁰⁰ Although the tuition costs paid by the individual students are somewhat higher in the more selective colleges, the difference is not significantly more expensive, and is often compensated for by more liberal and extensive student financial aid opportunities. Thus, the average student who is admitted to a selective public institution actually may invest less for a far more expensive education than the student who is admitted to a two-year college or nonselective four-year college and who is not the recipient of financial assistance.

In either case, the fundamental cost of the operation of the institution usually is the responsibility ⁶⁰⁰ of the taxpayers of the community or state, and the contribution of the individual student through fees or educational assessments is often a very limited percentage of the total education expense.

3. (C) The primary costs of public colleges are paid by the _____.
4. (M. C.) The overall investment in educational facilities and resources in the more selective schools as compared to the less selective schools is:
   _____(1) about the same.
   _____(2) a little less.
   _____(3) a little more.
   _____(4) more than twice as much.

5. (C) In terms of net cash investment for the average student, the individual per-student cost in the more select universities is _____ than $\xleftarrow{700}$ that in the less selective institutions.

A school for every need

The proliferation of state and community supported institutions of post-secondary education has brought higher education "closer to home" for many families in the middle or lower economic brackets and has contributed to an extensive acceptance of some of the less publicized aspects of selective admission and retention practiced by some public institutions.

Many college professors are supporters of the current meritocratic or elitist structure in higher education and they argue that effective selective admission procedures are essential to maintaining academic standards in higher education.

Some educators argue that students will develop $\xleftarrow{800}$ better academically if they are grouped with students of similar ability. Available research evidence offers virtually no support for this assumption. Thus, as far as learning is concerned, there seems to be limited interaction between the selectivity of the institution and the ability of the student. Excluding less able students at the point of entry may help assure universities that the graduates they turn out four years later will be of the quality to achieve success in the competitive job market.

Failing to admit a student, or discharging one whose grades are poor, denies the possibility of the $\xleftarrow{900}$ university or any of its personnel making any further educational impact on that student. By selectively screening out the lower performing students, an institution is implicitly taking the position that the education of these students is not worthwhile and that it has the foresight to predict what their long-range contributions might be. A study of history, however, reveals many contributions to science, literature, and public leadership by outstanding individuals who were never recognized as outstanding for achievement in secondary school. Many authorities believe that selecting and sorting can be performed much more effectively by graduate schools and by subsequent employers. $\xleftarrow{1000}$

6. (M. C.) Selective admission standards are least likely to be observed in:
_____(1) community colleges.
_____(2) state universities.
_____(3) graduate schools.
_____(4) private schools.

7. (T – F) Excluding less able students from admission is recommended as a way to conserve institutional resources.

Existence for education

Certainly most people would agree that the purpose of higher education is to *educate* students, with a responsibility to bring about certain desirable changes in their lives by helping them achieve more knowledge, more understanding of themselves and of their society. From this perspective, selective $\xrightarrow{1100}$ admission standards based on test scores and high school grades makes little sense. The real goal of education would seem to justify instead admission requirements designed to identify students who would be most influenced by the educational environment and process.

Rather than extensive emphasis on identifying students with the maximum demonstrated academic potential, universities should maximize the opportunities for improving the performance of all students and helping them develop the flexibilities for optimum adaptation to a changing society.

A common argument in defense of selective admissions is that any relaxation of admissions standards would lower the institution's "academic standards." The traditional view that academic $\xrightarrow{1200}$ standards are determined primarily by the abilities of the students admitted would seem to apply only to institutions that grade strictly on the curve.

Colleges certainly have the opportunity and the obligation to set any standards they wish, independent of their admissions practices. Academic standards are related to the performance levels required before the institution will certify that the student has passed certain courses and completed certain degree requirements. Critics might suggest that the only time academic standards are truly determined by admissions standards is when the college has no impact on performance—what comes out is simply what goes in!!

$\xrightarrow{1300}$ 8. (T – F) According to this writer the real goal in college education should be to bring about changes in students.

9. (T – F) Academic standards are directly dependent upon high standards of selective admission.

10. (T – F) This writer seems to be convinced that selective admission standards are $\xrightarrow{1350}$ really unnecessary.

——STOP——ASK FOR YOUR TIME——

Record time immediately.

SERIES VIII
Critical Thinking Exercises

Purpose

Merely scanning for main ideas or more intensive reading for facts will not develop the critical reading skills demanded in so many situations in adult life today. In addition to the development of assimilation and retention skills, certain basic abilities of critical reading must be developed. You must be able to grasp literal and implied meanings and to relate to them by generalization. You must form evaluative reactions to what you read as you inquire about quality and accuracy of material. You must learn to judge rationally what you read. You must develop insight and understanding in applying the ideas you acquire from reading.

A whole book could be developed around the concept of critical reading skills. To some degree you began to apply them in your Study Reading Exercises. Although critical reading skills involve a different approach to reading that does not result in a measure of efficiency, you should recognize this type of reading as a part of your pattern of flexibility. Therefore, this book has been expanded to include some brief introductory exercises of this type. Your library or Study Skills Center probably has several workbooks with more extensive materials on critical reading skills.

Instructions

In this series, rate of reading is not considered as being of primary importance. You may read these little samples as fast or slow as you please, but you must take time to *think* about them carefully, either during or after the reading process—or both. The articles are all short excerpts presented with only a number and no identification of source. Each one is followed by a few questions to focus your thinking. Try to draw from the content clues that will help you to make judgments. Consider also the rest of the critical reading questions presented here:

1. What is the author's purpose?
2. When was this written?
3. To whom is this appeal directed?
4. Who would have you believe this?
5. What do you question in this material?
6. In what ways does the writer reveal a bias?
7. What key words were used to influence your emotion?
8. To which of your basic needs does the writer appeal?

After you have answered as many questions as you can, turn to the "KEY" materials on pages 323 and 331. There you will find an identification of the source of the material and a few comments about the purpose of the presentation. Judge for yourself the accuracy of your responses.

Suggestions

The process of critical thinking in relation to reading is a never ending life process. One is deluged with communications of all kinds, many of which are loaded with emotional appeal and propaganda techniques. Series VI–12 in this workbook includes an analysis of several basic propaganda techniques and may be worth rereading in connection with these exercises.

The exercises in this book are only a token of the continuing work that you must do to be a critical reader. The ultimate dimension of effective reading is the skill of *reading critically*. Can you differentiate fact from opinion? Can you evaluate the validity of opinion? Can you detect unsound reasoning and propaganda techniques? Can you keep these points in mind, even when you are functioning at some of your higher levels of reading efficiency?

You need to develop the ability to comprehend ideas that authors do not state specifically, but that they expect you to infer. You need to develop skill in extending your thinking about ideas to such concepts as making generalizations, perceiving relationships, predicting outcomes, and anticipating authors' purposes. You need to make judgments about authors and their ideas. They can try to influence you, but *you* have the final word. You can choose to reject an author and his ideas, and he has no recourse. Good readers try to develop skill in identifying and understanding the ideas they encounter in reading, but ultimate acceptance and application of these ideas depend upon many personal factors that have nothing to do with the reading process itself.

You can be a good reader if you seek to make a personal application of the skills you have learned and if you maintain an alert inquiring mind. But you will not be reading in the deliberate concept of reading that sets 800 words per minute as a maximum. Neither will you be a good reader because you whiz through all materials at some fantastic rate of speed reading. You can develop a flexibility that enables you to make judgments and to adjust your reading skills to the needs and purposes of the moment.

You will discover that reading makes a great difference in your life. As you seek the ideas behind the words, you will find that flexible and polished reading skills are keys to a vast reservoir of knowledge and stimulation. Only you can determine your ultimate potential in using reading as a tool for personal development.

Even the "great books" are not gods: they are only tools for you to use. They may even be dull tools if you approach them with less than the sharpest of your wits. Authors are often dry and boring to some readers. They do not have the advantage of observing your reaction—responding to your enthusiasm—clarifying, when you look confused. They must go on monotonously with their one-sided monologue in total ignorance of *your* enthusiasm or boredom. If you remember this, you may be more tolerant and more effective in applying your skills to get the most from their work. You have the control of your reading, and you have the power to make it the kind of experience that you want it to be.

But what you need is not patience, but really an impatience with yourself that forces you to decide what you are reading *for* and then to read *for it!* You need to be impatient enough to center the energy for effective reading in your own head. True concentration in reading is not the effort to "keep other thoughts out"; it is a by-product of having a goal challenging enough to focus your full attention to the task of seeking it.

If knowledge is your goal, then you can attain it only when you think for yourself, not when you have merely understood what someone else thought. Knowledge is not something you learn or absorb: it is something you think about and use and bring to life in your own ideas.

In short, you will become a part of the reading you do. You will be able to read and to know what it is all about and how it bears on other things you have read or done. You will read in a way that makes you think, and finally produce some ideas with the look and mark of your own mind upon them. Then you will have achieved greater reading efficiency.

Exercise VIII–1

"They laughed when I wound up my shaver . . . " That's liable to happen to you when you first use it in front of anyone. A wind-up shaver may seem a plaything, or at best an emergency type of shaver (because it needs no cords or batteries). After all, how can a hand-cranked shaver rotate fast enough to do a clean and close job? And how many times do you have to wind the darn thing to finish one shave?

One answer at a time: the three-blade shaving head revolves at such a fast clip that it actually gives you seventy-two thousand cutting strokes a minute! Now, about the winding: the palm-shaped body is filled with a huge mainspring made of the same Swedish super steel used in the most expensive watch movements. You can crank the key just like a movie camera (about six turns) and the shaver shaves and shaves and shaves. From ear to ear, from nose to neck, without slowing down, it maintains its full shaving speed right to the end—and long enough to do the complete job. Hard to believe, but really true.

We have reason to believe that you will want to keep your shaver for the office, club, cabin or in a permanent place in your bathroom cabinet. Once you've tried it you won't let it go. The money that it leaves in your pocket; the dependability; the good, fast, clean shaves that you'll get—they'll give *you* the last laugh.

—— —— ——

1. What is the author's purpose? _____
_____

2. To whom is this appeal directed? _____
_____

3. Who would have you believe this? _____
_____

4. To which of your basic needs does the writer appeal? _____

Exercise VIII–2

Once again the annual guessing game is already underway. It is a guessing game I first became aware of eight years ago. This is the ninth playing of the game.

The reason I mention this is that each year for the past seven years I have proposed devices, resolutions, propositions, and so forth, to suggest that perhaps the time has come for us to give thought to what has been happening to families in this very uncertain process.

Somehow, somewhere, the master planners of the schedules and dates have not yet managed to coordinate these schedules with the schedule of the school year. The net result is that most have found it impossible to spend any of the summer vacation time of their children with them in the spirit each of us would like.

I have contended that there is no reason in the world why we could not take one month off in the summer while the kids are out of school, in order to be with them and to enjoy them to the fullest, and then come back and continue the business at hand.

I hasten to point out that each year when this proposal has been made, I have been approached by those who say, "Well, next year it will be different. Next year we will do it."

So far as I'm concerned, this is "next year" for the ninth time. "Next year" is now. The time is at hand for us to give this matter serious thought.

—— —— ——

1. What is the author's purpose? _____
_____

2. When was this written? _____
_____

3. To whom is this appeal directed? _____
_____

4. In what ways does the writer reveal a bias? _____
_____

Exercise VIII–3

Our life is frittered away by detail. An honest man has hardly need to count more than his ten fingers, or in extreme cases he may add his ten toes, and lump the rest. Simplicity, simplicity, simplicity! I say, let your affairs be as two or three, and not a hundred or a thousand; instead of a million, count half a dozen, and keep your accounts on your thumbnail.

In the midst of this chopping sea of civilized life, such are the clouds and storms and quicksands and thousand-and-one items to be allowed for, that a man has to live, if he would not founder and go to the bottom and not make his port at all, by dead reckoning, and he must be a great calculator indeed who succeeds. Simplify, simplify. Instead of three meals a day, if it be necessary, eat but one; instead of a hundred dishes, five; and reduce other things in proportion.

Why should we live with such hurry and waste of life? We are determined to be starved before we are hungry. Men say that a stitch in time saves nine, and so they take a thousand stitches today to save nine tomorrow.

———   ———   ———

1. What is the author's purpose? _____
_____

2. When was this written? _____
_____

3. To whom is this appeal directed? _____
_____

4. What key words were used to influence one's emotions? _____

Exercise VIII–4

So far, I had not opened my eyes. I felt that I lay upon my back, unbound. I reached out my hand, and it fell heavily upon something damp and hard. There I suffered it to remain for many minutes, while I strove to imagine where and *what* I could be. I longed, yet dared not to employ my vision. I dreaded the first glance at objects around me. It was not that I feared to look upon things horrible, but that I grew aghast lest there should be *nothing* to see. At length, with a wild desperation at heart, I quickly unclosed my eyes. My worst thoughts, then, were confirmed. The blackness of eternal night encompassed me. I struggled for breath. The intensity of the darkness seemed to oppress and stifle me. The atmosphere was intolerably close. I still lay quietly, and made effort to exercise my reason.

A fearful idea now suddenly drove the blood in torrents upon my heart, and for a brief period, I once more relapsed into insensibility. Upon recovering, I at once started to my feet, trembling convulsively in every fiber. I thrust my arms wildly above and around me in all directions. I felt nothing; yet dreaded to move a step, lest I should be impeded by the walls of a *tomb*. Perspiration burst from every pore, and stood in cold big beads upon my forehead. The agony of suspense grew at length intolerable, and I cautiously moved forward, with my arms extended, and my eyes straining from their sockets, in the hope of catching some faint ray of light.

———   ———   ———

1. What is the author's purpose? _____
_____

2. When was this written? _____
_____

3. What key words were used to influence one's emotions? _____

4. Who would have you believe this? _____
_____

Exercise VIII–5

The summer soldier and the sunshine patriot will, in this crisis, shrink from the service of their country; but he that stands it now, deserves the love and thanks of man and woman. Tyranny, like hell, is not easily conquered; yet we have this consolation with us, that the harder the conflict, the more glorious the triumph. What we obtain too cheap, we esteem too lightly: it is dearness only that gives everything its value. Heaven knows how to put a proper price upon its goods, and it would be strange indeed if so celestial an article as freedom should not be highly rated.

I have as little superstition in me as any man living, but my secret opinion has ever been, and still is, that God Almighty will not give up a people to military destruction or leave them unsupportedly to perish, who have so earnestly and so repeatedly sought to avoid the calamities of war by every decent method which wisdom could invent.

The heart that feels not now, is dead; the blood of his children will curse his cowardice who shrinks back at a time when a little might have saved the whole and made them happy. I love the man that can smile in trouble, that can gather strength from distress and grow brave by reflection. 'Tis the business of little minds to shrink; but he whose heart is firm, and whose conscience approves his conduct, will pursue his principles unto death.

_____ _____ _____

1. What is the author's purpose? _____

2. When was this written? _____

3. To whom is this appeal directed? _____

4. What key words were used to influence one's emotions? _____

Exercise VIII–6

Dear Member,

I'm enclosing a check for $40,500.

Unfortunately the check's not for you. It's for your Congressman.

Only you're paying for it.

That $40,500 isn't his salary either. It's the amount of new tax breaks he voted for himself. That's right, on top of everything else he gets, he just gave himself some fat new tax breaks.

But you can cancel out those new tax breaks by signing the "Stop Payment" sticker and placing it over the check, which is a postcard, and mailing it to your Congressman today.

That sticker also tells your Congressman that you want him to support HR 5525, a bill that will erase those fat tax breaks he just gave himself.

And, after giving himself the biggest tax break in U.S. history, he's trying to take your tax cut away from you.

_____ _____ _____

1. What is the author's purpose? _____

2. To whom is this appeal directed? _____

3. Who would have you believe this? _____

4. To which of your basic needs does the writer appeal? _____

Exercise VIII–7

We'd like to make your blood boil, to tell you things that will make you so angry you'll hardly see straight.

Just send us $10 and we'll guarantee to keep you angry for a whole year. (That's less than 94 angry cents a month!)

We've been studying for years the things that make any decent person's blood boil. Things like prejudice, injustice, and discrimination. Some of the things we publish aren't pretty. Some of our subscribers are upset when they read them.

That's too bad. But that's our job. There is always an element of outrage in telling the truth. And the materials you get from us are the most scholarly, hard-hitting, and factual to be found. We leave the namby-pamby social studies and the pat formula solution books to others.

Moreover, we'll get you mad four times a year, by sending you four shipments every year carefully selected in advance by specialists from our new publications. Next, we'll give you an opportunity to get madder yet, by letting you purchase additional material at a maddening 20 to 50% discount!

Wait till you read our publications on civil rights, civil liberties, black studies, Middle East tensions, books on race and politics, the radical right, the radical left, new works coming up on Israel and Jewish history, discrimination against women, plus some brilliant anthologies.

Wait till you read the publications on new developments in interfaith and interracial projects (OK, these particular things won't make you mad, they'll make you glad), an examination of some forgotten minorities, urban crisis, intelligence and race, to name a few.

Every year over 5,000 libraries trust us to get them mad. So do thousands of teachers and clergymen. And thousands of ordinary decent citizens, like yourself, fume because of us. What more can we do? Except to tell you to calm down. Relax. Slowly pick up your pen and fill out the enclosed coupon. Now mail it. We'll give you plenty of time to get angry once you get our first shipment of materials. Thank you.

——— ——— ———

1. What is the author's purpose? _____

2. What do you question in this material? _____

3. To which of your basic needs does the writer appeal? _____

4. What key words were used to influence one's emotions?

Exercise VIII–8

Okay, so you've had your automobile checked and you figure you are ready for winter. Not quite, for there are several more minor items that you can check yourself which are bits of knowledge that every motorist should carry with him from November through March.

In checking equipment items yourself, make sure your heater is working properly. Do you have a car jack in your trunk and a fully inflated spare tire? A flat tire on an isolated road during severely cold weather can mean serious trouble, if you suddenly discover that you don't have a jack or fully inflated spare.

Police and professional drivers experienced in winter driving say snow tires are far better than ordinary tires for both starting and stopping on snow and ice. Although heavy-duty chains are best of all, some motorists have been known to carry bags of sand in their trunks to give them extra traction. They suppose that the added weight gives the tires more pulling power on ice. Fact is, it doesn't, and if it's of considerable weight, it may even cause the rear end to sway severely. The only value of sand in the trunk is that it can be sprinkled on the ice for short-distance traction.

Health officers summed up advice to winter motorists with a warning to those over forty, those who are overweight, and those who have a record of heart problems. Go to great lengths to avoid overexertion in your efforts to free a stranded car.

——— ——— ———

1. What is the author's purpose? _____

2. What do you question in this material? _____

3. To which of your basic needs does the writer appeal? _____

4. What key words were used to influence one's emotions? _____

Exercise VIII–9

My strategy was to start a national war on apathy, to get people involved in community action in order to learn as well as help. For an educated person to think he is educated and pass the proverbial buck—well, you've had it. When you graduate, if you lack sensitivity, you are a vegetable. If the so-called educated don't become involved in the problems of the urban and rural poor, then they are going to become a part of our stale, stagnant power structure. Just another member of the status quo.

Our American colleges graduate two kinds of people: Those who memorize and swallow, and those who criticize and watch. I am critical of this intellectual, comfortable bull session attitude where one does an analysis of present American problems without getting his hands dirty.

You know, one of the most uncomfortable places to work in America is in middle-class America, because you are kind of worried about the peanuts and not the elephants. I think America is the sleeping giant. It isn't that we can't react to challenge; it's that we aren't challenging each other. We're in the land of the free, home of the afraid.

I want to draw people out, get them involved. When they become involved they become more inner-directed because the demand on the volunteer is to be creative, not to conform.

I want volunteers. We need field workers for the South this summer. They'll have to pay their own way, but we need them.

——— ——— ———

1. What is the author's purpose? _____
_____

2. To whom is this appeal directed? _____
_____

3. What key words were used to influence one's emotions? _____

4. In what ways does the writer reveal a bias? _____

Exercise VIII–10

You are walking toward your favorite store, thinking about a wedding gift you plan to buy. An unmarked car pulls up. Two men leap out, drag you into the back seat, plunge a hypodermic needle into your arm.

When you come to, you find yourself lying half-naked in a pool of dirty water on the floor of a windowless cell. Your captors keep beating you with truncheons, kicking you, pushing you up against the walls. Then they attack you sexually, mocking you and hinting that the other members of your family are undergoing the same horror.

You don't know *why* you've been imprisoned. You don't know *what* your torturers hope to make you say. You don't know *where* to turn. You've joined the nightmare world of the political prisoner.

It couldn't happen to *you?* It couldn't happen *here?* I hope not. But systematic torture is on the increase in more than 62 nations of the so-called "civilized" world. Hundreds of thousands of men, women and children are suffering the agonies of the damned in jails and concentration camps in Chile, the U.S.S.R., Indonesia, Uruguay, Iran, Brazil, Cuba, East Germany, South Africa and Spain and an unconscionable number of other countries around the globe.

Their crime? The vast number of these "prisoners of conscience" are members of legitimate political, social and religious organizations, trade unions, youth and other movements. They are professors, priests, women's leaders, lawyers and journalists—arrested for their political and religious sympathies. Others, more horribly, are ordinary citizens—housewives and little children— arrested for no good reason at all.

——— ——— ———

1. What is the author's purpose?_____
_____

2. Who would have you believe this?_____
_____

3. What key words were used to influence one's emotions?_____

4. To which of your basic needs does the writer appeal?_____

Exercise VIII-11

I give my pledge as an American to save and faithfully defend from waste the natural resources of my country—its soil and waters, its forests, minerals, and wildlife.

Conservation is a necessity in life today. The careful preservation and protection of our natural resources is the foundation of our country itself. But we are destroying these resources and they need help. The Great Plains and majestic mountains have provided sustenance for the human race since the beginning of time. Now I feel we should provide help and protection for them.

Man watches wildlife but he doesn't seem to realize that most animals rely on other species for survival. If one species becomes extinct, generally its dependent neighbor does too.

Our country is a country with more harsh punishments and beautiful rewards than any country in the world. Yet without a program to protect it from pollution and a generally worsening environment it will soon be destroyed—and all life with it.

Those concerned with conservation need help and support. The people are what make this whole thing tick. Those who realize the values of our rich natural resources and abundant wildlife must not be a silent majority. We cannot stand helplessly and watch waste products fill the sky and waters with ugliness like a victor over the defeated! Defeated? Not yet. But what about the future? We should start caring, not tomorrow, but today. We must be heard. Our pleas for clean air to breathe and clean water to drink have to be heard by the leaders of our great country; and they must echo in the heart of every citizen whether he be seven or seventy. This is vital not only for the preservation of our country's natural resources, but for our own existence as well.

———   ———   ———

1. What is the author's purpose? _____
_____

2. What key words were used to influence one's emotions? _____

3. In what ways does the writer reveal a bias? _____
_____

4. To whom is this appeal directed: _____
_____

Exercise VIII-12

The collecting of unusual rocks and semi-precious stones—rockhounding—is gaining momentum as a family sport in this country. One big reason: in addition to providing fun for everyone in the family, it also can be a "fringe benefit" for many, providing bonus adventures to their travel vacations. That's because rockhounding can be so easily combined with other outdoor sports—say, doing a bit of rockhounding while camping or fishing. (Or, maybe it's really the other way around—saving the fishing for when the rockhounding slows down.)

If you're interested in adding new variety and fun to your travels by graduating from the ranks of the "looker" to that of the real rockhound, you'll find the move much easier than you may have thought. A small rock pick, knapsack, a book or two, notebook, prospector's pan, a couple of small screens, plus a desire for a little adventure and a lot of fun are all you need to join the rockhounding clan.

Even the objects of your search often are much easier to find than many think. Today's rockhounds are, for the most part, content to search for materials which, though certainly far less valuable than gold or diamonds, are relatively abundant. Rocks like agate, jasper, petrified wood, chalcedony, onyx and sapphire are among the most popular and zealously sought after.

Join the mushrooming corps of rockhounds and you'll gain a hobby that promises rich bonuses in new adventures, some precious stones and a mother lode of fun.

———   ———   ———

1. What is the author's purpose? _____
_____

2. To whom is this appeal directed? _____
_____

3. What key words were used to influence one's emotions? _____

4. In what ways does the writer reveal a bias? _____
_____

Exercise VIII–13

Twenty years ago, had I chosen, I could have been declared legally blind, as my friends and business associates at the time well know. The trouble was a progressive disease of the cornea.

As a result of several operations by one of the most skilled surgeons in the country, my vision is now 20/20.

I *know* what it is to be nearly blind.

Because of that experience, I became interested in doing what I could to help prevent blindness. Few people have the disease that caused my difficulty, but many suffer from other diseases of the eye that are preventable or controllable if proper action is taken in time.

I'm thinking of glaucoma and cataract particularly, and of the eye disorders affecting small children that often go undetected until much damage has been done.

——— ——— ———

1. What is the author's purpose?_____
_____

2. To whom is this appeal directed?_____
_____

3. In what ways does the writer reveal a bias?____
_____

4. To which of your basic needs does the writer appeal?_____

Exercise VIII–14

You are cordially invited to use my new audiocassette program, "How to be a No-Limit Person," for 15 days at no cost or obligation. Simply sign this letter below and return it to me. I'll do the rest.

This cassette program was created to enable an already successful person like you to achieve even higher goals and enjoy greater rewards, every day.

"How to be a No-Limit Person" gives you a lifetime of research and first-hand experience in what makes a winner in any endeavor—how leaders in every field achieve their maximum potential.

You'll learn how to better utilize your tremendous energy and creative talent, how to let your own inner signals unerringly guide you to greater opportunities and more rewarding goals. You'll capitalize on the most important information in all three of my bestselling books, *Your Erroneous Zones*, *Pulling Your Own Strings* and *The Sky's the Limit*.

——— ——— ———

1. What key words were used to influence one's emotions?_____

2. To which of your basic needs does the writer appeal?_____

3. What is the author's purpose?_____
_____

4. Who would have you believe this?_____
_____

Exercise VIII–15

At the direct request of the President of the United States, I am calling upon you to make a most unusual sacrifice.

Not the kind of sacrifice that a national emergency might require of you or your children or your grandchildren to protect our shores from invasion.

I pray that will never happen. But today President Reagan and I must jointly ask you to voluntarily make a different kind of sacrifice—a sacrifice that will help us to protect our Republican majority in the Senate.

And so, on behalf of President Ronald Wilson Reagan, I have the honor of personally inviting you to become a member of the "Republican Presidential Task Force."

I won't insult your intelligence by pretending President Reagan mentioned your name specifically. But he did describe the kind of person he wanted at his side at this critical point in America's history.

He wants proud, flag waving Americans who've proven in their personal lives their readiness and willingness to sacrifice to keep our nation strong.

That's you, and President Reagan urgently needs you in his Task Force.

_____ _____ _____

1. What is the author's purpose?_____
_____

2. When was this written?_____
_____

3. What do you question in this material?_____
_____

4. To which of your basic needs does the writer appeal?_____

Exercise VIII–16

As regards my own education, I hesitate to pronounce whether I was more a loser or gainer by his severity. Much must be done, and much must be learnt, by children, for which rigid discipline and known liability to punishment are indispensable as means. It is, no doubt, a very laudable effort, in modern teaching, to render as much as possible of what the young are required to learn easy and interesting to them. But when this principle is pushed to the length of not requiring them to learn anything but what has been made easy and interesting, one of the chief objects of education is sacrificed. I rejoice in the decline of the old brutal and tyrannical system of teaching, which, however, did succeed in enforcing habits of application; but the new, as it seems to me, is training up a race of men who will be incapable of doing anything which is disagreeable to them. I do not, then, believe that fear, as an element in education, can be dispensed with; but I am sure that it ought not to be the main element; and when it predominates so much as to preclude love and confidence on the part of the child to those who should be the unreservedly trusted advisers of after-years, and perhaps to seal up the fountains of frank and spontaneous communicativeness in the child's nature, it is an evil for which a large abatement must be made from the benefits, moral and intellectual, which may flow from any other part of the education.

_____ _____ _____

1. What is the author's purpose?_____
_____

2. When was this written?_____
_____

3. What do you question in this material?_____
_____

4. In what ways does the writer reveal a bias?____
_____

Exercise VIII–17

Observe good faith and justice toward all nations; cultivate peace and harmony with all. The nation which indulges toward another an habitual hatred or an habitual fondness is in some degree a slave. It is a slave to its animosity or to its affection, either of which is sufficient to lead it astray from its duty and its interest.

The great rule of conduct for us, in regard to foreign nations, is, in extending our commercial relations, to have with them as little political connection as possible. Europe has a set of primary interests, which to us have none, or a remote relation. Hence she must be engaged in frequent controversies, the causes of which are essentially foreign to our concerns. Hence, therefore, it must be unwise in us to implicate ourselves by artificial ties, in the ordinary vicissitudes of her politics or the ordinary combinations and collisions of her friendships and enmities. Our detached and distant situation invites and enables us to pursue a different course. Why forego the advantages of so peculiar a situation? It is our true policy to steer clear of permanent alliances with any portion of the foreign world. Even our commercial policy should hold an equal and impartial hand; neither seeking nor granting exclusive favors or preferences, constantly keeping in view that it is folly in one nation to look for disinterested favors from any other; that it must pay with a portion of its independence for whatever it may accept under that character.

——— ——— ———

1. What is the author's purpose? ——————
——————————————————————

2. When was this written? ——————————

3. Who would have you believe this? ————

4. To which of your basic needs does the writer appeal? ——————————————

Exercise VIII–18

A. Corrupt the young, get them away from religion. Get them interested in sex. Make them superficial, destroy their ruggedness.

B. Get control of all means of publication and thereby,

   1. Get people's minds off their government by focusing their attention on athletics, sexy books and plays and other trivialities.

   2. Divide people into hostile groups by constantly harping on controversial matters of no importance.

   3. Destroy the people's faith in their natural leaders by holding them up for ridicule and criticism.

   4. Always preach true democracy, but seize power as fast and as ruthlessly as possible.

   5. By encouraging government extravagance, destroy its credit, raise fears of inflation, and general discontent.

   6. Foment unnecessary strikes in vital areas. Encourage civil disorders, and foster lenient and soft attitude on the part of government toward such disorders.

   7. By specious argument cause the breakdown of the old moral virtues of honesty, sobriety, continence, faith in the pledge and word, and ruggedness.

C. Cause the registration of all firearms in some pretext with a view to confiscating them and leaving the populace helpless.

——— ——— ———

1. What is the author's purpose? ——————
——————————————————————

2. When was this written? ——————————
——————————————————————

3. Who would have you believe this? ————
——————————————————————

4. What do you question in this material? ———
——————————————————————

5. What key words were used to influence one's emotions? ——————————————

Exercise VIII–19

Right now an entire generation of children run the risk of being scarred for life by the effects of semi-starvation and malnutrition—disease, mental retardation, stunted growth—unless massive emergency and long-range aid can be provided now.

These children, nearly 30% of whom will die before the age of 5, do not know why their existence is plummeting from barely tolerable to desperate. They do not know about:

*crop failures due to drought and flood,

*sharply reduced or exhausted reserves of wheat, rice and other grains,

*skyrocketing costs of fuel and imported foodstuffs,

*high prices and critical shortages of fertilizer, or

*women and children being given a lesser share of what food is available in order to maintain the already minimal diet of the family's wage earner.

In developing countries where the biggest single contributor to infant and young child mortality is malnutrition, *children desperately need your help.*

1. What is the author's purpose?_____
_____

2. To whom is this appeal directed?_____
_____

3. What key words were used to influence one's emotions?_____

4. To which of your basic needs does the writer appeal?_____

Exercise VIII–20

Consolidated worldwide net income for the first quarter of 1982 totaled $367 million, or $1.41 per share, compared with the Company's record high quarterly earnings of $658 million, or $2.45 a share, for the first quarter of 1981.

Revenues for the first quarter of 1982 amounted to $13 billion, compared with $15.5 billion for the 1981 quarter.

The first quarter reflects the adverse impact that certain economic factors are having on the petroleum industry, particularly international oil companies. Worldwide petroleum demand has weakened due to the severe business recession in the industrialized countries as well as strong consumer efforts to conserve energy.

At the same time, oil exporting nations have maintained high levels of crude oil production in relation to consumption despite high inventory levels worldwide. The imbalance between supply and demand has resulted in extremely low product prices. As a result of the continuing excess of oil supplies and weak petroleum demand, the downward pressure on operating margins intensified during the first quarter.

1. What is the author's purpose?_____
_____

2. When was this written?_____
_____

3. Who would have you believe this?_____
_____

4. In what ways does the writer reveal a bias?_____
_____

Vocabulary List

List all key words missed and all words underlined in error. *Look up* each word in the dictionary, *study* its meaning, see if it has different meanings in different contexts, *learn* some of its synoyms and *practice using* them in sentences. Many people find that "cue cards" are a valuable aid in vocabulary building. List the key word on the front of a small card and put definition and synonyms on the back. Carry a pack of these cards in your pocket to review at odd intervals.

Review this list periodically and check off those words you have added to your vocabulary.

1.

2.

3.

4.

5.

6.

7.

8.

9.

10.

11.

12.

13.

14.

15.

16.

17.

18.

19.

20.

21.

22.

23.

24.

25.

26.

27.

28.

29.

30.

31.

32.

33.

34.

35.

36.

37.

38.

39.

40.

41.

42.

43.

44.

45.

46.

47.

48.

49.

50.

Vocabulary List

List all key words missed and all words underlined in error. *Look up* each word in the dictionary, *study* its meaning, see if it has different meanings in different contexts, *learn* some of its synoyms and *practice using* them in sentences. Many people find that "cue cards" are a valuable aid in vocabulary building. List the key word on the front of a small card and put definition and synonyms on the back. Carry a pack of these cards in your pocket to review at odd intervals.

Review this list periodically and check off those words you have added to your vocabulary.

1.

2.

3.

4.

5.

6.

7.

8.

9.

10.

11.

12.

13.

14.

15.

16.

17.

18.

19.

20.

21.

22.

23.

24.

25.

26.

27.

28.

29.

30.

31.

32.

33.

34.

35.

36.

37.

38.

39.

40.

41.

42.

43.

44.

45.

46.

47.

48.

49.

50.

Vocabulary List

List all key words missed and all words underlined in error. *Look up* each word in the dictionary, *study* its meaning, see if it has different meanings in different contexts, *learn* some of its synoyms and *practice using* them in sentences. Many people find that "cue cards" are a valuable aid in vocabulary building. List the key word on the front of a small card and put definition and synonyms on the back. Carry a pack of these cards in your pocket to review at odd intervals.

Review this list periodically and check off those words you have added to your vocabulary.

1.

2.

3.

4.

5.

6.

7.

8.

9.

10.

11.

12.

13.

14.

15.

16.

17.

18.

19.

20.

21.

22.

23.

24.

25.

26.

27.

28.

29.

30.

31.

32.

33.

34.

35.

36.

37.

38.

39.

40.

41.

42.

43.

44.

45.

46.

47.

48.

49.

50.

Vocabulary List

List all key words missed and all words underlined in error. Look up each word in the dictionary, study its meaning, see if it has different meanings in different contexts, learn some of its synoyms and practice using them in sentences. Many people find that "cue cards" are a valuable aid in vocabulary building. List the key word on the front of a small card and put definition and synonyms on the back. Carry a pack of these cards in your pocket to review at odd intervals.

Review this list periodically and check off those words you have added to your vocabulary.

1.
2.
3.
4.
5.
6.
7.
8.
9.
10.
11.
12.
13.
14.
15.
16.
17.
18.
19.
20.
21.
22.
23.
24.
25.

26.
27.
28.
29.
30.
31.
32.
33.
34.
35.
36.
37.
38.
39.
40.
41.
42.
43.
44.
45.
46.
47.
48.
49.
50.

EXTENSION OF READING PROGRESS CHART

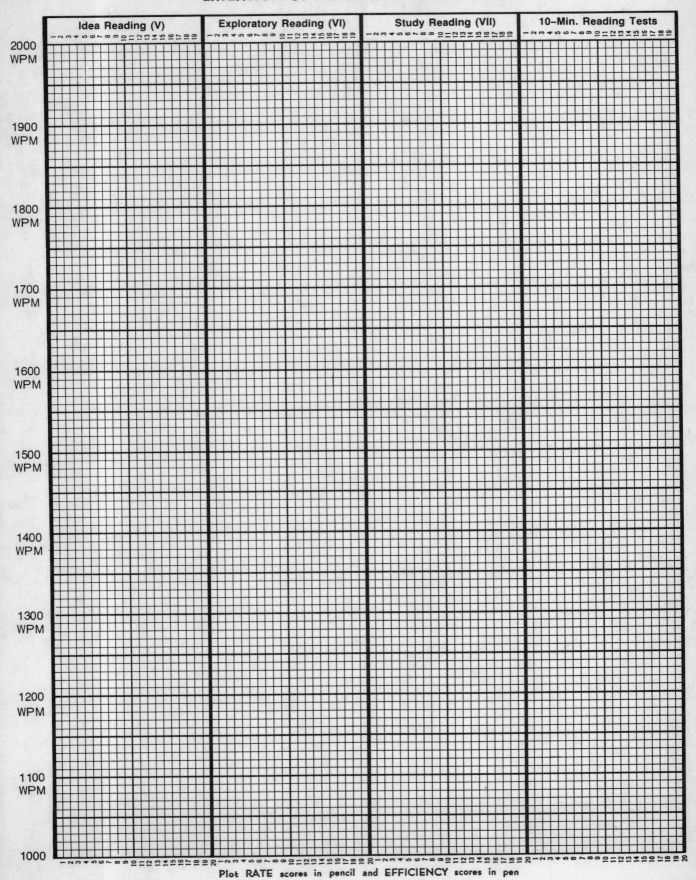

Plot RATE scores in pencil and EFFICIENCY scores in pen

EXTENSION OF READING PROGRESS CHART

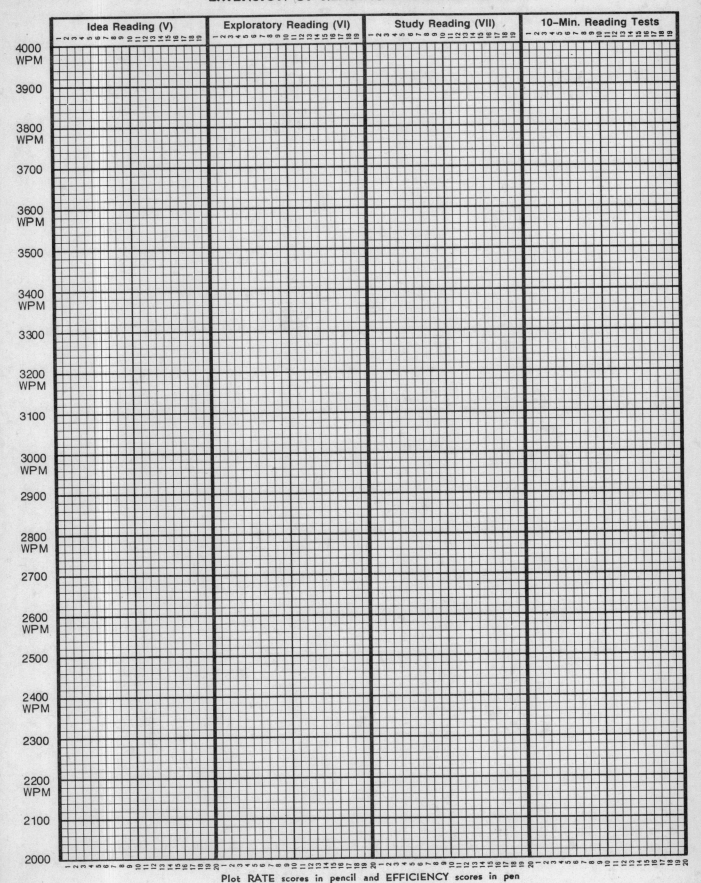

Plot RATE scores in pencil and EFFICIENCY scores in pen

EXTENSION OF READING PROGRESS CHART

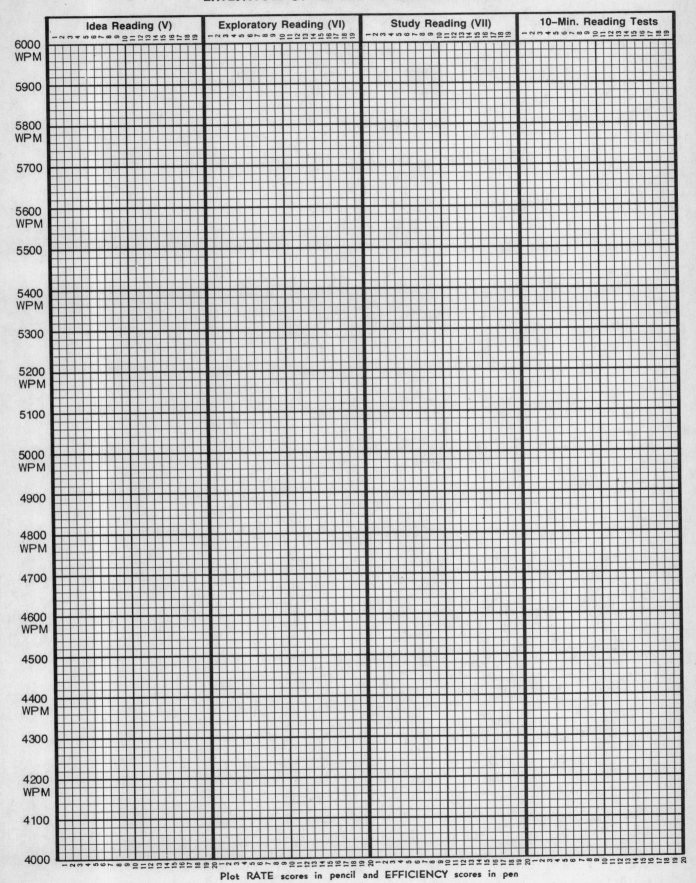

Plot RATE scores in pencil and EFFICIENCY scores in pen

Use for the word recognition drills and the word meaning drills.

Look up your time in Column I and read your rate in Column II.

I	II	I	II	I	II	I	II	I	II
				61	148	101	89	182-185	49
				62	145	102	88	186-189	48
				63	143	103-104	87	190-193	47
				64	141	105	86	194-197	46
				65	138	106	85	198-202	45
				66	136	107	84	203-206	44
				67	134	108-109	83	207-211	43
				68	132	110	82	212-216	42
				69	130	111	81	217-222	41
				70	129	112-113	80	223-227	40
1	9000	31	291	71	127	114	79	228-232	39
2	4500	32	281	72	125	115-116	78	234-240	38
3	3000	33	273	73	123	117	77	241-246	37
4	2250	34	265	74	122	118-119	76	247-253	36
5	1800	35	257	75	120	120	75	254-260	35
6	1500	36	250	76	118	121-122	74	261-268	34
7	1286	37	243	77	117	123-124	73	269-276	33
8	1125	38	237	78	115	125	72	277-285	32
9	1000	39	231	79	114	126-127	71	286-295	31
10	900	40	225	80	113	128-129	70	296-305	30
11	818	41	220	81	111	130-131	69	306-315	29
12	750	42	214	82	110	132-133	68	316-327	28
13	692	43	209	83	108	134-135	67	328-339	27
14	643	44	205	84	107	136-137	66	340-352	26
15	600	45	200	85	106	138-139	65	353-366	25
16	563	46	196	86	105	140-141	64	367-382	24
17	529	47	191	87	103	142-144	63	383-400	23
18	500	48	188	88	102	145-146	62	401-418	22
19	474	49	184	89	101	147-148	61	419-439	21
20	450	50	180	90	100	149-151	60	440-461	20
21	429	51	176	91	99	152-153	59	462-486	19
22	409	52	173	92	98	154-156	58	487-514	18
23	391	53	170	93	97	157-159	57	515-545	17
24	375	54	167	94	96	160-162	56	546-580	16
25	360	55	164	95	95	163-165	55	581-620	15
26	346	56	161	96	94	166-168	54	621-666	14
27	333	57	158	97	93	169-171	53	667-720	13
28	321	58	155	98	92	172-174	52	721-782	12
29	310	59	153	99	91	175-178	51	783-857	11
30	300	60	150	100	90	179-181	50	858-947	10

RATE TABLE FOR SERIES III—PHRASE MEANING

Look up your time (to the nearest 5 seconds) in Column I and read your rate in the Column under the appropriate exercise number. If your time is more or less than the limits of the table, or if you desire to compute your time more accurately to the exact second, divide the time (No. of seconds) into the "Division Constant" for that exercise.

Time	Exercise #1-4	Exercise #5-8	Exercise #9-12	Exercise #13-16	Exercise #17-20
# words	300	350	400	500	600
Division Constant	18,000	21,000	24,000	30,000	36,000
# seconds					
5	3600	4200	4800	6000	7200
10	1800	2100	2400	3000	3600
15	1200	1400	1600	2000	2400
20	900	1050	1200	1500	1800
25	720	840	960	1200	1440
30	600	700	800	1000	1200
35	514	600	686	875	1029
40	456	525	600	750	900
45	400	467	533	667	800
50	360	420	480	600	720
55	327	382	436	545	655
60	300	350	400	500	600
65	277	323	369	462	554
70	257	300	343	429	514
75	240	280	320	400	480
80	225	263	300	375	450
85	212	247	282	353	424
90	200	233	267	333	400
95	189	221	253	316	379
100	180	210	240	300	360
105	171	200	229	286	343
110	164	191	218	273	327
115	157	183	209	261	313
120	150	175	200	256	300
125	144	168	192	240	288
130	138	162	185	231	277
135	133	156	178	222	267
140	129	150	171	214	257
145	124	145	166	207	248
150	120	140	160	200	240
155	116	135	155	194	232
160	113	131	150	188	225
165	109	127	145	182	218
170	106	124	141	176	212
175	103	120	137	171	206
180	100	117	133	167	200
185	97	114	130	162	195
190	95	111	126	158	189
195	92	108	123	154	185
200	90	105	120	150	180

RATE TABLE FOR SERIES IV—SENTENCE MEANING

Look up your time (to the nearest 5 seconds) in Column I and read your rate in the Column under the appropriate exercise number. If your time is more or less than the limits of the table, or if you desire to compute your time more accurately to the exact second, divide the time (No. of seconds) into the "Division Constant" for that exercise.

Time	Exercise #1—6	Exercise #7—14	Exercise #15—20
# words	120	160	200
Division Constant	7200	9600	12,000
# seconds			
5	1440	1920	2400
10	720	960	1200
15	480	640	800
20	360	480	600
25	288	384	480
30	240	320	400
35	206	274	343
40	180	240	300
45	160	213	267
50	144	192	240
55	131	175	218
60	120	160	200
65	111	148	185
70	103	137	171
75	96	128	160
80	90	120	150
85	85	113	141
90	80	107	133
95	76	101	126
100	72	96	120
105	69	91	114
110	65	87	109
115	63	83	104
120	60	80	100
125	58	77	96
130	55	74	92
135	53	71	89
140	51	69	86
145	50	66	83
150	48	64	80
155	46	62	77
160	45	60	75
165	44	58	73
170	42	56	70
175	41	55	69

Since all the exercises in this series have been standardized at 900 words, this table can be used for all 20 exercises. Look up your time (to the nearest second interval shown) in Column I and then read your rate from Column II. For an approximate rate, you may use the time figure nearest your actual time. For any time figures beyond the limits of this table, or between the intervals given, the actual rate may be computed by dividing 54,000 by the time *(in seconds)*.

I	II	I	II	I	II	I	II
5	10,800	45	1,200	205	263	405	133
6	9,000	46	1,173	210	257	410	131
7	7,710	47	1,149	215	251	415	130
8	6,750	48	1,125	220	245	420	129
9	6,000	49	1,102	225	240	425	127
10	5,400	50	1,080	230	235	430	125
11	4,909	51	1,059	235	230	435	124
12	4,500	52	1,038	240	225	440	123
13	4,153	53	1,019	245	220	445	121
14	3,857	54	1,000	250	216	450	120
15	3,600	55	982	255	212	455	119
16	3,375	60	900	260	208	460	118
17	3,176	65	831	265	204	465	116
18	3,000	70	771	270	200	470	115
19	2,842	75	720	275	196	475	114
20	2,700	80	675	280	192	480	113
21	2,571	85	635	285	189	485	111
22	2,454	90	600	290	186	490	110
23	2,348	95	568	295	183	495	109
24	2,250	100	540	300	180	500	108
25	2,160	105	514	305	177	505	107
26	2,077	110	491	310	174	510	106
27	2,000	115	469	315	171	515	105
28	1.929	120	450	320	169	520	104
29	1,862	125	432	325	166	525	103
30	1,800	130	415	330	163	530	102
31	1,742	135	400	335	161	535	101
32	1,688	140	386	340	159	540	100
33	1,636	145	372	345	156	545	99
34	1,588	150	360	350	154	550	98
35	1,543	155	349	355	152	555	97
36	1,500	160	338	360	150	560	96
37	1,460	165	327	365	148	565	96
38	1,421	170	318	370	146	570	95
39	1,385	175	309	375	144	575	94
40	1,350	180	300	380	142	580	93
41	1,317	185	292	385	140	585	92
42	1,286	190	284	390	138	590	91
43	1,256	195	277	395	136	595	91
44	1,227	200	270	400	135	600	90

Since all the exercises in Series VI and VII have been standardized to a length of 1350 words, rates for any of these exercises can be found by looking up the time in Column I of this table and reading the rate from Column II. Times are given at 5 second intervals. For an approximate time you may take the time figure nearest your actual time.

For any time figures beyond the limits of this table or between the intervals, the rate may be computed by dividing 81,000 by the time *(in seconds)*.

I	II	I	II	I	II	I	II
5	16,200	105	771	305	266	505	160
6	13,500	110	736	310	261	510	159
7	11,571	115	704	315	257	515	157
8	10,125	120	675	320	253	520	156
9	9,000	125	648	325	249	525	154
10	8,100	130	623	330	245	530	153
11	7,333	135	600	335	242	535	151
12	6,750	140	579	340	238	540	150
13	6,231	145	559	345	235	545	149
14	5,786	150	540	350	231	550	147
15	5,400	155	523	355	228	555	146
16	5,063	160	506	360	225	560	145
17	4,765	165	491	365	222	565	143
18	4,500	170	476	370	219	570	142
19	4,263	175	463	375	216	575	141
20	4,050	180	450	380	213	580	140
21	3,857	185	438	385	210	585	138
22	3,667	190	426	390	208	590	137
23	3,522	195	415	395	205	595	136
24	3,375	200	405	400	203	600	135
25	3,240	205	395	405	200	605	134
26	3,116	210	386	410	198	610	133
27	3,000	215	377	415	195	615	132
28	2,893	220	368	420	193	620	131
29	2,793	225	360	425	191	625	130
30	2,700	230	352	430	188	630	129
35	2,314	235	345	435	186	635	128
40	2,025	240	338	440	184	640	127
45	1,800	245	331	445	182	645	126
50	1,620	250	324	450	180	650	125
55	1,473	255	318	455	178	655	124
60	1,350	260	312	460	176	660	123
65	1,246	265	306	465	174	665	122
70	1,157	270	300	470	172	670	121
75	1,080	275	295	475	171	675	120
80	1,012	280	289	480	169	680	119
85	953	285	284	485	167	685	118
90	900	290	279	490	165	690	117
95	853	295	275	495	164	695	117
100	810	300	270	500	162	700	116

SERIES II (ODD NUMBERS)

NO. 1	NO. 3	NO. 5	NO. 7	NO. 9
1. forehead	light	parched	trifle	crocodile
2. tease	support	inferior	obscure	stigma
3. bed	smell	hood	mark	devote
4. tranquillity	cupola	twist	port	salary
5. ice	fowl	economical	manservant	affection
6. sound	furnish	overlook	bent	lift
7. brisk	honor	prevent	rodents	discourse
8. dent	bare	goddess	dynamo	need
9. fine	cut	victim	remember	rule
10. tatter	wealthy	soothe	leg	danger
11. stick	ravage	song	vowed	vast
12. direction	slope	blemish	mist	sign
13. tired	stay	scribe	relieve	hum
14. mournful	degrade	stick	youthful	pretend
15. father	signal	scorch	yield	law
16. dash	postpone	bear	ball	hook
17. trip	avid	get	thigh	voice
18. score	anger	dress	costume	adorn
19. hotel	cage	chart	stately	power
20. powder	crazy	threat	enigmatic	form
21. heathen	ancient	pageant	drudge	verbal
22. craft	liable	headlong	penitence	bow
23. rare	scour	clean	criminal	pastoral
24. trap	dough	brace	seduction	chipmunk
25. dictator	daze	pure	eruption	shake

NO. 11	NO. 13	NO. 15	NO. 17	NO. 19
1. heard	shoeless	fuss	terrify	indignantly
2. bovine	estimate	flower	benevolent	concerned
3. woman	cheat	truism	conclusion	convert
4. style	condone	distribute	forever	lasting
5. gaze	seriousness	pecuniary	mournful	cyclone
6. fever	drunk	weighty	killer	yet
7. limestone	intellectual	observe	recede	also
8. excursion	bundle	hill	hurtful	bias
9. clear	estimate	spoil	railroad	chickens
10. isolate	wise	oppose	subservient	litter
11. hidden	uncertainty	sully	replace	stainless
12. rude	escort	silent	rare	convey
13. nut	front	cascade	illiterate	feast
14. box	lift	rub	cutter	spine
15. limpidness	entrust	tuber	university	waterfall
16. mature	refuse	vicious	scholar	formal
17. starve	haze	serious	prolific	trap
18. shout	dully	liberty	sense	renounce
19. pitcher	infirm	throw	powerful	hellish
20. change	city	solitary	rural	stonework
21. endure	melancholy	incubator	region	disregard
22. ruin	taste	pretense	trellis	origin
23. pretense	soft	bone	trust	satisfy
24. distrust	tuft	ruler	fabric	stop
25. helpful	strength	diplomacy	distant	rational

SERIES III (ODD NUMBERS)

NO. 1

1. a precious stone
2. to say something
3. an opening for
4. divide evenly
5. quite happy
6. about medium
7. one fully grown
8. a violent wrong
9. to go ahead of
10. articulate sound
11. view critically
12. a rascal
13. rather meager
14. to lean down
15. to amuse
16. a big tree
17. for smelling
18. has mild temper
19. morning hymn
20. a search for game

NO. 3

1. physical vigor
2. even surface
3. scarcity of food
4. exhibiting envy
5. close at all times
6. to reveal openly
7. in great need
8. a cheerful person
9. true to life
10. a modest person
11. with promptness
12. quickness of action
13. lighter than water
14. made imperfectly
15. open to view
16. act of dominating
17. show preference
18. brought about by
19. to frighten suddenly
20. to set free

NO. 5

1. some incentive
2. to move ahead
3. man of decision
4. not using care
5. a sudden calamity
6. act of forgetting
7. the threshold
8. completely worthless
9. gain full meaning
10. no set price
11. show satisfaction
12. confirm the deed
13. to take turns
14. something odd
15. in all probability
16. on the offensive
17. make a thrust
18. a trivial matter
19. have no boundary
20. serve as a guide

NO. 7

1. a common junction
2. to bid farewell
3. eternal existence
4. act of liberation
5. keeping a secret
6. comes to an end
7. an exhibit of humor
8. in correct position
9. that which is beyond
10. being very busy
11. to fascinate
12. likely a quarrel
13. considerable amount
14. with promptness
15. regular procedure
16. a severe look
17. join in a group
18. absence of sound
19. honesty of mind
20. not completed

SERIES III (ODD NUMBERS—*continued*)

NO. 9

1. to mix confusedly
2. to be outstanding
3. a decisive moment
4. more than is needed
5. thought to be absurd
6. especially suitable
7. covering all phases
8. to comprehend
9. usual way of doing something
10. where one lives
11. the last in the series
12. boundary line
13. a sound like a moan
14. a scenic painting
15. not public in nature
16. to set back
17. a solitary existence
18. provide financial aid
19. a tidy person
20. an act of good will

NO. 11

1. a feeling of thirst
2. not certain to occur
3. to be obedient
4. that which is to come
5. showing hilarity
6. an acquired holiday
7. one who is a criminal
8. pass quickly from sight
9. to be in right accord
10. of his own free will
11. choosing from several
12. to come together
13. simplicity of style
14. roughly sketched
15. state of being strong
16. a short hurried view
17. only one of a kind
18. changed in appearance
19. to stand still
20. to be thankful

NO. 13

1. associated with the press
2. usual course of events
3. capacity of receiving impressions
4. one who displays strength
5. one who is not selfish
6. overwhelming amazement
7. an amiable person
8. an ample amount of anything
9. set apart from others
10. adhering to a set plan
11. all over everywhere
12. to anticipate the outcome
13. becoming more complex
14. that which is dispersed
15. thought to be significant
16. related to the truth
17. authorized by proclamation
18. to withhold a privilege
19. an act which is illegal
20. to be potentially obtainable

NO. 15

1. considered to be brilliant
2. a surface injury to flesh
3. that which is awarded
4. something awkward or unhandy
5. in a contrary or reverse way
6. a perplexing and frustrating experience
7. buildings for lodging soldiers
8. not capable of producing vegetation
9. a battle between two individuals
10. be reduced to a state of beggary
11. rise and fall of the voice
12. cancel out the effects of
13. the capital city of a state
14. a state of being careful
15. the cause of an event
16. taking a census of the population
17. that which is indisputable
18. a summons to fight
19. to assemble or accumulate together
20. to contend in rivalry

SERIES III (ODD NUMBERS—*continued*)

NO. 17

1. the monarch of a kingdom
2. that which is relatively low
3. to enlarge either in fact or appearance
4. a representation of the surface of the earth
5. a martyr for the sake of principle
6. using the faculty of remembering
7. reproduced on a miniature level
8. the sixtieth part of an hour
9. which is within reasonable limits
10. a system of teaching morals
11. a moderately feeble-minded person
12. a complex situation or mystery
13. to have very narrow limits
14. quality or state of being neutral
15. a state of being nominated
16. does not deviate from the average
17. that which stands in the way
18. counted as obsolete in style
19. to vindicate or justify an act
20. under the oppression of a tyrant

NO. 19

1. the earth upon which we live
2. to develop and cultivate the mental processes
3. the practice of referring overmuch to oneself
4. to be envious of the other person
5. to be equal in quantity or degree
6. an error in the way a person thinks
7. that which becomes extinct
8. to be supported by evidence based on facts
9. to have a prescribed or set form
10. terror excited by sudden danger
11. to be full or complete in quantity
12. the accumulation or increasing of profits
13. a gesture used to enforce an opinion
14. to give a gift to someone
15. the act or action of gliding
16. the goal to obtain in winning the race
17. a meeting face to face with a client
18. to supply water to the land by canals
19. that which is regarded as an island
20. January, named after the Latin deity, Janus

SERIES IV (ODD NUMBERS)

	NO. 1	NO. 3	NO. 5	NO. 7	NO. 9	NO. 11	NO. 13	NO. 15	NO.17	NO.19
1.	S	D	S	D	D	S	D	S	S	S
2.	D	D	D	S	S	D	S	D	D	D
3.	S	D	S	S	S	S	D	D	D	D
4.	D	S	D	D	S	D	D	D	D	S
5.	D	S	D	D	D	S	D	D	S	D
6.	S	D	D	S	D	D	S	D	D	S
7.	D	S	S	D	D	D	D	S	S	S
8.	D	D	D	D	D	D	D	D	S	S
9.	D	D	D	D	D	S	S	D	D	D
10.	S	D	S	S	D	S	S	S	S	D

SERIES V (ODD NUMBERS)

	NO. 1	NO. 3	NO. 5	NO. 7	NO. 9	NO. 11	NO. 13	NO. 15	NO. 17	NO. 19
1.	F	T	T	F	T	F	F	T	T	F
2.	2	4	1	1	3	3	2	1	3	4

SERIES VI (ODD NUMBERS)

	NO. 1	NO. 3	NO. 5	NO. 7	NO. 9	NO. 11	NO. 13	NO. 15	NO. 17	NO. 19
1.	T	Automation	T	light	1	Philadelphia	T	T	T	F
2.	F	T	magma	F	T	F	physical	4	2	plaque
3.	T	math	2	gas	T	3	3	Sandstone	T	T
4.	decibels	T	F	T	E.P.A.	F	T	F	environment	F
5.	1	F	T	T	T	T	F	T	3	1
6.	F	F	F	2	decompose	T	F	F	F	T
7.	swim-bladder	2	F	3	4	4	F	1	T	1
8.	F	T	Iceland	F	F	F	T	T	F	calcium
9.	T	F	1	F	F	museum	4	springs	F	T
10.	2	3	T	T	F	T	psychosomatic	F	activity	F

SERIES VII (ODD NUMBERS)

	NO. 1	NO. 3	NO. 5	NO. 7	NO. 9	NO. 11	NO. 13	NO. 15	NO. 17	NO. 19
1.	T	melancholia	T	people	F	4	responsibility	T	degree	T
2.	F	F	Wardian	F	climate	T	F	4	F	2
3.	F	T	2	T	F	Florida	F	F	2	Global 2000
4.	4	2	F	1	4,000	F	moral	strict	T	F
5.	button	T	T	T	T	T	T	F	T	deforestation
6.	T	F	F	F	2	F	3	T	illumination	T
7.	50	severe	F	3	F	atrium	3	T	4	T
8.	1	F	T	T	T	2	T	F	F	F
9.	T	T	4	story	1	T	T	3	F	F
10.	F	3	mold	F	T	F	F	affirmative	T	1

In this series there are no exact or "right" answers. You were asked to read critically in an effort to understanding underlying purpose, emotional appeal, bias and propaganda techniques. You were asked to try to identify time and place of appeal.

As a key to checking on your own critical thinking, this key section consists of the identification of the source of the material and a few comments about the setting from which it was taken.

See how close you were to identification of basic factors. Think about those which you missed, and go back and read the material again to check out your own sensitivity to key words and ideas.

VIII–1

(an advertisement by the Haverhill's Company of San Francisco, California, in *Natural History*, February 1968, p. 22)

The purpose of this article is to sell the Haverhill's new shaver, which the company claims will give the consumer dependable, fast, and economical service for some time. The advertiser appeals to the reader's need for quick, convenient shaves.

VIII–3

(an excerpt from *Walden* by Henry David Thoreau. Boston: Houghton Mifflin Company, 1893, p. 32)

Henry David Thoreau was a transcendentalist who believed that simplicity is the key to a happy life. He went to Walden Pond to live for several months to "suck out all the marrow of life and to live deep." In this book *Walden,* Thoreau is trying to sell appreciation for the simple life as he experienced it in his Walden experiment.

VIII–5

(an excerpt from "The Crisis" by Thomas Paine, as it appears in *The Great Works of Thomas Paine*. New York: D. M. Bennett, 1878, pp. 382–383)

Thomas Paine wrote "The Crisis" to attract, interest, and involve people in the causes of the Revolutionary War. In this particular passage, he is condemning those who give up when the going gets rough. He warns that they will live to regret their "cowardice."

VIII–7

(A general mailing advertisement for a subscription service offered by the Anti-Defamation League of B'nai B'rith, 315 Lexington Avenue, New York, New York 10016)

The writer's purpose is to convince the reader that the firm that he represents will stir him up by exposing many of the shortcomings of today's society through hard-hitting and provocative articles, which the reader can obtain by subscription to the firm's series of studies. Words such as "blood boil," "angry," "prejudice," "discrimination," "upset," "outrage," "namby-pamby," and "fume" are used to sell the reader on the author's materials. His appeal is directed to the reader's intelligence by indicating that the studies are not the usual clichés generally available, but are exposés written by some of this country's best authors. Thus, the appeal is also to one's sense of honesty and integrity.

VIII–9

(taken from "Slum Lord, Sunny Side Up," by Marlise James and Ned Coll, the *Moderator*, April 1968, p. 51, with permission of the editor)

The author is the founder and director of the Revitalization Corps, which seeks to combat the problems of the poor through community action. The purpose of the selection is to make the educated aware of their obligation to help with the War on Poverty, and the author is making a particular plea for help the following summer.

VIII–11

(an article from the September 1970 issue of *Wyoming Wildlife*, reprinted by permission of the editor)

This article was prepared from a contribution by a 13-year-old schoolboy from Ranchester, Wyoming, David Seibert, and is an appeal to the readers to take some positive action to support conservation activities and to preserve some of the beauties he enjoys for the use of future citizens.

VIII–13

(taken from a letter from Eli Ferguson sent out in May 1982 in a mass mailing—a noncopyrighted form letter)

Mr. Ferguson is writing as the Treasurer of the National Society to Prevent Blindness and is soliciting funds to finance the activities of the organization which he describes in the succeeding paragraphs of the letter. Enclosed with the letter was a copyrighted brochure titled "Why all the Bother about Wills," which was published by the American Foundation for the Blind.

VIII–15

(taken from the introductory section of a letter signed by Howard Baker—a noncopyrighted mass-produced form letter dated May 21, 1982)

With special "gold seal" letterhead of the "Republican Presidential Task Force" this is an impressive document. In subsequent pages of this three-page letter, promises are made of a special golden "medal of merit" lapel pin and personal American flag to be presented to all Charter Members. Also offered are listings on an "unprecedented honor roll" and access to a "toll-free, unlisted hot line" to keep you up to date on "hot Senate issues!"

And on the last page is the definition of the sacrifice—a $120 per year membership subscription to the Republican cause—or a regular monthly payment of $10 or more.

VIII–17

(an excerpt from George Washington's *Farewell Address to the People of the United States*. Boston: Old South Leaflets, General Series, V. I, number 4, 1888, p. 15)

Before leaving office as the first president of the United States, George Washington made a speech to the people in which he offered advice on how to preserve the new nation. In this passage, he suggests that our country should refrain from interfering in any way with foreign countries.

VIII–19

(taken from a letter signed by Hugh Downs, dated "Spring 1982"—a noncopyrighted form letter used for mass distribution)

This letter was an official publication of UNICEF, the United Nations Children's Fund of which Mr. Downs was chairman. In subsequent paragraphs, worldwide operations and needs were described, and a need for $550,000,000 for current annual programs was identified, with the usual closing of many such letters to "please send your check in the enclosed reply envelope today."

SERIES II (EVEN NUMBERS)

NO. 2	NO. 4	NO. 6	NO. 8	NO. 10
1. cot	glimpse	cook	keen	humiliated
2. polite	charlatan	house	ministers	headland
3. mount	settlement	fish	eat	boast
4. falsehood	steps	gutter	empty	dominion
5. resin	hamper	blaze	pork	deny
6. predicament	cry	grass	jangle	incompetent
7. memory	sharp	level	lose	enrage
8. dromedary	sop	affront	medicine	inflexible
9. measure	hat	braid	concerning	possessions
10. conceal	afflict	intended	cutlery	muffler
11. contaminate	killer	weep	levy	stalks
12. green	melt	saving	disgusting	bag
13. dabbler	salary	plant	gas	biological
14. price	friendship	prayer	brush	see
15. shell	child	chest	vanquish	cheat
16. doctrine	short	inlet	pigeon	divinity
17. dart	drop	revise	holder	hasten
18. fortunate	struggled	scowl	pawn	dealer
19. contract	practice	assert	smaller	concept
20. tidy	ignited	chance	trap	hash
21. gait	cornucopia	western	harbor	resound
22. dwell	choose	advance	fury	restoration
23. pat	answer	part	furtive	form
24. befall	exhausted	cover	coagulate	wooer
25. pocketbook	taut	ripped	squander	useless

NO. 12	NO. 14	NO. 16	NO. 18	NO. 20
1. embarrass	plentiful	wrong	obscure	covetous
2. testimony	stake	bearer	assemble	rustic
3. morn	teach	heal	consider	naive
4. outbreak	industrious	guide	homemaking	robin
5. temerity	plume	crepe	penalty	cloth
6. ask	listen	angry	nose	inscrutable
7. weighty	succulent	spite	vegetable	elevation
8. foreign	wet	path	immunity	grateful
9. adventure	tormentor	wisdom	tolerable	manufacture
10. elder	depend	secure	fanciful	gratify
11. element	site	adhered	person	acknowledge
12. compassion	compassion	below	esteem	base
13. receive	oscillate	foolish	competency	road
14. injured	change	perplex	watch	disaster
15. staff	wife	perimeter	law	science
16. delve	official	relate	closet	producer
17. cringe	bureau	get	beguile	trade
18. tools	anticipate	chasm	final	thankfulness
19. house	useless	jewel	statement	consultation
20. ray	probable	accident	teacher	fair
21. aspect	torment	confined	degraded	hunter
22. director	bag	denial	buyer	mend
23. manifested	quit	tray	unite	depression
24. expanded	drench	shrewd	grand	exist
25. conquer	flung	unaffected	confusion	omnipresent

SERIES III (EVEN NUMBERS)

NO. 2

1. to recognize again
2. precious metal
3. a high polish
4. to empty out
5. a belief held
6. prose fiction
7. of little breadth
8. to belong to
9. infinite in size
10. entertains another
11. surface of earth
12. to poke something
13. made independent of
14. to make peace
15. leave it out
16. possessing dignity
17. an enormous animal
18. administer justice
19. not correct
20. one who expects

NO. 4

1. correct position
2. gentle animal
3. a gradual decline
4. diminish in size
5. abundant harvest
6. be flustered
7. upright position
8. to be stable
9. rather sleepy
10. ruinous condition
11. neglect of duty
12. expressive of pain
13. marked boundary
14. to annihilate
15. this very instant
16. ramble along
17. most valuable part
18. being clumsy
19. to collapse
20. to complicate

NO. 6

1. hurrying for aid
2. nearly as easy
3. more than needed
4. very small quantity
5. one or the other
6. a great error
7. plain to see
8. not interested in
9. scandalous conduct
10. just the opposite
11. at the beginning
12. a surviving part
13. obviously clear
14. about dawn
15. he who is a criminal
16. craving something
17. offer your service
18. avoiding something
19. being historical
20. dislike to work

NO. 8

1. rising in power
2. should be allowed
3. according to facts
4. to dispose of
5. to reach the peak
6. brought about by
7. prepared to go on
8. exclusive of others
9. not very busy
10. death by violence
11. decent in character
12. free from reproach
13. keep from falling
14. a great outcry
15. very necessary
16. completely exhausted
17. place for vacations
18. one who is punctual
19. one who is courageous
20. shattered to pieces

SERIES III (EVEN NUMBERS—*continued*)

NO. 10

1. punishment for an offense
2. an act of entering
3. in complete contrast
4. to pronounce guilty
5. to complicate matters
6. free from blame
7. to throw with violence
8. from this time forward
9. a military foe
10. to come to an end
11. the art of carving
12. a large river barge
13. to have an aversion to
14. to be part of an audience
15. anything very old
16. rough in countenance
17. pleasant salutation
18. one mad dog
19. to rush some place
20. to be in a safe place

NO. 12

1. consecrated as sacred
2. betray a trust
3. not according to facts
4. bottom of the scale
5. training for an event
6. that which is immense
7. an act of teaching
8. prove to be right
9. an orderly arrangement
10. one of the seasons
11. a table in a room
12. in a close-by vicinity
13. to answer yes
14. to be against
15. one noble in spirit
16. lack of attention
17. that which is interior
18. retain ownership of
19. to present for acceptance
20. to pause undecidedly

NO. 14

1. possessed with a severe handicap
2. soon to be indispensable
3. as often as necessary
4. an annual event or happening
5. the appendix of a book
6. to engage with close attention
7. close to correctness
8. to submit to arbitration
9. a military organization
10. something made without skill
11. to assault another person
12. the acceptance of an assumption
13. quality of being atrocious
14. to make trials or experiments
15. sale of goods to highest bidder
16. that which is authentic
17. to establish by authority
18. that written by his own hand
19. feeling of aversion toward something
20. a belief of some sort

NO. 16

1. to have and to keep
2. that which is tormenting
3. that which is done instantly
4. a confusing predicament
5. be on your guard
6. the part that is taken away
7. having gone astray
8. to arrange into chapters
9. idle chat in a conversation
10. the leader of the organization
11. to clarify the issue or report
12. to group or segregate in classes
13. instrument such as a clock
14. any system of rules or principles
15. that which is beyond
16. that which lies next to
17. to receive with intention of returning
18. that which is the bottom
19. to apply a brake to
20. characterized by brevity

SERIES III (EVEN NUMBERS—*continued*)

NO. 18

1. to make plain by means of interpretation
2. closely acquainted or familiar with
3. that which is in fashion
4. that which is without strength or solidity
5. a kind of a watertight structure
6. the foot of an animal or a person
7. to be eternal or infinite in duration
8. that which happens or occurs
9. a person who gives evidence as to what happened
10. extremely good of its kind
11. that which exceeds what is usual
12. personal conduct motivated by expediency
13. something considered as abnormal
14. living under false pretenses
15. sequence with no interval or break
16. in the nature of an enchantment
17. consecrated to a noble purpose
18. a habitual course of action
19. that which has a deceptive appearance
20. that which happens early

NO. 20

1. an allowance to one retired from service
2. that which is perplexed
3. pertinent to the present condition
4. formative in nature as clay or plastic
5. quality or state of being popular
6. the duties of a porter
7. within the powers of performance
8. a precaution taken in advance
9. a query relative to a problem to be solved
10. safeguarded by divine care and guidance
11. to puzzle out a mystery
12. a vessel holding one quart
13. to ramble or wander with no set goal
14. a place where anything is kept in store
15. a long loose outer garment
16. a part presented for inspection
17. to separate in different directions
18. coming first in logical order
19. to be slow or tardy in action
20. the guard going the rounds

KEY FOR INCREASING READING EFFICIENCY

SERIES IV (EVEN NUMBERS)

	NO. 2	NO. 4	NO. 6	NO. 8	NO. 10	NO. 12	NO. 14	NO. 16	NO. 18	NO. 20
1.	D	D	D	S	S	D	D	S	S	S
2.	D	S	S	D	S	D	D	D	D	D
3.	S	S	D	D	S	S	S	S	S	D
4.	S	S	S	D	S	S	S	D	D	D
5.	D	D	D	D	D	S	S	D	D	D
6.	D	D	D	S	D	S	D	D	D	D
7.	D	S	D	D	D	D	S	S	S	D
8.	D	D	D	D	S	S	D	D	D	S
9.	S	D	D	S	D	D	D	S	S	D
10.	D	D	S	D	D	D	D	D	D	S

SERIES V (EVEN NUMBERS)

	NO. 2	NO. 4	NO. 6	NO. 8	NO. 10	NO. 12	NO. 14	NO. 16	NO. 18	NO. 20
1.	F	T	T	T	F	F	T	T	F	F
2.	1	1	2	4	3	1	4	3	2	2

329

SERIES VI (EVEN NUMBERS)

	NO. 2	NO. 4	NO. 6	NO. 8	NO. 10	NO. 12	NO. 14	NO. 16	NO. 18	NO. 20
1.	T	sudden	T	F	F	individual	T	F	visitors	4
2.	2	F	quarreling	F	community	F	3	1	T	T
3.	F	neurotic	1	T	T	T	4	T	T	N.A.S.A.
4.	F	T	F	jetport	F	propaganda	F	addressability	F	T
5.	3	2	F	T	mind	4	Colorado	F	3	4
6.	distinctive	F	F	photographs	1	T	T	subscriber	F	T
7.	special	F	emotions	3	T	F	turnout	F	designers	F
8.	T	1	T	T	3	F	F	T	F	F
9.	T	T	2	F	T	T	T	2	T	F
10.	F	T	T	2	F	1	F	T	4	Space Center

SERIES VII (EVEN NUMBERS)

	NO. 2	NO. 4	NO. 6	NO. 8	NO. 10	NO. 12	NO. 14	NO. 16	NO. 18	NO. 20
1.	2	cause	F	T	T	1	F	F	F	F
2.	T	1	4	F	plastic	T	T	T	F	T
3.	suicide	T	50	F	F	fish	hydrogen	T	T	taxpayer
4.	F	F	T	Bible	F	F	1	F	Slavic	4
5.	T	T	interior	F	T	4	F	T	F	less
6.	escape	17th	T	T	2	F	T	oil	2	1
7.	3	F	F	3	low	T	F	3	T	F
8.	F	2	1	4	F	Alaska	water	F	empire	T
9.	T	F	F	T	4	F	T	3	T	F
10.	F	T	T	cross	T	T	F	tabled	2	T

In this series there are no exact or "right" answers. You were asked to read critically in an effort to understand underlying purpose, emotional appeal, bias, and propaganda techniques. You were asked to try to identify time and place of appeal.

As a key to checking on your own critical thinking, this key section consists of the identification of the source of the material and a few comments about the setting from which it was taken.

See how close you were to the identification of basic factors. Think about those which you missed and go back and read the material again to check out your own sensitivity to key words and ideas.

VIII–2

(taken from the *Congressional Record*, Vol. 113, No. 7, January 19, 1967, p. S558, by Senator Gale McGee, Wyoming, Democrat)

The purpose of the speech is to persuade the Senate to recess for the summer, although no formal measure is proposed. The appeal is made to the legislators' feeling for family unity by keeping families together at their homes in the summertime.

VIII–4

(an excerpt from "The Pit and the Pendulum," Edgar Allan Poe, as it appears in *The Works of Edgar Allan Poe*, Volume II. New York: A. C. Armstrong and Son, 1902, pp. 465–466)

Poe's story, "The Pit and the Pendulum," tells of the terror invoked upon men by the Spanish Inquisition. The character in this story has been arrested and thrown into the dungeon for heresy. The terror he feels upon awakening is a very real part of this story.

VIII–6

(taken from a letter written by Jim Davidson, and mailed in April 1982 to all members of the National Taxpayers Union—a noncopyrighted form letter mass-produced and distributed)

The author is the National Chairman of the National Taxpayers Union and he was soliciting support for a national attempt to get a reversal of a congressional action that he felt was very unfair. The excerpt was the lead section of a form letter explaining the implications of the legislation in critical detail and asking all members to contact their Congressmen expressing opposition to the action. The letter also pleads for contributions of $25 to $1,000 to finance a campaign to repeal the legislation. The goal was to raise $146,000. The public response was so great that within two months both houses of Congress had passed bills to repeal the "Congressional Tax Break" bill.

VIII–8

(taken from "Weathering the Winter," by A. R. Roalman, *Americana*: The American Motors Magazine, November/December 1967, p 15, with permission of the editor)

Appealing to the reader's need for knowledge of driving safety hints, the purpose of the article is to advise readers of some precautions for winter driving and car maintenance. The author of the article represents an automotive company which has an interest in making driving as pleasurable and safe as possible.

VIII–10

(taken from a letter from Genetta Sagan which was undated but which was distributed in a mass mailing in August 1976 under the letterhead of "A.I.U.S.A."—a noncopyrighted form letter)

This excerpt is the beginning section of a four-page letter which was headed "Dear Reader" and which began after a quotation from "The National Observer" about torture in Turkey. The letter describes in detail many activities and several case histories. Then it describes the organization and function of *Amnesty International—U.S.A.* and pleads for subscriptions and generous contributions.

The writer in a postscript identifies herself as an Italian resistance worker who was picked up by the Gestapo in World War II and held and tortured as a prisoner for 45 days. At the time of writing this she was an active member of *Amnesty International.*

VIII–12

(taken from "Rockhounding" by Pete Czura in *Americana: The American Motors Magazine,* November/December, 1967, p. 17, with permission of the editor)

The author, who represents a motoring magazine, appeals to the reader's sense of adventure and desire to make traveling more enjoyable and interesting by collecting rocks.

VIII–14

(taken from a promotional letter signed by Dr. Wayne Dyer and mailed out in a mass mailing in May 1982—a noncopyrighted form letter)

The letter is a personalized letter on personal, colored stationery printed only with Dr. Dyer's name and address but with no company name. At the bottom of the letter, however, is a signature line for the recipient to order the $39.95 cassette series at the "15-day risk free" audition. Enclosed with the letter is a four-page colored business brochure from Nightingale-Conant Corporation about the cassette program and Dr. Dyer and a prepaid envelope for your order. In the advertising folder, the company claims to be "the World's Largest Producer of Audio-cassette Programs" and the company address is the same as that shown on the personalized stationery of Dr. Dyer.

VIII–16

(an excerpt from John Stuart Mill's *Autobiography.* New York: P. F. Collier and Son, 1909, p. 39)

John Stuart Mill's education is unique in many ways. He was a genius who was educated by his father. Although he received no formal education from an institution, Mill makes some comments on education that are meaningful to educators today. He believes the old "brutal and tyrannical" system was not effective, but he also condemns the new system for being too easy.

VIII–18

(taken from the *Congressional Record,* July 19, 1968, p. H7114, by Representative Saylor, Pennsylvania, Republican)

Representative Saylor, having been given permission for extraneous remarks, brings to the attention of the House the Communist Rules for Revolution, as he took them from the Scottish Rite Masons' publication entitled "Youth: Have We Failed Them?" These Rules were among the captured papers taken in Dusseldorf, Germany, in May 1919. The Florida State Attorney recently obtained a new copy of them from a known Communist party member, who admitted that these Rules were a part of their unit plans.

VIII–20

(taken from the stockholders report for the first quarter of 1982 from Texaco, Inc., a noncopyrighted form report printed and distributed to all stockholders with their quarterly dividend checks)

This material was presented early in the twelve-page report, and was presented from the text of a "Texaco news release on first-quarter earnings." This was followed by detailed comments on market trends, functional breakdown, international activities and related items, three pages of tables on financial details and a summary of the annual meeting of the corporation.

SUGGESTED SEQUENCE FOR A TWENTY-HOUR READING PROGRAM

All basic series and numbers refer to basic exercises in this book. Pretests, posttests, and the supplementary exercise book, *Maintaining Reading Efficiency*, may be ordered from Developmental Reading Distributors, 1944 Sheridan, Laramie, Wyoming 82070.

(Schedule is designed for ten two-hour periods. For a 50- to 60-minute class, plan only about half the material scheduled. The "5-minute break" divides the material in two sections requiring approximately the same amount of time.)

FIRST PERIOD

Use a standardized, 10-minute reading test such as the *Maintaining Reading Efficiency Tests*.

(Score and collect.)

Discuss potential goals and materials to be used.

SERIES #	EXERCISE #
I	2, 4, 6

Explain Charts

5-MINUTE BREAK

II	2
V	2
VI	2
VII	2

SECOND PERIOD

I	8, 10, 12, 14
II	4, 6, 8
III	2

5-MINUTE BREAK

V	4
VI	4
VII	4

THIRD PERIOD

I	16, 18, 20
II	10, 12, 14
III	4, 6

5-MINUTE BREAK

V	6
VI	6
VII	6

Supplementary Reading Exercises from *M.R.E.*

FOURTH PERIOD

II	16, 18, 20
III	8, 10, 12, 14
IV	2, 4

5-MINUTE BREAK

V	8
VI	8
VII	8

Supplementary Reading Exercises from *M.R.E.*

FIFTH PERIOD

III	16, 18, 20
IV	6, 8
V	10

5-MINUTE BREAK

VI	10
VII	10
VIII	2, 4

Supplementary Reading Exercises from *M.R.E.*

SIXTH PERIOD

IV	10, 12, 14, 16
V	12

5-MINUTE BREAK

VI	12
VII	12
VIII	6, 8

Supplementary Reading Exercises from *M.R.E.*

SEVENTH PERIOD

IV	18, 20
V	14
VI	14

5-MINUTE BREAK

VII	14
VIII	10–12

Supplementary Reading Exercises from *M.R.E.*

EIGHTH PERIOD

V	16
VI	16
VII	16
VIII	14, 16

5-MINUTE BREAK

Supplementary Reading Exercises from *M.R.E.*

NINTH PERIOD

V	18
VI	18
VII	18
VIII	18, 20

5-MINUTE BREAK

Supplementary Reading Exercises from *M.R.E.*

TENTH PERIOD

V		20
VI		20
VII	(If time allows)	20

5-MINUTE BREAK

Use a final, standardized, 10-minute reading test such as one of the *Maintaining Reading Efficiency Tests*.

(Score in class and discuss comparisons with beginning tests.)